W9-BIO-363

THE OLD-PRUSSIAN CHURCH AND
THE WEIMAR REPUBLIC

THE OLD-PRUSSIAN CHURCH AND THE WEIMAR REPUBLIC

A Study in Political Adjustment, 1917-1927

DANIEL R. BORG

**PUBLISHED FOR CLARK UNIVERSITY BY
UNIVERSITY PRESS OF NEW ENGLAND**
Hanover and London, 1984

UNIVERSITY PRESS OF NEW ENGLAND

BRANDEIS UNIVERSITY UNIVERSITY OF NEW HAMPSHIRE
BROWN UNIVERSITY UNIVERSITY OF RHODE ISLAND
CLARK UNIVERSITY TUFTS UNIVERSITY
DARTMOUTH COLLEGE UNIVERSITY OF VERMONT

Copyright 1984 by Trustees of Clark University

All rights reserved. Except for brief quotation in critical articles or reviews, this book, or parts thereof, must not be reproduced in any form without permission in writing from the publisher. For further information contact University Press of New England, Hanover, NH 03755.

Printed in the United States of America

LIBRARY OF CONGRESS CATALOGING IN PUBLICATION DATA

Borg, Daniel R., 1931–
    The Old-Prussian church and the Weimar Republic.

    Bibliography: p.
    Includes index.
    1. Church and state—Germany—History—20th century.
2. Germany—Church history—20th century. 3. Evangelische
Kirche der Altpreussischen Union—History—20th century.
4. Germany—Politics and government—1918–1933. I. Title.
BR856.B595 1984 322'.1'0943 83-40559
ISBN 0-87451-292-1

To my wife,
   MARJORIE MACINTOSH BORG,
and to my parents,
   HELEN SEASTRAND BORG *and*
   RAYMOND E. BORG

CONTENTS

PREFACE

THE PAGES THAT FOLLOW attempt to explain why the Weimar Republic failed to elicit the loyalties of German church leaders and active parishioners. For the purposes of concentration, the study centers around the Old-Prussian church during the years 1917–27. Its formal membership—18,718,876 according to the 1925 census—constituted over 47 percent of all German Evangelical church members and slightly under 30 percent of the total German population.[1] Among Protestant churches the world over, the Old-Prussian church in those years loomed the largest only after the Church of England.

The significance of the inquiry becomes apparent from the course and fate of the Weimar Republic. Ushered in by the Revolution of 1918, the Republic lacked power to assemble a dependable democratic constituency long before the Nazis occupied the resulting political vacuum. To explain the Republic's tarnished appeal, Karl Dietrich Erdmann suggested years ago that historians examine the substratum of political belief in all areas, not least of all in the churches.[2] The overwhelming majority of Germans formally belonged to traditionally established churches (the Landeskirchen), which claimed to provide a necessary point of value integration for all of society.

In the small but growing monographic literature on the Evangelical churches, two sets of interpretations have rubbed against each other. The "optimists" have argued that the Old-Prussian church tried to accommodate the Republic or that the potential for an accommodation existed.[3] Thus, Claus Motschmann contended that Socialists and Democrats alienated the goodwill of the Old-Prussian church by appearing to persecute it.

J.R.C. Wright pointed out that some major church leaders turned into pragmatic republicans (Vernunftrepublikaner) and sought good relations with the Republic.

The "pessimists," on the other hand, have contended that aversion for the Republic was well set beforehand or that Evangelical churchmen made little progress in adjusting to the Republic.[4] Gottfried Mehnert elaborated this theme in the initial revolutionary phase, and Herbert Christ pursued it throughout the entire Republican period while arguing his main thesis that "political Protestantism" significantly influenced the voting behavior of Protestants. In his comprehensive survey of political attitudes, Kurt Nowak documented the persistence of antirepublicanism despite efforts of some church leaders to accommodate the Republic in the years 1925–31. Karl-Wilhelm Dahm contended that the political ideologies of German pastors fed on their social and professional insecurities. Out of a common crisis mentality crystallized four ideologies, two of which, including the predominant one, contested the principles of the Republic. In his study of the disestablishment and reconstruction of the Old-Prussian church, Jochen Jacke added an institutional motive for church antirepublicanism. Even the privileges that the Republic allowed the Old-Prussian church, he argued, could not satisfy that church's craving for institutional, political, and social power at the expense of the Republic.

It is possible to fault certain aspects of these interpretations. Motschmann and Wright, relying largely on archival sources, did not see the antirepublicanism that the pessimists tried to gauge in printed sources such as periodicals. The duties of church officials, as reflected by church archives, compelled a policy of accommodation with the Republic. On the other hand, pessimist versions are not entirely convincing. Since most Protestants had little contact with their churches, it may be too much to suggest that churchmen were capable of influencing their voting behavior significantly. Still perplexing is how a common crisis mentality could propel similar churchmen, who had experienced similar conditions, into such different ideological camps. A concentration on power and resentment does not appear a broad enough interpretation to do adequate justice to church motives.

This book finds antirepublicanism grounded in the institutional ideology and aspirations of the church itself. Accordingly, chapter 1 examines the institutional structure and value system in which churchmen acted. Subsequent chapters demonstrate the persistence of this institutional ideology in many areas: wartime disputes, church disestablishment and reconstruction, school politics, morality legislation, nationalist movements, attitudes toward Jews and socialists, and a welter of other foreign and domestic political issues. The broad pattern that eventually emerges attests to the vitality and extent of the institutional ideology that sustained antirepublicanism. Though siding with the pessimists, I recognize that antirepublicans held no corner in the Old-Prussian church and that the Republic's performance sometimes confirmed the ideological charges of antirepublican churchmen.

Among the study's conclusions is the thesis that the Republic challenged Old-Prussian churchmen to shed a legacy of political quietism. Some who would explain the activism of West German churchmen since 1945 locate the turning point in this respect in the Barmen theological declaration of 1934.[5] The Barmen synod condemned the "hyphenated Christianity" of the German Christians and, by implication, the various forms of hyphenated Christianity that Dahm delineated. In point 5, the declaration stressed the duty of the church to remind "rulers" and the "ruled" of their responsibility.[6] This interpretation is not so much wrong as it is one-sided. Another, quite as persistent, strain of activism — a conservative predisposition likewise chastened by the Nazi experience — entered the post-World War II scene by way of the Weimar Republic.[7]

Perhaps, therefore, one ought to speak of two qualitatively dissimilar turning points — the first roughly in 1917–21, the second in 1933–34. The former oriented most Old-Prussian churchmen, ideologically at least, against the first republic, while the second eventually moved church leadership toward a more nonpartisan support of the second republic (in West Germany). The differing thrusts of the two suggest that, from the perspective of the Christian proclamation, an activist church is not necessarily commendable, and a quietist church deplorable.

I chose the time frame circumscribing this study for the following reasons. The war period, especially 1917, raised crucial issues that churchmen would confront again and more directly in the Republic. By 1927–28, the institutional issues that the study pursues were either resolved (promulgation of the new Old-Prussian church constitution in 1924), stalemated (the school issue by early 1928), or indefinitely deferred (commutation of state contributions). Also by then both the church and the Republic had reached their most confident and secure years in the republican period. If by 1927 churchmen could not willingly accept the

Republic, they were not likely to do so in its final destructive phase (though some did). The political strains of the final phase polarized the Old-Prussian church and undermined the church solidarity engendered by conflict over the status of the church within the Republic. An attempt to relate political attitudes to church institutional aspirations, accordingly, makes more sense until roughly 1927 than it does later.

To avoid confusion with six other Protestant Prussian churches, this book refers to *the* Prussian Landeskirche as the Old-Prussian church. After 1815 "old Prussia" spread across the north German plain from the Rhineland to East Prussia. This sprawling territory was the domain of the Prussian Landeskirche, which claimed the membership of almost all Protestants in an area that was largely Protestant. Six other Protestant Landeskirchen became Prussian when Prussia assimilated their states as a result of the wars of German unification. But these six retained their independence of the Old-Prussian church as well as their old names.[8] A clarifying "Old-Prussian" found its way into the new name that the Prussian Landeskirche adopted in its constitution of 1922: The Evangelical Church of the Old-Prussian Union.

The territorial cessions of two world wars considerably reduced the geographical expanse of the church and its formal membership. After World War I, Prussia lost the bulk of the provinces of West Prussia (including Danzig) and Posnania, part of Upper Silesia, Memel, and several other smaller areas. Prussia reorganized the remnants of the lost provinces of West Prussia and Posnania into a province known as the Border Mark (Grenzmark). After World War II, church territory lying east of the Oder-Neisse line fell to Poland and the U.S.S.R. From 1955 until the early 1970s, Communist policy managed to separate—in practice if not in name—the territory of the Old-Prussian church (now called the Evangelical Church of the Union) lying in East Germany from that in West Berlin and West Germany.[9]

Within Germany during the Weimar period, the Old-Prussian church consisted of the following eight church provinces, ranked in order of membership size as determined by the 1925 census: Brandenburg (5,402,417), Saxony (2,901,977—not to be confused with the adjacent state of Saxony), Silesia (2,236,256), Westphalia (2,222,558), Rhine (2,137,028), East Prussia (1,851,167), Pomerania (1,761,956), and the Border Mark (205,517). When suburbs were incorporated into metropolitan Berlin in 1920, the Evangelical population (3,039,390 in 1925) exceeded that of every church province, including the remainder of Brandenburg, but constituted only 75.53 percent of the total metropolitan Berlin population.

With this and several other urban exceptions, the relative density of the Evangelical population was thickest in the core provinces of Pomerania (93.78 percent), Brandenburg exclusive of Berlin (91.15), and Saxony (88.54). The relative density of Protestants was less thick in the eastern provinces of East Prussia (82.04), Silesia (Lower Silesia 66.85; Upper Silesia 10.32), and the Border Mark (61.81), and most sparse in the western provinces of Westphalia (46.20) and Rhine (29.16), where the Catholic population predominated.[10]

Generally, a distinct sense of Protestant identity was most advanced where challenged by Catholicism in mixed confessional regions or by Socialists and Communists in urban areas. Together the Protestant and Catholic confessions could boast of a formal membership accounting for 95.62 percent of the entire German population (Protestants 63.26; Catholics 32.36) and 95.21 percent of the total Prussian population (Protestants 63.89; Catholics 31.32). Enrolling but 0.86 percent of the entire German population, Protestant free churches and sects (free Lutheran, Baptist, Adventist, etc.) had done little to shatter the near monopoly that the historic Evangelical Landeskirchen of the Reformation still enjoyed over Protestant loyalties.

The word *union* in the name of the Old-Prussian church refers to the union that the Prussian king began to forge in 1817 of the largely Lutheran population and of the Reformed (Calvinists) concentrated in the western provinces. Since most congregations formally retained either Lutheran or Reformed identities, the union remained incomplete in the Weimar period as an organizational, sacramental, and liturgical union. The union church sought to allay differences between Lutherans and the Reformed by referring to both as Evangelical (meaning biblically based). In the Weimar period and earlier, the term also distinguished Protestants collectively from Catholics. The words *Evangelical church* do not connote in their German context a crusading, evangelizing church, as some historians of American history are apt to employ the term.

I could not ignore other Evangelical churches whenever organizational ties, similar interests, and the church press bound all twenty-eight Evangelical Landeskirchen together in a common cause. Organized in a Church Federation (Kirchenbund) in 1922, the Evangelical churches made a significant effort to deal with common problems. The focus of this work enlarges to include the political lobbying of the Church Federation wherever it was authorized to represent the Old-Prussian church and other member churches collectively. Church free associations extended beyond individual church borders. Influential church periodicals read in the Old-Prussian church were by no means exclusively Prussian in scope and origin.

By contrast, the book's focus is considerably smaller than these interrelations may suggest. The political views of the millions belonging to the Old-Prussian church faded into public opinion. One must seek out those who by their leadership positions tried to set the tone for the church at large. Attention has focused, therefore, on church leaders of various orientations around whom political opinion crystallized as well as on church parties, the EOK (Evangelischer Oberkirchenrat, the central administrative organ of the Old-Prussian church), synods, Church Federation Assemblies (Kirchentage), and church free associations. Accordingly, the terms *churchmen* and *church leaders* are used loosely to indicate those voicing characteristic views in representative periodicals and at sessions of synods and various church-related organizations.

Finally, it is well to stress what this volume is *not* as a way of emphasizing what it *is*. It does not purport to offer a comprehensive or general history of the Old-Prussian church or of formal church-state relations. Nor does it survey systematically the metamorphosis of Protestant theology and social ethics in the 1920s. But the book does reconstruct all of these areas to the extent needed for answering its main question: Why the Weimar Republic failed to attract the loyalty of Old-Prussian church leaders and active parishioners.

ACKNOWLEDGMENTS

I HAVE ACCUMULATED scholarly debts in the preparation of this book, and now I have the opportunity to thank publicly those who have helped me.

My wife, Marjorie, must head the top of this list. She bore, without complaint, the many hours this book took from family activities. More important, she encouraged me whenever necessary. My children also deserve my deep thanks for their forbearance.

My debt is to institutions as well as to individuals. I wish to thank the American Theological Library Association, which, at my behest, micro-filmed many periodicals I used as original sources. The Andover-Harvard Theological Library provided me with a haven for research when I first began this study. I marvel at the high quality of its holdings in German church history. Especially I wish to acknowledge my gratitude to the former librarian, James R. Tanis, and present librarian, Maria Grossmann, for their readiness to help, interest in my work, and warm hospitality.

No less am I indebted to the National Endowment for the Human-ities. It provided me with a grant to do research on the background of the Church Struggle (Kirchenkampf) under the Nazis in the Archiv der Evangelischen Kirche der Union in West Berlin. There I was hospitably received by the archivist, Dr. Gerhard Fischer, who willingly interrupted his own work to honor my frequent requests.

Once the manuscript neared completion, George A. Billias, my col-league at Clark, and Henry A. Turner, Jr., of Yale University read it and gave me the benefit of their experience, insight, and knowledge. I acknowledge here also a much earlier debt to my late mentor, Hajo

Holborn. Two other colleagues at Clark gave me special encouragement: Paul Lucas, who taught me more about history than he may suspect, and Gerald J. Karaska, who encouraged me to submit this book to the University Press of New England.

There are many others who warrant my thanks at Clark University. The late Marion Henderson, Jean F. Perkins, Mary M. Hartman, Irene W. Walch, and Mary A. Powers helped me with references at the Goddard Library. Several times Terry Reynolds, Rene Baril, Roxanne Rawson, and Karen Shepardson collaborated to type the manuscript. Anne E. Gibson and Timothy H. Fast of the Cartographic Service at Clark were good enough to prepare the map of the Old-Prussian church for me.

Editors of the following journals graciously gave permission to use materials from articles that I had published: "*Volkskirche*, 'Christian State,' and the Weimar Republic," *Church History*, 35 (1966), 186–206; "German Protestants and the Ecumenical Movements: The War-Guilt Imbroglio, 1919–1926," *Journal of Church and State*, 10 (1968), 51–71; and "The School Civil War until 1927–28: Protestant Political Efforts to Retain Confessional Education," in *Proceedings of the Citadel Symposium on Hitler and the National Socialist Era*, ed. Michael B. Barrett (Charleston, S.C., 1982).

THE OLD-PRUSSIAN CHURCH AND THE WEIMAR REPUBLIC

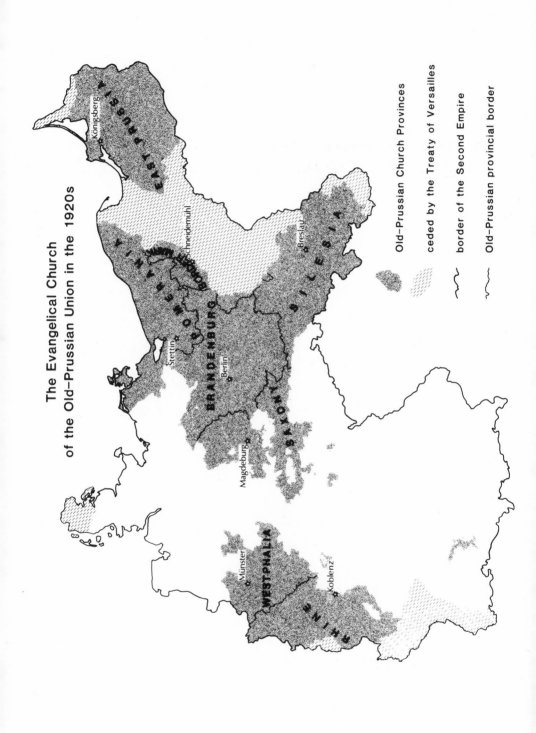

The Evangelical Church
of the Old-Prussian Union in the 1920s

EAST PRUSSIA

Königsberg

POMERANIA

Schneidemühl

Stettin

BRANDENBURG

Berlin

SILESIA

Breslau

SAXONY

Magdeburg

WESTPHALIA

Münster

RHINE

Koblenz

Old-Prussian Church Provinces

ceded by the Treaty of Versailles

border of the Second Empire

Old-Prussian provincial border

1

INTRODUCTION
From Political Quietism to Activism

IT IS NOT ONLY historians who have preoccupied themselves with the extent to which the German Revolution of 1918 broke with the past. As perceived victims, most Old-Prussian churchmen saw in the revolution both continuity and discontinuity. Long before the Kiel mutiny sparked revolution in November 1918, the progressive secularization of German life seemed to have threatened the Landeskirche as a "Volkskirche." The revolution and the Republic did not unleash this process so much as cater to it. By contrast, the revolution felled the Volkskirche's ally and protector, the monarchical "Christian" state, and introduced the "religionless" Republic. As a result, the Volkskirche faced alone the challenge of secularization under seemingly hostile political conditions. Given this frame of reference, the Old-Prussian church sought to shed the political quietism that it had cultivated under a benevolent state, to fend for itself politically, and to set its stamp on public values.

It is this theme that this chapter elaborates by focusing on the terms *Volkskirche*—literally, "people's church"—and *Christian state*. Both concepts admit to core assumptions that most Old-Prussian churchmen made about the public role of their church, the proper functions of the state, and the quality of church-state relations. It cannot be argued that all Old-Prussian churchmen shared these assumptions in like measure. Their views divided according to their position in the spectra of both church parties and political parties. Yet the large bulk ranged themselves in the political Right of church and state alike. One can see continuity and discontinuity alike in the response of churchmen to the Republic. Fundamental values remained largely unaltered after the revolution; but political behavior changed to keep pace with changed circumstances.

THE AMBIGUOUS REALITY OF THE VOLKSKIRCHE

The Volkskirche concept served as a continuing point of orientation for Old-Prussian churchmen in the Weimar Republic. They defined the term in its historical and most basic sense as an involuntary association to which one belonged by virtue of one's birth and the beliefs of one's parents. The concept derived from the Middle Ages, when the church embraced the entire political community. To preserve this type of church organization, Martin Luther eventually turned to the Saxon elector. Without his support, wrote Luther in 1525, "in a short time there will be nothing left of pastors' holdings, schools, and pulpits, and thus God's Word and service will go to ruin."[1] The adoption of the principle cuius regio, eius religio (religion determined by ruler) in the Peace of Augsburg in 1555 sustained the external unity of the Lutheran Volkskirche in Brandenburg. As Catholics and the Reformed grew more numerous as Brandenburg-Prussia expanded and ideas of toleration developed in the eighteenth century, the traditional Volkskirche began to give way to religious pluralism. The Woellner edict of 1788 placed the three major confessions (Lutherans, the Reformed, and Catholics) on a par, but the edict would merely tolerate sects. After Lutheran and Reformed congregations joined in the Old-Prussian Union, the medieval concept of Volkskirche persisted into the twentieth century as the church of almost all Protestants.

Beyond comprehensive membership, the term *Volkskirche* suggested an intimate though imprecise relationship between folk and church. As the Old-Prussian church reconstituted itself in the first years of the Republic, church liberals fought for a democratic Volkskirche to stimulate folk participation in church governance. The church Right fought back with the authoritarian argument that the church should serve the folk but not derive its governance from the masses, who could be expected to subvert the church's message. No matter how much church leaders differed on structure, all aspired to a church that enjoyed the trust and participation of the Evangelical folk. Such was the goal of a different connotation of Volkskirche that almost all church leaders from left to right could share: Christian values, nurtured by the Volkskirche for centuries, had historically molded German culture. Church leaders articulated this claim to justify the privileges of the Landeskirche that the revolution placed in jeopardy.

Strictly speaking, one cannot view the Old-Prussian Volkskirche as an involuntary association after 1873. In that year a Prussian law granted citizens the right to contract out of established churches. But relatively few had done so by 1900. Custom dictated church membership. In this sense, the Volkskirche remained involuntary even after membership had become legally voluntary. After the turn of the century, however, a movement set in to contract out of churches (Kirchenaustrittsbewegung), advancing in four waves until 1927.[2] The largest wave, the third, followed Germany's defeat and revolution. In 1920, when it swelled, 163,819 left the Old-Prussian church for "confessionless" status. Reaching its height in 1926, the fourth wave failed to match the previous one, perhaps because those most easily influenced had already contracted out. From 1919 to 1927, 4.05 percent or 758,590 members left the Old-Prussian church, and 4.03 percent or 1,592,089 left German Evangelical churches.

The movement advanced in waves partly because a number of associations mounted periodic and intense campaigns. These organizations grew out of those groups most indifferent or hostile to the churches—university graduates and workers. To promote the movement, middle-class "freethinkers" and Monists formed a loose federation in 1922 with two lower-class Marxist organizations, which merged in 1927 to constitute a formidable association of almost a half-million proletarian freethinkers.[3] Inasmuch as Marxists far outnumbered others in the federation, the general movement appeared inspired primarily by atheistic Socialists.

Those who framed the Socialist Erfurt program in 1891 were quite as hostile. For theoretical and tactical reasons, however, they refused to declare war on the churches and religion. Since religion was no more than a psychic reflection of class interests, one could expect it to disappear in a classless society. Until then, a struggle with the churches would thrust up an unnecessary barrier against potential Socialist voters. The Erfurt program asserted that "religion is a private matter" not so much to endorse religious toleration as to parry accusations that Socialists wished to suppress religion. The program urged a secularization of schools, the reduction of established churches to the status of private associations, and an end to state financial support of churches. By these means the program aimed at breaking the Christian ideological bond between state, church, and school, thereby transforming Christianity from a "public" into a "private matter." In this limited sense, the Socialist party could share the goals of the movement without endorsing it.[4]

From the turn of the century, Socialists disagreed increasingly in their attitudes toward religion. Some came to appreciate religious values, if not established churches, and to see a clear endorsement of religious neutrality in the party program. Others wished to marshal the party for an attack on churches. In the Weimar period, the parent Socialist party stood by the principles of its Erfurt program, now more clearly emphasizing religious toleration as a value in itself. But radical Socialists—Independent Socialists and Communists alike—promoted the cause of the two proletarian freethinker organizations as a necessary attack on middle-class society.

Each campaign against church membership was distinctive in its approach. Elements of these organizations cooperated in a "Committee Confessionless" to set the 1912–14 wave in motion. In mass assemblies impassioned Socialists assaulted churches as bulwarks of the monarchical order and bourgeois society. The movement's advocates launched the third and largest wave by pilloring "war theologians" for heedlessly helping to prolong the war. By leaving churches, taxpayers helped to impoverish them by avoiding church taxes, left intact by the Weimar constitution. The movement served the cause of secular schools, which the Weimar constitution had not endorsed as the norm, as well as recurring drives to persuade parents to withdraw children from religious instruction in public schools. Later, during the fourth wave, these groups attacked the stance taken by most churchmen in the presidential campaign of 1925 and in the inflammatory issue of dispossessing royal families in 1926.[5]

Old-Prussian churchmen were as relieved as they were alarmed that 4 percent of church membership contracted out between 1919 and 1927.[6] They had good reason to suspect that more of the many who had already broken covertly with the church would now take the overt step as well. The movement hardly touched rural areas. But churchmen feared greater success for the movement in urban areas, where its sponsors unleashed their most perfervid agitation, particularly among workers. Apparently many Socialist parents recoiled from severing the bond with traditional values and still desired religious instruction and confirmation for their children. Residual ties moved about 10 percent of those contracting out to return to the fold. That the Volkskirche could withstand such systematic attacks gave some credence to its claim of having molded German values.

The consistency with which a large majority of church members availed themselves of church rites supported this claim as well. Over 80 percent of all members of the Old-Prussian church who married in 1925 took their vows in a church ceremony after the obligatory civil ceremony.[7] In that same year, the number of children baptized constituted about 95 percent of all children born into families belonging to the Old-Prussian church.[8] It may be inferred that many parents, increasingly married outside of the church, placed a premium on baptism and church membership for their children. Church statistics indicated that the practice of confirmation extended well into the Socialist camp, which competed by holding youth dedication ceremonies. More than 1.8 percent of the total membership of the Old-Prussian church was confirmed in 1925.[9]

Wedding, baptismal, and confirmation statistics did not, however, indicate a flourishing church life. The Volkskirche could hardly be considered the people's church if church attendance were the measure. In Berlin a count of church attendance showed that only 3.5 percent of the Evangelical population had attended services on February 22, 1914. In Moabit (Berlin), a pastor reported that on an average Sunday .5 to .75 percent of his almost exclusively working-class congregation attended church, most of them from the lower middle class. A periodical writer remarked in 1926 that only 1 to 2 percent of the Evangelical population in a city near Berlin worshipped regularly. In 1927 General Superintendent Otto Dibelius estimated that perhaps as many as 1 percent of the Evangelical population in Berlin and 3 percent in much of northern Germany attended church on the average Sunday. Of course, the surge of attendance at church festivals, such as Christmas and Memorial Sunday, might register an average as high as 8 percent.[10]

In which groups did the Volkskirche inspire the greatest loyalty? In the course of the nineteenth century, the Volkskirche had increasingly lost the inner loyalty of the nation's cultural and economic leaders. German idealism or romantic spiritualism became the private religion of some, scientism of others. Churchmen acknowledged that the Volkskirche, on a second front, had lost a major battle with Marxism for the loyalty of workers at the end of the nineteenth century. Still the war had yet to end, and a small minority, especially those in Evangelical workingmen's clubs, remained loyal. A slowly maturing third front assumed crisis proportions in the 1920s: the indifference of parishioners in rural areas. Custom seemed most to encourage active church participation in small cities. Here and in larger cities the Volkskirche could count most heavily on the loyalty of small tradesmen and lower-ranked public officials. The middle classes, especially the lower middle class, appeared as the backbone of the Volkskirche sociologically. But defections riddled the middle classes as well.[11]

Women and older people attended church more regularly and in far greater numbers than men and younger people, a clear sign of a church on the decline.

The prerevolutionary Prussian state and the Old-Prussian church alike must be held partly responsible for this decline. Neither had managed to find sufficient resources to provide adequate pastoral services for an expanding population that migrated to ever-growing large cities during Germany's rapid industrialization. General Superintendent Dibelius called Old-Prussian Protestants the "worst cared-for church population in the world."[12] According to him, the pastor-parishioner ratio of 1:1,627 in 1849 had risen to a startling 1:2,500 by 1925. Before 1914 the Old-Prussian church failed to utilize in the parish ministry hundreds of theology students who had passed their final examinations. Large congregations in cities grew mammoth at the same time that urban life dissolved church customs. In the 1890s the Old-Prussian church embarked on a sustained effort to carve up urban congregations, build new church facilities, and employ more pastors and parish workers in cities. Still urban congregations remained incredibly large and understaffed.

During the Weimar period, the Old-Prussian church suffered the consequences of its past failure. In 1920, 6,857 congregations with under 2,000 members ministered to about 4.5 million parishioners and only 1,766 with over 2,000 to about 14.5 million. The relatively small number of large congregations presented the problem, for their parishioners averaged out to about 8,200 a congregation. A pastor-parishioner ratio of 1:10,000 could be considered quite normal in large Berlin congregations. In 1920, sixteen pastors cared for 230,000 parishioners in the largest Old-Prussian congregation, a ratio of 1:14,375.[13] Under such circumstances, pastors, like firemen, responded to emergencies and ceremonial occasions, and congregations, like fire stations, offered reassuring services that most citizens would expect to use only occasionally.

Somehow, Dibelius insisted, failing resources must be found. But the Weimar period was a poor time to redeem past mistakes. State and church finances remained in a considerable muddle, and lack of capital reduced the postwar church building program to about an eighth of its former capacity. By 1920 the surplus of available pastoral candidates had run out. Until late in the Weimar period, not enough students enrolled in theology faculties to supply the Old-Prussian church with the approximately 300 clerical replacements that it needed annually.[14] By 1925, financial problems and the cumulative shortage of pastors had left 691 of 7,692 pastorates vacant.[15]

Still the picture of church life in the Weimar period was not one of unrelieved gloom, particularly in cities. If only 2 percent of 24,000 in a large urban congregation worshipped on an average Sunday, enough people attended to stimulate a sense of corporate identity and to sustain a variety of activities centered around the congregation. Church associations abounded, appealing to certain groups (such as women or youth) or to all groups interested in a particular cause (such as confessional education or foreign missions). So plentiful were these activities that many churchmen deplored the time-consuming round of meetings. These associations and the activities of congregations themselves gave churchmen reason to believe that the decline in church participation had bottomed out and that better days lay ahead for urban churches. As the 1920s wore on, this optimism was encouraged by a shift in public mood that churchmen often interpreted as a growing aversion to materialism and a craving for lost spiritual bearings. Finally, a sense of church solidarity unknown to the prewar church set in as the Volkskirche confronted the perils that lay in its path.

This blending of light and dark areas in the picture of church life cannot but cloud our perception. Do we see a declining sect that ministers to a relatively few in an alien society? An affirmative answer appears reasonable if we emphasize relatively low church participation, systematic assaults on the church, and failing pastoral services. Or do we see a crippled Volkskirche still capable of influencing public life? Here, too, an affirmative answer seems plausible if we stress the comprehensive structure of the church, the frequency of church rites, and the reluctance of the many to shed church membership.

What Old-Prussian churchmen generally saw was a Volkskirche that could still generate energy enough to illuminate the dark areas in the future. So long as the state lent its benevolent support to sustain church structure and so long as the great majority desired church membership, there could be no realistic choice between sect and Volkskirche. As the Old-Prussian church entered the Weimar Republic, the big question was whether both prerequisites would prevail or whether the Volkskirche would collapse into sects.

Old-Prussian churchmen regarded sects as inherently abhorrent and the Volkskirche as infinitely preferable. At the Church Federation Assembly (Kirchentag) in 1921, Julius Kaftan endowed the Volkskirche with a justification that most churchmen expressed from one angle or another in periodicals and synods. Two years earlier, Kaftan, a Berlin theology professor, had reached the vice-presidency of the EOK (Evangelischer Oberkirchenrat), the highest clerical position in the largest German Evangelical church. From this position he brought authority to a subject that had sorely troubled the consciences of Evangelical churchmen—the relationship of the Volkskirche to the new Republic.

Kaftan's justification of the Volkskirche amounted to an endorsement of Christian folkish nationalism, which served as a lodestar for the Old-Prussian church. For centuries the proclamation of God's Word had shaped the moral content of the German character and German institutions, values that Kaftan described as "Christian imponderables." He contended that God's word acted more effectively on those rooted in Christian imponderables, and that the Republic threatened these values. For these reasons, the Volkskirche must resolve to persist as the custodian of German culture. Inasmuch as genuine culture stemmed from religious roots, German culture had also benefited from the church's stewardship. A society cut off from the creative source of its own culture degenerated into a lifeless shell of its former creativity. Kaftan concluded that, for the sake of church and society alike, the Volkskirche must nurture Christian imponderables by preserving and strengthening the vital connection between Christianity and "Germanness" (Deutschtum).[16]

Obviously Kaftan saw more in the picture of church life than the eye can detect. He and other like-minded church leaders interpreted the lighter areas to signify the persistence of a Christian cultural residue upon which the Volkskirche could yet flourish. Had they concluded that the church amounted to no more than a sect or, at most, a missionary Volkskirche in an alien society, they might have raised more modest claims on German public life. Then the folk was to be won, not lost. It was reassuring to believe that Christian folk values, if revitalized, could still sustain a viable Volkskirche. With this interpretation in mind, Old-Prussian churchmen anxiously scanned the horizon of public life in the Weimar Republic and summoned their wrath to condemn forces destructive of the Christian folk.

CHURCH GOVERNANCE BEFORE 1918 AND POLITICAL QUIETISM

Only superficially did the Old-Prussian church appear to have won its independence from the state before 1918. By 1876 the monarch and the state had reconstituted the church on a corporate basis with its own organs of self-administration. The state bureaucracy, in that same year, relinquished the last of its authority over internal church matters to the EOK. By 1876 one could no longer regard the Old-Prussian church as formally a state church.

The Old-Prussian church was nevertheless subjected to considerable state control and influence. The Prussian constitution of 1850 had indeed secured the theoretical independence of the church from the state, but not from the king, who as summus episcopus (highest bishop) remained the primary source of organizational authority within the church. In theory, his churchly office formed no more than a private annex to his kingly authority. For many, however, the legal distinction between the king's two roles was little more than sleight of hand to conceal his advancement of Protestant and conservative interests and his continuing control of the Old-Prussian church. It is little wonder that revolutionaries in 1918 verged on claiming the king's personal prerogatives within the church. The schizoid functions of the king could even alarm the contending church parties that had emerged with church self-administration. The "ruler's church government" (landesherrliches Kirchenregiment) could not help favoring one or another of these parties. Many churchmen feared that the king, for the sake of confessional parity, neglected the legitimate interests of the Old-Prussian church.

The institution of a political summus episcopus dated from Reformation practices. German Lutheran rulers preempted the defunct authority of Catholic bishops not as a private annex to, but as a constituent part of, their responsibilities as Christian rulers of a Christian society. Luther had urged the Saxon elector to intervene as an "emergency bishop" — as one provisionally occupying a *church* office — to restore stable church conditions. Whatever thought was initially given to Luther's counsels was soon forgotten as Lutheran rulers imposed their permanent control, often shared with noble patrons, upon congregations through consistories. Anxious concern for the new church, which characterizied the intial "episcopal" period, gave way under the "territorial system" to the supremacy of state over church interests. In Brandenburg-Prussia east of the Elbe River, the privy council, through consistories, governed passive Lutheran congregations as arms of the state, charged with nurturing proper moral behavior and obedience to state decrees. There existed no corporate organization known as the church beyond individual congregations. The territorial system culminated in the suspension of Lutheran consistories in 1808 and in the incorporation of their functions into a newly created ministry of state. More clearly than ever before, a state church had emerged.[17]

In retrospect, the administrative reorganization of 1808 appears as the first stage in the incremental development of the Old-Prussian Union. By suspending Reformed organs as well as Lutheran, the crown forged an administrative union. When the monarch reestablished provincial consistories in 1815, he drew no administrative distinction between Lutheran and Reformed congregations. Ever since Johann Sigismund had converted to Calvinism in 1613, rulers of Brandenburg-Prussia had aspired to forge a union church of their Reformed coreligionists and their predominantly Lutheran subjects. The administrative union consummated, this goal now lay within reach. Reformed and, with some pressure, Lutheran congregations responded affirmatively to the appeal of King Friedrich Wilhelm III in 1817 for a sacramental union, the essence of the "union." Concurrently, the king imposed a common liturgy upon this largely voluntary union by royal decree.[18]

Only gradually did the church acquire an administrative independence as the king, pressed by circumstances, distinguished ever more clearly between his prerogatives as a ruler and his authority as summus episcopus. This perception rested on a distinction that natural-law jurists had drawn since the end of the seventeenth century. They distinguished between the sovereign rights of the ruler over the church (jura circa sacra) and the legal autonomy reserved to churches in their own religious affairs (jura in sacra). In the reorganization of 1808 the king recognized these two spheres of law in practice by reserving jura in sacra to the Catholic church. The king's effort to impose a common liturgy upon the union forced him to regard the church as a corporation of congregations. If the state controlled the church, the interconfessional provincial assemblies (Landtage) established in the 1820s might logically claim a share of control. To avoid this danger, the king had to regard the church as a corporation distinct from the state and under his personal control. The constitution of 1850, which proclaimed the independence of churches, obliged the king to establish his own church government as separate from the state bureaucracy. Thus the EOK sprang to life in 1850 to govern the church through the consistorial apparatus. But the Kultusminister, soon deprived of exercising the king's authority within the church, retained his traditional function of representing the king's sovereign rights over the church.[19]

The synodical structure imposed upon the entire church in the 1870s did not significantly impair the power of the preexisting church bureaucracy.[20] Fully developed by 1876, the new system of self-administration (not self-government) stemmed from the model provided by the Rhine-Westphalian Church Ordinance of 1835. Since the Reformation in the west, Reformed and Lutheran congregations had governed themselves through congregational presbyteries and territorial synods. In compromising with the king in 1835, the westerners retained their presbyteries and synods, but only at the price of losing their former self-government, accepting a modicum of self-administration, and receiving the king's liturgy. The compromise clamped together Lutheran consistorial and Reformed presbyterial-synodical systems in such a way as to award decisive authority to the former. This model was later copied in the Congregational and Synodical Ordinance of 1873 that applied to the other—the eastern —Prussian provinces. In 1876 the General Synod Ordinance crowned the provincial synodical structure with a General Synod for the entire realm.

The three ordinances gave the Old-Prussian church a complete presbyterial-synodical system of self-administration that ranged from local congregational councils to the General Synod. While consistorial organs derived their authority from the summus episcopus and organized from the EOK downward, the organs of self-administration organized upward. On the congregational level, qualified adult males elected two administrative church councils. The ruler's church government made its first appearance on the next level in the person of the superintendent, the highest clerical and administrative official of the district (Kreis). The general superintendent, who sat on the provincial consistory, supervised the clergy and religious life of the districts in his province (or part of it). Synods—district, provincial, and general—met periodically to discharge their duties as prescribed by their enabling ordinances.

In this system the powers of the ruler's church government outweighed those of synods. As summus episcopus, the king appointed EOK and consistorial officials as well as general superintendents and superintendents (except in the west). They were not responsible to synods in a constitutional sense. The three ordinances detailed and restricted the authority of synods and congregational councils but not those of the ruler's church government. Church government intruded into the legislative domain by way of the king's privilege of appointing a sixth of the deputies in eastern provincial synods and in the General Synod. By the same token, synods participated directly in church government through their executive committees, the GSV (Generalsynodalvorstand) voting on certain matters within the EOK. The system of self-administration allowed elected church organs to help manage the church without giving them a determinative influence.

By opening up church governance to popular participation, the presbyterial-synodical system, it was hoped, would arouse an active interest among parishioners in church life. Generally this hope remained unfulfilled. Elections from one synod to the next higher, derisively known as the "filter" or "sieve" system, tended to shut out undesirable elements from representation. The "filtered" General Synod of 1915 consisted of 202 members, of whom 105 were clergymen of the Middle and Right church parties. Only one liberal pastor attended. Of the 97 laymen, seven were consistorial officials; 48, high state officials; 13, owners of large estates; 8, businessmen; and 4, professional men. Almost half of the laymen were of the nobility.[21] Since the more conservative elements of society evidenced the greatest interest in the church, democratic elections by parishioners to synods would hardly have denied these elements a preponderate representation in any case. But the filter system, along with the king's right to synodical appointments, contributed to depriving synods of a popular aura under which church issues could arouse a sympathetic public response.

When the revolution forced the church to rebuild its governance system, the church Middle party and especially church liberals, the main casualties of the filter system, showed the greatest willingness to criticize past failings. The Old-Prussian church had exhibited efficient and conscientious synods and officials, concluded Professor Adolf Deissmann of the Middle party, but lacked creative leadership, active congregations, and contact with church members. This debility Professor Wilhelm Bousset, a liberal, partly ascribed to authoritarianism, which, he claimed, had left an even sharper imprint on the Old-Prussian church than on German political life.[22]

State influence was more directly brought to bear on the church in the domain of jura circa sacra. Although the EOK and consistories were church organs, their officials were state officials. The Kultusminister confirmed their appointments and subjected them to the state's discipline. He had an opportunity to veto a church law before its enactment, ostensibly to ensure that church legislation did not transgress state law. But he was not obliged to state reasons for his objection, and state law did not delimit the full scope of jura circa sacra. Finally, as a public corporation enjoying public financing, the church submitted to narrow state controls on the disposition of church property, the raising of church taxes, and a wide range of administrative matters.[23]

Because the king largely controlled the church internally through his church government and externally through the Kultusminister, it is hard to imagine how the Old-Prussian church could have embarked on an activist course that could have run counter to interests of state as conceived by the king. It is true that Wilhelm II left matters of church policy largely in the hands of the EOK, which exercised great power because of this benign neglect as well as because of the impotence of synods. But the EOK, dependent on royal favor, steered the church clear of issues that bordered on politics, even as the Old-Prussian church made a conspicuous display of its loyalty to the monarch. A church aspiring to an activist role in society must possess a corporate sense of identity as well as the freedom to act. The Old-Prussian church acquired such an identity in the nineteenth century, but did not gain the requisite freedom until the Revolution of 1918.

THE CHRISTIAN CONSERVATIVE LEGACY AND THE REPUBLIC

Conservative ideology provides yet another explanation for the Old-Prussian church's prerevolutionary political quietism. Conservative churchmen upheld an authoritarian conception of society and a corresponding sense of community, both of which they saw reflected in the old order. Moreover, conservative ideology tended to hallow existing conditions and to mask the blemishes of the conservative order. The revolution relieved conservative churchmen of the need to defend the old order, and their conservative convictions gave them a platform on which to criticize the new.

The Christian conservative conception of an authoritarian society as well as its matching sense of community can be traced back to Martin Luther. Largely because of prevailing church conditions in Germany, his distinctive conceptualization of social ethics resulted in political quietism.

Luther held that God ruled His creation through a spiritual Regiment (government) and a worldly one.[24] Within the first, Christ called men into the fellowship of His church (communion of saints) through the gift of faith; within the second a concealed God ruled through persons and institutions, His masks, according to His purposes. The worldly Regiment embraced three divinely ordained forms of social organization, which

nineteenth-century Lutherans generally referred to as orders of creation—
the magistracy, the household (including economics), and the constituted
church (though limited to Christendom). Each order embodied a divine
purpose that Christians and non-Christians alike could perceive through
reason and conscience. Here God utilized man's reason to create law and
justice. No order was specifically "Christian," since it did not derive its
organizational principles from gospel even though the orders operated
under God's providence.

From this theological cosmology came certain practical consequences
and attitudes. Just as faith descended from Christ in the spiritual Regiment, so too did authority flow from God into the worldly Regiment. Just
as man's efforts to save himself resulted from sin, so too did his attempts to
assert himself against divinely ordained, worldly authority (Obrigkeit)
stem from the Devil. God used even sinful authority to maintain order
against the disorder that the Devil sowed. For Luther obedience to secular
authority was mandatory in all cases except in an unjust war and in matters
of religious conviction.

Theoretically a sense of community within an authoritarian society
should result from Luther's doctrine of the calling, which bridged the
distance between the two Regimente. Within the orders of creation were a
variety of offices (such as father, shoemaker, prince) that served the
commonweal. Through reason an officeholder perceived the inherent
purposes of his office, but his will to act accordingly might be corrupted.
Whether one served or misused his office depended largely on whether one
belonged to Christ or to the Devil. Luther conceived of an ethos of selfless
service by those in authority that, matched by selfless obedience, could
bond a community. The concept of inviolable civil liberties within the
political order was as utterly foreign to Luther's thinking as it was to his
age. To later nineteenth-century conservative Lutherans, political liberalism, by catering to individual rights, not only defied divinely ordained
authority but also subverted a Christian sense of community.

Luther did not believe that man could create the ideal society toward
which Christian ethics pointed. Sin permeated the orders of creation; even
saints sinned. Hence the persisting need to distinguish between the two
Regimente. The true Christian ought to follow the love ethic embodied in
the Sermon on the Mount, but in his offices he must act by their inherent
purposes and, be he a man of authority, employ compulsion to punish evil
out of love for neighbor. Luther's was a dualistic ethic reflecting the two
ways in which God ruled the world through the Regimente. One could

not determine "what" the nature of one's office was from the gospel, only "how" that office should be exercised. As H. Richard Niebuhr noted, the dualism was fraught with tension, "for technique and spirit interpenetrate, and are not easily distinguished and recombined into a single act of obedience to God."[25]

Luther's dualistic ethic can be enfeebled in two ways—by fusing or by isolating its two elements. Were the two fused, a unitary ethic would result by which gospel is transformed into law or law into gospel and imposed upon the orders of creation, in the first case, or upon the sphere of faith. The danger for German Lutheranism came traditionally from the other direction. If the two elements were separated, the concept of the calling would give way to a double morality.

Several years before the First World War, Ernst Troeltsch contended that Luther's dualism had degenerated into a double morality among modern-day Lutherans.[26] Luther's formulations had left his followers in a quandary. Should they seek to transform the sinful spirit of the "world" as it permeated the secular orders, or accept it because these orders were divinely ordained? The main thrust of German Lutheranism, according to Troeltsch, was to release the tension of the dualism. Lutherans extolled secular institutions as God given, accepted existing conditions as beyond the scope of a specifically Christian social ethic or motivation, and cultivated religious inwardness.

Yet Luther's thought and example expressed the potential for a different response—an activist church. The church could not compel secular authority to alter its behavior, but the church could raise a warning voice. No matter how divinely ordained, secular authority could not escape the impact of sin. Luther understood the pastor's calling to include responsibility for passing moral judgment on the actions of the magistrate. His personal example showed a rejection of political quietism.[27] An activist church that operates out of the Lutheran dualist framework is one that is moved by the Christian love ethic to judge existing conditions by purposes inhering in the orders of creation. Luther's approach, however, required Christians to judge the moral implications of policies of state without prescribing their content, the difficulty to which Niebuhr alluded.

In an extended form, Luther's social thought constituted the point of departure employed by perhaps most Old-Prussian churchmen in the Weimar Republic in two general respects: his authoritarianism and the prospects for activism that his social ethics adumbrated. Churchmen commonly condemned the revolution, disparaged liberal emphasis on individual rights for ignoring a necessary inner commitment to the whole, and distrusted democratic theory for deriving authority from the masses. Historical circumstances help to explain why Luther's authoritarianism could persist centuries beyond its initial conception into a less congenial age. Unlike Calvinists in the West, German Protestant churches found reassuring protection in their authoritarian states and little need to contest them. Luther's authoritarianism and the state morality that Prussian rulers cultivated showed an affinity through which the one reinforced the other. The state's domination of the Protestant churches choked any possibility for them to sit in judgment over state and society. When the revolution cast aside this solicitude, ideological bond, and control and introduced a seemingly hostile form of government, the church was challenged as well as free to follow an activist path.

The seedtime of the resolute conservatism held by most Old-Prussian churchmen in the Weimar Republic was the period from the War of Liberation to the Revolution of 1848, when religion and conservatism fused into a compact ideology. In this period Lutherans and pietists found in each other kindred allies against rationalism.[28] Under the aegis of a religious revival known as the Awakening, the two nourished a Christian conservatism that set its stamp on the Old-Prussian church, especially in the eastern provinces. Characteristically, Christian conservatives argued that rationalist political theories of the French Revolution — popular sovereignty and an external concept of individual freedom — had acted as a solvent on the traditional social and political community to which men owed basic allegiance, the same type of solvent that had weakened faith in revealed religion.

By mid-century Christian conservatives had exchanged their earlier romanticizing of feudalism for a more rational concept of state and constitutionalism, a shift promoted by the persuasive jurisprudence of a Lutheran legist and Berlin professor, Friedrich Julius Stahl. It was his political theory, infused, after the Wars of Unification, with nationalism (loyalty to the nation state), that many Weimar churchmen cherished as their own.

Anticipating Julius Kaftan, Stahl postulated the reality of a Christian moral continuum, developed historically through the folk, that should bind the errant individual to the community. Stahl contended that liberalism inculcated a self-centered individualism that would shatter this moral continuum and atomize the Christian community. Primary political authority must reside in the monarch, responsible to God, not in the people. The monarchy could qualify as a "Christian" state if the Christian moral continuum motivated it to act in accordance with God-given purposes inhering in the state.[29]

Implicitly Stahl appears to have added another order of creation to the three enumerated by Luther—the folk, an order that underlay his concept of the Christian state. His was a cultural definition of the folk, allowing the interaction of a folkish ethos and Christian morality to produce a distinctively Christian moral continuum. The intrusion of folkish nationalism into nineteenth-century Christian conservative thought created an extended base for an authoritarian community. It appears that folkish nationalism compensated for the failing power of the Christian faith to engender a sense of community in this secularizing century, and recast the claims of Christianity for prominence in German society in a more broadly acceptable manner.

In the nineteenth century, Christian conservatives grafted on to Lutheran and Prussian authoritarianism a historical justification of the conservative order. Through the historical process God had ordained existing political authorities, who bore an aura of legitimacy that defied Christian subjects to mount criticism. Nineteenth-century German Evangelical churches never seriously entertained the alarming prospect of criticizing the use of power by divinely ordained authority.[30] For the same reason, conservative churchmen censured emergent political movements—particularly liberalism and socialism—that would transform the Christian state. Political commitment narrowed the church's appeal to an increasingly smaller segment of the Prussian population.[31] To Stahl's conservative contemporaries, apostasy and materialism, not political idealism or economic need, fired these movements. Selfish individualism held sway where apostasy deprived the individual of proper motivation to serve the commonweal and to honor established authority.

Not until the exhilarating Wars of Unification did conservative churchmen, who dominated the Old-Prussian church, begin to acquire the political nationalism that characterized most of the church in the 1920s.[32] Before Bismarck's military successes, political nationalism had sounded too Jacobin. Moreover, the political goal of liberal nationalists, German unification, could be attained seemingly only by violating the principle of historical legitimacy. But Christian conservatives eventually rallied around Bismarck's banner when he effectively demonstrated that political nationalism could be tapped for authoritarian purposes in a unified Germany.

According to Stahl's "monarchical principle," rulers must assert the community's interests against the masses and estates alike. In the Second Empire churchmen set great store by the Kaiser's authority, which seemed to tower above the grasp of political parties and fleeting parliamentary majorities, presumably seeking narrow interests.[33] One may praise parliamentarianism for accepting conflict as both natural and inevitable and for superimposing rules of the game for resolving conflict. To many churchmen in the Empire and then the Republic, however, social conflict seemed as natural and inevitable as original sin, and just as contemptible for venting man's egoism at the expense of the commonweal.

The Republic appeared congenitally incapable of accepting the mantle of the Christian state, for two principal reasons: the religious neutrality of the Republic, and its parliamentarianism. At the Church Federation Assembly in 1921, Vice-president Kaftan elaborated both reasons. As for the first, he indicted the Republic for proclaiming its "religionless" nature. Since the Volkskirche functioned as the custodian of German culture, the state must consciously promote Christian values and eschew religious neutrality. Kaftan's critics at the assembly complained that he had exaggerated; the Weimar constitution, accepted two years earlier, had guaranteed most traditional church privileges. But Kaftan insisted that "the religionlessness of the state is a brutal fact."[34] The churches had to fight for what the state should have willingly conceded, and the National Assembly had left largely unresolved the fate of Christian education in public schools. "Have we really still a state that in its own interests concerns itself with promoting Christian faith in God and Christian morality? No one can seriously assert that." A Christian folk ought to promote Christian values, since the state requires a pervasive morality that it cannot itself produce. Here Kaftan restated the old claim that Christian values can bind together the national community and counteract the corrosion of materialism and individualism.

Accordingly, Kaftan drew the conclusion that the relationship of Volkskirche to state should ideally be one of interdependence, a necessary "symbiotic relationship." Through this theory of symbiosis Kaftan and others bound the concepts of Volkskirche and the Christian state tightly together. The Christian state, in its own interests, nurtured the Volkskirche. Religion was no mere private matter, as Socialists would have it, but a matter of paramount public importance as well. Perhaps reluctantly, Kaftan recognized that separation of church and state was bound to come eventually and the summus episcopus go. The revolution, detested by conservative church leaders, had emancipated the churches. But their leaders would have cherished a different scenario: a separation that left the Volkskirche with its privileges and the state with its Christian character.[35]

Kaftan left no doubt that he looked upon the traditional monarchy as a Christian state. Shortly before the revolution a conservative church leader described the monarchy in these words: "With justice none of us has ever spoken of the 'Christian state' in its most actual sense, only in the sense that even the state, its legislation, and administration are strongly influenced by Christian [morality]. The educative and social idea, which has indirectly imbued even state institutions, stems from the spirit of Christianity. When one, therefore, examines our legislation, one comes across it everywhere."[36] Lutheran social ethics prevented this church leader—as well as Stahl earlier and Weimar churchmen later—from identifying the monarchical state as inherently Christian. Only its motivation seemed distinctly Christian.

Kaftan denied that a republic could be similarly motivated because of its perverse political process—parliamentarianism, the second major ideological reason for contesting the Republic. Rule by parties rendered the state incapable of fostering a symbiotic relationship with any promise of permanence. Kaftan would surely have agreed with the classic conservative analysis purveyed by Friedrich Brunstäd, an Evangelical professor of philosophy.[37] To Brunstäd, the social-contract theory and parliamentarianism catered to individual selfishness instead of upholding the God-given moral purposes of the state. As a social atom, the individual founded with others a state through contract so that he could pursue his own designs without regard for his moral obligations to the whole. But in parliaments power cliques and monied interests gained control of the state and trampled the rights of individuals as well as those of the community.

Nor could Kaftan see any hope for such a republic in theory:

The religionless state recognizes no authority over it. The truth, which we Christians apprehend in the word of scripture [Romans 13:1−7] that authority [Obrigkeit] is from God and must act accordingly, is consigned to the rubbish heap in it [in the religionless state]. The religionless state recognizes no authority over it; this means, however, that it no longer believes in its own authority. It cannot if it excludes faith in God for itself as a state.[38]

Here Kaftan identified another mark of the Christian state: It recognized that God had ordained the state as an order of creation. The state drew its authority from Him and ought to acknowledge its responsibility to Him, not to the materialist masses.

By its very nature, a parliamentary republic could not serve these purposes as God intended: "It is but the birth of the day, everything is valid for the present until the next election when a new state is again born that perhaps desires and regulates everything differently. It is a tottering entity, does not stand on firm feet, offers no guarantee beyond the immediate hour. Basically this is the way things are with the religionless state."[39] Lack of continuity caused by perpetual competition of parties representing special interests rather than the divine purposes of the state condemned a parliamentary republic to the status of an indelibly religionless state. The state, beholden to God, must rule its citizens with an appropriate sense of responsibility, not co-opt them in a political process that debased the moral ends of the state. Suitably motivated, a monarchy could qualify as a Christian state because of its structure; the parliamentary republic never, because of its political process. The precise form of government did, after all, bear directly on the state's potential for functioning in a Christian manner, even though no form could be regarded as inherently Christian.

Like Kaftan, who looked forward to a restoration of the Christian state, Old-Prussian churchmen overwhelmingly entered the republican period as staunch monarchists. The ideal of monarchism remained the fulcrum of political orientation for most of them.[40] When Germany forsook the foundations on which monarchy presumably reposed, churchmen confronted a republic that seemed to flaunt its "religionless" nature and to indulge party rule at the expense of the commonweal.

THE SHIFT TO POLITICAL ACTIVISM

It would be wrong to suggest that, in the decades before the war, most Old-Prussian churchmen were thoroughly quietistic, paying scant attention to how Christian social ethics could shape their world. The church preached social sensitivity to the needs of others as well as moral and civic virtues, such as loyalty to the monarch and devotion to the nation state. The Inner Mission, which spun an amazingly large and effective network of Evangelical charities throughout Germany, found welcome support in the Old-Prussian church, attracting a small army of volunteers. Together with the Inner Mission and other church free associations, Old-Prussian churchmen lobbied for morality legislation, as they would continue to do in the 1920s.

But the official church balked at proposing social reform, especially if the reform ran counter to the wishes of government or the church's conservative membership. Such was the implied message of the EOK in 1895, when it closed the damper on the Christian-social movement, spearheaded by Adolf Stoecker since the late 1870s. It was none other than the EOK's vice-president, Julius Kaftan, however, who proposed to lift the damper on political activism after the Revolution of 1918. Before the revolution Old-Prussian churchmen leaned toward political quietism, afterward toward political activism.

Stoecker as well as Kaftan feared for the future of the Volkskirche under the impact of secularization, and counseled the church to act in its own interest against this threat. Kaftan found much to fault in the existing "religionless" and republican state, while, four decades earlier, Stoecker wished to shore up the existing Christian and monarchical state, especially by winning workers for the church and the conservative order.

As social evils historically associated with rapid industrialization multiplied, the conservative world view of an organic community cemented by legitimate authority and Christian faith seemed more than ever anachronistic in the second half of the nineteenth century. But church social concern failed to advance beyond Evangelical charities at a time when the Socialist party, antagonistic to religion and the prevailing political order, firmly entrenched itself. The beguiling assumption that the state remained governed by legitimate Christian authority seriously hampered social and political criticism, even though the Kulturkampf of the 1870s aroused fears that Bismarck, in alliance with National Liberals, had failed to defend principles upon which the Christian state must take its stand.[41]

It is against this background—a politically quietist church controlled by a state seemingly acting more and more in its own interests—that Stoecker's startling appearance on the political scene must be viewed. Though appointed court chaplain in 1874, Stoecker longed for a church freed of state influences so that it might attack the social question on its own terms. By himself he tried to enlist workers in a Christian-Social Labor party (later called Christian-Social party), which he founded in 1878. But workers ignored his summons. Only in several pockets in western Prussia did his party eventually strike deep roots.[42]

Stoecker deplored the tendency of EOK pronouncements to follow the political course of the state. Of course, he agreed with the harsh condemnation of socialism in the EOK decree to the clergy in 1879 and in its circular to pastors in 1890. But the EOK decrees of 1879 and 1895 strongly discouraged social-political activity by pastors and, together with the circular of 1890, suggested to contemporaries that state influences rather than church interests dictated the intent of these pronouncements.

Thus, the decree of 1879 seemed to endorse Bismarck's attempts to suppress the burgeoning Socialist party. The decree also discouraged other pastors from following Stoecker's example by picturing Jesus as one who submitted to state and society without judging them. When Bismarck embarked upon a policy of social legislation in 1881 to counter Socialist growth, however, the EOK seemed to alter its emphasis by commending social legislation to the clergy.[43]

Stoecker's chance to lure the church into more of an activist course came in 1890. Wilhelm II allowed anti-Socialist measures to lapse with the alternative strategy in mind of courting working-class favor through social legislation. At the urging of the Kaiser, the EOK followed suit in a circular to the clergy. It indicted socialism for infecting the "folk soul" with materialism and hostility to religion and fatherland and for sowing conflict between labor and management. Yet the circular commended the cause of worker welfare to the clergy. Over the church's efforts loomed the goal of amicable social reconciliation within the existing order. Encouraged, Stoecker helped found in 1890 the Evangelical-Social Congress, which aimed to stimulate Protestant social responsibility by investigating and assessing social conditions.[44]

Once more optimistically set in motion, the Christian-social movement soon met disaster, owing to a reversal of state policy and dissension within the Congress. Alarmed that his efforts by 1894 had not stemmed Socialist growth, Wilhelm II returned to the strategy of political suppression. In the meantime, the ranks of the Congress divided between the more liberal younger generation led by Friedrich Naumann and the more orthodox older one under Stoecker. An Inner Mission pastor, Naumann had come to the jarring conclusion that conservative allegiances and values obscured economic injustices and thwarted social justice, a concept that he sought to derive from the moral teachings of Jesus.

The two factions developed differing attitudes toward the Socialist party. To Naumann and his followers, the Socialist party did represent legitimate interests of workers, and should be encouraged to follow its reformist tendencies within the state. Such a position could only appall Stoecker and his friend Pastor Ludwig Weber, who had taken the lead in founding Evangelical workingmen's clubs in the 1880s. Both considered the social question largely solved if workers, having been won for the gospel, could find social justice within the existing order. From this perspective, socialism could not be indulged because of its anti-Christian ideology or assimilated because of its class egoism.[45]

Stoecker, discharged as court chaplain in 1890, was now able to pursue within the General Synod his agitation for a church freed from state and summus episcopus alike. His project would inevitably shift church governmental authority to synods controlled by the church Right, which already dominated higher synods by way of "filtered" elections. But liberals and the Middle party could only fear for their doctrinal freedom in a synodically controlled church. For his part, Wilhelm II, fearing dissension in his church, refused any thought of relinquishing his power. But could the church pursue a social program if he did not? Intertwining the independence movement and the church's social course, both sparked by Stoecker, was the growing realization that the church's social message could not appear credible to the alienated so long as state ties remained in place.[46]

Faced with a choice, the EOK was prepared to sacrifice its social program rather than disrupt church-state ties. This predisposition hardened as the king set a course that could collide with that followed by many clergy in response to the EOK's circular of 1890. At the Congress's convention in 1894, the younger generation criticized conservative agrarians for exploiting agricultural labor, and soon took issue with the pending bill to suppress Socialists. As a result, conservative industrialists and agrarians condemned not only the Congress but also the entire Christian-social movement for promoting the interests of one social group against the whole and for playing into the hands of Socialists.

The EOK issued its 1895 decree to prevent a rift with its summus episcopus and another rift within the church's constituency.[47] The decree warned of excesses, particularly among the younger clergy, who had allegedly grown so involved in social-political problems and agitation as to neglect their pastoral responsibilities. The church could make an indirect social contribution by stimulating social sensitivity among all groups. But "it cannot be emphatically stressed enough," the decree continued, "that all attempts to make the Evangelical church into an authoritative cooperating factor in political and social conflicts of the day must divert the church from the goals set by the Lord of the church: generating spiritual happiness." The decree advised pastors to encourage the submission of the needy to "God's world order and world government" with the fillip that "envy and lust after one's neighbor's goods violate God's commandment."[48] Especially these words staked out a retreat to quietism. Similarly, Wilhelm II, in a publicized telegram, expressed the view that "pastors should worry about the souls of their congregations, cultivate love-to-neighbor but stay out of politics, for it does not concern them."[49]

Caught in a bewildering cross fire, Stoecker felt forced to leave the Conservative party when its leaders pressed him to disavow the movement that he had begun. But he also came to the honest conclusion that he could no longer cooperate with Naumann without denying his own heritage. Accordingly, Stoecker and his orthodox friends left the congress in 1896 to reorganize the Christian-Social party without Naumann's following and to found the Church-Social Conference (after 1918 called the Church-Social League) as a conservative and orthodox counterpart to the now largely liberal congress. In actuality, however, the Christian-social movement, as a movement, ceased in 1896. No longer could Stoecker stir significant sections of the Old-Prussian church, and no longer did Naumann give serious consideration to the movement.[50]

In the decade and a half before the First World War, only the congress, the conference, and several associated organizations kept alive the concerns of the Christian-social movement. But they differed in approach, composition, and general attitude. The congress, continuing to meet as an open forum, tried to analyze social problems in a detached manner and to understand socialism rather than condemn it. By contrast, the conference, true to its origins, appeared more as a closed ideological group. The conference was much more successful than the congress at creating a strong sociological base. To a large extent, the Inner Mission, the workingmen's clubs, the Evangelical component of the Christian unions, the Christian-Social party, and finally the Church-Social Conference shared the same conservative church support and, to a lesser extent, the same leaders.[51] After Stoecker's death in 1909, the husband of his niece, Pastor Reinhard Mumm, assumed the leadership of the small Christian-Social party. Also active in the Inner Mission, Mumm served as the conference's general secretary from 1900 through the Weimar era. The conference's sociological base, its conservative and orthodox composition, its strong commitment to the church (though a free one), its tendency to view politics as a continuing struggle over basic values, and the singular appropriateness of Stoecker's general program after the revolution ensured that the Weimar church would draw much more strongly on Christian-social assumptions than on Evangelical-social.

Discouraged from social activism, the Christian-social clergy, Pollmann hypothesized, may have devoted itself all the more to nationalist causes. Pollmann noted that these pastors affected nationalist as well as social concerns.[52] In 1896 Naumann entered professional politics by founding the National-Social Association, which combined both motifs. Church nationalism and social activism complemented each other in the sense that both fostered social reconciliation. It is worth emphasizing that the primary goal of the EOK and Christian-social pastors alike in 1890 was social reconciliation which, like nationalism, united, not social politics, which divided and begat internal conflict. Later, in the Weimar period, the motifs of "social" and "national" became virtually interchangeable in the minds of many churchmen because of this affinity.

Why strong nationalist feelings prevailed within the church before the war may in part be explained by the failure of the church to act as a dynamic force in Prussian society. Membership declined or lapsed into indifference, doctrinal dissension abounded, attacks from the outside proliferated, and state ties spiked chances for a social counterattack. Through nationalism, however, it was still possible to associate the destiny of the nation with Protestantism, a claim central to the concerns of the Evangelical League for the Protection of German-Protestant Interests (Evangelischer Bund zur Wahrung der deutsch-protestantischen Interessen).

By 1914 the Evangelical League had grown into a mammoth organization, enrolling some half-million members. The league, founded in 1886, aspired to set a Protestant political defense against the growing power of "Rome" as the Catholic Center party emerged from its pariah status during the Kulturkampf to a position of considerable importance in the calculations of the Prussian and imperial governments. Protestants could take great pride in the mighty empire forged and ruled by the Protestant Hohenzollern family and dominated by Protestant Prussia. Yet political necessity obliged the Kaiser and king, their summus episcopus, to follow a policy of confessional parity, which, the league complained, worked out to the disadvantage of Protestantism. As a consequence, the league took the initiative in defending, advancing, and lobbying for perceived Protestant interests. The heady nationalist claims fostered by the league well suited this purpose: Protestantism had historically nurtured the German or Prussian ethos and given the state its moorings and values.[53]

The frustrations and sense of impotence of the prewar church reached their alarming peak during the first months of the revolution when Socialists, now ensconced in government, seemed about to disestablish churches and shatter the Volkskirche. The path to a politically activist church in the Republic began with the political struggle to preserve the Volkskirche — the preferential status of established churches and Christian education in public schools. This path branched into many areas, sometimes more in intention than in actual performance, once the survival of the institutional church was assured.

By necessity and design, the activism of Old-Prussian churchmen in the Weimar era led far beyond Stoecker's concentration on the social problem. More than any event, the revolution brought home to churchmen the debilitating social divisions and political animosities that afflicted German public life. The chaotic economic and political condition of Germany during much of the Weimar period filled them with darkest despair, challenging the church to respond. Quite as important, the separation of church and state, which the revolution and National Assembly initiated but left incomplete, accorded churches enough freedom to pursue an activist program. No longer need Old-Prussian churchmen feel hampered by political concern for the monarchical order to which the church had been tied organizationally, ideologically, and emotionally. Now a new effort, fueled by the frustrations of the past, could be launched to win back lost ground. But the most provocative reason for the development of an activist Volkskirche stemmed from the assumption that the centuries-old Christian state had come to a dismal end with the emergence of the Weimar Republic. The religionless state seemed out of place in a Christian folk and morally harmful to it. Changed circumstances after the war rather than any new theological insight accounted for the resolve of many Old-Prussian churchmen to inter the ghost of political quietism.

Such was the conclusion that Vice-president Kaftan drew in his speech at the Church Federation Assembly in 1921.[54] In the absence of a Christian state and until "the old symbiotic relationship with the Christian state is restored," the Volkskirche must alone carry unprecedented responsibilities for nurturing Christian imponderables. Kaftan would even endorse passive resistance against the religionless state if it thwarted the Volkskirche's aspirations. To him the defense of Christian imponderables was an act of obedience to the Word of God, their creator.

Kaftan feared lest Protestant "glorification" of the state in the past conceal the inner transformation of the present state and the hollowness of its cultural pretenses. The new state hardly warranted such devotion. A religionless state can cater only to a spiritually void civilization. The Volkskirche must reclaim its creative role as the generator of culture. Accordingly, the religionless state must be forced back into the specific tasks reserved by God for the state as the guarantor of public order. Here

Kaftan had particularly in mind the current question (as framed by church leaders) of whether the culturally creative spirit of Christianity or the secular spirit of the religionless state should imbue public education.

Clearly Kaftan wished to justify and inspire the closed-front mentality that had seeped into the Old-Prussian and other Evangelical churches since the revolution. The churches and the associations that they had spawned fostered harmony within in order to close fronts to the outside and to mount a collective resistance against the sallies of the religionless state. Expressing this siege mentality, Kaftan called for a comprehensive Evangelical people's league (Volksbund) spanning Germany to shield Christian values wherever and however imperiled. A discussant would close fronts against "Rome" as well. For Catholicism, especially the Catholic Center party, seemed allied with the "modern state" to the disadvantage of Protestantism.[55] Indeed, a smaller second front closed against "Rome" soon after the revolutionary threat to both confessions had passed.

Kaftan's summons to activism admits one to the core of predominant assumptions within the Old-Prussian church.[56] Yet he did not explicitly forge a link to the more narrow social concerns of preexisting strains of activism. Obviously he had little sympathy for the less noticeable Evangelical-social strain, perpetuated in the congress, which eschewed conceptualizing social problems from the point of view of a Volkskirche fighting for its values in public life. But he shared the Christian Socials' conception of an authoritarian society bonded by Christian faith and Christian nationalism. For Kaftan, as for Stoecker, the crucial question was whether Christianity could prevail in private and public life and still bond a national community.

What consequences attended the new role that Kaftan would fashion for the Volkskirche? The discussion following his address prompted questions that would recur and had already risen.[57] Martin Rade, editor of the influential liberal periodical Die christliche Welt, entered the lists as the most prominent republican churchman. He debunked the metaphysical notion of state that permitted Kaftan to denounce the Republic as religionless. Because of his nominalist view of political authority, Rade could argue that criticism of the Republic as religionless was misplaced and, in any event, unwarranted. One must rather realistically judge the state by what it did, not by what it tended to do because of some alleged essence. The dispute over what constituted proper political authority for the Christian would persist throughout the Republic.

Several other enduring issues cropped up as well. Kaftan had asserted that proclaiming the Word of God should also include the nurturing of Christian imponderables into which the Word had historically breathed its life. He meant to defuse the inevitable objection that the Volkskirche had no mandate to reach beyond the literal proclamation of the Word. His argument partially countered another objection as well: If the Volkskirche organized its members in defense of Christian imponderables, would it not forfeit its spiritual role as it struggled to emerge as a power in public life? Indeed, such became the bitter complaint of some church liberals as the closed-front Volkskirche tried to close them in against their will.

Another dilemma—that of political neutrality—confronted Evangelical churches in an acute form because of Kaftan's contention that the Volkskirche itself and not merely its members as citizens must actively enter the political struggle. If the Volkskirche must do battle with the religionless state, in what sense could it retain a semblance of political neutrality indispensable for a church embracing a large membership of diverse political loyalties?

Kaftan's response characterized the ambiguous policy of the Old-Prussian church. Two discussants drove home one point that Kaftan doubtless intended. Both called for an end in the church to the old, widely accepted slogan, "Politics do not concern the church." One commented that such a slogan would entrench the "princes of this world" in their power at the expense of Christians. The other, Reinhard Mumm, now a Nationalist Reichstag deputy, added that the slogan complemented the Socialist position that religion was a private matter, both dangerous errors. The Volkskirche may legitimately fight for its own political cause, Kaftan counseled, but not for that of any party. Even pastors might preach political sermons if conscience compelled, provided that they thereby proclaimed the Word of God (in Kaftan's broader sense). Kaftan claimed to have delivered such a political sermon during elections to constituent assemblies in 1919. Within that context, however, the effect of a political sermon amounted to a decided endorsement of the political Right and repudiation of the Left. In fairness to Kaftan, one must add that only political quietism in a politically free church could effectively have exorcised this problem. But, as subsequent chapters show, the Old-Prussian church balked at paying the price that intentional neglect of its political interests would carry.

2

THE WAR

OLD-PRUSSIAN CHURCHMEN tended to look back upon the Second Empire as a model government cemented by monarchical authority and moral purpose. Such a judgment, however, was qualified. Church leaders knew that the very forces that wrought instability in the young Republic had issued directly from the Second Empire that they extolled. Prewar Germany was deeply divided politically. Precisely because of these divisions, churchmen cherished the sense of community (Volksgemeinschaft) that the war initially aroused in all segments of the German people. Even Socialists, traditionally hostile to military appropriations, voted for war credits and joined the party truce.

But as the war grew more desperate, the united front against the enemy began to crack and hostility toward the church resumed. The year 1917 alerted Old-Prussian churchmen to both external and internal dangers. In that year, the Reichstag accepted a peace resolution that churchmen considered inimical to German war aims, and the Kaiser's Easter proclamation, promising electoral reforms in Prussia, seemed to portend a disestablishment that could destroy the Volkskirche. If one compares the expectations of Old-Prussian churchmen at the onset of war with their disappointment at the end, one can begin to fathom their aversion for the ill-fated Weimar Republic. The same socialist and democratic forces that, in their opinion, had shattered the Volksgemeinschaft and thus Germany's capability of prosecuting the war were also those that had swept away the Christian monarchy and erected a republic.

PREWAR POLITICAL COMMITMENTS

For conservatives and Bismarck, Stahl's monarchical principle had been axiomatic: towering over the parties, the monarch acted to modulate opposing interests of classes and parties and to ensure continuity of policy independent of these interests. The history of the Second Empire documented the failure of the monarchical principle to function as expected. Spared the necessity of composing differences that parliamentary responsibility would compel, parties acted to represent and defend group or class interests against the government, while at the same time espousing a distinctive Weltanschauung against the others. Under these circumstances, the monarchical principle operated to accentuate divisions rather than to bridge them.

These divisions proved fateful for the Protestant churches. Of the six major parties that organized nationally in the Second Empire, most churchmen could muster sympathy for only three — the two conservative parties and the National Liberals.[1] Of these three, the German Conservative party (Deutschkonservative Partei), originally a Prussian party, drew the greatest support from Old-Prussian churchmen. Conservatives posed as guardians of church interests in accordance with the theory of symbiosis delineated above. From the predominantly Protestant rural areas east of the Elbe River the party drew its greatest strength, though it lost ground in Reichstag elections from 1887 to 1912. German unification at first drove a wedge between Bismarck and the main conservative party. Its offshoot, the Free Conservative party (Freikonservative Partei), extolled Bismarck's leadership for nationalist reasons. But main-line Conservatives posed as nationalists only when they believed that imperial and Prussian interests coincided. As the National Liberal party (Nationalliberale Partei) muted its demand for parliamentary responsibility, it became a real option even for conservative Protestants west and south of the Elbe. It appeared, in fact, as the conservative party in these regions. After its contretemps with Bismarck in the late 1870s, the importance of this party for the government declined, as did its mandates in the Reichstag.

Hardly an option at all for most churchmen was the Progressive party (Deutsche Fortschrittspartei). The left-liberal party's opposition to clerical influence on education and its indifference, even hostility, to church life were reprehensible. Still, Friedrich Naumann and some of his followers chose to join one of the three parties into which left liberals had split, after Naumann's attempt to found his own party, the National-Social Association

(Nationalsozialer Verein), aborted in 1903. Small in numbers though once more united in 1910, the Progressive party acted increasingly as a bridge between National Liberals and the growing reformist wing of the Socialist party.

The Socialist party—the Social Democratic Labor party (Sozialdemo-kratische Arbeiterpartei)—remained beyond the pale for almost every Protestant pastor and loyal church member. The party did not take on a decidedly Marxist hue until the adoption in 1891 of its Erfurt program, which, however, did not condemn Christianity explicitly. But churchmen, who often equated socialism with atheism, grew alarmed as the Socialist party increased its mandates in the Reichstag from 2 in 1871 to 110 in 1912, becoming the largest Reichstag faction with over a quarter of the seats.

As the Socialist party burgeoned, a social and political chasm widened between Socialist workers and the remainder of German society. It is true that the party's right wing welcomed the prospect of achieving socialist goals within the framework of parliamentary democracy. But the party stood on record as opposed to revisionism, voted against military appro-priations, and on ceremonial occasions preached the need for continuous class struggle—all of which could not help but put off potential liberal allies. Moreover, as party leadership shifted toward a reformist tactic, the left wing grew more radical, anticipating the wartime split that produced the dissident Independent Socialists and Spartacists.

Because of confessional rivalry, the Catholic Center party (Zentrums-partei) offered at best a very limited option to German Protestants, though it also shared a concern for church privileges. Compared with its Protestant counterpart, the social Catholic movement, which formulated the Center's social program, took shape earlier, marshaled greater support from workers, and found greater response among church leaders. Accordingly, the Christian trade unions that formed in the 1890s embraced many more Catholic workers than Protestant. Before the war, conservative Centrist leaders had come to see in the existing political structure a strong defense of Catholic interests. But a growing democratic wing, influenced by Matthias Erzberger, favored a change of fronts toward the political Left, enabling the Center to collaborate with Progressives and Socialists in the political crises of 1917.

To a considerable extent, the political-party loyalties of Old-Prussian churchmen varied according to their position within the church-party spectrum. The exceptional size of the Old-Prussian church, its synodical structure, and frequent doctrinal disputes stimulated the growth of four major church parties, which continued to act out their traditional roles during the Weimar era. Certain affinities predisposed members of a particular church party to favor a corresponding political party according to a more-or-less common Weltanschauung.

Most conservative of all in theology as in political belief, confessional Lutherans longed for an unblemished confessional church rooted in Reformation creeds.[2] They deplored the doctrinal vagueness of the Union. Confessional Lutherans upheld an ideal episcopal church largely independent of the state. Constituting the church Right, confessional Lutherans and Positive Unionists dominated the General Synod and provincial synods after 1879.

Liberals occupied the other end of the church-political spectrum. Founded on a national basis in 1863, the liberal Protestant Association (Protestantenverein) aspired to reconcile religion and culture and thus stay the defection of intellectuals from the church. The affinity that liberals professed to see between the Christian and the German spirit, even the identification of the two, predisposed them to a preference for a national church and to a religiously tinged nationalism. More than nationalism linked political and religious liberals. At the 1909 convention of the Protestant Association, Friedrich Naumann explained that individualism and a shared abhorrence of authoritarianism constituted the common denominator of both movements.[3] The association never struck deep roots in Prussia, where only a thousand of its membership of twenty-five thousand resided in 1890.

Part of the Protestant Association's weakness lay in its inability to capture the membership of a new breed of religious liberals who rose to prominence after 1875 — those impressed by the theology of Albrecht Ritschl (1822−89). Ritschl's followers saw in his theology a means of transcending the conflict of church parties and their theological disputes by interpreting scripture and Luther in an ethical sense. But they soon joined older liberals in a common struggle against doctrinal restraints that nettled the liberal clergy. Martin Rade, Friedrich Naumann's brother-in-law, helped to found the impressive periodical of this group, *Die christliche Welt,* which spawned the Association of the Friends of *Die christliche Welt* in 1903.

Liberals encountered considerable hostility within the Old-Prussian church, though not enough to threaten their survival. The liberal concept of an immanent God working through culture (dubbed "culture Protestantism") undermined set Reformation doctrines. The church Right's domination of synods and intolerance of liberalism forced liberals to look to the king's church government for protection. But church government, though trying to balance off conflicting pressures in the church, did not quite recognize liberals as a legitimate church party.

Even more galling was disciplinary action, or after 1910 trial for heresy, to which radical liberals exposed themselves if they vaunted their convictions publicly. In the two decades before the war, younger liberal pastors, trained in critical and historical theology, increasingly assaulted the doctrinal norms of the church, and some soon found themselves in deep trouble with church authorities. In 1911 Pastor Karl Jatho of Cologne, a liberal, was defrocked, and in 1912 Pastor Gottfried Traub of Dortmund, a prominent liberal, was released from pastoral service for allegedly abusing church authorities in his spirited defense of Jatho. It is little wonder that liberals sought a democratic church, congregational autonomy, and even state controls to assure minority rights against church government and synods in doctrinal matters. For opposite reasons both confessional Lutherans and liberals found much to deplore in the prewar church.

Between confessional Lutheran and liberal extremes lay the moderately liberal Evangelical Association (Evangelische Vereinigung) and the moderately orthodox Positive Union, both of which stemmed from an older middle party that had taken a firm stand for the Prussian Union.[4] More than the Positive Union, the association tolerated liberals for the sake of church unity, and posed as the party of reconciliation between contending church factions. Precisely for this reason the association, also known as the Middle party, could appreciate the mediating role of the summus episcopus and a strong church government largely independent of synodical majorities. Its members tended to support National Liberals politically. The Positive Union was no sooner constituted in 1876 than it emerged as the largest and most important church party, a position that it held throughout the Weimar era. From its very beginning the Positive Union sought to confine the authority of church and state bureaucracies in order to extend that of clergymen and synods. Naturally liberals feared changes that would increase the power of their orthodox opponents, fears that rose with the fall of the summus episcopus in 1918. More so than others, leaders of the Positive Union bore the brunt of responsibility for Evangelical workingmen's clubs, the Church-Social Conference, Stoecker's Christian-Social party, and the Inner Mission. The Positive Union also drew strength from the Reformed in western Prussia, where the latter for historical reasons found their greatest support.

Pietists were another group that, like the Reformed, constituted no church party but still made its weight felt in synods. After 1875 English and American revivalism sparked the proliferation throughout Germany of pietist societies (Gemeinschaften) formed outside of the official church by born-again Christians. Stoecker's party found some of its most devoted followers among pietists in western Germany. In 1897 the older German pietist societies and the newer formed the Gnadauer Association, a loose confederation that in the mid-1920s embraced about six thousand societies and 225,000 registered members in Germany and Austria. The sectlike organization of born-again pietists generated great tension with the comprehensive and more coldly formal Volkskirche.[5] In the Weimar period, after initial confusion, pietists took a more active role in church affairs, aligning themselves with the church Right in Old-Prussian synods. The church paper, Licht und Leben, edited by Josef Gauger, held pride of place in molding or expressing pietist opinion in Prussia.

Deepening doctrinal divisions aroused the fear that the Landeskirche as a Volkskirche could not long survive. A Volkskirche embracing almost all Protestants of differing beliefs seemed irreconcilable with the confessional church that the church Right deemed essential. A repetition of the Jatho "affair," to which liberals took angry exception, seemed likely to break up the Volkskirche. A liberal proposal to salvage the Volkskirche, widely discussed until the war, suggested that the Landeskirche devolve into a merely administrative association (Zweckverband), leaving doctrinal matters to congregations.[6] But the church Right would not assent to a church stripped of creeds, and others feared so radical a departure from the traditional Volkskirche. Doctrinal controversy induced a sense of impotence within the church as well, already heightened by the defection of the church masses and by the failure of the church to grapple with the social question. How could such a church combat unbelief in public life, with its own ranks in disarray and its own beliefs contested from within?

In the public controversy over the "affairs" of 1911–12, the political liberal press defended the principle of religious liberty, and conservative papers argued the need for doctrinal authority. This response demonstrated a traditional alignment of political liberalism and conservatism with corresponding church parties within the Old-Prussian church. Inasmuch as the church Right dominated prewar synods, the general political complexion of the Old-Prussian church appeared largely conservative. While pastors tending toward the liberal church camp favored National Liberals or Progressives (following Naumann), the more orthodox voted overwhelmingly for conservative parties. Clerical political preferences could also vary regionally. In southern Germany, pastors could readily throw their support to the National Liberals or even the Progressives. In the rural areas of Prussia, especially east of the Elbe, pastors consistently voted conservative along with landlords and peasants. Most pastors shied away from Progressives, though left liberals muted their hostility as Naumann and some of his followers entered their ranks. The few pastors who turned Socialist found it impossible to stay in the ministry.[7]

The Reichstag elections of 1912 revealed a political cleavage between the large mass of nominal church members on the one hand and prevailing church sentiments on the other. While Conservatives and National Liberals lost mandates, Socialists gained, finding their strongest response in Protestant areas.[8] In seventeen electoral districts where Protestants numbered over 80 percent of the total population, Socialists captured 44.9 percent of the vote, Conservatives only 20.7, and National Liberals a scant 12.8.

The 1912 elections were ominous for the Bismarckian system as well as for Protestant churches. The dramatic increase of Socialist mandates and the growth of the Center's democratic wing meant that a majority combination of nonconservative parties — Socialists, Progressives, Centrists, and National Liberals — might press successfully to alter the existing political structure. Especially since 1908, nonconservative parties did form tactical alliances in the Reichstag and in the south German states in support of suffrage and tax reform, parliamentary responsibility, and social legislation. The bloc came unstuck as the war approached, but the collaboration of these parties revived again in the political crises of 1917.

A pall of political stagnation descended upon Germany during the Wilhelmian era, for neither the executive nor the legislature could provide decisive leadership.[9] The almost continuous increase of hostile Socialist deputies limited sharply the government's field of maneuver in the Reichstag. Increasingly the government failed to steer its own course, tacking instead with the wind of majority opinion. For their part, parties had become so accustomed to their traditional roles as a largely negative check upon government policy and so conscious of their own differences as to make a concerted attempt to introduce parliamentary responsibility well-nigh impossible. Only the crises of 1917 could prod nonconservative parties to take the initiative in constitutional reform, and then only halfheartedly.

Compounding the pervading sense of political stagnation was the adamant refusal of conservative parties to consider a fundamental revision of the Prussian three-class suffrage system. The warped effects of this system can be seen in the results of the 1913 elections to the House of Deputies: With only 14.75 percent of the popular vote, Conservatives received 143 seats, while Socialists with 28.38 percent managed to capture a mere ten.[10] From their political base in the House of Deputies and in the House of Lords, Conservatives had managed to entrench themselves in the Prussian government and to help shape imperial policy through Prussia's preeminent position in the imperial Bundesrat (upper house). Nonconservative parties in the Reichstag deplored what for them amounted to a pernicious influence upon imperial policy. They saw in the three-class suffrage a national issue of paramount concern and in the decade before the war pressed for suffrage reform—Socialists and Progressives for an equal franchise, National Liberals for a system of plural voting. The issue would soon surface in the war and plague church leaders. Through an equal suffrage and more equitable districting, Socialists could expect to supplant Conservatives as the largest faction and contest Volkskirche privileges.

WARTIME NATIONALISM

The nationalism displayed by many churchmen and much of the German public appropriated and secularized Christian motifs. Their religiously tinged nationalism dated from the War of Liberation in 1813, when Prussian pastors preached a holy war against the "anti-Christ," Napoleon. Through this struggle against the French, they thought, God had unexpectedly wrought a moral and spiritual renewal of Prussian society. In the process, He had blessed Prussian arms with success.[11]

Later, German idealists, following Herder and then Fichte, abstracted a metaphysical concept of folk that also focused nationalism in Evangelical churches. Through membership in the German folk, all Germans shared a mystical sense of identity and an obligation to serve and sacrifice. Christian conservatives, such as Stahl, might accept the concept of folk in a cultural sense. But they feared its political consequences. Not from the folk did political authority stem, but from God. Beginning in the 1880s, Prussian conservatives could join liberals with fewer reservations in extolling the nationality that the Second Empire served. A flood of nationalist feeling overwhelmed remaining reservations within the Old-Prussian church as the war began. Only later did the war force upon churchmen the problem of reconciling war and a Christian predisposition toward peace.

At first the circumstances surrounding the outbreak of war overshadowed this social-ethical problem. Uncritically, Old-Prussian churchmen accepted the "encirclement" explanation propounded by the Kaiser: "During a time of complete peace, we have been attacked in that word's truest sense. By the envy of our enemy who encircles us. For twenty-five years I have secured and maintained peace. Now the sword had been thrust into my hand."[12] By attacking as it did through neutral Belgium, he claimed, Germany acted only in self-defense. Throughout the military struggle and later, German churches never admitted any specific German responsibility for engulfing Europe in war. Characteristically, the 1924 social proclamation of the Evangelical churches alluded to a "war forced upon us."[13]

Belief in Germany's innocence released a tide of national feeling. Even the official church history, written by Martin Schian, admitted that pronouncements of churchmen sometimes reflected a colossal national egoism.[14] Schian published his two-volume work after the war when the political Left condemned the churches for their chauvinism and support of an increasingly hopeless war. Against this criticism, Schian argued that the churches properly felt obliged to bolster the will to victory insofar as victory seemed possible. But neither the military stalemate in the West nor the oppressive length of the war shook the confidence of most churchmen that victory could be had if only the German folk could muster the will to win. Accordingly, pastors preached "holding out" (Durchhalten) until the very end of the war.

Though he argued that wartime sermons generally kept a salubrious balance, Schian admitted their tendency to err on the side of Pan-German nationalism. He openly cited excesses found particularly in three types of sermons: (1) The "victory" sermon, given frequently at the beginning of the war, praised God for success and showed little religious depth. (2) Only a little less dangerous was the "hope and trust" sermon, which assured the congregation of ultimate victory by appealing to the righteousness of Germany's cause. In 1917 an assemblage of church officials addressed the Kaiser in the same vein: "God the Lord wishes soon to give Your Majesty, our German people, the desired noble victorious peace."[15] (3) The "folkish" sermon contended that God's special blessing had legitimated the German cause so that the superior values of the German folk might enrich human culture. A variant of this type of sermon was that God had chosen Germany to punish His enemies.

All three types had in common a nationalist self-righteousness running athwart the ground theme of Christian repentance, which might imply coresponsibility for the war. Preachers prone to such exaggeration were often dubbed "war theologians." The term makes theological sense only when limited to those who purveyed a distinctive war theology. Yet published wartime sermons, Wilhelm Pressel has concluded, generally reflected a war theology that justified the motifs enumerated by Schian as excesses; his exceptions were more the rule. War theology appears to have set the tone for Protestant homiletics.[16]

War theology, according to Pressel, mated theological liberalism, particularly the theology of Albrecht Ritschl, with folkish nationalism. Ritschl fostered an ethical interpretation of Christianity by which God worked immanently through history and culture to liberate men from materialism in order to realize His moral kingdom on earth. War theology reduced the sphere of ethical activity to the folk, conceived as a vessel through which God revealed His will. In the ecstatically sensed folk solidarity of the first war months, war theologians, according to Pressel, heard the summons of God for folk renewal. War theology did not so much refute Reformation theology as shift its accent: grace became God's offer of folkish renewal; faith, trust in God's guidance of the folk; the communion of saints, the community of the folk; God's covenant, a special bond with the German folk; law, obedience to folk necessities and values; and sin, dereliction to folkish responsibilities. War theologians, bolstered by German victories, could assume that God favored German arms and that the war amounted to a clash of values as well as arms.

It is little wonder that Protestant churchmen condemned the enemy in harsh moral terms. They similarly lashed out at Allied stories of German atrocities—"war lies"—and claims to a higher political morality. With such ruses the vengeful Allies turned world opinion against the just German cause and forced an innocent Germany to defend itself against much of the world.[17]

German churches lent the war effort their full support. Statements by church organs absolved the Kaiser of any war guilt and enjoined parishioners to hold out to the all-but-certain victorious end. A widely used war liturgy and patriotic songs lent color to many types of services. From pulpits, pastors encouraged thrift, scored war profiteers and food hoarders, and urged parishioners to subscribe to war bonds. The EOK, church institutions, and congregations invested heavily in war bonds, funds for the most part irredeemably lost following Germany's catastrophic inflation in 1923. Thousands of church bells—Schian estimated 18,668—and countless organ pipes were donated to the war effort.[18] Wherever possible congregations sought to ameliorate local hardships, comfort the bereaved, and send letters and church periodicals to the front.

In several ways the war experience quickened Old-Prussian church life.[19] Church parties concluded a truce for the duration of the war, pledging to end party strife and forgo press feuds. Soon the formidable prewar movement against church membership came to a halt. As the first exhilarating battles took place, church attendance rose precipitously. Some argued that "war religiosity" lacked genuineness. Others sensed a religious stirring in the war experience and claimed that the war had helped bridge the growing prewar gap between church and folk. But that gap widened again as the heady nationalism of the first war years waned and gave way to a desperate longing for peace.

As 1917 began anxious churchmen had some reason to believe that Germany might soon break the military stalemate. Prospects of ultimate victory, however, clouded over when the Reichstag on July 19 adopted a nonannexationist peace resolution that signaled to many churchmen a distressing lack of determination to prosecute a successful war.

At the outbreak of war, Germany had proclaimed that it fought a defensive war. But its political and military leaders soon developed extensive war aims that, if realized, would secure for Germany a hegemonic position on the continent. As German armies descended on France, a war-aims movement took shape to fasten these goals upon the government and to bolster public morale in their support. But Chancellor Theobald von Bethmann-Hollweg would define war aims only ambiguously in public so as to retain a free hand in diplomacy and to avoid public debate. He pursued a policy of the "diagonal" meant to appease Socialist and Pan-German political extremes, hoping to smooth over prewar animosities. Socialists had voted war credits in the belief that Germany fought only in self-defense. Grateful to Socialists, Bethmann intended to wed them to the nation by promising a "new orientation" politically after the war. What this might mean he also deliberately left vague, so as not to provoke the political Right.

By the spring of 1917 the policy of the diagonal had lost its charm.[20]

The two issues of war aims and political reform had blended into the more ultimate question of whether and to what extent a democratic order would supplant the traditional constitutional monarchy. It seemed improbable to the exponents of the old order that the middle and lower classes would tolerate the Bismarckian system in the event that the costly war ended in defeat or even in a negotiated peace. As the swell of war-aims propaganda enveloped Germany and attacked Bethmann-Hollweg, a growing minority of Socialists balked at supporting an "imperialist" war. One group of left radicals, later known as Spartacists, hoped to exploit the war for revolution. A larger group rejected war credits in order to constrain the government into accepting a negotiated peace. The two split off from the parent party (thereafter known as Majority Socialists) and organized in the spring of 1917 as the Independent Social Democratic party (Unabhängige Sozial-demokratische Partei Deutschlands).

These defections from the main Socialist party fed on the resentment of the lower classes as the war stalemated. Food shortages compounded by the British blockade, the toll of deaths, compulsory labor, the harsh siege law, and the apparent success of war-aims propaganda discredited the Majority Socialist policy of war support. Threatened by defections, Majority Socialists had all the more reason to hold the government to a war of defense and commit it to concrete political reform. But in July 1917, when war credits came up for renewal, the imperial government had moved in the opposite direction to pursue the full scope of its war aims.

By then it had become clear that German submarines had failed to knock Britain out of the war, while forcing the United States into it. It had also become apparent to the Centrist Erzberger that the Central Powers verged on collapse. In his speech on July 6, he proposed that the Reichstag proclaim its support for a peace of reconciliation. His alarming speech catalyzed Center and Progressive factions, which had favored extensive war aims, and Majority Socialist deputies, painfully aware of their dilemma, into a Reichstag majority that sought to commit the government to a negotiated peace and predispose the enemy toward it. The result was passage of the Reichstag peace resolution of July 19 that proclaimed Germany's wish to conclude a peace without total victory, a peace of reconciliation without annexations, the "Scheidemann peace" supported by most Socialists. The groups within the war-aims movement, including many Protestant churchmen, countered by preaching a "Hindenburg peace," one of total victory and extensive war aims. Such a peace General

Erich Ludendorff, the dominant figure in the Supreme Command and in the government from July 1917 on, insisted that he could deliver until the very last months of the war.

During the course of these developments the resistance of many church-men against a negotiated peace hardened. Earlier, in December 1916, Bethmann had tried to move the Allies toward a negotiated settlement. When this attempt failed, churchmen feared that the Allied rejection signaled the determination of the enemy to destroy Germany.[21] The peace resolution and subsequent Vatican peace overtures struck them as both dangerous and futile and led many into the ranks of the Fatherland party (Deutsche Vaterlandspartei), founded in September 1917. This ostensibly nonpartisan party, organized to marshal popular protest against the peace resolution, advocated a continuation of the war to a victorious end, opposed political reforms, and eventually enlisted over 1.25 million members throughout Germany.

This dispute over the war and its aims brought into the open the opinions of a small, concerned minority of largely liberal churchmen, whom Martin Rade had encouraged to take a public stand. Before the war, Rade and other Friends of *Die christliche Welt* had actively participated in the German peace movement, which otherwise had made little headway within Protestant churches. The war prompted intense debate and deep-ened political divisions among the Friends, who split into three groups. Some tended to view the spirit of the Sermon on the Mount as unreservedly binding. The other extreme extolled loyalty to folk as the more immediate obligation of Christians. Caught between extremes, Rade urged peace as a Christian duty while taking Germany's just interests into account.[22]

Since the onset of hostilities, Rade had deplored the failure of the churches to work for peace. Every nation could consider itself the aggrieved party and argue that it fought merely in self-defense. European churches, like most Socialists initially, adopted the position of their governments. The war experience of the Church of England was remarkably similar to that of the Old-Prussian church.[23] In both, churchmen converted the rationale of a war of defense into an ideological crusade, a holy war against the evil that the enemy embodied. For such a mentality, a negotiated peace amounted to compromise with evil. That the churches seemed to promote hatred rather than peace signaled to Rade the bankruptcy of Christendom.

Encouraged by the peace resolution, Rade proposed on July 26, 1917 that Christians in warring nations bring pressure to bear upon their governments in the interests of peace. Karl Aner and four other Berlin pastors responded with an appeal to Christians throughout the world to work for a peace of reconciliation by opposing the distrust, intentional lies, avarice, and deification of naked power that made war possible. Several other peace declarations soon issued from the embryonic peace movement within the Evangelical churches.[24]

That these appeals would arouse violent controversy becomes apparent when one examines the war aims that tempted Evangelical churchmen. Schian overshot the mark when he claimed: "[The sermon] never preached a war of conquest; he slanders who would assert [the contrary]."[25] War sermons, according to Pressel, "not infrequently" launched hopes for a larger Germany.[26] Annexationist and reparation demands appeared in church periodicals, including the liberal *Protestantische Monatshefte* and *Protestantenblatt,* which refused to join other liberals in the peace movement. Convinced that a determined enemy sought to annihilate an innocent Germany, possibly most churchmen regarded annexations as necessary if future wars were to be avoided. Thus a declaration of the Evangelical League asserted: "A victorious Germany alone can secure the peace of Europe."[27] One can sometimes find the argument that failure to obtain annexations amounted to losing the war. The Christian-Social party demanded the dismemberment and partial annexation of Belgium, adjustment of Germany's borders according to military need, German control over central Africa, and reparations.[28] Churchmen argued for imposing a considerable indemnity on their enemies, only to decry that subsequently forced on Germany. One, for example, reasoned: "It is only fair if our enemies, who have caused war damages, also pay for them."[29]

The war experience and an acute sense of aggrieved honor bolstered an already strong commitment to folkish nationalism and aversion to Western "internationalism" in church quarters. Much of the church press, various church organizations, congregational councils, and church districts endorsed the Fatherland party. Appalled, Rade deplored the announced intention of a Breslau pastor to preach on the theme "Christians to the front against the worst enemy: the black-red-golden international" in support of the Fatherland party.[30] Traditionally leery of conspicuous political activity, pastors naively lent the Fatherland party their support, persuaded as they were that allegiance to the fatherland could scarcely be construed as partisan. Against the impression that pastors enrolled in that party spoke for the church, seven Württemberg pastors issued a protest declaration rebuking the party for insinuating that those who refused to join lacked patriotism.

Increasingly it became clear that the summer storm over the peace resolution had split liberals politically along the same lines as the debate over nationalism had earlier. Gottfried Traub's frenetic promotion of "holding out" persuaded Old-Prussian church authorities to restore him to pastoral service, and this former Progressive found a new political home in the Nationalist party after the war.[31] At the other extreme, such pacifist liberals as Karl Aner found their way into the postwar phenomenon of religious socialism.

Because of their nationalism, the bulk of Evangelical churchmen appeared to condemn both the peace resolution and the papal peace offer. War theology, according to Pressel, provided a characteristic stimulus to "hold out." Though God favored the German cause, He would not assure victory if the folk did not respond to His summons for self-renewal. Accordingly, acceptance of a negotiated peace short of total German victory amounted to a rejection of God's will and proffered grace.[32] In October 1917 the Saxon Provincial Synod urged parishioners to disregard "agitation for a premature end of the war."[33] Churchmen argued that the necessary victory could yet be won if only the German people possessed a determined will, that enticing thoughts of peace short of victory undermined this will, and that hasty peace resolutions convinced the enemy of Germany's inability to carry the war farther.

Annexationist churchmen added confessional concerns to their criticism of the papal peace offer.[34] Some claimed that the Pope was partisan, favoring the interests of the Allies. If troops pulled back to the boundaries of 1914, as the Vatican suggested, Germany would forfeit the fruits of its hard-won victories. An outspoken official of the Evangelical League reasoned that the Pope wished to prevent the Protestant Hohenzollern from dominating central Europe. Quick to link the peace resolution inspired by the Catholic Centrist Erzberger with papal peace overtures, some argued that the Vatican had schemed to foist the resolution upon a gullible Germany. They watched with alarm as the Center party made common cause with Socialists and Progressives after the July peace resolution. This shift also meant that Protestant churches more than the Catholic provoked the anger of those who yearned for a negotiated peace.

Under these circumstances, the peace appeal of Aner and his brethren could make little headway in Evangelical quarters. The churches, according to Schian, could react in no other way, for such declarations encouraged the false belief that an "honorable" peace depended merely on the goodwill of Germany.[35] If Germany had acted righteously from the beginning, what more could it do for peace now that its very existence seemed at stake? Some 160 irate Berlin pastors signed a protest statement contending that Germany must choose between complete victory and ignominious defeat.[36] They could not imagine extending the hand of brotherhood to "shameless slanderers," foreign church leaders who condemned Germany for the war. They regretted that Aner's declaration lent moral support to the Reichstag majority. Both liberals and the more orthodox condemned the illicit fusion of religion and politics that they professed to find in the declaration. Appealing to Luther's authority, Professor Hermann Jordan of Erlangen argued correctly that Christianity may not be invoked to determine the rules by which God's moral order operated, but he also gave the erroneous impression that Christians might not sit in moral judgment over the actions of the state. Likewise, the *Protestantenblatt* resurrected the old thesis that pastors should not meddle in politics and that Christianity could have no bearing upon specific state policies.[37]

It was against this radical separation of public and private morality, against a double morality, that Rade and Aner protested. If the Christian owed uncritical allegiance to the state, he was obliged to sanction a power struggle fought out among nations according to reasons of state. Rade eventually joined some 250 churchmen in signing the Aner appeal (whose wording he did not quite approve) because the ideas invoked against it "are impossible for Christians and damaging to the church."[38]

Obviously, a moral declaration of this sort had political implications just as much as an endorsement of the Fatherland party. But Aner and Rade hewed more closely to Luther's dualistic ethic than their antagonists. Many of the latter, admittedly, accepted the continuation of war as unavoidable under the circumstances, while deploring the spectacle of Christian nations locked in destructive combat.[39] But the war-peace debate exposed a double morality that absolutized and sanctified the nation state or that, at least, denied to Christians responsibility for passing moral judgment.

THE THREAT OF DISESTABLISHMENT

It was during the year 1917 that Old-Prussian churchmen became suddenly aware of internal dangers confronting the fatherland, the Christian monarchy, and the Volkskirche. The Reichstag peace resolution in July epitomized the first of these dangers, while the political reforms announced in the Kaiser's Easter proclamation seemed to herald the other two. The year looms as a watershed between the prewar era, characterized by intramural squabbles, and the postwar period, marked by political preoccupation and the struggle to keep the Volkskirche intact within a "religionless" democratic state.

Prompted by Bethmann-Hollweg, the Kaiser promised in his Easter proclamation to abolish the Prussian three-class suffrage system and to reform the House of Lords. Bethmann's promise of a "new orientation" had alarmed Conservatives while encouraging Majority Socialists and Progressives in the spring of 1917 to press for immediate reforms. For the sake of the war effort, National Liberals in the Reichstag also joined the reformers. Bethmann fully realized that he had to concede to the Left in order to shore up public morale and to work with the new Reichstag majority. He hoped to avoid immediate controversy by delaying reform until after the war. But the Reichstag majority pressed him to issue on July 12 a decree that committed the government to an equal franchise in Prussia and electoral reform even during the war.[40] (The Reichstag was already elected by an equal franchise.)

The July crisis had thus forced the government to accept the peace resolution and suffrage reform, both vehemently contested by the war-aims movement. That neither was successfully pursued may be charged largely to the account of the Supreme Command. Bethmann's successor, Georg von Hertling, could not induce the Prussian Landtag to introduce the equal vote so long as the Supreme Command dangled the prospect of total victory, as it did before and after the Brest-Litovsk peace with Russia in March 1918 and during the spring offensive of 1918. Accordingly, the Conservative tactic in the Landtag was to delay suffrage legislation until victory could deflate pressures for reform. The initiative taken by the Reichstag majority in July 1917 promised at least some hope of extricating Germany from war and of promoting domestic unity. But the policy of the Supreme Command drove the two domestic fronts that had solidified in 1917 still farther apart. Should victory now elude Germany, political reforms promised in 1917 could scarcely satisfy the nation in defeat.

In November 1917 the Prussian ministry submitted to the House of Deputies three bills for an equal franchise and a reconstitution of the House of Lords. But a majority of Conservatives and National Liberals settled instead on a discriminatory plural voting system, at a time when workers staged massive strikes against the war. Conservatives would not see that an equal franchise had become a state necessity for prosecuting the war. Accordingly, they condemned the reforming parties for exploiting the war situation, while Hertling recognized the imperative need for reform and gave Majority Socialists due credit for asserting control over dissident workers. Hertling tried to win over National Liberals by enlisting the aid of their Reichstag faction and to persuade Centrists by conceding constitutional guarantees that would safeguard established churches and confessional schools. Even these gambits failed when, on July 5, 1918, the House accepted a combination of constitutional guarantees and a discriminatory plural franchise.

Old-Prussian church leaders watched the struggle over the Prussian suffrage with foreboding. If Socialists managed to eclipse Conservatives as the largest faction, the reform could conceivably result in a disestablishment that could shatter the Volkskirche. Wilhelm Philipps, editor of *Die Reformation,* concluded: "The dream of a Christian state is dreamed out." He predicted that the proposed democratic suffrage would produce a "revolution in the church... the likes of which have not been experienced in Germany since the Reformation," resulting in a gradual "dechristianization" of the German people. "Anti-Christianity is arming and all those who pave the way for democracy give it aid," he charged. Indeed, "if democracy gains ascendance in the world, then begins the great fight between Christianity and anti-Christianity."[41]

Fear lest the gathering political cloud unleash its lightning upon the church fed such fulminations. If the "Christian" state were incapacitated by a Landtag hostile to the church, one might expect the privileged status of the church as well as confessional schools to go by the board. A brief look into each area reveals the dimension of this fear.

The privileged status of the Old-Prussian church was most conspicuous in its intricate system of church finance, which corresponding church and state laws consolidated in the years 1898 to 1909. In setting its annual budget, a congregation would estimate income from its property and incidentals, then levy a church tax on its members up to a level acceptable to the state, and finally draw subsidies from the state budget to cover the remaining deficit, if any. State officials determined whether a congregation warranted a "covering" subsidy, intended to guarantee clerical salaries that ranged between 2,400 and 6,000 marks annually. In 1918, income from property accounted for 34 percent of total budgeted income throughout the church, taxes 39 percent, and state contributions 27 percent. Thus, two-thirds of total budgeted income rested on two privileges—church taxing and state contributions.[42]

The great wealth of the Old-Prussian church obviated the need for drawing even more income from privileged sources. As 1919 began, the Old-Prussian church and its congregations owned 270,000 hectares of land (or 667,170 acres, about the size of Rhode Island). The amount of church capital investments (securities, loans, mortgages) totaled about 460 million M. An additional 118 million had accumulated in funds for clerical raises, pensions, and survivor benefits to which congregations, the church at large, and the state contributed.[43]

Church taxes and state contributions seemed more threatened by the prospect of a hostile Landtag majority. Like the six Evangelical churches in the "new" provinces and the Roman Catholic church as well, the Old-Prussian church enjoyed the legal status of a public corporation (*Korporation des öffentlichen Rechts*) replete with the "sovereign" right of raising taxes. Because of their large memberships and historical roles, the justifying theory ran, these established churches had exerted a greater impact on society than other religious bodies. Accordingly, they warranted special privileges. By granting them, the state ostensibly acknowledged the theory of symbiosis. The church tax, levied largely through the Prussian income tax and collected by the state, may appear trifling. In 1913 the per capita church tax came to a mere 1.97 M. or 3.8 percent of a total (federal, Prussian, community, and church) per capita tax load of 51.57 M. But the tax was no head tax. It varied widely by income as well as by congregation. Congregations shared their tax and property income with the church at large by way of a general assessment (Umlage). Together with income from capital accumulated in general and specific church funds, the Umlage laid the financial base for meeting a multitude of general church expenditures. In the years before the war, the Prussian state contributed annually about 12 million M. to the common clerical funds and another 9–10 million to subsidize pastor salaries, to pay the cost of church administration, and to support many specific church needs.[44]

A reformed Landtag might weaken or topple one or both of the two threatened pillars—church taxes and state contributions. Of the two, the collection of church taxes might seem beyond immediate danger because of its incorporation into the public tax system. Church fears began with the insecurity of state contributions, which the Landtag voted annually.

The legal claims of the church to state contributions were as obscure as they were complicated. Annual appropriations for clerical subsidies, the most important state contribution, lay anchored in material law and not merely in the annual state budget. But this legislation, in turn, did not rest upon contractual legal claims that the church could press upon the state. Rather, the state conferred its largess in this case because the function of the church coincided with state interests. Such, after all, was one justification of the Christian state, recognized by church and state alike. As for other appropriations, the church might need to argue its contractual legal claims item by item or fall back on the possibly less substantial grounds of customary law (as in the case of administrative costs).[45]

Given the legal insecurity of state contributions, a skeptical and hostile Landtag might deny any legal obligation to maintain them. It might also deny any moral obligation that stemmed from confiscating church property twice in the distant past (in the Reformation and Napoleonic periods) and from forcing the church overnight to rely on the voluntary giving of parishioners. Even loyal church people were unaccustomed to such a role, and beyond them lay a host of indifferent and even hostile members.

Beyond financial privileges lay another imperiled vested interest: confessional education in public schools. Nine-tenths of all Prussian children attended free public elementary schools (Volksschulen) during the period of obligatory attendance from ages six through fourteen, when Evangelical children were confirmed. The remaining tenth attended "middle schools" (Mittelschulen), largely upgraded Volksschulen, or "higher schools" (Gymnasia, Realgymnasia, and Oberrealschulen and their preparatory schools), which led to university study. All three tracks included religious instruction in their curricula. Old-Prussian churchmen worried most about elementary schools because they were largely organized along confessional lines and enrolled the great bulk of Prussian pupils.[46]

Most elementary schools were confessional—Evangelical or Catholic— in the sense that pupils and teachers, as a rule, attended and staffed the schools of their confession. Beyond this normative organizational definition in the "school maintenance law" of 1906, church leaders assumed that a discernible Christian spirit imbued the entire course of instruction. Prayers were said, religious services held, and church festivals observed. Instruction in German and history took due account of confessional loyalties. But it was compulsory and exclusively Evangelical religious instruction that put a distinguishing stamp on the Evangelical confessional school. Very much the exception in Prussia as a whole, interdenominational Simultan elementary schools prevailed in West Prussia, Posnania, Hesse-Nassau, and, beyond Prussia, in the state of Baden. Staffed by Protestants and Catholics alike, Simultan schools offered children of both confessions a common curriculum, except in religious instruction given separately according to confession. Though not confessional, Simultan schools were nonetheless "Christian," likewise ostensibly permeated by a Christian spirit. There were no "secular" schools in Prussia.

Before the war, confessional schools and religious instruction had come under severe attack.[47] It was the more alarming to church leaders because schoolteachers themselves carried its brunt. Most reform-minded teachers favored Simultan over confessional schools. Increasingly, teachers had also grown unsympathetic toward the religious education curriculum prescribed in the general curriculum outline with the approval of the church. Yet teachers were obliged to give religious instruction along with other subjects. Few advocated abolishing religious instruction outright. Some argued for a common religious or moral instruction encompassing both confessions, and others for less catechetical memorization. These and other sallies put church leaders on the defensive, prompting them to question the confessional reliability of many teachers.

Still the church could exercise some control in practice over religious instruction, since local clergymen enjoyed the right to visit and inspect it. Moreover, though the state possessed the exclusive right of "supervising" schools, it usually commissioned clergymen in villages and small cities as inspectors of local elementary schools and as district (Kreis) school inspectors. Finally, local clergymen sat as ex officio members on local school boards.

Clerical influence and control, however, embittered most teachers. Fighting for their professional independence, they demanded supervision by the pedagogically trained, ruling out clergymen. Well organized in the German Teachers' Association, elementary schoolteachers discussed and drew public attention to these issues. In the Landtag they could count on the sympathetic ear of the two liberal parties, which had bitterly contested clerical influence over the half-century before the war.

From the rapidly growing Socialist party had come even more radical attacks. Everywhere Socialists favored secular as opposed to Christian schools of either type, though Socialists might yet differ on the value of some religious or moral instruction. Church leaders viewed Socialists as well as progressive educators as dangerous enemies of the church, and considered Christianity a natural enemy of "materialist" socialism.

Because so much appeared at stake, the Kaiser's Easter proclamation sounded the tocsin and threw church leaders into a shocked state of confusion as they grasped for ways of safeguarding the Volkskirche. They had to reckon also with the possibility that in a democratic Landtag an atheist might wield the extensive powers of the Kultusminister over church public corporations. Against this danger, some leaders of the dominant church Right advocated an immediate disestablishment that would at once sever state controls and secure church privileges before the implementation of constitutional changes. But others cautioned against precipitous action that might well lead to both disestablishment and the collapse of the Volkskirche.[48]

Even those liberals who favored a democratic franchise dismissed any thought of disestablishment entertained by leaders of the church Right. In this respect all liberals appeared united. They, of course, deplored the frustrating restrictions imposed upon them by the ruler's church government. But they considered an independent, dogmatic church controlled by the Right infinitely worse.[49]

The suffrage issue thus raised again the perplexing prewar problem of how to reconstruct the Landeskirche as a comprehensive Volkskirche without sacrificing its spiritual unity. Under the church party truce, doctrinal conflict, though muffled, had persisted. In 1916 General Superintendent Wilhelm Zoellner of Westphalia, a Lutheran leader, brought this conflict more into the open. He proposed that the Landeskirche restrict itself to administration and organize two subchurches, one orthodox and one liberal, pastors and congregations joining one or the other. Apparently he calculated that most would enter the orthodox subchurch, which could then entrench the confession in most of the Landeskirche.[50] Thus, debate over the future church had already arisen in the war before the Prussian suffrage issue suggested that church constitutional reform might prove more imminent and hazardous than anyone had expected.

While the lower house deliberated, the church Right took the initiative. "Through the introduction of an equal franchise they [the undersigned] fear such a large increase of elements indifferent or even hostile to the Christian religion in the Assembly [lower house] that the preservation of the confessional...school is in extreme danger," wrote 454 Westphalian pastors in a petition to the king. "Dechristianizing the youth means dechristianizing the folk and endangers ultimately the existence of Your Majesty's leadership of the Prussian Landeskirche entrusted to you by the grace of God."[51] Favorably disposed toward Simultan schools, however, the liberal

Protestantenblatt charged the Right with equating its particular interests with those of the church as a whole.

Moved to action primarily by the church Right, several district synods in the spring and summer of 1918 finally began to cope with the constitutional threat. Finding widespread approval was the proposal of the Düsseldorf Presbyterium, designed to curtail state controls while salvaging church privileges.[52] These privileges the EOK and GSV hoped to see guaranteed in legislation proposed by the Center party to safeguard Catholic, and thereby Protestant, interests in the event of suffrage reform.[53]

At first Conservatives rejected such constitutional safeguards, hoping to make an equal franchise as disagreeable as possible for the Center. But, isolated, Conservatives soon broached the compromise passed on July 5, 1918 that acceded to the Center's repeated demands. Still more than half of the Center deputies rejected the compromise on plural voting in the belief that a reactionary franchise must fail to defend the churches despite constitutional guarantees.

No less divided than Catholic leaders were their Protestant counterparts.[54] The church Right objected to constitutional safeguards on two counts: A qualified majority might still abolish or alter them; and moreover, the proposed safeguards might well make it impossible for the church to cut state ties. The alarming possibility existed that neither the Volkskirche would be preserved nor a desirable separation attained. By the same token, the safeguards might later defend the Volkskirche structure, without which a disestablishment appeared undesirable anyway. Confessional rivalry also put Protestant leaders on guard against the guarantees. At least the left wing of the Center party could take credit for helping to introduce an equal franchise. Yet the Center tried to obviate a possible result of the reform that it advocated—a radical disestablishment— through constitutional safeguards. To die-hard church Conservatives especially, this maneuver smacked of two-faced opportunism.

At the beginning of the war, Protestants and Catholics had made a shaky truce under which many Protestant tempers simmered, especially from 1917 on. Before the war, Conservative and Center parties had shielded church interests in the Landtag. But now the Center party made common cause with reforming parties in both the Landtag and Reichstag. Protestant churchmen accused the Center of extorting political concessions from the hard-pressed government, an impression heightened when on April 19, 1917, the Bundesrat abolished restrictions that yet remained from the Kulturkampf on Jesuits (prohibition of Jesuit institutions). Indeed, several Prussian provincial synods protested, but, according to Schian, this rumbling would have assumed more deafening proportions in time of peace. The Central Committee of the Evangelical League issued a public statement, charging that Bethmann-Hollweg "during the fatherland's time of need surrenders to improper pressure from the Center party and saddles the justified feelings of the Evangelical people with the bitter fact: the first inner-political fruit of the World War is the greater freedom of movement that the blood enemy of German Protestantism enjoys." The statement concluded: "German Protestants could almost be proud that its unreserved patriotism is expected to undergo such a test of endurance if this event did not so clearly indicate a completely unbearable neglect of Evangelical quarters . . . which are politically ineffectual but irreplaceably patriotic."[55]

This impression drew substance from the fact that the remainder of the anti-Jesuit law was abolished precisely in the year marking the quadricentennial of the German Reformation. Because the war caused difficulties with arrangements, military authorities persuaded the Evangelical churches to postpone festive public celebrations in Wittenberg and Eisenach. Some disturbed churchmen regretted that the government so obviously neglected Protestants while hastening to mollify Catholics.[56]

The impression that the Evangelical churches no longer counted in public life and indeed faced an ominous future led church leaders to consider how to organize parishioners for the defense of church interests. In the dawning age of democratic politics the collective voice of church members could be politically effective. Adolf Deissmann, chairman of the German Evangelical Pastors' Association, summed up the opinion of many:

While Germany is two-thirds Evangelical, the influence of the Evangelical church on public life has become nil. . . . Should separation of church and state . . . come about, it [the Evangelical church] would become in the eyes of the world a group of fragmented sects; Rome and the other unevangelical and unchristian forces would develop their influence all the more. I refer only to the facts: abolition of the Jesuit law, peace offer of the "Father of Christendom" [papal peace offer of 1917], Erzberger-Scheidemann [Centrist and Socialist respectively] the consultants of a German imperial chancellor [Hertling, a Catholic]. A good Evangelical imperial chancellor [Georg Michaelis] left helplessly after a few days and a Center leader replaced him. These events would have been impossible if there were in the German Empire a corpus evangelicorum that could raise its voice and whose voice must be heard.[57]

Actually, the Protestant churches already had a national organization through which they could act collectively. Church governments met periodically for discussions in the Eisenach Church Conference (Kirchenkonferenz), founded in 1851. In 1903 the German Evangelical Kirchenausschuss (Church Committee) was created to function as the Conference's executive committee. Neither suited Deissmann's purposes. He had in mind a popular representation that could speak for the churches independent of the state. In the past, the Old-Prussian church, pastors' associations, and the Evangelical League, among others, had pressed for a national synodical representation to supplement the Church Conference without intruding upon the internal affairs of member churches. These overtures had been thwarted by non-Prussian particularists, especially Lutherans, who feared for the integrity of their Landeskirchen under the domination of the giant Old-Prussian Union. During the war, calls for a closer and more popular national church organization had increased.[58] By 1918 the political situation had grown ominous and the issue critical.

Reflecting this concern, the German Pastors' Association endorsed Deissmann's proposal for a national synod existing alongside the Kirchenausschuss. Anticipating that proposal, the Kirchenausschuss in its session of June 11, 1918 decided to study the possibility of augmenting the Church Conference with such a synod. The Kirchenausschuss shared the association's agonizing concern.[59] National church representation needed a popular base to confront postwar dangers expected from ultramontanism and radicalism alike. The events of revolution, however, overtook these prods to action, and the initiative fell to other hands.

THE DEMISE OF THE SECOND EMPIRE

Under Prince Max of Baden, who replaced Hertling as chancellor on October 3, 1918, the Bundesrat proceeded to introduce the principle of parliamentary government and thus fix upon the reforming parties responsibility for shaping government policy. Persuaded that the war could not be won, the Supreme Command, not these parties, demanded this transformation in order to facilitate armistice negotiations with President Wilson, who had repeatedly lashed out at Germany's leaders for their militarism.

Even church liberals sympathetic to a democratic franchise in Prussia had stopped short of endorsing parliamentary government. But now some —such as Alfred Fischer of the *Protestantenblatt,* Otto Baumgarten, and Martin Rade—welcomed this revolution from "above" with astonishing optimism, dimmed only by the impending defeat. What distinguished the three was a combination of practical counsel and idealism. On the one hand, resistance against constitutional reforms would prove futile and most likely injurious to the church. On the other, they believed that reforming parties, even the Majority Socialist, had demonstrated their political maturity during the long war. A democratic state appeared morally preferable to tutelage under authoritarian forms. Finally, they denied that a democratic spirit violated a distinctively German ethos. But the great majority of church leaders, including other liberals, could scarcely envision a future for Germany once the mainstay of Bismarck's constitution had given way under Prince Max. Bruno Doehring, a royal court chaplain, could even assert: "The monarchy in Prussia is a thousand times more than a political question for us Evangelicals, it is a question of faith."[60]

In December 1917 a Lutheran editor had asserted that a military setback need no longer be feared.[61] But almost a year later Germany verged on military collapse, even though its armies occupied vast stretches of enemy territory. If the army appeared invincible, it seemed logical to conclude that the cause of this startling change of fortune must lie in the unwillingness of the home population to support the war effort adequately. It appeared as though the enemy had brought Germany to the verge of collapse not only by dint of armed force but also by the infection of non-German values.

This conclusion found confirmation in war theology. Military collapse plunged war theologians into an acute religious crisis. Why should the benevolent God who had inspired folk solidarity at the onset of war allow defeat at the end? One could not conclude that God had failed the folk without losing faith in God's rule through history. War theologians, according to Pressel, concluded that the folk had failed God.[62]

Ever since the Easter proclamation and the peace resolution, the ingredients of what later became fully expressed in the stab-in-the-back (Dolchstoss) charge germinated in the minds of nationalist Old-Prussian churchmen.[63] The Reichstag majority and especially the Socialist parties seemed to have exploited Germany's tribulations for partisan purposes, as Socialist involvement in munitions strikes in January 1918 appeared to illustrate. The first known public articulation of the stab-in-the-back charge came in a sermon preached by Bruno Doehring on February 3, 1918, in which he scored those responsible for these strikes as "venal and cowardly creatures who have treacherously desecrated the altar of the fatherland with [their] brother's blood, . . . who . . . have poisoned the good spirit of our folk, who have lured those deplorably misled from their place of productive work into the street, put the murder weapon in their hands and directed them to attack their...brothers, who still face the enemy, in the rear."[64] On October 20, two weeks before the revolution, the Lutheran *Evangelische Kirchen-Zeitung* charged: "Collapse behind the front—not the collapse of our heroes' front. That is the shocking development of the last days.... The homeland has not held out."[65] The stab-in-the back interpretation of the last year gave many churchmen all the more reason to anathematize parliamentary democracy, for in its German form it seemed born of treason.

Through the exchange of armistice notes with President Wilson in October it became clear that the enemy would demand the Kaiser's abdication before consenting to negotiate a peace. The result was mounting public pressure on the Kaiser to abdicate.[66] Monarchist churchmen now feared desperately for the monarchy, the ostensibly Prussian Protestant form of government. On October 31, 1917 Old-Prussian general superintendents had telegraphed the Kaiser: "And though...from foreign countries an impudent and clumsy attempt was made...to loosen the indissoluble bond that couples our folk with Your Majesty, we now vow...unshakeable loyalty to Your Majesty."[67] But alas, the monarchy sank in the quicksands of the November Revolution.

When the Majority Socialist Philipp Scheidemann proclaimed the Republic in November 1918, the great majority of Old-Prussian churchmen could scarcely be expected to accept the new regime willingly. Their commitment to the old order flowed far too deep to change course overnight. For centuries their political ethics had incorporated monarchism and authoritarianism and, for over a century, conservatism and antiparliamentarianism. They felt a special debt to the Hohenzollern, the main casualty of the revolution, for centuries of benevolent service to the church. In the war they perceived the perils that might await the Volkskirche if the suffrage system and the monarchical mainstay gave way. The war's outcome and the Republic's birth seemed to result from national betrayal and an unconscionable collapse of the national community. Under these circumstances, normal political attitudes in the church could only have reflected hostility to the incipient Republic. One need not attribute their initial antirepublicanism to psychic disabilities, such as strong resentments, a quest for institutional power, or insecurity induced by crisis, though all three certainly conditioned the church's response. Rather, one must keep fully in mind the preexisting mentality of churchmen as they entered the Republic.

3

RECONSTRUCTING THE VOLKSKIRCHE

"THE SPLENDOR of the German Empire, the dream of our fathers, the pride of every German has departed. Therewith the exalted vessel of German power, the ruler, and the royal house that we loved instinctively."[1] Thus did President Reinhard Moeller of the EOK pay tribute to the Hohenzollern monarchy at its passing, before equally distraught churchmen at the first postwar national Church Assembly (Kirchentag).

Between the revolution from "above" in October 1918 and the first assembly eleven months later, a revolution from "below" forced the abdication of the Kaiser in November, ushered in the Republic, and plunged the nation into turmoil. The two revolutions were certainly among the strangest in history. In the first, the existing regime engineered its own fall so as to facilitate armistice negotiations. In the second, the masses overthrew their own government, though it had already assumed parliamentary form and had committed itself to the enemy's armistice terms. The November Revolution was fortified by the suspicion that the military's intransigence and the Kaiser's refusal to abdicate were thwarting the peace that the masses craved. As governmental authority evaporated, local workers' and soldiers' councils sprang up everywhere. Socialists assumed power on all levels of government.

In Berlin on November 9, Prince Max transferred his prerogatives as chancellor to Friedrich Ebert, Majority Socialist party chairman, so that Majority Socialists might curb the growing threat of social revolution and lower-class dictatorship. That they would succeed was not apparent for some time. Majority Socialists felt compelled to accede to the proposition of their coalition partners — Independent Socialists — in the provisional ministry (Council of People's Commissars) that all political authority flowed from revolutionary councils. But Majority Socialists soon managed to extricate the Revolution from these councils. They prevailed upon a national congress of councils in December to set January 19, 1919, as the date for elections to a constituent national assembly. This decision frustrated efforts of left-wing Independent Socialists and Communists to erect a class dictatorship through the loosely organized nexus of revolutionary councils.

What violence there was came not from a clash between the old order and the new but from sharp disagreements among Socialists over the course of the revolution. Left-wing Independents fell in with attempts of Communists to spark insurrection from December 1918 to June 1919. Independent Socialists resigned from the provisional ministry on December 29 and from a similarly constituted Prussian government on January 3, leaving Majority Socialists alone in power until the Weimar Assembly — the constituent National Assembly — convened in February and the Prussian Constituent Assembly met in March. In both Majority Socialists aligned with Centrists and Democrats in the historic Weimar coalition, which set its stamp on the constitutions that each assembly framed.

The Weimar constitution could not help but repel Prussian monarchists. Authority derived not from a monarch but, as Article 1 stated, "from the people," who elected a Reichstag every four years and a president for a seven-year term. To remain in power, the federal cabinet required the confidence of the Reichstag and its parties. German federalism persisted in the shape of a largely advisory Reichsrat, representing state governments. The Prussian Constituent Assembly framed a constitution that similarly established a popularly elected Landtag and a Staatsrat that represented the provinces.

The course that the November Revolution followed obviated the radical disestablishment that churchmen had begun to fear in 1917. Having brought about a National Assembly in which Marxist parties lacked a majority, Majority Socialists found themselves forced to compromise on constitutional principles governing churches and schools. Since the constitution obliged states to reconstitute church relations and school systems according to its principles, Old-Prussian churchmen soon feared less a dissolution of the Volkskirche than government intervention to prevent the framing of a church constitution in a form seemingly hostile to the Republic. Controversy, accordingly, accompanied each step in the process of disestablishment over a span of six years, ending as late as 1924 when the Prussian Landtag accepted the new church constitution.

The following chapter focuses alternately on two sets of issues: the external problem of securing favorable disestablishment terms from the Republic and the internal one of reconstructing the Old-Prussian church. Throughout the chapter, the spotlight is thrown on the controversies attending both processes that brought to light underlying political attitudes.

THE ALARM OF REVOLUTION

Far from preaching resistance to the enveloping revolution, surprised church leaders meekly submitted. They realized that they had no realistic choice between the old order and the revolution. They could, however, aid Majority Socialist efforts to restore order. The East Prussian Consistory, for example, denied on November 15 that pastors should feel obliged to resist the new regime.[2] On November 30, the EOK and GSV, augmented by a newly co-opted Council of Confidants (Vertrauensrat), went so far as to counsel parishioners that the church "is not bound to a particular form of state constitution."[3] Through these and other statements, which in no way recognized revolutionary government as legitimately constituted, church leaders also tried to withdraw the church from the political struggle and to guide it unscarred through the revolutionary period.

But the Old-Prussian church was much too obvious a target for revolutionaries to ignore. By formally assuming executive power on November 14, the Prussian Socialist government claimed the state's prerogatives over the church, the situation dreaded by church leaders in 1917. The Socialist government might claim even more. If it also seized the fallen monarch's prerogatives within the church, Socialists might paralyze Old-Prussian church leadership while shattering the church from without.

Actually indecision rather than determined action characterized Socialist behavior from the very beginning. For six weeks the dispute between Majority and Independent Socialists played itself out within the Kultusministerium over whether to defer restructuring church-state relations until constituent assemblies convened or whether to preempt that settlement by decree. This issue provoked bitter public controversy as well when the Socialist Kultusministerium issued decrees stripping schools of their confessional garb.

The Prussian Kultusministerium enacted the most radical and comprehensive of these decrees on November 29. For the sake of religious freedom, the decree prohibited prayers and religious celebrations in schools, liberated teachers and pupils alike from the obligation of giving or taking religion classes, and forbade testing in religious doctrine and homework for religious instruction.[4] One would expect a Socialist Kultusministerium to have introduced secular schools instead. Still, the decree unleashed a massive protest movement among loyal Protestants and Catholics because it augured others that might soon follow.

Previous Socialist initiatives had reinforced this suspicion. On November 12, Ebert's ministry ominously pledged "the Socialist program" and religious freedom.[5] On the following day, November 13, the new Prussian Socialist government promised "liberation of the school from any church domination" and "separation of church and state."[6] In the proclamation of November 12, however, church leaders were relieved to discover that the people's commissars anticipated a constituent national assembly and, until it convened, confined decrees to securing order. If so, church-state relations might avoid alteration by decree until constituent assemblies met, at which time political parties friendly to churches could help shape the terms of the anticipated separation. The Prussian government, by contrast, pledged itself "to transform old, basically reactionary Prussia as quickly as possible." In this case, perhaps little could be done to prevent Socialists from wreaking their will by decree. On November 15, the Kultusministerium decreed the release of dissident children from compulsory religious instruction and, on November 27, the abolition of clerical school supervision.[7] With the November 29 decree, the Kultusministerium seemed to assault the citadel of the Volkskirche more directly. Soon alarming reports of similar actions in other German states tended to confirm suspicions that the revolutionary wave might now sweep over the churches.

The new composition of the Prussian Kultusministerium gave further grounds for concern. The Executive Council of the Berlin revolutionary councils had appointed the Majority Socialist Konrad Haenisch and the Independent Socialist Adolf Hoffmann to lead the Kultusministerium. Haenisch professed appreciation for Christianity and the churches as a cultural force. In contrast, Hoffmann had long distinguished himself as an outspoken leader of the movement against church membership. He was already notorious in church circles for his polemical brochure, *The Ten Commandments and the Ownership Class*. In the wake of these appointments, freethinkers and other dissidents entered the Kultusministerium as either officials or consultants. Church leaders shuddered at the mere thought of their power, for "Ten-Commandment Hoffmann" gained the upper hand in the Kultusministerium.[8]

Soon after his appointment, Hoffmann declared at a meeting in the Kultusministerium that it should decree a separation of church and state without delay and stanch the flow of subsidies to churches by April 1, 1919. Soon word leaked out about a memo, composed by Alfred Dieterich, an Independent Socialist dissident, who sketched out a plan of action for Hoffmann. Dieterich projected the ultimate goal of reducing churches to the status of private associations, expropriating part of their property, and saddling them with state controls to curtail their freedom.

Quickly the Center party and the Prussian Catholic episcopacy entered the field against Hoffmann with blunt protests. For the Prussian bishops, Cardinal von Hartmann of Cologne protested that reform by decree would breach the people's commissars' proclamation of November 12: the Prussian government could issue decrees only to preserve order, not to preempt decisions of forthcoming constituent assemblies. The only legal argument, and yet most effective one, that the churches could conceivably muster was that the revolution had set and then broken its own ground rules. The Catholic hierarchy, press, free associations, and Center party also accused the Kultusministerium of waging a new Kulturkampf and summoned loyal Catholics to massive demonstrations and protests. The charge implied that Socialists aimed not at liberating conscience but at suppressing the Christian churches. This insinuation galvanized Catholics by conjuring up memories of persecution under the Second Empire, while casting Socialists, likewise once persecuted, in the new role of oppressor.[9]

In the Protestant wing of the Christian counterattack, a cloud of illegitimacy hung over the EOK and GSV, paralyzing church leadership at its very center. Without their summus episcopus, could the two legitimately speak for the Old-Prussian church? True, the authority of both rested on state law that the revolutionary government had not abolished. But their authority hardly encompassed the powers of the summus episcopus on whose behalf church government functioned. In a democratic era the GSV suffered the same liabilities as its parent body, the "filtered" General Synod, from which liberals were all but excluded. Should it manage to meet, the General Synod could not confer legitimacy on church government or legally claim the powers of the summus episcopus. In the clamor of local and regional Evangelical protest movements, then beginning to mushroom throughout Prussia, the EOK and GSV heard disturbing claims that the prerogatives of church government had expired with the monarchy and that authority to reconstruct the church had devolved upon parishioners. Clearly the EOK and GSV could not delay to resolve the riddle of their legitimacy.

At their joint meeting on November 18, the EOK and GSV agreed to draw into their deliberations an advisory body of churchmen broadly representative of church groupings, including liberals. By calling this body a Council of Confidants in the heyday of revolutionary councils, the EOK and GSV sought to demonstrate that they enjoyed the confidence of the mass of church people, whom they now claimed to represent. While informing congregations of this decision on November 23, the EOK and GSV preached the need internally for church solidarity and externally for a unified front under their leadership. Together with the Council of Confidants, the EOK issued on November 30 a protest to the Kultusministerium that followed the line of argument already probed by the Catholic episcopacy. [10]

Lack of clearly legitimate central leadership in the Old-Prussian church partly explains why Catholics more than Protestants spearheaded the Christian counterattack. Moreover, political parties, which had catered to loyal Protestants, were in the throes of dissolution and reorganization and could not mobilize a defense of the churches. Finally, the revolutionary Prussian government viewed Catholic opposition as the more formidable. The Kultusministerium's decrees had inadvertently helped to fire a separatist movement in the predominantly Catholic Rhineland and Upper Silesia. Not wishing to drive Catholics into the maw of separatists, the Prussian government had more reason to appease Catholics than Protestants. [11]

Though Catholics had a more powerful political muscle, the corresponding movement among Protestants was more remarkable for a different reason. More so than the Catholic church, the Old-Prussian church had yet to learn how to shift for itself politically and how, in a democratic age, to mobilize the masses in support of the Volkskirche ideal. The dramatic rise of Socialists to power and the challenges of the Hoffmann era goaded local and regional church leaders to action. In desperation and without central direction, they appealed for the loyalty of nominal church members. The declining influence of the Protestant churches under the Second Empire had augured ill for the prospects of a mass Volkskirche movement.

But local and regional church leaders soon discovered the reality of the Volkskirche that they proclaimed. The bulk of the Protestant middle classes and large sections of the working classes, even Socialists, would part only reluctantly from the Volkskirche pattern, however little they might participate in the life of the church. The EOK and GSV might suspect the Volkskirche movement of bolting their authority, but the ambiguous legitimacy of church authorities spurred the initiative of lesser church leaders, without which the EOK and GSV would have little political muscle to flex.

The beginning of the Volkskirche movement in Breslau and distant Göttingen typified the pattern that the movement assumed throughout Prussia. As early as November 12, Breslau pastors and laymen organized makeshift committees and later an action committee to coordinate agitation. Pamphlets denouncing "Hoffmann's decrees" were hastily printed and distributed, and angry mass demonstrations held. Later the action committee sent speakers hither and yon to apprise church members of the significance of the forthcoming elections to constituent assemblies and to promote the circulation of petitions. Much the same happened in Göttingen, where local congregational boards, at the suggestion of Professor Arthur Titius, founded a People's League (Volksbund) on November 18.[12]

The People's League and other Volkskirche associations wished not only to defend Volkskirche privileges but also, looking beyond the immediate crisis, to project Protestant values into public life by activating nominal church members. Volkskirche groups might accentuate one or the other of these twin goals, but throughout Prussia the common danger solidified church ranks. Thus aroused, the Volkskirche movement assumed gigantic proportions as it sought to influence elections to constituent assemblies and then the assemblies themselves. Later it tailed off into support for various Protestant public causes, most notably the movement to preserve confessional education.

Both churchmen and Socialists knew that the liberal principle of individual religious freedom, highlighted in the decree of November 29, undercut church privileges as well as confessional education. Like Catholic spokesmen, Protestant leaders construed the decree as an assault upon religious freedom by arraying the individual rights of the majority against the individual rights of the minority. Looked at in this way, dissidents in the Kultusministerium imposed their narrow religious prejudices by decree against the individual rights of the vast majority.

This message was implicit in the first mass petition, circulated by the Berlin Volkskirche Auxiliary (Volkskirchendienst), organized on November 14 under the chairmanship of Wilhelm Kahl, a Berlin law professor. A consultant in the Kultusministerium while yet a member of the GSV, Kahl had early fathomed the intentions of the first and the constitutional weakness of the second in what loomed as an unequal struggle. The auxiliary's petition demanded Christian schools and regular Christian religious instruction. By claiming to represent the will of congregations constituting nine-tenths of the population, the petition pitted the rights of the majority against the individual religious freedom espoused by Socialists.[13]

As protests poured into the Kultusministerium, Haenisch finally took a public stand against Hoffmann. He had agreed to the November decrees to prevent Hoffmann from seeking the endorsement of a radical course from the Executive Council of the Berlin revolutionary councils. As early as November 30, however, Haenisch declared publicly that he would resign if the separation issue were not reserved for constituent assemblies. He hastened to assure Catholics and Protestants of his conciliatory intentions in subsequent letters and press statements. These assurances were cast in a bad light, however, when, on December 5, the Kultusministerium set out to appropriate the powers of the former summus episcopus and when, on December 13, it enacted a "law" to facilitate leaving churches. Moreover, Haenisch continued to vindicate the decree of November 29 in the name of individual religious freedom rather than suspend it for the sake of orderly legal procedure.[14] His oblique tactics, however, failed to put a damper on the spreading protest movement. Nor could they, of course, endear him to Hoffmann. Eventually Hoffmann resigned when Independent Socialists deserted their Prussian coalition with Majority Socialists on January 3. Now under Haenisch, the Kultusministerium staged a careful, though embarrassing, retreat.

While in retreat, the Prussian government and Haenisch repeatedly asserted their intention of placing the entire bundle of church-state issues in the hands of the forthcoming Prussian Constituent Assembly. In a letter to Cardinal von Hartmann on January 8, the Prussian government, at Haenisch's prompting, invalidated the decree of November 27 abolishing clerical school supervision. On the next day, the government, again following Haenisch's recommendations, responded to the protest of the EOK, GSV, and Council of Confidants of November 30. Before broaching the issue of separation in the assembly, the government promised to consult church authorities in order to obviate any lingering sense of religious persecution.[15]

But Haenisch's retreat was no rout. Two days later, on January 11, he enacted a decree that converted religious instruction into an optional subject within teacher-training institutions. Moreover, he balked at completely suspending the controversial decree of November 29. In Hoffmann's absence because of illness, Haenisch, on December 28, merely suspended the decree wherever its implementation met difficulties.[16] He finally withdrew it on April 1, while the Prussian Constituent Assembly met, only to decree the continuation of optional religious instruction for pupils and teachers alike until a future law would settle the issue.[17]

Haenisch's consistent behavior suggests that optional religious instruction represented for him the point of no retreat. Despite his condemnation of Hoffmann's tactics, Haenisch appeared to believe that this issue, a matter of civil libertarian principle, was fair game for resolution by decree. Much as church leaders dreaded reform by decree, they saw the need to concede on the substance of the issue. The EOK, in its letter to the Weimar Assembly on March 13, would limit compulsory religious instruction to pupils belonging to churches. A strong stream within the Council of Confidants would, however, endorse optional religious instruction for all pupils. Neither would deny teachers a freedom of choice.[18]

What gave pause to Protestant church leaders as they shaped their demands on constituent assemblies and to Haenisch as he turned a difficult corner were the radical views of elementary schoolteachers grouped in the large German Teachers' Association. Teachers gave clear warning signals that they would not be ignored. Meeting in June 1919 before the Weimar Assembly had set the school provisions of the future constitution, the first postwar teachers' convention threw its weight behind secular schools by demanding that religious instruction be excised from the curriculum as a regular subject.[19] Uppermost in the minds of most who accepted this plank was antagonism to any church control over religious instruction. The EOK was relieved to discover that few elementary schoolteachers had actually opted out of religious instruction. That few pupils also withdrew suggested a pervading acceptance among parents of regular religious instruction, even if optional. The passionate resistance of teachers to church influence, however, threatened to rupture their relations with the churches. The association contended that "school supervision is exclusively the affair of the state." By voicing again this old argument, teachers shielded their vaunted professional autonomy under cover of higher state interests, thus exposing churches as ideological pressure groups.

It is of course true that churches, no less than teachers' associations, acted as pressure groups in the Weimar Republic. In fact, the great lesson learned by church leaders in the crucible of revolution was that they could successfully pursue the interests of the Volkskirche with the prospect of mass support. The information sheet of the Council of Confidants hailed Haenisch's retreat from the decree of November 29 as "the first victory of the church movement of our day over the church-hostile policy of the new government." The Hoffmann fiasco showed "that the church is still a power in the life of the folk, that the menacing of our folk's religious institutions [Heiligtümer] provokes a resistance with which the new rulers feel they cannot cope."[20]

Quite as important was a second lesson. In the future the church must remain ever alert and assert itself against the religionless Republic for the sake of Volkskirche ideals. "Hoffmann's carelessness in disclosing existing plans," commented one church periodical, "opened the eyes of many, and for this we wish to be thankful."[21] Undeterred by political considerations to which Haenisch reacted, Socialists would presumably have destroyed the Volkskirche. From this perspective, churchmen concluded that Haenisch differed from Hoffmann merely in tactics.[22] Throughout the life of the Republic, churchmen would recall Hoffmann's attempts as revealing the true, malevolent intentions of Socialists, a memory that colored their attitude toward the Republic no less than toward socialism. Socialists most clearly articulated the intrinsic "religionless" nature of the Republic.

Yet this assessment hardly did justice to Haenisch and Majority Socialists. Churchmen tended to judge political parties by whether they would harm or aid churches, and to impute motives accordingly. Haenisch's primary concern, however, was neither to harm nor to aid churches, but to consolidate the young Republic. He found himself caught in a cross fire between radical Socialists, with whom Majority Socialists cooperated for the sake of the revolution, and outraged churchmen, whom he wished to appease for the sake of political stability. Neither antagonist appreciated Haenisch for the statesman that he played. Shortly after Hoffmann's resignation, Haenisch published an article to persuade Socialists of Hoffmann's folly and churchmen of Socialist respect for religious conviction.[23] Haenisch asserted that it would be "as undemocratic as politically immoral" to resolve church issues by force. At a time when "thousands of the most difficult problems" beset the Republic, he wrote, it had been a "fateful mistake" to compound these difficulties by also "broaching the hotly contested question of separation of state and church." For this mistake he blamed the narrow obstinacy of freethinkers: "Everything else may [be permitted to] collapse if only free-thinker clericalism can gather its wheat into the barn, this free-thinker clericalism that is just as bad as any other."

Haenisch hoped that this article and his beginning retreat would improve Majority Socialist prospects in the impending elections, especially with Catholic voters. Breaking privately with Hoffmann in a letter on December 31, Haenisch complained: "Each day of retaining the religion decree [of November 29] especially would have cost both of our parties hundreds of thousands of votes."[24] Some churchmen interpreted his retreat as merely an attempt to recoup party losses. But even before Hoffmann's tactics eroded Socialist strength, Haenisch had disapproved of them. Though he unwillingly agreed to the November decrees, he regarded them as a means of liberating conscience rather than of harming churches out of hatred.

Though misreading Haenisch's motives, church leaders correctly concluded that Haenisch and Hoffmann agreed on goals while differing on tactics. At constituent assemblies, both Socialist parties could be expected to press for the implementation of their Erfurt program. It made good sense, therefore, to emphasize common Socialist goals in order to dissuade parishioners from helping to vote a Socialist majority into power. The dispute of the two men over tactics, however, did not disclose a *mere* difference, but one of crucial importance. Unlike Hoffmann, Haenisch would accommodate churches as they wished, by granting them an opportunity to lobby for their cause through the parliamentary process. For most churchmen, however, Haenisch's retreat signified their momentary victory over socialism rather than an improbable victory of the churches and Majority Socialists together over radical revolutionaries.

DISSENSION IN CHURCH RANKS

Confronted with the task of renovation while facing the threat of disestablishment, the Old-Prussian church seemed paralyzed. A nonexistent king was needed not only to put constitutional changes into force but also to summon the General Synod to initiate them. To whom did the king's authority in the church fall? Conceivably the new Prussian Socialist government might seize the powers of the summus episcopus. While the various church parties and groups fairly bristled at this thought, they disagreed over who within the church should wield those powers. Their answers turned not a little on which solution might lead to cherished constitutional ideals. Now the stormy debates and arguments of the prewar years returned, but with greater urgency, because real constitutional decisions had to be made. In the ensuing debate, four contenders laid claim to leadership within the church: existing church government, the Prussian state, various groups agitating for a democratic church, and elements of the church Right that dominated synods.

The EOK and GSV made their first move on November 18, 1918. President Bodo Voigts of the EOK claimed for the GSV and EOK the powers of the summus episcopus so long as the General Synod was not convened. Claiming to speak for the church—also because of the Council of Confidants that they formed—the EOK and GSV protested the school decrees "in the name" of the Old-Prussian church. Also making the same claim in a letter to congregations on November 23, the EOK urged them to desist from any divisive efforts to reconstitute the church. The EOK and GSV capitalized on a powerful argument: If the church dissolved into factions or departed from the present legal framework, the new state might not recognize the new church structure as the legal claimant of the old church's privileges and property.

At first the Kultusministerium ignored the claims of the EOK and GSV. On December 5, however, it appointed Pastor Ludwig Wessel of Berlin as the "government representative for the Evangelical church authorities in Prussia," responsible for countersigning all important internal church decisions. Two days later Wessel was even appointed an officer in the EOK, formerly an appointment carrying the king's consent. In accepting these appointments, Pastor Wessel apparently acted with honorable motives toward his church. By a fluke he had drawn Hoffmann's attention and then trust. Worried about the impact of revolutionary government upon church finances, the Berlin clergy had organized a pastors' "council" and deputized three clergymen, Wessel among them, to contact and even negotiate with the Kultusministerium independent of the EOK.[25]

Though he tried to mediate between church authorities and the Kultusministerium, Wessel soon found that, because of the EOK's protests, he had become part of the problem. The EOK was legally correct to defend its prerogatives against the intrusion of a government veto over its internal administrative decisions. Wessel's sudden appearance also crossed the political strategy of the EOK and GSV. Until constituent assemblies convened, the EOK and GSV wished to avoid controversy with the state that could jeopardize the legal claims of the church to privileges. Wessel's appointment, however, might herald a disestablishment by decree. In any event, Wessel's veto right might hamper their efforts to take church interests in tow against the state. No wonder a group of Elberfeld and Barmen pastors wrote him: "We are ashamed that an Evangelical pastor decided to place himself at the disposal of *Herr* Hoffmann for his purposes as you have done, and feel that your conduct is betrayal of the church."[26] Finally, Wessel—and Berlin pastors, for that matter—had eluded the front that the EOK and GSV had begun to close against the Kultusministerium. Wessel's appointments passed with the Hoffmann era at the beginning of January 1919.

Recognition of the preeminent leadership of the EOK and GSV came slowly within the church also. Since church government derived its authority from the king, the argument ran, it had lost its legality with the king's abdication. Such an argument led nowhere, however, since the competence of church government remained anchored in state law. As the EOK and GSV, aided by the Council of Confidants, parried the blows of the Kultusministerium, respect for church government and its claims grew apace. By mid-December, the Berlin authorities had managed to impose their leadership on most groups forming the Volkskirche movement.[27] Still church authorities had difficulty in blazing a common trail to constitutional renovation. To disillusioned liberals, existing church government was too authoritarian, and to defiant Lutherans, proposed renovations seemed too democratic to leave uncontested. Both extremes drew on current political experience and used political terminology to argue for either a democratic or a more authoritarian church, revealing a common frame of reference for both ecclesiastical and political problems. Still, the total spectrum of attitudes toward church government and contemplated church reforms was hardly so clear.

Among themselves liberals agreed on constitutional goals, but were divided on strategy. They promoted doctrinal freedom, congregational autonomy, democratic elections, an end to the hated "filter" system, and a national church. Leaders of the Protestant Association (Protestantenverein) urged their liberal colleagues to accept EOK and GSV leadership. Now represented in the Council of Confidants, these leaders expected to exert some influence on the future church constitution. At first suspicious of the new regime, the *Protestantenblatt* cautioned the church not to accept democratic constitutional principles merely because they seemed politically fashionable.[28]

By ignoring church authorities, Martin Rade and his liberal circle of friends hoped to unleash a democratic revolution in the church and to attract church members long since alienated. These liberals feared that their gullible colleagues unwittingly aided existing church government in imposing an authoritarian constitution that would discourage mass participation. To Rade the argument against divisive organizing seemed inconsequential compared with the overriding need to renew the church from below.[29]

On November 14, Rade and Pastor Bernhard Gay of Chemnitz issued an appeal, later signed by many prominent liberals, for Volkskirche "councils," a term connoting the appeal's revolutionary character. The revolution had swept away the Landeskirche with the old regime, the appeal claimed. Rade's first set of principles called for a national church democratically constituted and paid little attention to any need for salvaging Volkskirche privileges. By the end of December Rade appeared much less certain that the old church had been shattered. Instead of a revolutionary national church, he now called for a popularly elected national Church Assembly (Kirchentag), where liberals could fight for their cause. Other liberals followed Rade's lead in founding Volkskirche councils. But Rade failed to inspire a movement. Most congregations rejected revolutionary councils, their name offending conservative church people.

Rade and many of the Friends of Die christliche Welt became Democrats in spirit or affiliation. They refused to regard Socialists with the righteous indignation of the church Right. In a second set of principles, Rade, for example, urged church people to assume roles in the Democratic and Socialist parties as a means of influencing the state's attitude toward organized religion. The fact that Democratic liberals tried to engineer a democratic church revolution made it easy for the conservative orthodox to tar liberal constitutional ideals and the recent political revolution with the same brush.

Almost as revolutionary was a group of pietists. Some denied that church government legally existed after the king's abdication. And Münster theology professors Karl Heim and Otto Schmitz caught the fancy of some pietists with their sweeping proposals.[30] Published on December 1, the Heim-Schmitz plan combined a voluntary communion fellowship with the traditional Volkskirche, organized nationally and united only by the simple confession, "Jesus is the Lord." The two authors struck a revolutionary note by calling for "Evangelical councils" without regard for existing church structure.

Generally the church Right—confessional Lutherans, Positive Unionists, and, more clearly later, pietists—abhorred the radical edge of the
Volkskirche movement for promoting democracy in the church and threatening the church's confession. For the same reasons the Right's faith in the
leadership of the EOK plummeted in the spring of 1919. In February the
Constitution Committee of the Council of Confidants proposed constitutional renovation by way of a constituent assembly elected directly and
democratically by adult parishioners (Urwahlen).[31] Two realistic considerations tipped the scales in the committee's calculations. The republican
state, whose approval was required for constitutional change, might reject
proposals from a General Synod that appeared reactionary and unrepresen-
tative. Also, democratic elections would elicit the loyalties of parishioners
now that the church depended on them more than ever. It now became
clear that the EOK, which strongly influenced this recommendation, had
not fought divisive organizing in the church to avoid democratization. On
April 10, the EOK and GSV, meeting with the Council of Confidants,
accepted the committee's recommendation for submission to the General
Synod. Liberals of the Protestant Association had won their bet with Rade
that the church's highest authorities could be won for a democratic
church—or so it then seemed.

Having helped defend the church from the political revolution, the
church Right in the Council of Confidants was not about to help engineer
a revolution in the church from above. Led by Friedrich Winckler, the moderator of the General Synod, the church Right predicted dire consequences.
A democratic suffrage would allow Socialists and other hostile elements to
infiltrate church leadership. The number of elected liberals was bound to
increase, placing the church's confession in jeopardy. Surely the EOK
should see that the cause of legal continuity could best be served by convening the General Synod for the purpose of constitutional reform and not
merely for empowering a constituent assembly.

Likewise opposed to a democratic church, the Reformed argued for the
old "filter" system, holding that only devoted Christians ought to be eli-
gible for election. Traditionally the Reformed had questioned consistorial
government and extolled synods. Understandably, some liked to think that
the competence of church government had dissolved while that of the General Synod remained intact. Some suspected the EOK of maneuvering to
retain consistorial domination and argued that church government must
bend to the will of synods.[32]

The ecclesiastical and political views of rock-ribbed confessional Lutherans were the most inflexible of the church Right. Denouncing the simple Heim-Schmitz confession as insufficient, their official program called for a confessional church under any circumstances and a Volkskirche if possible. Soon they supported wholeheartedly a confessional Volkskirche. Lutherans looked forward to the greater freedom that the Volkskirche—confessional and at last independent—was to enjoy. But the same prospect made liberals blanch, for there was no room for them in such a church.

As they abhorred democracy in the state, confessional Lutherans detested it in the church. Political authority emanating from "below," from the irresponsible masses, cannot be accountable to God "above." In the church only pious men, not nominal members, should wield authority. The task of the church "often consists in opposing the natural inclinations of the folk or cleansing and sanctifying them," wrote the Lutheran editor Wilhelm Laible. "This task can be accomplished only if God's will, attested to in His Word, not the will of the masses, prevails in the church." For Laible the defense of the church's confession also meant resistance to the principles of the revolution: "Under no circumstances may the church be torn away from the ground on which it alone can stand . . . by the introduction of a suffrage stemming from one of the Revolution's main principles [that are] completely alien to . . . Christian principles."[33]

Within the much larger Positive Union, aversion for a democratic church appeared almost as pronounced, and for the same reasons. An appeal of the Positive Union in April 1919 called for a confessional Volkskirche and rejected a democratic church suffrage. Like the Reformed and Lutherans, Unionists agitated for a speedy convening of the General Synod for the purpose of enacting constitutional reforms, some even contesting the legality of the former king's church government.[34]

Members of the traditionally conciliatory Middle party, the Volkskirche Evangelical Association, tended to take a pragmatic attitude toward constitutional problems. They disapproved of both radical liberal efforts and the Heim-Schmitz proposal, fearing that both stirred up undue dissension. Preaching church unity in dire times, they rallied around the efforts of church government and the majority within the Council of Confidants to defend and reconstitute the church.[35]

While all groups defended the church against the revolutionary state, they differed internally on the means of reconstituting the church, and on ends. From these starting points the internal struggle to renovate the Volkskirche proceeded.

THE VOLKSKIRCHE MOVEMENT AND THE CHURCH FEDERATION

The above melange of attitudes also pervaded the Volkskirche movement, which followed two goals: (1) externally, the defense of the Volkskirche against the new state; and (2) internally, a renewal of church life, especially by activating nominal church members. The first goal was obviously conservative, the second innovative and potentially controversial. Of the two goals, Rade's liberal group and the pietists Heim and Schmitz placed a decided emphasis upon the second. In addition, Rade and other Democratic liberals hoped to neutralize the church politically in order to draw alienated members of republican parties into the communion of the church. To dislodge the more politically conservative, genuine democratic elections appeared indispensable. This hope soon faded, however, as the external goal of preservation largely triumphed over the internal goal of renewal during the first year. Still the external threat galvanized the loyalty of church members—a renewal of sorts, but hardly the kind cherished by the radical wing.

Actually the conservative thrust powered the Volkskirche movement from its inception, and accounted for the hundreds of thousands who swelled its ranks. Arising more or less spontaneously in the November Revolution, the movement in Prussia soon accepted the leadership of the Berlin authorities as they sought to orchestrate protests to the Kultusministerium, to promote parties favorably disposed toward the church in elections, and to lobby at the Weimar Assembly.

The movement organized nationally as the German Volkskirche Federation (Volkskirchenbund) on April 29, 1919.[36] The new federation of Volkskirche associations chose Professor Arthur Titius as chairman and August Hinderer of the Evangelical Press Association as business manager. By promoting the Volkskirche Auxiliary earlier, and now the Volkskirche Federation, the Press Association expanded well beyond its original function as a news bureau to mobilize Protestants for political purposes. The Press Association's main offices in Berlin-Steglitz doubled as the federation's national headquarters. Within Prussia some half-million parishioners had enrolled in Volkskirche associations within three months of the revolution —an index of popular support, according to Otto Dibelius, "unparalleled in the history of German church life."[37] By September 1919 more than a million had swelled organizations leagued in the Volkskirche Federation.

Likewise in the federation, emphasis upon entrenching the Volkskirche outweighed that upon internal renewal. Chairman Titius, himself a Democratic liberal, acknowledged that the federation's principal task was political: "In politics today one has respect only for the masses. . . . For a number of years the federation will have the task of revealing the existing forces [of Protestants] and allowing them to be politically effective."[38] Though the federation could not avoid "certain internal questions," Titius conceived of its role more as a moderator than as a protagonist within the churches. Had the federation meddled in church constitutional affairs, it would have lost its mass following. Except for affiliates in the states of Saxony and Württemberg, the Volkskirche Federation began to lose mass support after the Weimar Assembly had fixed principles for an advantageous disestablishment.[39] The circumstances surrounding the rise and decline of the Volkskirche movement suggest that it projected more the goal of external preservation than that of internal renewal. Its mentality, however, continued to pervade the Old-Prussian church—that of closing church fronts against external threats.

The same mentality pervaded the Church Federation (Kirchenbund) of Evangelical Landeskirchen as well. In fact, the official church institutionalized the movement's twin purposes in the assembly (Kirchentag) of the Church Federation. At Elberfeld in January 1918, a conference of Volkskirche groups and church free associations endorsed Rade's suggestion for a popularly elected national church assembly and asked the Kirchenausschuss to summon it.[40] The Kirchenausschuss proved amenable. Even before the revolution, in June 1918, it had considered augmenting the Eisenach Church Conference of church governments with a synodical organ to lend more force to the church's public voice in the portended democratic state.

From all church quarters after the revolution had come an oft-repeated demand for greater national church unity and for national organs that effectively represented church members, not merely church governments. Churchmen discovered the power of the masses in the new democratic state. But what specific form should these organs assume? After the revolution liberals seemed willing to settle for a federalist national church.[41] For them the real crux was whether the Church Assembly would be chosen by direct elections from parishioners and thus represent more accurately the broad composition of the Landeskirchen. Because the more orthodox, who cherished territorial churches for the sake of confessional autonomy, sensed the political need for greater church unity, the two could more easily come to terms. But the church Right had only contempt for direct—"democratic"—elections.

The Kirchenausschuss responded quickly to the initiative of the Elberfeld conference. To its representatives, President Bodo Voigts suggested more than a mere church assembly—a permanent church federation —since no one knew when the revolutionary crisis would end.[42] At a "preconference" in Kassel on February 27 and 28, representatives of free church associations and church officials endorsed this proposal and chose a committee to plan for the Church Federation and Church Assembly, as well as to suggest how the Landeskirchen ought to be reconstituted.

The shape and function of the forthcoming Church Assembly now depended largely on the recommendations of the planning committee as endorsed by the Kirchenausschuss. The committee could prescribe direct elections to the Church Assembly and suggest to a broadly composed assembly that it similarly commend direct elections to guide the reconstruction of the Landeskirchen. But the committee and the Kirchenausschuss chose to compose the Church Assembly of delegates largely from existing church governments, synods, and church free associations. Moreover, the two suggested that the Church Assembly claim only an "indirect" influence over the internal affairs of member churches and a "direct" jurisdiction only in representing the churches externally. Clearly, the conservative thrust of the Volkskirche movement weighed heavily in the committee's scale of priorities.

Hastily Martin Rade assembled disappointed liberals in a pressure group, called *Volkskirche und Kirchentag*. By June 1919 the groups rallying to it claimed a membership of thirty-six thousand.[43] Rade's new lobby hoped to marshal mass support for liberal constitutional principles at the Church Assembly. The pressure group also promoted the attendance of nominal church members, specifically Socialists. Rade prevailed upon Voigt's successor, Reinhard Moeller, to invite three Socialists.

As Democratic liberals especially had feared, the Church Assembly, convened in Dresden in September 1919, fell under the thrall of the more conservative and orthodox churchmen. The three Socialists refused to attend. Of the 320 delegates, Rade estimated, only about 50 drew together in the liberal component. To the consternation of perhaps most delegates, Arthur Titius contended that the church, under God's guidance, must accommodate itself to changed conditions, bitter defeat, and the republican era:

He [God] has destroyed the Kaiser's might, our pride and joy, and placed us upon a long, difficult, and incalculable path of suffering. We are ready to follow Him, certain that the paths on which He wishes to lead us are nevertheless paths of mercy, of blessing. We, whose weapons held back the entire world, should learn to go weaponless through an armed world. We, who were conquered by empty words of justice, freedom, and happiness in a coming League of Nations, we should learn to believe that these words can become true. Be it therefore!"[44]

Summing up the opinion of perhaps most members, Wilhelm Philipps exclaimed: "It has not yet been shown that the spirit of the new era stems from above."[45]

To the dismay of liberals, the Church Assembly refused to commend direct elections to member churches, even though some churches had already adopted the principle. Under pressure from the Right, the assembly took no position at all. The moderator of the Westphalian provincial synod explained: "In political elections we have seen sufficiently what is attained through direct elections. Our people are whipped up, instincts and passions are aroused, necessary inner unity and love of fatherland have not grown thereby. . . . Direct elections lead to radicalism, and will not result in a blessing for our church."[46]

The display of conservative political attitudes at the Church Assembly moved the Democratic liberal Otto Baumgarten to wonder whether the Evangelical church was "really to become a rear guard of the political reaction." At the Church Assembly he received the uncomfortable impression of associating with "a hidebound, so-to-speak pre-March [pre-1848] monarchially disposed society."[47] Similarly, Ernst Troeltsch commented: "The Conservatives have lost their rule in the state, in the churches they wish to keep it. The ideal is to make the church into a citadel of a type of spiritual counterrevolution."[48] Rade worried about the failure of the Church Assembly to draw upon wider segments of the church's membership. "Consequently we are no representation of the people," he stated, surveying the assembly, "no representation of the *Volks-Kirche*."[49]

This liberal commentary prompts two questions. First of all, did the church Right intend to misuse the church politically for the cause of antirepublicanism, as Troeltsch suspected? One can find comments in the church press that suggest this conclusion. Now that the revolution had "destroyed" Prussia, wrote a Lutheran in early 1919, the church must remain a solid "pole" in the flux of events and not yield to democratization.[50] But the church Right was oriented defensively against the intrusion of revolutionary principles in this case, not offensively against the Republic. In the church Right ecclesiastical and political constitutional principles were generally cast of the same mold. One may infer political antidemocratic convictions from them but not, given the circumstances, a conscious political misuse of the church.

Second, could Rade legitimately claim that only a democratic church could create a "Volks-Kirche"? It is true that authoritarian Landeskirchen had grown unpopular, but the case for a democratic church had yet to be proved. The church Right, too, craved a popular church and believed that only the traditional message of Christianity — certainly not democratic principles — could generate one. The Right feared to admit the masses to political power out of concern for the church's confession, without which renewal must falter. Rade's claim, in short, was not without an answer.

One is tempted to conclude, however, that both Right and Left overestimated the importance of direct elections. The debate over democracy revolved around the composition of synods, far removed from the ordinary concerns of most active parishioners. But the debate foreshadowed the direction that the Old-Prussian church would take. It tried to close fronts against the outside in pursuit of interests that the church Right largely defined. If the Old-Prussian church could have activated nominal church members by way of democractic elections, it might well have accommodated itself more readily to the Republic. All the same, it seems highly unlikely that even democratic elections could have elicited enough interest from others to sap the formidable strength of the church Right.

The emergence of the Church Assembly in 1919 completed the shift in the church's attitude toward the state, occasioned by the revolution. No longer could German churches rely on summi episcopi to safeguard vital interests. They sought instead collective action, in the words of Wilhelm Philipps, "to fend off...all state incursions and encroachments into the realm of the church."[51] Comments made in joint EOK and GSV meetings alluded to the Church Assembly as a means of defense against "the assault of the pagan-materialist world view," "the advance of Rome," and the "church-hostile state."[52] But the Church Federation was not meant to remain forever on the defensive. Consistorial President Boehme of the Saxon Landeskirche explained that the projection of religious convictions and church interests against the state "can be secured better if the powerful forces of Evangelical Germany can be set in motion in one direction by one agency." Previously the regulation of churches and schools had rested exclusively with the states. But now, wrote Boehme, "since the new federal constitution drew church and school questions into the competence of the federal government, unity is frankly a necessity."[53] Also the Church Federation was conceived as an instrument of the closed-front Volkskirche.

Several years passed before all arrangements could be made to constitute the Church Federation. A statement of competence, accepted by the 1919

Church Assembly, was later incorporated into the final constitution passed by the 1921 Church Assembly. After all twenty-eight Evangelical Landes-kirchen agreed to a Church Federation treaty, church dignitaries officially promulgated the Church Federation constitution on May 25, 1922, at the historic Castle Church in Wittenberg.

Finally the Evangelical Landeskirchen wielded an effective, though cumbersome, instrument with which to make their weight felt politically. When member churches experienced difficulties with hostile state governments, the former could call upon the Church Federation to represent their case to state and federal governments. The federation lobbied as well for morality and school legislation. The old Kirchenausschuss was retained as a permanent executive to carry out joint decisions of the assembly, which represented church members, and the council (Kirchenbundesrat), the successor to the old Church Conference, which represented church governments. Churchmen ascribed great weight to decisions of the Church Assembly inasmuch as it ostensibly functioned as a popular forum to formulate and express church opinion.

But the four church assemblies held from 1919 to 1927 fell shy of functioning as popular forums. Members were not chosen by direct elections, and the Church Federation was conservatively structured to accord church governments a considerable influence. Moreover, the assemblies did not usually act as open forums for the discussion of vital issues. They did indulge in heated debates on direct elections in 1919 and on religious education in 1921. But, as one periodical put it: "The Stuttgart [1921] Church Assembly was more a parade than a scene of battle. Actual disputes were transferred to committee sessions."[54] In most cases, assemblies approved committee suggestions with little debate. Apparently church leaders sacrificed free discussions in order to present a determined and undivided front behind assembly resolutions. Church leaders exalted in the new found enthusiasm of laymen for attempts of the churches to assert themselves since the revolution.[55] But such was usually the enthusiasm of those willingly enrolled in a closed-front Volkskirche.

CHOOSING POLITICAL PARTIES

Since Socialists had placed disestablishment on the political agenda, churchmen could expect forthcoming constituent assemblies to grapple with this issue. This ominous prospect raised the question of how active church members might ultimately help shape future church-state relations by channeling their influence through political parties. In choosing parties, the relatively small camp of church liberals fractured between the tug of the political Right and the Democrats; a Nationalist liberal might feel torn between the political program of his party and the church and school policy of the Democrats. The church Right, however, discovered that political preference and concern for the Volkskirche converged, narrowing the choice to one or two parties on the political Right. These political elections, held at the end of January 1919, gave Old-Prussian churchmen little time to make choices. But the choices they made persisted for the most part throughout the period under consideration.

The immediate problem facing active Protestants was that parties to which they had previously thrown their support had broken up during the revolution. Protestantism seemed to have lost its political advocates at a time when the fate of the Volkskirche hung in the balance. Uncertainty encouraged churchmen to consider a number of options. Should they go it alone by founding an Evangelical party, collaborate with Catholics in the Center, or attempt to mold the policies of newly formed parties?

The idea of an Evangelical party, a counterpart to the Catholic Center party, appeared to some to be an attractive possibility. It seemed possible that the burgeoning Volkskirche movement might expand such a party. Scattered attempts to found an Evangelical party miscarried, however. Before the revolution, active German Protestants had ranged themselves in several political parties. The threat of disestablishment could not catalyze these diverse elements into one Evangelical party, especially since other political issues would intrude to accentuate differences. The example of the small Christian-Social party showed that the Protestant electorate might diffuse even more with the founding of an Evangelical party. A broad, inclusive Volkskirche, contended the liberal *Protestantenblatt,* could not act like a narrow sect in political matters. The theological argument that an Evangelical party could not take positions on current issues in the name of gospel was on the lips of many. Finally, the inability of these attempts to draw a mass following on such short notice induced even those who endorsed the idea to shift to the newly founded Nationalist party, lest the Evangelical vote split.

Through a process of elimination, members of the church Right often settled for the Nationalist party. This process could continue to eliminate even the Nationalists, at which point an Evangelical party loomed as the only remaining alternative. Only in 1929, beyond the period here analyzed, did the national quest for an Evangelical party come to fruition in the shape of the Christlich-Soziale Volksdienst.[56]

If for the moment an Evangelical party seemed impracticable, collaboration with the established Catholic Center party might marshal broad political strength that both denominations required to advance common interests in constituent assemblies. To encourage this possibility the Center and its offshoot, the Bavarian People's party, took steps to transform themselves into interconfessional parties, the Center adopting the name "Christian People's party." This attempt reached its goal, however, only in the Christian Democratic Union (CDU) after the Second World War. Only a few active Protestant churchmen entered the rechristened Center before the January elections. Soon almost all of them had departed. Reverting to its old name, the Center had failed to accommodate Protestants sufficiently in its organization. The Center's republican orientation, qualified though it was, certainly put off monarchist Protestants. Apparently the bulk of church leaders, conditioned by the anti-Catholic feeling of prewar days, would agree with *Der Reichsbote* that the renamed party was really a "wolf in sheep's clothing," exploiting Protestant apprehensions. This conservative daily, in fact, condemned two Protestant proselytizers of the rechristened party as "betrayers of the Evangelical faith,"[57] and spread warnings of the Berlin Pastors' Association and a Berlin district synod against the Center's overtures. Churchmen could question whether a bond forged at a moment of crisis could endure beyond that crisis. It seemed also that the theological objection to an Evangelical party must also apply to an interdenominational one. Against the competition of the Nationalist party, finally, the Center could win little ground in Evangelical church quarters.

Rather than blaze new political trails, active Protestants followed old ones by affiliating with newly formed parties of prewar vintage. The mounting appeal of the German National People's party (Deutschnationale Volkspartei), especially, discouraged new departures. Toward the Nationalist party gravitated a collection of prewar rightist parties—the two conservative parties, Stoecker's Christian-Social party, the German Folkish party, several small anti-Semitic groups, and a clutch of former National Liberals. By threatening large estates in the East with expropriation, heavy industry with nationalization, the churches with radical disestablishment, the revolution galvanized these groups to seek the protection of a larger umbrella. Churchmen found it easy to transfer their loyalties to the new conservative party inasmuch as several of its components had drawn their votes previously and as it aspired to restore the monarchy. Moreover, its program promised to shield the Volkskirche and extolled Christian nationalism.

A sure sign that church leaders understood the stakes involved in the elections was the large number who volunteered their services as candidates of several parties. Of these the Nationalist party drew the largest share, electing eight of the thirty who campaigned under the Nationalist banner for seats in the Weimar Assembly. Nationalists also placed four general superintendents and a pastor in the Prussian Constituent Assembly. The most prominent Nationalist in church quarters was the former Landrat Friedrich Winckler, chairman of the Old-Prussian GSV, who later rose to the temporary chairmanship of his party. As leaders of the Christian-Social party, among them Reinhard Mumm, entered the Nationalist party, the political allegiance of most Evangelical members of Christian unions and Evangelical workingmen's clubs shifted accordingly.

Despite initial scruples against women's suffrage, won by the revolution, Nationalists soon formed a committee to campaign for the women's vote in the elections. Pastors' wives, deaconesses, and Evangelical women's associations fell in with these efforts. At the head of the Association of Evangelical Women's Clubs stood the Nationalist politicians Magdalene von Tiling and Paula Mueller-Otfried. Later the movement of Evangelical parents to preserve confessional education indirectly promoted the Nationalists' cause among Evangelical women, for the Nationalists posed as intrepid defenders of the movement's principles.[58]

Running a poor second in competition with the Nationalists for the vote of active church members, the German People's party (Deutsche Volkspartei) consisted of the bulk of the old National Liberal party, reorganized under the leadership of Gustav Stresemann. It also longed for a restored monarchy and showed a strong nationalist slant. But it muted the sharp Nationalist thrust against the Republic. Like the Nationalist party, it took established churches in tow at the Weimar Assembly, differing, however, on school policy; Nationalists pressed for confessional schools. Initially sanctioning both Christian Simultan and confessional schools, the German People's party later insisted upon making the former normative, much to the ire of Nationalist churchmen. In the Weimar Assembly, four churchmen sat as politicians of the German People's party, among them the eminent law professor Wilhelm Kahl, who played a major role in deliberations over churches and schools.[59]

Inasmuch as the two Socialist parties appeared as the Volkskirche's most dangerous enemies, church leaders scarcely considered any accommodation with them before the elections, apart from Rade and his following. Rather, the campaign for favorable disestablishment terms had to be waged primarily against Socialists. Two sets of values, Christian and anti-Christian, seemed ranged against each other in the political realm. From this restricted angle of vision it seemed only logical to lump all Socialists in the same category; yet differences cut deep among Socialists. Both Haenisch and Heinrich Schulz, state secretary for school affairs in the federal Ministry of the Interior until 1927, appeared to appreciate the moral and cultural impact of historical Christianity, and wished to retain religious instruction in some form.[60] Majority Socialists, moreover, refused to consider their programmatic positions on churches and schools so important as to rule out compromise in Weimar. But Independent Socialists took a more uncompromising position, training their guns not merely on church privileges but on Christianity itself.

Between the socialist Left and the conservative Right, the German Democratic party (Deutsche Demokratische Partei) appeared to most churchmen as only a limited alternative. A group of intellectuals and members of the former Progressive and National Liberal parties founded this avowedly republican party a week after the outbreak of revolution. Emerging as its leader, Friedrich Naumann won a seat in the Weimar Assembly and in July 1919 rose to the position of party chairman. Though a heart attack a month later struck him down, Naumann had lived long enough to render established churches an invaluable service in Weimar. With Naumann a group of liberal theology professors and pastors entered the party; but men holding high church positions could not be found among them. To a great extent, the Friends of *Die christliche Welt* joined the party. To accommodate churches after his falling-out with Hoffmann, Haenisch appointed Ernst Troeltsch and a Catholic Centrist as state secretaries in the Kultusministerium. The Democratic party succeeded in placing two Democratic liberals in the Weimar Assembly and three, including Rade and Troeltsch, in the Prussian Constituent Assembly.

What impelled these men to defy the tide of church opinion by fastening onto the Democratic party? For them political isolation within the church was no new experience. Like others, Rade had earlier joined Naumann in the National-Social Association after the break with Stoecker, and now followed him into the Democratic party. Democratic liberals professed to see the wisdom of the policy pursued by the Reichstag majority since July 1917. Now they accepted the Republic out of a sense of responsibility, after the revolution made any other form of government short of a socialist dictatorship seem impossible.

Like their Nationalist colleagues, Democratic liberals sought political office out of concern for the church. Rade hoped that the Democratic party might allow "church members such as I to influence its position if we ourselves are sincerely and honestly Democrats."[61] His hopes were not misplaced. Within the Old-Prussian church, however, a pall of suspicion enveloped the Democrats, a pall that they could never shake off. After all, Democrats, through their liberal theologians, seemed to espouse the democratic church abhorred by the church Right. The "enlightened" world view of Progressives, their hostility to confessional schools, and the indifference of liberal intellectuals to the church combined to tarnish the image of the fledgling Democratic party. The readiness of Democrats to collaborate with Socialists in government and to endorse the Republic meant, by implication, condoning the repugnant revolution that had undercut the "Christian" state. Before the adoption of the party's first program in December 1919, halfhearted attempts by Democrats to use the Prussian state to impose democracy upon the Old-Prussian church outraged the church Right.

The party's program clarified the Democratic stand on schools, only to blur that stand on churches. In the section on culture, which church liberals such as Rade helped shape, Democrats advocated a Simultan school wide enough to include both confessional and nondenominational religious instruction. More alarming to the church Right was the stance of the program on church-state relations. To be sure, the state should cut off subsidies only in a manner that spared the churches financial hardship. But "historical, convictional, and practical connections" between church and state must endure, and the state must draw church minorities under its protective wing.[62] Did such vague phraseology, however, mean that the "religionless" state should retain a governing hand in church affairs, and even foist democracy upon the church? To this proposition the indignant church Right would never agree.

To sum up, the impact of the revolution restricted the party preferences of Evangelical churchmen before the January elections. It did so because the constitutional crisis facing the Landeskirchen demanded the closure of political fronts for the sake of election success. Actually, the revolution simplified the picture of party preference, in the sense that Nationalists drew into one fold not only several conservative parties but also a group of church liberals fired by an extreme nationalism. Moreover, Democratic liberals had not yet experienced the pull to the left that later led to the growth of religious socialism within the churches. One can imagine that party loyalties would have shown greater fragmentation at the outset had the attention of the churches not been riveted on their constitutional fate.

ESCAPING DISASTER AT WEIMAR

In the Second Empire, Old-Prussian churchmen had little reason to advise parishioners how to vote.[63] Now that constituent assemblies would determine the fate of the Volkskirche, expediency moved churchmen to try their hand at influencing the outcome of the January elections. What gave them pause, however, was the realization that such a campaign could affront many church members and goad parties attacked—particularly the two Socialist parties. Church leaders tried to resolve their dilemma by isolating church-state issues from others, by urging parishioners to vote for parties friendly to the church, and by neither endorsing friendly parties nor attacking others by name. If the church was partisan, it was formally partisan for itself.

This strategy lay behind the questionnaire that the Berlin Volkskirche Auxiliary and several other organizations sent to parties, with the promise or threat that the church press would publish replies. The two Socialist parties ignored the questionnaire or simply referred to their Erfurt program. But the other parties gave generally satisfactory, though vague, answers. The result of the inquiry, therefore, was to distinguish sharply between middle-class and Socialist parties, with the implication that Socialists hardly warranted consideration. In this way, the church closed political fronts against Socialists without ostensibly violating its political neutrality.[64]

Of course, the sponsors of the questionnaire also intended to apply pressure on the newly formed parties by flaunting the voting power commanded by church demands. The protest movement against the recent Hoffmann decrees and the burgeoning Volkskirche movement advertised the voting potential of church people. So did the aggressive mood that prevailed throughout the Old-Prussian church as the election campaign took shape.

Church free associations and Volkskirche groups carried the brunt of the campaign, and the Public Relations Committee of the Council of Confidants orchestrated the common effort in congregations by way of its information sheet. The church press mobilized its resources for the same purpose. Well-attended assemblies met in churches throughout Prussia to apprise loyal Protestants of dangers looming at the forthcoming constituent assemblies. From the Public Relations Committee issued advice to congregations: Promote the election of suitable candidates and parties, but do not endorse any party; get out the women's vote in this their first election; impress on parishioners their duty to vote; march to the polls as a group after special church services.[65]

Despite these preparations, the outcome of the elections disappointed church leaders of the church and political Right. They could, of course, take some comfort in the moderate success of pastors and active laymen who campaigned as candidates. In the 1912 Reichstag election, 21 pastors had campaigned, and 2 had won mandates. Thirty-nine pastors appeared as candidates in the election of the Weimar Assembly, and 7 won seats. Out of a total of 59 candidates, 16 lay leaders and clergymen received mandates to the Weimar Assembly.[66]

What most discouraged churchmen was that the political Right, to which they had thrown their greatest support, failed to penetrate deeply into the electorate as mass parties, while Socialists scored strong gains. In the 1912 Reichstag election, the Right (including National Liberals) had garnered almost 30 percent of the vote; but now the two Right parties gleaned a scant 14.7. By the same token, Socialists had raised their percentage from 34.9 to 45.5 (Majority Socialists 37.9; Independents 7.6). Despite the agitation of the Volkskirche movement, the greatest Socialist increase came from largely Protestant areas, which even in 1912 had loomed large as Socialist strongholds. The elections, nevertheless, had yielded some encouraging results. Now split into two parties, Socialists had not gained the majority they needed to incorporate the Erfurt demands into the new federal constitution. And the two Right parties, together with the Christian People's party (Center), had marshaled 34.4 percent of the vote. If to this was added the 18.5 percent that the surprisingly successful Democratic party received, the major middle-class parties had cornered a 52.9 percent majority, and would control 229 out of 423 seats at Weimar.[67] Clearly, much depended on how Democrats chose to treat established churches. Fortunately for the latter, a former Lutheran clergyman—Friedrich Naumann—now led the Democrats.

The results of the election, when compared with the public outcry against the November decrees, suggested that church interests could command greater popular support if separated out from other political issues. A Socialist, for example, could be expected to vote for his party even though he favored Christian religious instruction for his children. If church leaders had not reached this conclusion by January 1919, they soon came to it as a consequence of the massive petition drive that they subsequently launched.

The Public Relations Committee decided to promote a petition drive through local pastors as a final effort to bring popular pressure to bear upon constituent assemblies. No doubt the committee, well aware of public reaction against the November decrees, concluded that a petition on behalf of religious education stood a better chance of attracting signatures than one promoting the narrower privileges of the Landeskirchen. The committee reasoned that church groups could be expected to shower constituent assemblies with petitions. But too few signatures might signal to parties a lack of public interest in the fate of Christian public education. For the sake of concerted action, therefore, the committee asked pastors to solicit signatures to the following petition: "We, the undersigned members of the Evangelical church twenty years of age and over, demand that our children receive, as before, an education in public schools that rests on the foundation of Christianity and that aspires toward Christian growth and culture."[68] The petition was vague enough to attract adherents of Simultan and confessional schools alike.

The success of the venture, promoted also by other churches, amazed church leaders, who had of course worked hard to ensure its success. On June 14, 1919 the Kirchenausschuss could inform member church governments that total signatures thus collected came close to 7 million, the Old-Prussian church contributing over half of this number.[69] The 7 million who signed the petition or others like it—all presumably of voting age —represented 23 percent of the total votes cast in the election of the Weimar Assembly, over half again as many signatures as the two Right parties had together gleaned in votes.

Could this incredible feat help compensate for the relative weakness of the Right at Weimar? Could it induce Socialists to compromise, deter Democrats from following the radical course of elementary schoolteachers, and punctuate church demands in this area as well as in others? These and other questions preoccupied EOK officials and members of the GSV and the Council of Confidants. Together they staffed the four operational committees of the Council of Confidants. Together they struggled to steer the church between the Prussian state and contentious church politics, while hoping to outrun the storm forming at Weimar. Clearly internal consensus was needed to weather the storm and to chart a course toward church reconstruction. As a device to generate this consensus, the Council of Confidants was no cosmetic graft on the body of church government. Its Public Relations Committee, assisted by the Evangelical Press Association, revealed a talent for political agitation, and its Constitution Committee marked what seemed like a promising path out of the present constitutional morass. The Disestablishment and Education committees trained their attention respectively on church and school deliberations at Weimar. They sought to frame the demands that the EOK should submit, lay contingency plans, and help develop the church's lobbying effort at Weimar.

Fortunately, the EOK, GSV, and Council of Confidants disposed of ready-made contacts at the heart of the decision-making process at Weimar — in the Constitution Committee. Three members of the Council of Confidants participated in the committee's deliberations on churches and schools: pastors Reinhard Mumm and Gottfried Traub, both as Nationalist deputies, and Professor Adolf von Harnack, as an expert summoned by the government. Mumm especially remained in close contact with the EOK throughout these deliberations.[70] A fourth churchman, Professor Wilhelm Kahl, a People's party deputy and expert on church law, fought tenaciously in this committee for church privileges. As a member of the GSV and of the Disestablishment Committee, he was, of course, privy to discussions within the Council of Confidants.

When the Weimar Assembly convened on February 6, no one could be sure what course it would pursue. The drift of the ensuing deliberations is easier to follow if one keeps in mind that the assembly considered four options in settling the constitutional issues posed by churches and schools: (1) yielding to the particularism of the states by reserving the entire complex of issues for state legislation; (2) leaving to federal legislation the formulation of principles by which states should proceed to reconstruct church-state relations, a position endorsed by both Socialists and Democrats in line with their unitary constitutional ideals; (3) anchoring in the constitution itself the principles governing disestablishment on the state level, much as the Center party had tried to safeguard church privileges in Prussia immediately before the revolution and now tried again at Weimar in collaboration with the political Right; and (4) reaching a compromise between those favoring federal legislation and those advocating constitutional safeguards. Eventually the Democrats forged the compromise suggested in the fourth option by first tipping the majority balance in favor of the second option and then the third. But the first alternative weighted the scales initially.

As provisional minister of the interior, Democrat Hugo Preuss had framed a draft constitution. He included the second option in his draft, by which federal legislation would establish principles for the states, a provision deleted, however, in deference to particularist objections from states. Other aspects of the draft were also modified when churches protested. On February 22 the EOK contested the statements that "no religious society enjoys privileges over others" and that "authorities" may no longer inquire into confessional affiliation. The EOK claimed that the church faced bankruptcy if deprived of its privileged status and thus of church taxes, and that without confessional statistics the state could hardly collect the church tax.[71] Subsequently the draft underwent revision to omit any mention of church privileges and to permit the collection of confessional statistics.

After Preuss presented his revised draft to the assembly, on February 24, the Left was surprised to hear the Catholic Center and the Right parties, contrary to their avowed particularism, argue for the third option of securing church privileges and Christian education directly in the federal constitution itself. In several states (but not in Prussia) Socialists commanded legislative majorities after the recent state elections. In such states, wrote Mumm, "church people face . . . an almost hopeless fight against the materialist rule of the masses if the Reich does not come to their aid."[72] Even eventual federal legislation, subject to the whim of the Reichstag, might prove hostile to churches. The only sure recourse was to build guarantees into the constitution itself, thereby setting limits on future legislation and obliging the federal government to shield the status of churches and Christian schools wherever attacked.

The assembly's Constitution Committee rewrote church and school provisions during its forty-two sessions between March and June. On crucial issues Socialists were pitted against the Catholic Center and the Right parties, and neither side could command a majority in the committee without the Democrats. To the dismay of church partisans, Democrats sided with Socialists on March 17 to vest the federal legislature with authority to establish principles governing religious societies and schools. The Kirchenausschuss followed this dispute with foreboding. On March 13, several days before, the Kirchenausschuss had written the assembly to bolster the position of the Catholic Center and the Right parties. Elaborating on the familiar theory of symbiosis, the Kirchenausschuss requested that the Volkskirche come under the protection of the federal constitution itself. Essentially, the Kirchenausschuss argued for the status quo, guaranteed by the constitution. "Any intervention in the religious consciousness of our folk . . . would enkindle a storm of indignation," it warned. As proof for its threatening claim, the Kirchenausschuss pointed to 3.4 million signatures already collected in support of the Christian education petition.[73]

Under Naumann's leadership, the Democrats proved amenable to these demands when the committee shifted its attention to the section of the draft dealing with basic rights. Majority Socialists moved to relegate churches to the status of free associations, while the Catholic Center and the Right parties moved to incorporate church privileges. The latter tried to squeeze so many guarantees into this section as to render federal legislative competence relatively harmless. Majority Socialists saw through this strategy, but as the impasse deepened they expressed a willingness to compromise. Actually they had little choice, since Naumann and the Democrats were prepared to tilt the majority balance again, this time in favor of the Catholic Center and the Right parties. Still, it was to Naumann's credit that he managed to persuade Majority Socialists to introduce with Democrats on April 3 the decisive motion that granted the Landeskirchen the privileged status that the revolution had placed in jeopardy.[74]

The compromise thus reached favored church constitutional guarantees at the expense of federal legislative competence, and Kirchenausschuss minutes record Evangelical church leaders' satisfaction with the results.[75] Not surprisingly, the compromise embodied several smaller ones. The compromise solution left established churches as public corporations (authorized to levy taxes), while, as a gesture to Socialists, allowing other religious societies the right to apply for this privileged status. Thus, bowing to the principle of equality, the committee retained privilege. Since state contributions rested to a considerable extent on complicated legal claims, Majority Socialists reluctantly agreed to honor these claims and to allow federal legislation to establish principles governing their commutation. But only Majority Socialists compromised. Independent Socialists condemned the various compromises and insisted on an end to subsidies, church taxes, and the protection of church property.

Though the committee reached quick agreement on church provisions, it struggled hard to find acceptable compromises on school issues. The contending parties came to terms more readily on religious instruction than on school type.[76] Party differences extended from Socialists, who wished no religious instruction, to Catholic Centrists, who wished to subject it to church control as much as possible. All could agree that religious instruction, if retained, should become optional for teachers and pupils alike. But on the critical question of content and church controls, the parties soon found themselves at loggerheads.

In the committee, Richard Seyfert advocated nondenominational Christian cultural and ethical instruction, the character of which would render superfluous any church influence on religious instruction. He took aim not only at confessional but also at Simultan elementary schools, in which pupils attended religious instruction by confession. Seyfert and two other teachers (another Democrat and a Majority Socialist) moved to reserve the issue for future federal and state legislation. His views and their motion strengthened the resolve of the Catholic Center and the Right parties to secure confessional instruction within the constitution.

This resolve the EOK also sought to bolster when, on March 13, it submitted to the assembly a list of ten demands.[77] The EOK demanded the "German" school, historically the "Christian" school, in which religious instruction centered around the truth of Christianity. If school officials now assumed exclusive control (Leitung) over religious instruction, the EOK recommended that they include theologically trained officials whom church authorities had a hand in choosing. The church should also play a role in choosing texts and in determining the curriculum.

The EOK delivered an ambiguous message to the assembly. Its letter neither advanced the cause of confessional schools outright nor insisted on the church's right to control religious instruction. Previously, the Prussian state had conferred this right through church officials upon local pastors, authorizing them to attend and even intervene in religion classes, to evaluate and correct the teacher, and to lodge complaints with school supervisory officials. Church control of religious instruction as well as general supervision by local pastors had embittered teachers. Hoping to appease them, the EOK and the Council of Confidants took no interest in retaining clerical supervision, but control of religious instruction was a different matter. Here the EOK, worried lest large numbers of teachers refuse religious instruction, tried to recommend an inoffensive substitute for church control. The EOK letter suggested that the Old-Prussian church might settle for Simultan schools and confessional religious instruction with weakened safeguards, though the wording did not bar confessional schools or, for that matter, church control of religious instruction.

In the committee, Seyfert's views ran afoul of the persuasive logic of Professor Harnack, who insisted that only the churches, not a religiously neutral state, could determine the content of religious instruction. He doubted that most teachers could isolate the elements of belief that confessions held in common, and asserted that these elements could thrive only within a confessional ambiance. As both a respected liberal churchman and a Democratic sympathizer, his words weighed heavily. Accordingly, Naumann proposed the decisive motion by which religious instruction would be given in accordance with the beliefs of the churches as a regular, though optional, subject. Even Majority Socialists agreed to confessional religious instruction if religion were included in the curriculum. But they rejected Naumann's motion out of abhorrence for any religious education given under state auspices. As Naumann explained his motion, churches might determine the general character of religious education but not physically inspect religion classes. The committee—eventually even Seyfert —concurred. But Seyfert and other Democrats insisted on an amendment to Naumann's original motion to assert the state's right to supervise religious instruction. As accepted in the constitution, this provision (in Article 149) read: "Religious instruction shall be given in conformity with the principles of the religious society concerned, without prejudice to the State's right of supervision."[78]

Despite the committee's understanding, the chosen formulation merely held two conflicting principles in tension, without delimiting either. It is not surprising that varying interpretations later arose. On the one hand, Old-Prussian church leaders argued that means short of control over teachers, such as those already suggested to the assembly, must be found to assure the church that religious instruction conformed with its principles. On the other, teachers contended that such means jeopardized the state's right of supervision and that Article 149 merely obligated each teacher to conform with church principles as he understood them.[79]

An even greater Delphic vagueness suffused the eventual constitutional provision on school type, because of party disagreements.[80] After the first two committee readings, Weimar coalition parties took matters into their own hands, the Catholic Center and Majority Socialist parties negotiating the "first" compromise without Democrats and then the "second" with them. How could cherished school types—confessional for Catholic Centrists, secular for Socialists, and Simultan for Democrats—find expression in a formula for a unified school system?

The solution toward which the committee initially groped satisfied Democrats only. Tilting the balance toward the Catholic Center and the Right parties, Democrats formed a majority for confessional religious instruction. They turned toward Majority Socialists to consolidate a majority for the common elementary school (Grundschule) "for all." Taken together, the two tentative decisions portended Christian Simultan schools, a prospect that made Catholic Centrists as well as Socialists bristle.

To advance the cause of confessional schools, the Center party moved to reserve the choice of school type to parents. Most Catholic parents could be expected to choose confessional schools. Opponents found themselves at a disadvantage in responding. Socialists had made parental release of children from religious instruction a big issue during the revolutionary period. How could they quail before the next step along the path of parents' choice? Moreover, the Center party advocated parents' choice as a matter of religious freedom, a democratic right that the November decrees in Prussia claimed to assure. The principle of parents' choice, however, ran athwart the common school "for all" that Socialists had long since endorsed and now championed along with Democrats and elementary schoolteachers. In the past, conflicts over schools had surfaced largely as legislative battles. The principle of parents' choice, however, could carry strife over school type into every community. Such was the civil discord that the Center party would tolerate in order to retrieve confessional schools.

Though the motion lost, it soon flamed into life again under extra-ordinary circumstances. When Democrats dropped out of the Weimar coalition rather than sanction the Versailles treaty, they also dropped out of the pivotal position that they had manipulated so successfully. Catholic Centrist leaders reached for the plum by threatening to follow Democrats unless Majority Socialists came to terms. Sufficiently intimidated and likewise disappointed with the results of committee deliberations, Majority Socialists gave way. The two parties (which together enjoyed a necessary majority) settled on the principle of parents' choice to determine which of three types of elementary school — confessional, secular, or common (presumably with confessional religious instruction) — each community might establish.

The two parties had, however, reckoned without the highly vocal advocates of common schools. The "first" compromise, accepted by a slim majority at the second plenary session on July 18, aroused such a public furor as to imperil a majority at the third and final plenary session on July

31. The two compromising parties thereupon negotiated with Democrats, only to tarnish them as well in a "second" compromise, Article 146 of the constitution, which combined common schools and parents' choice.

The first paragraph seemed to prescribe common schools, defended by Democrats, as the norm: "The public school system shall be developed organically. The intermediate and higher school system builds upon a common elementary school [Grundschule] for all." The second paragraph, however, seemed to qualify the norm so heavily as to supplant it with the principle of parents' choice, in which case one could argue that the constitution actually placed the three types on a par:

Within communities, *however*, upon the application of parents and guardians, elementary schools of their confession or Weltanschauung [secular schools intended here] are to be established insofar as the organized school system [ein geordneter Schulbetrieb], in the sense also of paragraph 1, is not thereby jeopardized. The will of parents and guardians is to be taken into consideration *as much as possible*. State legislation determines specifics according to the principles of a federal law.[81]

Especially the teaching profession contended that the first paragraph clearly presented common schools as the norm, for the second paragraph allowed deviating types only as exceptions (only upon application, significantly not required for common schools). If Article 146 postulated no normative school at all, why then had the "second" compromise superseded the "first"? Since the words *"organized school system"* in the second paragraph referred to common schools in the first, other types might be permitted only where common schools already flourished—thus ruling out deviating types in a small community that could maintain but one school and stifling their development in cities.

The case for parents' choice sounded quite as persuasive. The word *however* followed later by the words *as much as possible* in the second paragraph clearly raised parents' choice above the normative stipulation in the first. Common schools may be established wherever parents wanted nothing else. The words *organized school system* referred not to common schools at all but rather to educational standards, merely ruling out small, inferior schools of whatever type.

But how did the three parties of the Weimar coalition interpret their own compromise? Heinrich Schulz, a Majority Socialist deputy, read an interpretation in their name at the final plenary session.[82] Later the Federal Court (Reichsgericht) would cite as authoritative the interpretation that he now gave. According to Schulz, the three parties recognized common schools as the norm. But they intended to make deviating types conditional not upon the viability of common schools in each community, but rather upon the educational capacity of deviating types themselves.

The moderate interpretation of the three parties proved decisive in certain related court challenges but not for legislators (even those from the three parties), who still drew their preferred interpretation from the ambiguous text. For other reasons as well, it seemed improbable that even in 1919 the prospects of normative common schools loomed large. The three parties acknowledged the likelihood that confessional schools would persist as the norm in practice because of tradition and the apparent will of parents. The large minority of the assembly (or large majority, if one includes Majority Socialists), which favored parents' choice, grew shortly thereafter as the fortunes of the political Right waxed and those of the Democratic party waned. If most parents and increasing numbers of deputies opted for parents' choice, the probability that the anticipated federal law could clearly stipulate normative common schools faded considerably.[83] Had the assembly also left the fate of churches in the hands of the Reichstag, one can easily imagine that a church conflict on the federal level could have persisted as well.

What then had the Landeskirchen not lost at Weimar, and why? Apart from a greater measure of independence, they could only lose under the circumstances. Pastor Mumm commented in his memoirs that he and his political friends had secured provisions more favorable than church officials had expected, crediting the Volkskirche movement and petition drive in part for this success.[84] But shifting party relationships within the Weimar coalition on specific issues produced the decisive results. Without the opportunistic role played by the Center party, it is hard to imagine how confessional schools could have been salvaged. The Catholic Center and the Right parties enjoyed the advantage of having their case argued by men skilled in church constitutional law. Fortunately for the Evangelical churches, these experts and other churchmen also led or influenced parties other than the Nationalists, the main beneficiary of church political loyalties. Naumann had found a compromise formula for both church-state relations and religious instruction, and Kahl and Harnack had contributed the weight of their arguments and prestige.

If the torrent of Evangelical petitions, which, according to Mumm, arrived in "piles,"[85] influenced anyone, one wonders whom. As an unmistakable mandate from the people, these petitions had a great impact on the Constitution Committee, Mumm claimed, even on Socialists. But Majority Socialists conceded nothing on schools that they thought they could carry. They conceded obligingly what they had to yield on church status in the hope of extracting concessions from others on schools. Yet the school issue was the target of the massive Evangelical petition drive. Catholic Centrists hardly needed persuasion from Protestants, and Independent Socialists remained far beyond the pale of any persuasion. One suspects that the petition served the same purpose as the petition of the Volkskirche Auxiliary had earlier—that of pressuring the newly formed middle-class parties, scrambling to establish a reliable mass clientele, to stand by church interests. The Evangelical churches had demonstrated in a remarkable way, and perhaps to everyone's surprise, that they could generate mass political support on their own.

Evangelical churches pressed hardest and lost most on school issues. The threat of normative secular schools passed with the January elections, as did that of Simultan religious instruction several months later. As a result, confessional instruction was to remain a regular subject in common as well as confessional schools. Article 146 ruled out local clerical supervision by placing school supervision under full-time trained officials. Likewise church control of religious instruction in its old form went by the board. Both had proved increasingly ineffective anyway, souring the clergy for provoking teachers. What church leaders particularly regretted was that the state could no longer assure the church that baptized members would attend religion classes.[86] At this point, especially, the constitution created in the Volkskirche a fissure that could widen with time.

Optional religious instruction appeared inevitable. Secular schools did not. One wonders why Old-Prussian church leaders finally embraced the principle of parents' choice by which secular schools could poach on others. When the "first" compromise broached that principle, Old-Prussian church leaders must have questioned whether the bargain was worth the intrusion of secular schools. The Constitution Committee's version of the Christian Simultan school had much to commend it. Confessional religious education would prevail in every school as a regular though optional subject, for the committee version projected Simultan schools not as the norm but as the exclusive type. The committee's solution, accordingly, would obviate the hazards of periodic school battles in local communities. It would force several states to restore the confessional religious instruction that they had dropped and permanently remove this temptation from others. The EOK letter of March 13 was noticeably silent on school type, dangling the prospect that Christian Simultan schools might prove acceptable.

The switch in the position of Nationalists, acutely sensitive to church wishes, between the second and third plenary sessions may have indicated a shift in the calculations of church leaders as well. In the second, Pastor Traub rejected the first compromise out of aversion for secular schools, preferring the committee's version. In the third, however, Pastor Mumm acclaimed the second compromise as the best that the political situation would allow, though he disliked common as well as secular schools. Subsequently, most Old-Prussian church leaders heartily endorsed the confessional schools that the second compromise yielded, arguing as well that federal legislation must put all three types on a par on the basis of parents' choice.[87]

If church leaders had shifted their position, their subsequent judgments on the new common school may explain why. The common school, later called Gemeinschaftsschule, could hardly warrant the name *Christian* as the traditional Simultan school could. Common schools would employ dissident teachers as well as teachers of either confession. Article 148 stipulated that "the feelings of those who differ in opinion" must be spared. Under such circumstances, could consciously Christian teachers still express Christian values? Could school prayers and religious observances continue, religious instruction appear as anything but an appendix on the curriculum, and a Christian spirit suffuse the entire curriculum?[88] Such liabilities did not mar the confessional school as much. The interests of the Volkskirche might indeed be better served by writing off secular schools in exchange for "the" Christian school and by counting on Evangelical parents to keep the growth of secular schools and the dropout rate from religious instruction within narrow bounds. Pastor Mumm had little doubt that Evangelical confessional schools would ultimately prevail in the local school battles that would necessarily follow. As he wrote to the EOK on August 6, "I see in the introduction of parents' rights a great gain and do not rate the vitality of secular schools very high, [a judgment] for which I may cite the petition movement, sponsored by the Council of Confidants in Berlin, that has already yielded 6,886,000 signatures."[89] In the end, the magnitude of the petition drive may have influenced the calculations of its sponsors more than it did the major decisions of the Weimar Assembly.

Mumm had in mind the school strife that subsequent federal legislation would unleash because of the principle of parents' choice. Article 174 regulated the intervening period: "Until the enactment of the Reich law provided in Article 146, Paragraph 2, the present legal situation shall continue."[90] For Prussia this transitional provision froze the legal status of school types spelled out in the school maintenance law of 1906. That law established confessional schools as the norm. Since the Reichstag struggled unsuccessfully to pass the implementing legislation, Article 174 closed the door on common and formally secular schools alike for the duration of the Prussian Republic.

With respect to their own status, the Landeskirchen enjoyed their greatest success. The constitution preserved traditional church privileges intact, apart from state contributions for which churches had reason to expect a just commutation. Whether the constitution actually separated church and state, however, is problematic. It sliced one bond that did not exist and left others intact.

Article 137 entrenched in the public mind the notion that the assembly had separated church and state. This article began by asserting that "there is no State Church" and continued with these words: "Every religious society regulates and administers its affairs independently, within the limits of the law applicable to all. It appoints its officers without the cooperation of the State or the civil community."[91] Since the 1870s, however, the Old-Prussian church had relinquished its status as a "state church." If it still qualified as one because of its summus episcopus, the abdication of the Prussian king, not Article 137, cast aside the state's (actually the king's) prerogatives. Article 137 confirmed the essential autonomy of the Old-Prussian church that the revolution had ironically won for it from the king.

On the other hand, the constitution failed to destroy bonds that did exist, foremost of all church privileges. And the republican state only partly released its grasp on church affairs. Article 137 did not prevent the Prussian Republic from claiming the former ruler's prerogatives until 1921. Even afterward the Republic tried to retain a right to contest high church appointments. Since commutation did not ensue, the state continued to determine the subsidies that it would grant, the extent to which churches could raise taxes, and the use of church property.[92] One must heavily qualify the thesis that the disestablishment terms of Weimar liberated the churches while binding the state to perpetual servitude.[93] In their external form church-state relations changed amazingly little as a result of Weimar deliberations.

The Weimar Assembly provided a generally favorable settlement of almost all basic church and school constitutional issues, thus preempting basic decisions on these matters in state constituent assemblies. "How we feared for the immediate future of the church when the church-hostile Revolution broke out!" wrote a conservative churchman. "And yet how smoothly—if we overlook some outbursts and agitation—the deliberations went in the National Assembly."[94] Even though Stoecker's vision of a free Volkskirche poised now on the threshold of reality, the revolution yielded other less beneficial by-products. "We Christian-Socials fought for decades," wrote Pastor Mumm, "for a disestablishment of the church without a dechristianization of the state."[95] Because the constitution considered all world views of equal value, the state had lost its distinctive "Christian" quality. Yet, though Nationalists rejected it, Mumm denied that "the new federal constitution stems from a purely materialistic spirit."[96]

CHURCH ELECTIONS AND BUNGLING DEMOCRATS

While the Weimar Assembly labored in the spring of 1919, church liberals in the Democratic faction of the Prussian Constituent Assembly precipitated a constitutional conflict between the Old-Prussian church and the Republic. They acted in March to transfer the prerogatives of the defunct summus episcopus to three ministers in the Prussian cabinet. Later, in November, Democratic liberals urged the three ministers to intervene by imposing democratic elections upon the Old-Prussian church in order to shake the dominance of the political and church Right. In the course of both disputes, the outraged church Right, fighting for the independence of the church under its control, revealed its disdain for the Republic.

Ever since the revolution the EOK had promoted the thesis that the prerogatives of the summus episcopus reverted to the church with the passing of the monarchy. To be sure, the EOK did not dare to touch these powers for fear of acting illegally and jeopardizing church financial privileges. Its argument was meant to forestall a repetition of the Wessel affair. Through Johann Victor Bredt, a Nationalist law professor, the EOK learned that Haenisch and the Prussian Socialist cabinet, following Hoffmann's departure, agreed to the EOK's proposition. No doubt the Socialist government proved obliging because Bredt assured Haenisch that the church planned to elect a constituent assembly democratically; Bredt also returned with the news that the Socialist government expected such elections.

Because of this "informal agreement," as Jacke called it, the EOK was not prepared for the abrupt turn of events on March 20. On that day the Prussian Constituent Assembly considered a provisional "emergency constitution" that disposed of the king's power with these words: "The state government for the present is to exercise the prerogatives that were held by the king according to laws and ordinances." Worried lest this general formulation also include the powers of the summus episcopus, Nationalists moved an amendment: "The rights of the king as bearer of the ruler's church government do not pertain hereto [to prerogatives transferred to the government]."

It may be that church liberals in the Democratic faction—professors Rade, Otto, and Troeltsch—wished to reserve these rights for the state as a political check on the church. A Democratic colleague in the Weimar Assembly, Walther Schücking, also a law professor, had already advised the Prussian Kultusministerium that it might claim them as an annex to the king's power. Unfortunately, the Nationalist amendment did not make clear to whom these prerogatives belonged. Ostensibly to close the church's constitutional gap, Democrats moved to amend the Nationalists' amendment: "These royal church prerogatives are transferred to three state ministers of Evangelical belief, appointed by the state ministry, until the issuance of the constitution." When neither amendment carried, Nationalists and Democrats successfully proposed both. Together, at least, the amendments would close the highest office in the church to dissidents and Jews.[97]

A week later, on March 26, the EOK sent its sharp protests to the Prussian government along with two monographs that the EOK had earlier commissioned to refute Schücking.[98] The one by Bredt and the other by Max Berner of the Prussian Superior Administrative Court buttressed the EOK's argument: Inasmuch as the king had occupied a church office, his church prerogatives should now fall back to the church. Against Schücking, Berner contended that the state might not wield power within the church, since the Christian authority of Luther's day no longer prevailed in the Republic.

The EOK could not claim, however, that any organ in the church was constitutionally authorized to receive the powers that theoretically rebounded from the summus episcopus. By reconstituting the summus episcopus, the Prussian Assembly allowed the church to get on with its task of renovation while assuring legal continuity with the past for the sake of financial privileges. Wary of inflaming church opinion, the three ministers acted at first with tactful reserve, as Ernst Troeltsch had advised. By then he had become the government's chief consultant for Protestant church affairs as a state secretary in the Kultusministerium. Minister President Paul Hirsch replied to the EOK on June 11 by urging it to recognize the legality of the three ministers with the assurance that the government regarded the arrangement as strictly provisional.[99]

Even so, a storm of indignation swept through the Old-Prussian church, discrediting the Democratic party. Years later the pietist Josef Gauger would recall that Rade "had sold out the freedom of the church and betrayed [it] to the power of the ruling party [sic]."[100] It seemed incredible and offensive that now one Democrat (Rudolf Oeser) and two Majority Socialists (Wolfgang Heine and Albert Südekum) should function as the Old-Prussian church's highest bishops. Inasmuch as Democratic liberals had sponsored the arrangement, churchmen of the dominant Right feared lest the three ministers impose democracy upon the church. They regretted as well the church's dependency upon the whim of the "religionless" state.

Less critical of the Democratic initiative, church liberals were divided more on its underlying theory and purpose.[101] Some echoed Schücking's argument that the summus episcopus had always functioned in his capacity as ruler. Harking back to prewar arguments, they justified continued state controls within the church to safeguard freedom of conscience for minorities. Rade, too, ignored the church Right's Christian-authority argument. He reasoned that the present state, like Reformation Obrigkeit (authority), might help the church out of constitutional difficulties in emergencies. To Rade and his friend Erich Foerster, however, the big question was whether the state should eventually turn over the powers of the summus episcopus to existing nonrepresentative church organs or require democratic ones before relaxing its grip. According to Foerster, both the summus episcopus and his church government had forfeited their legality. As a sort of probate judge, the state must decide if church organs represented all church groups fairly. Obviously, existing synods, above all the General Synod, could hardly stand such a test. Rade shifted Foerster's argument onto strictly political grounds. Rade speculated, Republican parties, sensitive to the conservative voice of the church, could accede to a separation only when direct and democratic elections had superseded the indirect and conservative "filter" system. In his speculation the church Right began to see confirmed its most agonizing fears about the three ministers. To many, not without reason, Rade appeared as a scheming extortionist.

The Prussian Assembly's decision for the three ministers fell between February 13–14, when the Constitution Committee of the Council of Confidants recommended direct elections to a future church constituent assembly, and April 10, when the EOK, GSV, and Council of Confidants formally accepted this advice by a vote of 31 to 18. The majority was guided by the need to elicit popular support for the church and to allow for a proportionate representation of all minorities. Also influencing the majority was the well-grounded fear that the government might otherwise intervene. The three-minister arrangement made it the more imperative to establish a democratic system of church governance to which the state would relinquish the former ruler's church powers. Linking the three-minister arrangement with the decision, the church Right claimed that church government and the Council of Confidants had succumbed disgracefully to state pressure. The Right continued to insist that the General Synod itself undertake constitutional reform, even at the price of conflict with the state. Unable to win over the Council of Confidants, the church Right marshaled its strength that spring in provincial synods. All that met repudiated direct elections from adult parishioners to a constituent assembly. [102]

Confronted by this resistance, the EOK gave way. The unity front that it had assembled through the Council of Confidants had collapsed as liberals interpreted the Right's campaign as an effort to reconstruct a dogmatically intolerant church. The General Synod could be expected to reject the council's recommendation, and the three ministers might therefore refuse to summon it. The EOK sought a way out of this impasse by compromising with the church Right and by winning the indulgence of the Kultusministerium. To the GSV on May 14, Vice-president Reinhard Moeller proposed the submission of two bills to the General Synod: one to reelect congregational boards, the second to empower these to elect a constituent assembly. The compromise would remove two "filters" (district and provincial synod elections), while leaving in place the reconstituted third, perhaps the most effective of the three. The second bill also provided that the king's church prerogatives would temporarily revert to the EOK and GSV. Requested by the GSV only to draft the bills, the EOK asked the Kultusministerium at the end of May whether it approved, since legislative sanction was needed for changes in church ordinances. Apparently the EOK wished to confront the suspicious but dominant church Right in the GSV with a compromise that could win state approval. [103]

In his reply of July 21, Haenisch argued the need for establishing "a certain inner similarity between church and political sensitivities and customs of the folk," a representative, presumably democratic, church, authorized on behalf of parishioners to administer large sums of the "people's" money, accumulated by the church tax. He regretted that the two bills excessively favored the representation of the clergy and the conservative countryside. But he implied that the three ministers might summon the General Synod when he reserved judgment until it had acted. Strangely enough, he omitted comment on the contemplated transfer of royal church prerogatives. By this time, Troeltsch, who framed this letter, had concluded that the state could do nothing more, short of outright conflict, to press for a democratic church. Perhaps for that reason the Kultusministerium leaked Haenisch's letter to the press—to prod church liberals into action. [104]

Now the church Left began to marshal its resources as the Right had in the previous half year. During the summer and fall of 1919 liberals collected signatures and relayed petitions to the EOK, a campaign coordinated through a Berlin headquarters. Some, such as the *Protestant-enblatt* editors, saw the three-minister arrangement in a more favorable light, for the three loomed increasingly as the last hope for direct elections. [105]

As the constitutional dispute headed toward a crisis, the church Right and liberals, only recently united in defense of the church, locked horns over ecclesiastical principle. Occasionally both drew upon supposed political lessons from the recent past to underscore constitutional points. [106] Democratic liberals especially tended to accuse the Right of consciously promoting political conservatism in the church, and the church Right retorted that liberals would apply alien political principles to church reconstruction. These escalating charges of intentional misuse of the church for political purposes were largely inaccurate, however, since a common cast of thought often produced organizational principles equally applicable in church or state. Certainly liberals as a group were too fractured politically to subject to this blanket charge. Generally they kept to traditional ecclesiastical arguments that had not been invented with the revolution. In their eyes, moreover, an inclusive Volkskirche must reflect diverse political persuasions.

The church Right's logic, by contrast, led toward a politically conservative church, by excluding most of its alienated republican constituency from representation. This logic led as well toward an authoritarian state. If both church and state received their authority from "above," democracy could not constitute it from "below."[107] Christ "never entrusted Himself to the masses who cry 'hosanna' today and 'crucify' tomorrow," wrote Philipps, and neither should the church. He could just as well have spoken of the state. To Philipps, nominal church members represented the objects of the church's ministry, not the subjects of its authority. The church could not dispense with elections, certainly, but it could restrict them to bona fide Christians in order to protect its integrity. In most German states, wrote Troeltsch shortly before the fall crisis, German Protestantism combined "the ideology of qualified submissiveness to authority, of monarchical temperament, of the military social order, of conservative manorial rule so completely with its ethics and dogma, with its institutions and customs, that it could be considered the spiritual twin of the conservative-political system and feel itself as such with pride."[108] Philipps would not quarrel with this judgment, except to make virtues out of what Troeltsch considered vices.

To theoretic objections against direct, democratic elections, the church Right added practical ones. Direct elections might equip the Socialist masses with a ladder to scale the citadel of the church, wresting control from the hands of loyal Christians. Rade dismissed such fears (as had the majority in the Council of Confidants), since Socialists appeared far too indifferent to entertain such thoughts.[109] Indeed, church elections in Württemberg in July and in Baden in October bore out his contention, for here the crusading Right, despite direct, democratic elections, won resounding victories.

In early September the GSV agreed to the EOK's request for submission of the two bills to the General Synod. Because of Rightist pressure in the GSV, the drafts were not changed to accommodate any of Haenisch's criticisms. Nor did the EOK consult the three ministers or the Kultusministerium before publishing the bills in September. Not until October 30 did the EOK submit the bills to the three ministers, along with a request to summon the General Synod in early December, leaving little time for negotiations. Apparently the EOK snubbed state authorities as a demonstration of church independence. The church Right in the GSV had faulted the EOK for so much as consulting Haenisch earlier about the two bills.[110]

Goaded by Democratic liberals, who reacted angrily to the EOK compromise with the Right, the Democratic faction in the Prussian assembly resolved to contest the two bills.[111] On November 5, in the assembly's budget committee, Rudolf Otto proclaimed that the consent of Democrats to church subsidies would depend on the attitude of the EOK and General Synod toward the Volkskirche and the protection of minorities. On November 11, Protestant members of the Democratic faction formally requested the government to explain what it intended to do "to preserve the rights of the state and of citizens belonging to the Evangelical Landeskirche." The two bills contradicted "the democratic foundations of the Prussian state." Democrats also complained that the proposed transfer of the three ministers' competence lacked the force of law.

The Democratic position became more clear on November 13, when the faction posted ten theses. Thesis 8 stated candidly: "For the state a friendly solution would be fatefully more difficult if the church separating from it would assume constitutional forms that basically run counter to its own. The democratic state has an interest in a democratic church constitution." Thesis 9 advised Prussian churches to adopt direct elections and forgo suffrage restrictions for their own good. This veiled threat was accompanied by another. According to thesis 6, the state should dismantle controls over Evangelical churches only insofar as it scaled down its financial obligations to them.

Confronting the Republic was the dilemma of silencing the conservative voice of the church without laying itself open to the charge, already exploited by the political Right, of intervening in church affairs. Bolstered by the Democrats, the three ministers *in evangelicis* turned down on November 13 the EOK's request to summon the General Synod until they and the EOK could work out election procedures to a church constituent assembly that had promise of acceptance in the Prussian assembly. They pointed out that the proposed transfer of their powers blatantly contradicted the provisional constitution. "The functions of the ruler's church government have been transferred to the undersigned and will be exercised by them," they insisted, "for the purpose of having principles decided upon for the re-election of church organs, which correspond to the general political electoral principles of the present and [which] especially secure the right of minorities to the representation of their religious convictions in the church." All the same, the three ministers professed good intentions. They claimed to have acted to obviate a probable conflict between the Prussian assembly and the General Synod if the latter were to pass the two bills. On the same day, Minister President Hirsch informed the EOK that the church could receive its internal independence only with the anticipated financial settlement.

On December 3, the Prussian assembly debated both the Democratic inquiry and an opposing one submitted by the Nationalists. Represented by two general superintendents, Nationalists claimed that Article 137 of the Weimar constitution had already conferred independence on the churches, even though subsidies had yet to be commuted. The intervention proposed by the three ministers—indeed, the institution itself of the three ministers—appeared egregiously unconstitutional. The People's party criticized Democrats for sparking a Kulturkampf against the Old-Prussian church. Both parties deplored the differential treatment of Protestant and Catholic churches.

In his reply, Haenisch argued that Article 137 left the specifics of separating church from state to subsequent state legislation. Until then the three-minister arrangement remained well within constitutional bounds. Moreover, the Weimar constitution allowed the Prussian government to take the position "that separation . . . can only be carried through simultaneously in the financial and legal fields. So long as this does not take place, the former legal regulations remain in force."[112] Had the government persisted in this position, the three ministers would have manned their posts throughout the Weimar period. Subsidies were not commuted. The forthcoming General Synod might pass whatever it wished, Haenisch continued. But, likewise, the Prussian assembly enjoyed the same freedom to confirm or refuse whatever the General Synod passed. Moreover, Prussian law gave the state ministry responsibility for determining whether church law violated state law, as the proposed transfer of the three ministers' prerogatives obviously did. Technically, therefore, the state had not arbitrarily intervened in internal church affairs, nor would it. But technical justifications could not wipe out the main offense of the three ministers in the judgment of the church and political Right—the use of state power to democratize the Old-Prussian church.

Meanwhile, howls of protest issued from the indignant church Right. Philipps interpreted the intentions of the three ministers as "an open declaration of war on the Evangelical church by the religionless state."[113] He advised the church to "arm" for a scarcely avoidable Kulturkampf. A consensus prevailed in the church Right that the church could not truckle to such intolerable demands. Not since the Hoffmann era, still in vivid memory, had church-state relations been so strained. Now that the long-awaited constitutional struggle with the republican state had finally arrived, the temper of the church Right was vigilant and aggressive. Even politically conservative church liberals, appalled by the sudden threat to church independence, joined the church Right in lacerating protests. But unlike a year earlier, now the church's closed front against the state buckled. Democratic liberals had joined the oppressor (in the eyes of the church Right), and some politically conservative liberals recovered enough from their initial shock to think better of the Democrats.

Especially Democratic liberals bore the brunt of the church Right's attack. The conservative *Kreuzzeitung* accused them of betraying their church to the religionless state just as "the Socialists betrayed the fatherland for the sake of party."[114] If Rade had originally justified the three-minister arrangement as a means of filling the constitutional gap, he now appeared to reveal his true intentions. Rade claimed to wear two hats, one as an influential churchman, the other as a politician. Wearing his political hat, he could not risk the possibility "that in making the church independent a political direction is favored unilaterally."[115] At the Prussian assembly debate on December 3 he more bluntly asserted that the state might not concede the church to the Nationalists. The church Right, however, could see but one hat, for Rade seemed to manipulate state power for church and political reasons alike.

Like Rade, other Democratic liberals argued that their party intended neither to promote liberal church demands nor to cultivate Democratic support in the church. They acted, so they claimed, only to dislodge the conservative political hold on the church and to render it politically neutral. Even non-Democratic liberals could sympathize with this purpose. Discouraged by the scrapping of direct elections, the *Protestantenblatt* before the fall crisis saw "unexpressed, but demonstrable, conservative-partisan purposes as godfathers" behind the two compromise bills, a charge that Rade's *Christliche Welt,* of course, leveled continually. The fact that the chairman of the GSV, the Nationalist politician Friedrich Winckler, had led the fight against direct, democratic elections and that now the Nationalists worked feverishly to save the "Winckler bills" seemed to lead to such a conclusion. But, given the Democratic initiative, the church Right could argue more convincingly that Democrats manipulated the church for political purposes by inviting state intervention.[116]

As the press of the church Right gave vent to its indignation, Rade became appalled by the abuse heaped upon the republican state. He pointed out, correctly, that the new state had treated churches generously. If the Old-Prussian church provoked a Kulturkampf, he warned, the state could easily create difficulties beside which the Hoffmann measures would pale. Some church liberals—not just Democrats—eventually accused the church Right of exploiting the controversy for political gain. They held that the state was seriously interested in avoiding—not provoking—a Kulturkampf. [117]

One predictable effect of this crisis was renewed questioning by the Right of the legality of the three ministers. Viewing this arrangement as the best solution to a problem that held no correct answers, Rade and now Schubring of the *Protestantenblatt,* finally committed, stoutly defended it. They contended that the state might impose direct elections in order to determine to whom the three ministers' prerogatives should fall. [118]

But the thinking of some church liberals, best represented by Erich Foerster, went much farther. [119] In Foerster's opinion, a free church and freedom of conscience could not coexist; corporate freedom stifled individual freedom. Luther, he argued, had sacrificed church freedom to the state in order to gain freedom of conscience. Before the war, church liberals had similarly tended to regard the state as the embodiment of the cultural community, responsible for the defense of religious freedom within the Volkskirche.

With this line of thought in mind, Foerster, himself not a Democrat, sought to shore up the shaky position of the Democrats and the three ministers in the eyes of suspicious liberals. To guarantee religious freedom and in exchange for public corporation rights, the three ministers might rightfully demand a democratic church, one in which all members enjoyed equally the benefits conferred by the state.

Foerster claimed that his argument underlay Rade's assumptions. Rade merely commented that it did not sound absurd. By contrast, the church Right quailed at the mere thought. Foerster had written that Luther's views on a state-controlled church need not be jettisoned merely because the present regime rejected them. To this the Lutheran Wilhelm Laible commented acidly that early Christians had not regarded a hostile state as a positive gain, but as the "beast from the abyss" of Revelations 13. [120] The beast, represented by Rome, personified the Devil, the anti-Christ that would compel the worship of all. One can well imagine the parallel that Laible meant to draw with the Prussian Republic.

Wilhelm Schubring feared lest the Democratic initiative disrupt the liberal consensus on internal church reform. Liberals lacked enthusiasm for the initiative because the government singled out the Old-Prussian church for treatment as a delinquent ward of the state and refused to humiliate the authoritarian Catholic church in like fashion. The *Preussische Kirchenzeitung,* the periodical of the Middle party, which generally approached the liberal church position, held any General Synod preferable to one arranged by Democrats. Moreover, all liberals felt uneasy about the state's intended role as deus ex machina in support of their church aspirations. Justifying this role and suggesting that political neutrality alone had not led him to his position, Schubring wrote: "We friends of a free Volkskirche do not need to be ashamed of ourselves in the least by accepting the alliance of political forces in support of our church goals; the church Right has always gladly accepted and sought them."[121] If they spurned such an alliance, liberals could only expect a reign of political reaction and "blackest orthodoxy" in the church.

Enraged by the intentions of the three ministers and the Democrats, Philipps, like some others of the church Right, called for a General Synod "at the earliest possible date and under any circumstances, even without the approval of the three ministers."[122] He suggested that the forthcoming General Synod consider whether it should bear the burden of financing church government. In line with Haenisch's arguments, such a course would presumably free the church from state control. Philipps' extreme suggestions, however, fell foul of most of the church Right, for unilateral action might well dissolve the Volkskirche. Otto Dibelius, for example, cautioned Philipps to temper principle with insight. After all, the church still leaned heavily upon the state for financial support, and could ill afford to provoke the ire of the coalition parties. In reply, Philipps claimed to urge a unilateral departure only as a desperate last resort. But to Schubring the alarming proposals of Philipps, a dangerous demogogue, amounted to "revolution." Not the radical Left, but the church Right, appeared revolution prone after the advent of the three ministers.

Reinhard Moeller, now EOK president, came to the prudent conclusion that the church could hardly avoid negotiations with the three ministers if it did not wish to jeopardize its financial claims and rights. Friedrich Winckler and a majority in the GSV sided with Moeller, against those in the church Right who objected to negotiations for the sake of church honor and independence. In a letter of December 15, by which the EOK accepted the three ministers' offer to negotiate, Moeller put into sharp relief the arguments of the EOK against the legality of intervention and for restricting the state's authority. First, if prior agreement with the state were demanded before the General Synod could be called, the government would tie the synod's hands. Second, contrary to initial assurances and to Article 137 of the Weimar constitution, the declared role of the three ministers had shifted from facilitating constitutional reform to shaping the new constitution. Third, and most important, the Prussian assembly might not pass on the content of laws enacted by the General Synod regarding internal church matters, but only on whether these laws stayed, according to Article 137, "within the limits of the law applicable to all." As a consequence, the assembly might not impose direct elections to a constituent assembly, an issue that clearly fell within the sphere of internal church affairs. [123]

The negotiations held in January and February of 1920 demonstrated that the government wished to retreat hastily from the position of the three ministers and the storm of controversy that they had aroused. To be sure, the EOK and GSV conceded to the three ministers and Haenisch greater representation for large urban congregations and more restrictions on the number of elected clergymen. On the two critical issues, however, the EOK and GSV had their way. The government no longer insisted on direct elections. It agreed to liquidate the three-minister arrangement as soon as the church constituent assembly convened. The authority of the three ministers would go over, according to a special church law, to a Landes-kirche committee (Landeskirchenausschuss), consisting of the EOK and GSV. The EOK and GSV promised to press the General Synod to accept the compromise, and the three ministers and Haenisch agreed to do the same with the Prussian assembly once the General Synod passed the bills. [124]

Of course, the EOK exerted no direct control over the General Synod, held in Berlin on April 10–24, 1920. Many in the church Right were still resolved to vote down the compromise and to undertake reform through the General Synod. To block this movement, Moeller assembled the General Synod unofficially at the end of one of its first days to impress upon delegates the dire consequences of rejecting the compromise. Niedlich, a Berlin pastor and the only liberal to attend the unreconstructed General Synod, reported that Moeller put the problem bluntly to delegates in these words: "Either accept these drafts or thwart any possible reconciliation with the state!" [125] Eventually the General Synod acceded, passing the bills by a two-thirds majority. On July 8, 1920, the Prussian assembly confirmed the church laws after little discussion.

Finally, for the first time in its long history, the Old-Prussian church could enjoy the prospect of freedom from state influence in its own internal affairs. Church liberals, however, had little reason to cheer, for they feared for their existence in a free, primarily orthodox Volkskirche. The *Protestantenblatt* now regretted that the government had not insisted more vigorously on direct elections. But the indomitable Rade refused to give up the hope that the state might again apply pressure on the church. After all, he wrote, the church still relied upon the state for subsidies, and the state had yet to set its seal of approval upon the church constitution, still unwritten. But the government had already surrendered its trump card by agreeing to dismantle the institution of the three ministers before the constituent assembly had framed the new constitution.

Democratic and Nationalist church leaders differed fundamentally on the nature of the conflict that had ended with the defeat of the state's most recent church policy. For Democrats the struggle had been waged by republicans to wrest political control of the Old-Prussian church from antirepublicans, with the goal of neutralizing the church politically. Of course, democratizing the church also coincided with liberal ecclesiastical aspirations. For Nationalists, on the other hand, the beleaguered church had struggled courageously to liberate itself from the tightening grip of the religionless state. Of course, church independence and an authoritarian church structure would seal the control of the antirepublican church Right.

Democratic liberals had leveled three general charges against the church Right. The first—that antirepublicans controlled the Old-Prussian church—cannot be doubted. Less accurate was the second—that the dominant church Right intentionally misused its power politically against the Republic. Political conservatism formed an integral part of the church Right's social ethics, and its political and ecclesiastical views ran parallel. It was impossible to determine whether antidemocratic remarks were made intentionally for political effect or for principle's sake. Least accurate was the third charge—that the church Right deliberately manipulated the conflict in order to attack the Republic. After all, the church Right acted defensively and legitimately for the cause of church independence.

From the church Right's vantage point, church independence could not be compromised. It seemed preposterous that the religionless state claimed the highest position of control in a Christian church. It seemed unconscionable that such a state tried to foist alien—democratic—principles upon the church for political reasons. That the Republic would not subject the Catholic church to a similar humiliation made this demand the more unbearable. That the Prussian government expected the church to barter democracy for subsidies, already guaranteed (until commuted) by the Weimar constitution, seemed outrageous.

Even if the Democrats had correctly seen a menace to the Republic in the Old-Prussian church, they would have done well to look away. Their dilemma was that they had no satisfactory way of ending the conflict that they had provoked. Had the three ministers held their ground or remained in place to shape a democratic constitution, or had Democrats and Majority Socialists mobilized their followers for church elections, Democrats could have expected nothing less than some form of church civil war. They faced opponents who would not yield appreciably and who had prospects of winning even direct, democratic elections. Ironically, Democratic church policy, resolutely followed, would have intensified the politicization of the Old-Prussian church. Fortunately for the Democrats, the Center party and Majority Socialists had good reason not to follow the lead of their coalition partner. The Catholic Center party could hardly join a drive to impose democracy upon a Protestant church and not upon the Catholic. Majority Socialists acted with reserve after the Hoffmann fiasco.

One can speculate that the Democratic initiative had the opposite effect from that intended. Within the church Democrats provoked widespread hostility toward their party and the republican cause. Certainly Democrats squandered the goodwill that they had earned so recently at Weimar. For many Protestants after the revolution the Democratic party was the only possible political bridge to the Republic. The Center party loomed as the opportunistic political arm of their confessional rival. The Majority Socialist party, the third in the historic Weimar coalition, lay beyond consideration even before the Hoffmann era. By inviting state intervention in church affairs, Democrats may have contributed a specific religious reason for the general erosion of their appeal among middle-class Protestants in the course of 1919.

THE NEW CONSTITUTION OF THE OLD-PRUSSIAN CHURCH

Between the meeting of the General Synod in April 1920 and the Constituent Assembly (Kirchenversammlung) in September 1921, the requisite elections were held—first to congregational boards, in January 1921, and then to the assembly, in June. A noticeable lack of participation characterized elections to local church boards. Immediately fears passed that Socialists might storm the church, since reelected congregational boards chose delegates to the assembly. In these second-stage elections the so-called United Right—confessional Lutherans, Positive Unionists, and pietists—won almost two-thirds of the seats.[126]

The Constituent Assembly met from September 24 to 30, 1921, adjourned while its right-dominated Constitution Committee drew up a draft constitution, and finished its deliberations from August 29 to September 29, 1922. As finally accepted, the new constitution reflected the wish of delegates not to create a different, unfamiliar church structure, but to concentrate on filling the constitutional gap left by the departed summus episcopus. Thus the most important new feature was a Church Senate that fell heir to his prerogatives at the top of the governance structure, while the status of congregations at the bottom, the focus of the earlier Volkskirche movement, remained virtually unchanged.

Predictably, the new constitution was far from democratic. It did include women's suffrage and elections by proportional representation for the benefit of minorities—both innovations of the revolution—and it abridged the "filter" system by electing the eastern provincial synods directly from congregational boards. But the constitution omitted direct elections to synods from adult parishioners. Though theoretically the church was constructed from congregations "upward," administrative authorities did not derive their authority directly from "below." Church political authority ascended from congregations through synods to the Church Senate and funneled downward to the EOK, consistorial officials, general superintendents, and superintendents.[127]

Though the constitution embodied a number of compromises, these served to reestablish constitutional checks and balances formerly secured by the king's church government. The GSV had proposed its own draft constitution by which synods would subordinate and control the organs of church administration. Determined to salvage consistorial authority, the EOK argued successfully with delegates that synodical control of church government would introduce the parliamentary government that the church Right claimed to abhor. In turn, the GSV prevailed over the EOK in its formula for General Synod elections. Originally the GSV promoted the complete "filter" system. But its chairman, Friedrich Winckler, announced his willingness to settle for General Synod elections from provincial synods that had been elected directly by local congregational boards (thus bypassing elections from district synods), a stand backed eventually by most of the

Right. Delegates of the Right tended to assume that the more directly the church depended on the "masses" the less it could carry out its divine mission. Arguing that any democratic order was necessarily self-destructive, Walther Wolff, moderator of the Rhenish provincial synod, claimed that democratic states quickly "run themselves to death."[128]

The most significant compromise, however, concerned the disposition of the power that had formerly accrued to the summus episcopus. His administrative prerogatives transferred to the new Church Sentate. Since they had not been subjected to synodical control, the Senate possessed considerable power, particularly because it appointed to high positions in the church bureaucracy. EOK officials and representatives of the General Synod constituted the Senate along with general superintendents at the behest of the EOK and moderators of provincial synods at the insistence of the GSV. Now the EOK was obliged to share the powers of church government with leaders of synodical church parties, but it had largely avoided the danger that a majority in the General Synod could control church government. Because of its representation in the Senate and its expertise, the EOK could exert a strong influence over the church body to which it was formally subordinated. The EOK also managed to preserve its former prerogatives within church administration. As the example of the Senate showed, the EOK succeeded in keeping a balance among synodical, clerical, and consistorial elements in the constitution. In this effort the EOK was strongly supported by liberals and the Middle party, who feared giving unwonted authority to synods, easily controlled by the Right, or to the clergy.

None of these constitutional disputes, however, raised so much passion and controversy as the preamble. During the heated election campaign the church Right had raised the perennial cry that liberals endangered the church's confession. Accordingly, the United Right pushed through the assembly a preamble stipulating the church's confessional stand by listing traditional creeds.[129]

The EOK and GSV had proposed an extremely vague preamble, but one clear enough to indicate continuity with the past. Ardently upheld by liberals and the Middle party, the EOK charged that the Right's preamble violated Christian freedom. The confessional stand may be defended only in exceptional instances to guard against excessive subjectivism, the purpose of the "heresy" law of 1910. Because of the preamble, liberals and the Middle party voted against the final constitution. In the preamble the dissentients confronted the hazards, long anticipated, of coexisting as a minority in a free Volkskirche.

The political significance of the preamble was twofold. Though it was generated primarily by confessional concerns, the preamble also reflected the determination of the United Right to ensure for the church a missionary role that had indirect political implications. Some churchmen professed to see that Socialist and liberal values had demonstrated their bankruptcy in the Republic. The church seemed to have an unusual opportunity to fill the resulting spiritual void. To penetrate this void, the church needed agreement on its own objective principles—uncontaminated by liberal dilutions.[130]

Second, and of greater immediate importance, would the Right's preamble, contested by a third of the assembly, induce the Prussian government and legislature to reject the new church constitution? This possibility had indeed been suggested by enemies and scorned by friends of the preamble and of the modified "filter" system at the assembly. The EOK had marshaled another, similar argument against the preamble and electoral system. Both might so affront the political Left as to thwart the church's hopes for an eventual generous commutation of state subsidies.[131] The danger of "intervention" could become all the more acute if the large dissenting minority appealed to Prussian Democrats and more generally to the coalition government, which might again muster enough courage to intervene in church affairs.

Some outraged liberals did protest the preamble to the Prussian government, urging it to protect religious freedom and minority rights within the church. Most of the distraught minority, however, rejected this move after considering it seriously. The Middle party, the EOK, and the GSV counseled against an appeal to the state, and both liberals and the Middle party urged their disappointed sympathizers not to leave the church. To the Middle party an appeal for state intervention was too humiliating to contemplate.[132] Without a doubt the church Right would have considered such an appeal traitorous, and most of the minority had no desire to shoulder the responsibility for a possible Kulturkampf.

The danger still loomed that the government and legislature might withhold their recognition of the constitution with the now familiar argument that, since the state conferred benefits, it could require minority protection. Invoking the EOK's previous position, the United Right argued that Article 137 of the Weimar constitution permitted the legislature to pass only on external aspects of the church constitution—hence, not on the preamble and election procedures. This was the argument that President Moeller voiced against the conferred-benefits thesis of the government when both subsequently took counsel.

The upshot of these deliberations was agreement on a bill, presented to the Prussian Staatsrat in October 1923, which, in line with Moeller's argument, provided state confirmation of articles dealing with such matters as church taxes and property but not with the preamble and the electoral process. In the Staatsrat, Emil Hallensleben, a liberal leader at the church Constituent Assembly and a member of the People's party, moved unexpectedly to reject the bill. But it passed by a narrow margin because the People's party and the Nationalists agreed to propose a declaration to the effect that the preamble lacked any legal significance. Likewise in the Landtag the bill could marshal sufficient strength only with the appended declaration. The bill was passed on March 19 and decreed on April 8, 1924.[133] By this time the preamble issue had aroused the anger of Democrats and Socialists more than the election procedures.

In view of the furor over the preamble, it is ironic to note that it had little practical significance. Even the German Christians could later claim to accept the preamble. Apparently church government, which had contested the preamble, shied away from applying it in the legalistic fashion dreaded by liberals; in any event, no major heresy crisis involving the preamble arose for the remainder of the period under consideration. The preamble conflict also went against an opposite trend in the relations of church parties, which tried to compose internal disagreements in order to project a common front against the outside.

Only one seemingly minor obstacle now delayed the promulgation of the constitution. Technically, church administrative officials were still officials of the state, and subject to its regulations. If the church were to become administratively independent, as the Weimar constitution required, these positions had to be converted into church offices. The heart of the problem was funding church administration. The Reichstag had not yet (and would never) establish principles governing state commutation of subsidies. If the Prussian state chose to pay church officials, could it also demand some sort of control over them? This delicate question demanded an immediate resolution, for the Constituent Assembly had stipulated that it reassemble if the constitution had not been promulgated by October 1, 1924.

Only a week before the deadline, on September 23, 1924, the Landtag gave its consent to a temporary solution, enabling church authorities to promulgate the constitution in the nick of time.[134] The Prussian government obligated itself to pay an adjustable, annual lump sum to cover church administrative expenses, salaries, pensions, and survivor benefits. What disturbed church leaders was the wish of the republican state to retain some measure of control over high church officials. In the Landtag, Democrats and Socialists lobbied to arm the government with a veto over the appointment of politically objectionable church officials. Taking church interests in tow again, Nationalists properly argued that such a veto would violate Article 137 of the Weimar constitution. In July, Democrats and Socialists managed to include a veto right in the proposed bill. Then several leaders of the church Right again raised the specter of a Kulturkampf, and even suggested decreeing the church constitution without settling the matter of administrative costs. But liberals tended to welcome some check on the church for the sake of minorities and political neutrality. The *Protestantenblatt* even questioned whether the church provisions of the Weimar constitution, authored by "Roman calculation," had not carried the emancipation of churches too far.[135] Eventually a compromise, originally proposed by the government, passed. It authorized the government to negotiate with the Evangelical Landeskirchen in Prussia for the right to contest church appointments of presiding officers in high administrative organs. The Old-Prussian church took this threat to its independence in stride, since the compromise did not obligate the churches to concede this right or make financial aid contingent upon such a concession.

Because of the lack of a general commutation and continued state supervision of church finances, the Old-Prussian church did not quite succeed in throwing off the shackles of the republican state. The April law retained state controls over church property and taxes while confirming the external legal aspects of the new constitutions of the seven Evangelical Landeskirchen in Prussia. By 1927 this law had generated considerable friction between church and state authorities. The General Synod in 1927 passed a resolution to protest that state officials had exceeded their authority by encroaching on church independence.[136] A confessional Lutheran even protested provisions of the April law as flagrantly unconstitutional. By according state ministers a restricted veto over church financial legislation, the law allowed the state to preempt church decisions.

The republican policy of keeping the Old-Prussian church on a tight leash—promoted especially by mistrustful Democrats and Socialists—had at least two political consequences. In 1931 the Evangelical Landeskirchen in Prussia finally conceded a government veto over the appointment of high church officials in order to conclude a treaty with the state that paralleled the recent Prussian concordat with the Vatican. This veto right provided the legal pretext for the Nazi seizure of Prussian church government in June 1933. More generally, republican church policy forced the Old-Prussian church to struggle for its independence against republican parties (but not the Center), a phenomenon that redounded to the political advantage of the antirepublican Right, especially the Nationalists.

CHURCH FINANCES AND THE PRUSSIAN REPUBLIC

Constitutionally, the Old-Prussian church emerged largely free of state controls with the promulgation of its constitution in 1924. Financially, the church had grown more dependent on the largess of the state. The Reichstag never managed to pass legislation that would allow individual states to commute their contributions to the Landeskirchen. Thus in Prussia the former system of church finance, though thrown off base by inflation until 1924, continued to operate as before the revolution.

The Weimar constitution shored up the three main pillars of this system. Article 138 guaranteed church property, and Article 137 conferred upon the church the status of a public corporation with the right to raise taxes. By contrast, Article 173 left doubts about the strength of the third pillar—state contributions.

Article 173 stated that "present state contributions...based on laws, contract or special legal titles shall be continued" until the federal government enacted a law governing their commutation. The three legal categories, however, were as vague as they were seemingly inclusive. The federal legislation anticipated to refine them for the purpose of commutation was needed in the period pending commutation as well.[137] How each state chose to define its responsibilities to its Landeskirchen hinged on its dominant parties. Thus the state of Saxony and several small states, where Socialist governments held power, scaled down state contributions from prewar levels, reduced the clergy to a penurious existence, especially in the inflation, and involved their Landeskirchen in protracted legal conflicts.

Unlike Saxony, the Prussian Republic extended a generous hand to the

Landeskirchen. The Prussian state accepted the role assigned it in previous church and state legislation of "covering," in the case of clerical salaries, the deficits of needy congregations. This policy managed to pull the Old-Prussian church through the inflationary period without serious financial damage and resulted in increased contributions that even after the stabilization of the currency in 1924 did not quite drop to prewar levels.

Ironically, it was the pillar of state contributions, considered the most exposed to attack in 1917 and 1918 and constitutionally the most problematic, that proved most stable in Prussia. The other two pillars —church property and taxes—fell victim to economic collapse during the inflationary period. The large capital investments of the Old-Prussian church and its congregations (460 million M.) and of the clerical funds (118 million M.) were largely wiped out, and later subjected to legal revalorization at a small percentage of their original value. Reduced to 159,000 hectares by 1925, landed property yielded disappointing returns, partly because of the problem of adjusting leases and rents to an inflating currency. The pillar of church taxes, the stoutest of the three, likewise tottered. Tax sums devaluated between collection and use, and the collection machinery faltered after 1920, when the federal income tax replaced the Prussian as the base of the church tax assessment.

Shaken by its two tottering pillars, the Old-Prussian church tried to lean all the more heavily on the third, state contributions—and the Prussian Republic proved obliging. The Prussian Constituent Assembly passed a law late in 1920 that adjusted pastors' salaries to inflation. If congregations could not make ends meet with income from property, the church tax, and a state subsidy, "advances" (Vorschüsse) would cover the deficit. Through advances, the state extended its credit to the church at no charge in order to tide it over a period of unstable financial conditions. By the time that the authorization of advances was to expire in 1923, however, the economy and church finances faced catastrophe rather than improvement as the inflation reached its horrifying peak. In 1922 the Landtag had already seen the wisdom of extending advances until 1925 and of once again adjusting pastors' salaries by law.

As the inflation picked up momentum, congregations drew in less and less income from property and the church tax, and the clerical funds suspended payment because of evaporating capital and income. By December 1923, the state covered 85.6 percent of the total cost of clerical compensation through subsidies and a wholesale granting of advances that many had come to regard as a misnomer.[138] After all, who could expect an impoverished church to repay them? Advances amounted to concealed and unlimited state subsidies, given largely without a prior examination of congregational need, under conditions of dire emergency.

In the years immediately following the inflation, church officials and pastors' societies once again confronted the problem of securing state contributions. The switch from an inflated to a stabilized currency had rendered obsolete the sums determined by law in the inflationary period. They sought to persuade the government to set state contributions anew in material law for an indefinite period. But the government alarmed church leaders by preferring to determine state contributions anew each year in its budget. The government also took a dim view of extending advances, which church officials and pastors had come to regard as indispensable. Eventually, after considerable political maneuvering, the government's cause prevailed over the efforts of the political Right and Center party to perpetuate advances. These parties had to settle for a law in November 1925 that set the state's clerical subsidy for 1926 and retroactively for 1925.[139] Despite the fears of churchmen, the appropriations in the law were barely adequate to the church's basic needs. Eventually, in 1928, the church gained the security that it craved in a material law that assured state contributions at a level slightly higher than that of 1914.

By 1927 another cloud had formed over the General Synod — the problem of improving clerical salaries. This cloud had appeared regularly on the horizon in the postwar years. Pastors had grown alarmed whenever the state had not promptly adjusted their salaries to raises afforded state officials, and, together with them, had suffered when salary adjustments had failed to keep pace with the inexorable spiral of prices. Most pastors drew salaries at grade 10 on the state salary schedule, the lowest for academically trained state officials. Because of the relative inflation of the stabilized currency and their low position on the salary schedule, clergymen sensed that they had lost ground since the war. By 1927, they, as well as church authorities, had taken alarm at reports of growing indebtedness among impoverished pastors. The inflation had taken its toll of savings, and pastors, particularly in the countryside, despaired of providing their children with a secondary education. For these reasons, the General Synod enjoined the Church Senate to augment education grants to needy pastors and urged the state government to raise the clerical salary scale to grade 12.[140]

In the years 1925 to 1927, the Old-Prussian church had come to recognize the approximate limit of support that it could expect from the state. Now that income from capital investments had largely evaporated, the Old-Prussian church tried to cut expenses and to exploit the other two sources of revenue available to it—property and church taxes.

This effort had also been a condition that the state had earlier set for "covering" clerical salaries during the inflation. At that time, no one knew how much revenue church taxes might yield. Church landed property, by contrast, offered a likely target, in two respects. Its yield had plummeted far below prewar returns because of lax management and inflation. Moreover, about 10 percent of the pastorates enjoyed a return from local property that exceeded the guaranteed salary of clergymen. In the first instance, the church set about instituting better management practices and, with the legal aid of the state, revising leases. By 1925 returns had risen to 93.8 percent of the prewar yield, or 9,811,000 M. In the second instance, part of excessive local property income was drained off by a church emergency decree in 1922 to aid the general coverage of clerical salaries, much to the disgruntlement of wealthier country congregations and their pastors.[141]

Once the currency stabilized in 1924, church leaders could again tap the potential of church taxes, which rapidly resumed their role as the most substantial financial pillar. By 1925 the total budgeted tax need of congregations had risen to about 66 million M., an increase of 89 percent over 1914. The rise of church taxes, however, fueled the movement to leave the church and alarmed economic interests and state officials who regarded the church tax as the least justifiable tax during a period of economic distress and high taxation. Church taxes had, however, risen less steeply than the figures suggested. By 1926 the general cost of living had increased about 40 percent over 1914.[142]

Church taxes were bound to rise, for a number of reasons. State contributions hardly compensated for the massive losses sustained by church capital because of the inflation. The assessment on congregations (Umlage) had served to finance a host of general church expenditures. Now the church at large felt compelled to accept other financial responsibilities as well, such as the subsidization of its congregations in ceded areas.

Deprived of income from capital investments, the budget of the church at large collapsed into one borne chiefly by the assessment on congregations. In the postwar years, church leaders felt confined by mere "existence" budgets that cut out whatever could be safely neglected for the moment. The church's practice of closing out old pastorates and opening new ones illustrated its financial immobility. During the inflation the EOK complied with state wishes for retrenchment by withholding pastoral appointments to small country congregations. Retrenchment in the countryside was not, however, followed by expansion in city suburbs, which, following the inflation, often grew at an alarming rate. The EOK could not move the state to help endow new pastorates as it had in the past. In the six prewar years, 424 new church edifices had been built, as compared with merely 54 in the seven years 1919–25. [143]

Practical considerations as well as state pressure ruled out the last remaining path to financial mobility—church taxes. Pegged largely to the federal income tax, church taxes grew all the more conspicuous the higher they rose. Statistics suggested what many already sensed: An increase in the numbers contracting out coincided with the announcement of the church tax, resulting in a contraction of the tax base. The Church Senate and the EOK concluded in 1925 and 1926 that the tax rate had reached the point of diminishing return and set about lowering taxes. [144]

The church tax had grown extremely unpopular not merely because it seemed high. Its incidence seemed unfair as well. The per capita burden appeared small enough—3.38 M. in 1925, only 2.4 percent of the total per capita tax load (as compared with 1.97 M. and 3.8 percent in 1914). Unlike a head tax, however, the church tax was assessed by the congregation at a percentage of the federal income tax. As before, the percentage varied from congregation to congregation according to need. Federal finance offices, which administered the income tax, compounded this disparity with another. They resorted to the expedient of collecting the church tax by occupational categories (the "Pauschalsystem") rather than by actual income. To use an example cited at the 1927 General Synod, two engineers in the same congregation might pay the same church tax of 31 M. even though one earned a salary of 2,4000 M. and the other 12,000 M. a year. [145]

A narrowing of the tax base created a third disparity. Church leaders complained bitterly that finance offices failed to convey reliable tax data, by which congregations could more accurately assess their members, and allowed many to slip through the collector's fingers. An income tax that allowed generous exemptions, moreover, fell on fewer people, especially in a period of economic viscissitude. Church taxes tempted not only workers with relatively low assessments to contract out, but also the more wealthy because of the tax's strong progression. As a result, church taxes shifted increasingly onto the impoverished middle classes. Though by 1925 the per capita load of church taxes had grown by 72 percent over 1914, the amount that individual parishioners actually paid might have increased by 300–600 percent and even more because of these disparities.[146] A further tax increase might precipitate a movement to contract out even within the middle classes, where the church found its strongest resonance.

The main taxing problem, then, was not so much the rate of taxation as the inequity that resulted from faulty collection and from a largely one-tax base. When the General Synod assembled in 1927, delegates took great comfort from the promise of the Federal Finance Administration to end the inequitable Pauschalsystem after years of continual church prodding. This decision, together with the promise to make reliable data promptly available to congregations, created the prospect of future taxation according to actual income and congregational need. Under such conditions, the EOK calculated that total tax yield would mount even as the tax rate declined. By 1927, however, the Old-Prussian church would not settle for such concessions. The General Synod voted an overhaul of church taxation. It enjoined the Church Senate to seek state consent for an extension of the church tax base to property and corporations. Such an extension would seem to establish a more socially just tax base and spread the tax load away from the personal income tax that had invited attacks.[147]

By 1928 the Old-Prussian church had reached a position of relative financial security. The dire fears aroused in 1917 for the financial security and the continued existence of the Volkskirche had failed to materialize, even though the three pillars of church finance stood on less firm ground. Income from church investments and property had fallen off precipitously, but the pillars of church taxes and state contributions had expanded to support the structure of the Volkskirche. The EOK and the General Synod of 1925 and 1927 acknowledged with thankfulness the persisting solicitude of the state. With the 1928 law on state contributions in sight, the chairman of the Finance Committee could even bestow the ultimate of compliments at the 1927 General Synod: "We can be happy when the state perceives that the church is a cultural factor necessary and important for the state."[148]

It is tempting to conclude that the persisting suspicion or hostility that the Republic drew from many Old-Prussian churchmen was poor reward for the Republic's stewardship. But one must keep their ideological context in mind. The state was no longer "Christian," no longer one that fostered the churches as a "cultural factor necessary and important also for the state." The benefits conferred by the Republic appeared won by the political Right and Center party in contest with the political Left, by the intiative of churchmen as politicians, and by the pressure of church officials and assemblies.[149] Where such political activism proved unavailing, as for a time in neighboring states, the church had to pay the consequences. Where such political activism succeeded, should one credit the Republic, a mere party state? Still, churchmen did not usually fault the Prussian Republic for niggardliness. That many could still deplore the Republic leads to a negative conclusion: Financial need or greed cannot account for antirepublicanism in the church.

4

THE SCHOOL CIVIL WAR

IF OLD-PRUSSIAN churchmen could appreciate the Republic for its largess, they deplored it for subverting confessional education. At the National Assembly, the Socialist Heinrich Schulz had announced the intention of the Weimar coalition to enact enabling federal legislation on elementary school type within less than a year. Only then did politicians expect local school conflict to break out, as parents' groups vied with one another in elections over school type. Because of the delay and eventual frustration of that legislation, those hostile to confessional schools tried to bend existing state law to their advantage or where possible to ignore it. And the exchange of a religiously neutral state for the Christian deprived confessional schools of their guarantor. As confessional education deteriorated, churchmen yearned for deliverance from the resulting civil war that federal legislation could bring but never did.

THE LEGAL STATUS OF CONFESSIONAL EDUCATION

Of great importance was the degree to which Article 174 of the Weimar constitution froze Prussian school law in place. The article asserted that "the present legal situation" should continue until the Reichstag passed legislation on school type anticipated in Article 146. It was commonly argued within the Old-Prussian church that Article 174 should shield confessional education from subsequent deterioration. But court decisions made it clear that "the present legal situation" referred only to Article 146 on elementary school type, not to other school articles or collateral school issues.[1]

What, then, did Article 174 protect? It clearly shielded the school maintenance law of 1906, by which Evangelical teachers normally instructed Evangelical pupils and Evangelical principals administered Evangelical elementary schools. Article 174 also raised a bar against secular schools, for the law of 1906 had not authorized them. But other articles weakened this bar. Article 149 permitted teachers—and pupils, with parental consent —to opt out of religious instruction. If a teacher did so, however, he lowered his usefulness to his school, and therefore his chances for employment in another.[2] If he contracted out of his church, he could not legally retain employment in a confessional school or seek it in a secular school that could not exist. Socialist parents thought that Majority Socialists had won secular schools, if only as a deviating type, in the final Weimar school compromise (Article 146). But lack of enabling federal legislation thwarted their expectations.

In 1927 the Federal Court (Reichsgericht) held that state law on school supervision did not fall under the protection of Article 174.[3] If the Weimar constitution did not bar dissident inspectors of confessional schools, neither did the letter of the Prussian law. But then the Kultusministerium would appoint only church members before the revolution. Decrees dating from 1876, 1877, and 1880 could be expected, however, to contain the influence on religious instruction of the few dissident supervisors (Schulräte) whom the Kultusministerium dared to name in the Weimar period. By these decrees supervisors were limited to external surveillance of religious instruction, for the reason that its content required the agreement of the churches. Accordingly, local clergymen before the war usually took on the responsibility for visiting religion classes and lodging complaints. Another reason for this practice was that supervisors of one denomination had to wield authority over some schools of the other in confessionally mixed areas.[4]

Because supervisors carried heavy responsibilities, dissident supervisors could hardly spend much time meddling with religious instruction. The government of each administrative region (Regierungsbezirk) bore the main responsibility for supervising elementary schools in Prussia. A subdivision of the province, each region divided into city and country administrative districts (Kreise) in which a number of supervisors operated.[5] Assigned as many as 400 teachers, a supervisor was generally expected to visit each religion class in each school but once a year. Even so, appointing a dissident supervisor was rather like igniting a powder keg. The absurd idea of employing dissident supervisors of confessional schools struck Protestants and Catholics alike as a bad politcal joke.

What legal rights remained to the Old-Prussian church to influence Evangelical elementary schools? Article 149 asserted that religious instruction must conform with church principles. Accordingly, the Kultusministerium followed its old practice of consulting the EOK about religious instruction when the former undertook to revise instructional guidelines for various school levels and teacher training. But the traditional mechanism used to ferret out abuses went largely by the board. In the Prussian Constituent Assembly an adroit maneuver of the Center party preserved the right of local clergymen to participate ex officio in local school committees.[6] But the other two parts of this mechanism—local clerical school supervision and supervision of religious instruction—were scrapped.

Elementary schoolteachers had long deplored clerical school supervision. At the end of the "Hoffmann" era, the Kultusministerium abolished its own decree when Catholic protests arose. On July 18, 1919, the Prussian Constituent Assembly revoked the practice once more, and the Weimar constitution followed suit in Article 144. Unlike their Catholic counterparts, Old-Prussian church leaders repeatedly asserted throughout the Weimar period that they had no interest in reviving clerical school supervision.[7] The resentment of teachers far outweighed any dubious advantages that the practice could promise.

With local clerical school supervision gone and with the prospect of dissident supervisors in sight, the church's right to influence religious instruction assumed a new importance. But local pastors generally stopped visiting religion classes at the time of the Hoffmann decrees. The teachers' message was that they would decline religious instruction en masse if the church insisted on visits by local clergymen. As a result, the church's practice of supervising religious instruction fell largely into disuse.[8]

These developments virtually excluded the Old-Prussian church from direct knowledge of school conditions and from a corresponding influence. Only indirectly—above all through pupils and parents—could the church learn of abuses detrimental to confessional education. Understandably, the Old-Prussian church ultimately rose to the challenge hurled by teachers by insisting on its legal claim to some supervision of religious instruction, in a different and less offensive form.

The continuing search for a new form of supervision appeared important because the Old-Prussian church feared to leave religious education exclusively in the hands of teachers.[9] Large numbers seemed to have deserted Christian ties altogether. Even more Protestant teachers, seeing in a nondogmatic, nonconfessional liberal religious instruction the ideal form, felt trapped by Article 149's prescription of confessional religious instruction. In its own defense, the Old-Prussian church claimed to have taken on responsibility for the child's religious instruction at baptism. The Volkskirche required as much. But how could the church expect teachers to teach what they contested and to accept church controls that they scorned? These were the questions that raised teachers' hackles, even as the church renounced clerical supervision, sought a compromise on religious instruction, rejected a dogmatic shackling of teachers, and repeatedly extended the hand of reconciliation.

POSITIONS ADVANCED BY EVANGELICAL CHURCHES

Protestant church leaders throughout Germany recognized the necessity of constructing a common platform on schools as quickly as possible. By forming a united front they hoped to enter the struggle shaping up in the Reichstag over the future of elementary schools. Here the major issue was whether legislation would favor the common school or place all three types —common, confessional, and secular—on a par. A related question was whether the parties should resolve in the same piece of legislation a clutch of collateral issues as well, above all those centering on how churches could be assured that religious instruction conformed with their principles. Attempts to organize parents and others for the school conflict also necessitated a clear church program. At every level church solidarity had become the watchword.

Whatever the Church Federation Assembly decided on schools carried an aura of popular church approval, though the Kirchenausschuss largely shaped the two school declarations that obliging assemblies issued. The first, the Dresden declaration of September 5, 1919, anticipated the federal school legislation that the second, the Stuttgart declaration of September 15, 1921, confronted in the full glare of public controversy. Subsequently church leaders hailed both as the unanimously adopted position of Evangelical churches. One must accordingly analyze them as a whole, along with a third document, a set of guidelines issued by the Kirchenausschuss as a gloss on the suggested wording of the Stuttgart declaration.[10] The two declarations appealed to the broad public, the guidelines to the more private understanding of already committed churchmen.

The Dresden declaration identified the German school as the Christian school: for over a millenium Christianity had exerted an enduring influence on folk life that warranted preservation. By contrast, the Stuttgart declaration put into the limelight an Evangelical concept of education, which the corresponding guidelines explained within the context of the theory of symbiosis. Teachers had complained bitterly that the 1921 school bill would split school systems asunder by allowing deviating and narrowly sectarian school types (confessional and secular) to entrench themselves at the expense of the common school and commonweal. Against this charge, the Stuttgart declaration asserted that the highest product of education was "the person, pious and moral in the spirit of the gospel," shaped in Christian schools that neglected neither breadth nor commitment to the commonweal.

In the Kirchenausschuss's guidelines, however, the declaration's individualist stress gave way to education for service within the Gemeinschaften —within the historic, involuntary communities enumerated as the family, folk, state, and church. Each of these communities ought to recognize a common goal in educating Christians. For the individual, motivated by God's love, acknowledged his obligations to these God-given communities, spurning false freedom and false authority. Accordingly, church and school must cooperate in a spirit of mutual trust in service to these communities as well as to the individual. The formative role of the church in such an authoritarian society, however, would deprive teachers of the sovereignty they claimed over education and prove unacceptable to the broad public. More serviceable, therefore, was the pale shadow of the guidelines in the Stuttgart declaration, whose emphasis lay on educating character within the supporting framework of Christian schools.

The Dresden declaration supported confessional over common schools with the argument, more centrally focused in the Stuttgart declaration, that the entire spirit of the school, not merely religious instruction, conditioned Christian education. But the Dresden Church Assembly appeared hesitant to press full parity for confessional schools. This gap the Stuttgart declaration filled by alluding to its concept of education. Wherever it existed or parents wanted it, the confessional school must be assured a "full possibility of development," meaning complete parity with other types, or, more accurately, with the common school. Here the Stuttgart Church Assembly took direct aim at the 1921 school bill.

"Christian" Simultan schools constituted a notable exception to this recommended rule of thumb where they had settled in historically. It is clear that the two declarations begrudged Christian Simultan schools. Old-Prussian church leaders professed to find no place for genuine Christian Simultan schools in Article 146.[11] Once the enabling federal legislation passed, non-Christians could presumably teach in common schools. Article 148, solicitous of "the feelings of those who differ in opinion," would surely rule out traditional Christian observances and the Christian context of general education. Christian Simultan schools looked rather like a lost cause; common schools looked like secular schools with appended confessional religious instruction. This message Old-Prussian church leaders continually conveyed to parishioners, sometimes to dispel the claim of teachers that common schools could hardly alter existing schools. There was some truth to this claim, however. Apparently many Prussian teachers availed themselves of their constitutional right to drop school prayers and neglect religious observances, if not always to refuse religious instruction outright. Confessional schools had begun to resemble the common school of the constitution.

Finally, these declarations suggested how to assure churches that religious instruction corresponded with their principles. For the Dresden declaration, "internal guarantees" above all sealed this correspondence—the teacher's training and commitment to the congregation, his willingness to teach religion, his conscientiousness. The declaration hesitantly required "external guarantees" for churches as well. But external guarantees might look as unconstitutional as they seemed necessary. The declaration avoided the dilemma by reserving its solution to individual churches, while claiming for them a right to help select texts and frame syllabi as well as to expect representation on local school committees and the appointment of suitable supervisors of religious instruction. The Stuttgart declaration grasped one horn of the dilemma by stating flatly that the state could not decide whether religious instruction conformed with church principles. Logically, churches must decide; but how, without supervising religious instruction in some sense and angering teachers? The Stuttgart declaration suggested that churches form special "organs," partly staffed by religion teachers themselves, without explaining how these organs could proceed to "assure the church...an indispensable influence" on religious instruction.

The Kirchenausschuss's guidelines explained further the rationale for this solution, so far as it went. By itself, the "religionless" state surely could not decide. If churches did not directly assume this responsibility, they must resort to conveying binding dogma to the state for imposition upon religious instruction. Such was the worst of all possible solutions. Earlier the Kirchenausschuss had recognized that teachers abhorred the dogmatic religious instruction that this solution would necessitate.[12] Moreover, any attempt to compress Evangelical beliefs into manageable principles of dogma would doubtless provoke unending theological controversy and disrupt the inner solidarity that churches craved. Unwilling to settle for internal guarantees and unwilling or unable to formulate dogma, the churches had little choice other than claiming external guarantees that appeared to fall short of clerical supervision, administered by organs that co-opted reliable teachers.

Since Article 149 did mention "principles," the two church assemblies could hardly avoid some definition. The Stuttgart declaration referred to "the norms of Christian faith and life as these are contained in the gospel given in Holy Scripture and attested to in the creeds of the Reformation." This clever formula, carefully phrased to mention creeds without equating them with gospel, managed to solicit agreement from liberals and the more orthodox alike. Avoiding a listing of principles, it more resembled a statement of goals. But these would suffice for the guidance of special church organs, which would proceed by their own understanding of Evangelical principles without feeling obliged to elaborate them until tested in specific cases.

The two declarations had been framed broadly and vaguely enough to reach unanimity but narrowly enough to take specific positions. Those most dissatisfied were church liberals, who, however, had refused to break this attempt to close fronts. In Prussia, church liberals had preferred Christian Simultan schools as the norm. Since these now appeared constitutionally questionable, their ranks tended to divide over common and confessional schools, often endorsing neither wholeheartedly. "On the one side [that of common schools] threatens the danger of the subjection of religion," held the *Protestantenblatt* in 1921, and "on the other that of clericalism."[13] As the conflict deepened, deputies of the People's party insisted upon altering the shape of common schools to resemble traditional Christian Simultan schools in federal legislation. Accordingly, some church liberals could continue to promote Christian Simultan schools with some prospect of success.

In 1926 and 1927, Pastor Tribukait, a liberal in a Dortmund pastorate, found himself at loggerheads on this issue with the large majority of pastors in his district. The well-tempered arguments that he published for Christian Simultan schools covered the ground that similar liberals traversed.[14] Conceding the necessity of confessional religious instruction, he viewed any attempt to compel the convictions of teachers in other subjects as more Catholic than Protestant. He worried lest Evangelical support of confessional schools help Catholics to their goal of dogma-ridden confessional schools. Since Catholic pupils would try to avoid Christian common schools, the Evangelical churches could secure a dominant influence on them if the entire curriculum were taught in a generous free Protestant spirit. Certainly Socialists and dissidents would not prefer less capable secular schools (as a deviating type) to such schools, and they might well settle for Christian Simultan schools should Evangelical churches renounce any pretense of supervision. Christian Simultan schools would dispel the blind pathos that confessional schools were more likely to nurture, and they would generate a sense of folk solidarity sadly lacking in Germany, and appropriately begun with children.

THE FIRST CONFLICTS

Out of the declining Volkskirche movement at the end of 1919 emerged the Evangelical parents' movement, to counteract attacks on confessional education. The movement did not arise as spontaneously as was meant to appear. The EOK sparked it initially in Prussia, and the church bureaucracy and clergy continually nourished it behind the scenes. Publicly it was the Evangelical Press Association, formally independent of the churches but partially financed by them, that gradually took the initiative in organizing parents locally, regionally, and finally nationally. Together the Old-Prussian church and the Press Association launched drives after each of the first two Church Federation Assemblies.

A decree by Kultusminister Haenisch touched off the first drive. On November 5, 1919, he decreed the election of parents' advisory councils (Elternbeiräte) at each school. Elected every two years by proportional representation, and thus by the list system, the councils, albeit strictly advisory, could offer advice on any aspect of the school. It was widely believed in the Old-Prussian church that Haenisch decreed these councils to allow Socialists an influence on nominally confessional schools. Even Haenisch's successor in 1921, Otto Boelitz of the People's party, claimed as much in 1926.[15]

The EOK saw in the new institution a challenge as well as an opportunity. The challenge consisted in depriving Marxists and freethinkers of any great success in parents' elections, the opportunity in securing church interests through parents as partial compensation for missing local clerical supervision and church supervision of religious instruction. Shortly before Haenisch's decree, the EOK had asked each provincial consistory to establish advisory education commissions, which would draw teachers from various school levels into deliberations with the clergy. Once Haenisch's decree came to light, the EOK assigned consistories, advised by education commissions, responsibility for activating Evangelical parents. Anticipating elections as early as January, the EOK urged pastors to neglect Christmas preparations, if necessary, in order to promote confessional lists and to explain the gravity of the elections to parishioners.[16]

Consistories and their education commissions responded to the urgency of the EOK's summons. They also began to organize parents and others into permanent associations. The church press, fed by releases from the Press Association, plunged into the campaign as well. "To work!" admonished *Die Reformation.* "The spirit of the school depends on the composition of the parents' advisory councils. Christians to the front!"[17] Here at last was the church's chance to take the offensive against the incursions allowed or threatened by the religionless state.

Consistories and the Press Association invited selected pastors and reliable teachers to short courses on school issues, subsidized by the EOK. Those suitably trained fanned out systematically through the provinces to admonish local congregations and to summon local parents' associations into existence. It was this pattern of agitation, begun at the end of 1919, that the Old-Prussian church followed to prepare parents for subsequent elections as well, and to found new parents' associations and enliven older ones. Over these efforts, however, hung a dark cloud: the unrelenting hostility of perhaps most elementary schoolteachers, certainly of their elected leaders, to a movement that promoted confessional schools and monitored the behavior of teachers. A leading Breslau teacher predicted that teachers would refuse religious instruction if the church persisted in organizing such a movement.[18]

Confronted by hostile teachers during the campaign, the Old-Prussian church faced another enemy at the polls in March 1920: Socialists, who had similarly mobilized their constituencies and who now put forth party lists in support of secular schools. Since other parties did not follow suit, Evangelical parents' associations managed in many places to submit their own lists under the rubric "Christian nonpartisan lists," in conscious reaction against Socialist lists. The elections thus appeared, then and later, as a struggle over the religious character of elementary schools, shoving other issues aside.

The "Christian nonpartisan" label proved effective, attracting Socialist parents while implying that other lists were rather less than Christian and certainly partisan, whether submitted by supporters of secular or of common

schools. In the first years of the Republic, Socialist parties heavily dominated Berlin elections. Yet Christian nonpartisan lists in 1920 won most
of the advisory council seats in the Evangelical schools of metropolitan
Berlin. The results fairly astounded Old-Prussian church leaders. The reality of the Volkskirche seemed all the more clear. Comprehensive figures are
lacking, but a fair guess is that Christian nonpartisan and related lists won
at least an absolute majority of the advisory council seats in the Evangelical schools of the Old-Prussian provinces.[19]

General success was offset by local failures. Now Old-Prussian church
officials had to face the reality that Socialists and other enemies of confessional education dominated parents' councils in many nominally Evangelical schools. Where control of local government and school committees lay
in their hands as well, the church could expect flanking movements to
deprive elementary schools of their confessional quality: employment of
dissidents, dropping of prayers and religious observances, and dilution of
confessional religious instruction. Trust in the impenetrability of Article
174's shield, however, lulled church leaders into believing that endangered
schools would be spared a frontal assault. They reckoned without Konrad
Haenisch.

Appalled by the implications of Article 174, Kultusminister Haenisch
repeatedly pressed the federal government for quick passage of enabling
school legislation or for the enactment of an emergency law to permit secular schools. Finally, he hit upon an expedient device that served this purpose
— "assembled schools" (Sammelschulen).

Soon after the first parents' elections, some astonishing news filtered out
of the small city of Adlershof, south of Berlin: Haenisch would permit
Adlershof to set aside one of its three elementary schools to enroll pupils
released from religious instruction. Challenged by Nationalists in the Prussian Constituent Assembly, the Kultusministerium explained on July 6,
1920, that the school remained formally confessional and that religious
instruction would resume whenever any pupil asked for it. Presumably only
Evangelical teachers could find employment there. Legally, this administrative reassembling of pupils violated neither the school maintenance law of
1906 nor Article 174. Actually, the first secular school had been created in
the formal guise of a confessional school to circumvent Article 174. Nearby
Neukölln chose the accurate but preposterous term *Evangelical schools without religious instruction* to label the six schools that it transformed into assembled schools in the fall. By November 18, 1920, when the EOK formally
lodged protests, Oberschöneweide in metropolitan Berlin and Elberfeld in

Westphalia had announced similar assembled schools or classes. The contagion was beginning to spread.[20]

Sapping Article 174 of its meaning, these deceptive legal arguments enraged loyal church members. The EOK took a more comprehensive view of the developing situation in its discussions with the Kultusministerium on November 26, 1920.[21] In a joint press release, the EOK acknowledged the Kultusministerium's dilemma. By freezing the confessional norm, Article 174 had led to a "state of distress" (Notstand) for "a considerable number of teachers and pupils" who had opted out of religious instruction. The Kultusministerium could not prevent their "relief in individual cases by special transitional measures." Though the EOK could not publicly approve patently illegal secular schools, it could not in fairness condemn them either. Other motives for the EOK's ambiguous position crept in as well. On the one hand, the EOK could not publicly endorse assembled schools that it hoped to contain with the aid of the parents' movement. Fortunately, the Kultusministerium had promised restraint, limiting assembled schools to "individual cases." On the other hand, the EOK welcomed assembled schools in "individual cases" to relieve remaining confessional schools of disruptive influences.

Before it protested, the EOK had caught a glimpse of actual school conditions from a report submitted by a pastor in Oberschöneweide.[22] The community assembly, dominated by Independent Socialists, had decided on these schools with the oral permission of the Kultusministerium but without even consulting the local school committee. Teachers had dictated to pupils a declaration by which parents declared their willingness to enroll their child in assembled schools. Socialists had put peer pressure on factory workers, from whom most of the declarations had come. The pastor was as relieved by the outcome as he was alarmed. Now peace could return to the remaining confessional schools that had suffered from this agitation and from the "terrorism" of Socialist teachers, a position that the EOK could endorse.

The EOK could also applaud the fierce opposition of local parents' groups to what they persisted in regarding as illegal secular schools. In 1922 a distraught pastor in Ohligs, south of Düsseldorf in the Rhineland, summarized the school conflict that had disturbed his congregation for over two years.[23] Through house-to-house agitation, local Communists, "using all means of persuasion and terrorism," had managed to induce parents to withdraw a thousand children from religious instruction. Thereupon the school committee decided to transform two Evangelical schools into assembled schools, in the spring of 1921. The Evangelical parents' associations in both schools protested by withholding their children from school in a boycott popularly referred to as a "strike." A year later they discovered that the two schools planned to resume Evangelical religious instruction as a regular subject. No longer could one distinguish theoretically between confessional and secular schools in Ohligs. The pretense that secular as assembled schools enjoyed full legality in the shape of confessional schools had ended in the further paradox of secular schools offering Evangelical religious instruction.

The EOK realized its hopes for containing the contagion. By 1927 the number of assembled schools had reached 249 and by 1931 even 289 (in addition to many classes not grouped in assembled schools).[24] Yet by 1931 fewer than one percent of all Prussian elementary schools were assembled. They struck root especially in urban industrial areas, where Socialists and Communists were strongest. After the Kultusministerium permitted such schools, elections to parents' councils in urban areas revolved more immediately around the religious nature of local schools. Yet the percentage of assembled schools amounted to only a small fraction of the percentage of seats that Marxists captured on parents' councils.

Marxists and others faced the perplexing problem of establishing assembled schools as a deviating type, a problem that churches kept well in mind when arguing for parity. Administrative and political hurdles had to be scaled. The Kultusministerium gave no blanket permission to local school communities. Enough pupils had to withdraw from religious instruction to demonstrate "technical difficulties" within the existing structure. Parents had to agree to the transfer of their children, and teachers to volunteer. School committees had to agree and then demonstrate a necessity to the regional administration, which in turn sought approval from the Kultusministerium.

This process might break down at some point.[25] Persuading parents to withdraw their children from religious instruction and to send them to assembled schools proved exceedingly difficult. As an innovation, assembled schools might appear less legitimate and, being largely lower class, less qualified than confessional schools. In March 1922, only 2.2 percent of the pupils in Prussian elementary schools did not attend religious instruction, and only 0.5 percent of the teachers refused to offer it. Christian parents' associations tried to influence wavering parents and to reverse unfavorable decisions. Church leaders and parents' associations, perhaps with

some success, repeatedly denounced assembled schools as narrowly ideological party schools. School committees in the hands of non-Marxists might
offer another stumbling block, as could the regional administration. For
whatever reason, the administrative region of Arnsberg in Westphalia readily permitted assembled schools in 1922, but not the neighboring
administrative regions of Münster and Minden. Finally, the political Right
and the Center party in the Reichstag and Prussian Landtag exerted pressure on the Prussian Kultusministerium to hold the line against assembled schools.

Because of these difficulties, Marxists and others resorted to "strikes" to
punctuate their demands for assembled schools in some localities. As the
case of Ohligs illustrates, Christian parents' associations reciprocated to
forestall unfavorable decisions. Heinrich Schulz claimed in 1922 that strikes,
begun by either side, occurred frequently.[26] If assembled schools were not
always a proximate cause in Prussia, it is probably safe to conclude that
this issue usually lurked somewhere in the background. The largest of all
strikes exploded in 1926 when Evangelical parents struck near Dortmund
to remove a dissident supervisor in a unit where assembled schools had
steadily nibbled away at confessional schools.

The obvious failure of Marxists to legitimate assembled schools and the
confessional success in parents' elections shored up the claim of Protestant
and Catholic leaders alike that the majority of German parents preferred
confessional schools over other types. If granted full parity with common
schools, confessional schools would doubtless emerge in practice as the
norm. The first school bill on school type, however, would relegate confessional schools to a deviating type and deny churches the full measure of
success that seemed within their grasp. Not until April 22, 1921, did the
federal Ministry of the Interior manage to submit to the Reichstag this
bill, which the state secretary, the Majority Socialist Heinrich Schulz, had
formulated in consultation with state governments and the parties that had
framed the shaky and ambiguous Weimar school compromise. The bill
was a compromise to execute a compromise, satisfying no party. The nine
months between submission and discussion offered enemies of the bill a
welcome opportunity to organize public pressure on the Reichstag.

The German Teachers' Association entered the lists at its annual conference in June. Here the association—140,000 teachers strong—declared
war on the "Schulz" bill and set aside a half-million M. for its war chest.
The association charged the Schulz bill with gross violation of Article 146

by allowing much too great a latitude to deviating types at the expense of the common school. The impassioned campaign played directly into the hands of the attentive churches. Never again would the miscalculating association see a bill that so clearly prescribed common schools as the norm. The wave of protest set loose by teachers in the summer of 1921 soon gave way to a larger tide of protest on behalf of confessional schools.[27]

Again Catholics led the counterattack, as they had in the heyday of revolution. Like Protestants, they had early recognized the political power of parents. Unlike Protestants, they had systematically organized parents at all levels. Founded in 1911, the Catholic School Organization expanded after 1920 into a mass organization that drew together local associations of parents and others and structured these associations along diocesan, state, and national lines.[28] Protestants still lacked a comparable national organization, and only Brandenburg in Old-Prussian church territory could boast of a provincial parents' association. It was this organizational deficiency that Protestants now resolved to make good, in an effort to maximize their impact on the fate of the Schulz bill.

In November 1921, prodded by the Evangelical Press Association, the Old-Prussian church launched its second drive to organize parents, this time more methodically. Alluding to perils that beset confessional schools in the Reichstag, the EOK asked each provincial consistory to make certain that parents' associations had been organized "so generally and systematically" as to remove any doubt that one could rely "on their intervention at a given moment."[29] The Saxon consistory had complained that the mounting campaign of teachers and radicals against the bill had confused church people and pastors. One might not count on them to mobilize parents for confessional schools in later elections over school type. The Silesian consistory had stressed organizing parents systematically before the bill passed so that they might influence its terms. In either case, a second drive appeared as a political necessity, and, in the second case, one that could brook no delay.

Under the direction of the Press Association, twelve pastors worked over Lower Silesia, after attending short courses on school issues and organizing techniques. The Silesian consistory intended to promote this pattern until a provincial association had emerged before Christmas. Pastors had bridled at the thought that organizing parents would antagonize local teachers and disturb the peace of their congregations. To overcome this reluctance, the consistory went so far as to impose such activity upon pastors as a duty. The consistory also disclosed the ultimate purpose of the drive—a national parents' association that could muster the will of millions in a lobby for satisfactory school legislation.[30]

This association, the Evangelical National Parents' League (Reichselternbund), came into existence on January 27, 1922, less than a week after the Reichstag had addressed the Schulz bill in plenary session. On March 6, 1922, the National Parents' League made its appearance on the political stage by petitioning the Reichstag for quick passage of a school law that would oblige the Stuttgart school program.[31] The petition struck a note of exasperation that would resound with increasing volume in subsequent petitions as federal legislation stalemated. The petition cited instances in which Article 174 had not prevented certain states from assaulting confessional education, creating intolerable school conditions that the desired school law must rectify. "There can be no federal school law in which our demands of conscience are not met," the petition defiantly proclaimed, "and there will be no school peace if the inalienable rights of parents are not assured by federal school law."

The assertiveness of the petition stemmed from the confidence of the National Parents' League that it had assembled a formidable political lobby, one that the Reichstag could not easily ignore. Comprised of provincial parents' associations in Prussia and similar organizations in other German states, the league soon claimed to embrace two million parents and other concerned church members. August Hinderer, the national director of the Press Association, doubled as the general secretary of the National Parents' League, and the national staff of the new organization took up quarters in the Berlin offices of the Press Association. Now permanent and skilled leadership could augment the haphazard efforts of the Old-Prussian church to mobilize parents by putting pastors on temporary leave.

All provinces followed the pattern of organization pursued by Silesia in close collaboration with the Press Association, inevitably antagonizing teachers.[32] The other provinces aspired to reach the level of organization that Brandenburg had already achieved as a result of the first drive. The Berlin parents' league represented in microcosm what the National Parents' League hoped to become for the whole of Germany. In metropolitan Berlin, local parents' associations had been systematically organized and nourished, tactics conceived to ward off dangers in individual schools, and trends and enemies scrutinized. In February 1922, the consistory could report more than 100 local Berlin parents' associations with a membership of 70,000 and 128 associations with 60–70,000 members in the remainder of the province. After the second drive, Westphalia managed to draw larger numbers into its new provincial association—230,000 in May 1922.

The intense public debate over the Schulz bill narrowed the maneuverability and will of parties to compromise. In fact, the Center party deserted the Weimar school compromise altogether, by interpreting Article 146 to mean full parity for confessional schools.[33] And the Socialist and Democratic parties pressed in the opposite direction to restrict deviating types wherever they might jeopardize common schools in a given community. As a result, the Reichstag's Education Committee reached near paralysis as the sides forming around individual provisions and amendments roughly balanced out. Still, with the Center's endorsement, the parity principle moved into the range of political possibility. Earlier signs of the Center's shift doubtless explain why the Stuttgart Church Assembly in 1921 could so emphatically commend the parity principle that the Dresden Church Assembly in 1919 had merely hinted at.

With a deadlock in sight and the Center party holding firmly to the parity principle, Old-Prussian church leaders had more reason to demonstrate in biennial elections to parents' councils in May 1922 how little parents favored the common school that the Schulz bill projected as the legal norm.[34] The EOK concluded that partisans of confessional schools had captured about 75 percent of all council seats in Evangelical schools (not including assembled schools) and that common-school lists had generally suffered a dramatic defeat. The real battle seemed to lie between confessional and secular schools. Lists endorsing secular schools had won most of the remaining 25 percent. Why shackle parents with a common-school norm when the vast majority rejected it?

But did parents genuinely reject common schools, or did they merely appear to do so at the behest of the churches and Socialists? In Brandenburg confessional lists had won about two-thirds of all council seats and had virtually shut out common-school lists, while in the province of Saxony partisans of confessional schools had captured only 42.5 percent and conceded common-school lists 27 percent of the seats. In Brandenburg a well-organized parents' movement had championed the Evangelical cause in the elections, but in Saxony this movement had faltered. The conclusion drawn by the EOK and Saxon consistory alike was that success in these elections varied directly with the vigor displayed by congregations and pastors. Such vigor had less prospect of success with the Marxist working class than with the middle classes, which otherwise, the Saxon statistics suggested, would partially endorse common schools. That as many as 75 percent of Prussian Protestant parents wholeheartedly endorsed confessional schools was highly questionable. The impression that the Reichstag fought the school battle along totally false fronts was also debatable. Though the 75 percent average encouraged the EOK, it was alarmed by the vote of 25 percent of parents against Christian schools. Clearly, the Volkskirche was eroding.

Shortly before the council elections, the Reichstag's Education Committee performed its first operation on the Schulz bill, voting by a slim majority to place all school types on a par. Then its deliberations stagnated until February 1923. Because of the general stalemate and delay, the National Parents' League considered the use of a referendum, permitted by the Weimar constitution, to break the legislative logjam. If most parents readily accepted full parity and adequate safeguards for confessional schools, would not most voters? Church leaders read disturbing signs in the last council elections that Evangelical parents had grown weary of the continual school struggle. How long could one expect to maintain the momentum of parents organized in the huge National Parents' League? A referendum might cut the Gordian knot at a stroke and release this tension as well.[35]

During the week of January 14–20, 1923, the National Parents' League launched a massive drive to invigorate its member associations if possible, to goad the Education Committee into action, and if necessary, to prepare Evangelical parents for a decisive referendum. During that week mass rallies in Prussian cities fired off thousands of resolutions to Reichstag deputies, protesting the legislative stalemate. But a referendum failed to follow this barrage, perhaps because deliberations of the Education Committee resumed in the following months. But one can readily surmise why church leaders then and later regarded a referendum as a desperation strategy of last resort. The apparent majority for confessional schools might well vanish as voters faced, in some cases, a choice between their parties and their school preferences. Past experience taught that church causes fared better when severed from party politics.

Then, too, after having carefully weighed the political odds, the Catholic School Organization eventually turned a deaf ear to the formidable undertaking.[36] The results of a massive signature drive, prompted by south German bishops to commit Catholic deputies of whatever party, seemed to increase the chances of such a referendum. Almost 9 million Catholic voters—78.62 percent of the total Catholic electorate—signed statements endorsing maximum Catholic school demands. But when deliberations of the Reichstag's Education Committee petered out in July 1923, the Catholic School Organization refused to exercise its option, for fear of failure. An unsuccessful referendum could significantly set back further legislative attempts in the Reichstag. Nine million Protestant voters had to be found to match the 9 million signatures of Catholics if a referendum were to attract the requisite majority. But not even the People's party, though moderately conservative and largely Protestant, fully subscribed to the Stuttgart program, preferring Christian Simultan schools as the ideal. Prospects for marshaling 9 million voters were at least as dim on the Protestant side as on the Catholic, even though Protestants outnumbered Catholics almost two to one in Germany as a whole.

The death of the revised Schulz bill left Protestant leaders bitter and frustrated. It also left them with an army of parents and others resolved upon entering a new campaign. The National Parents' League was a characteristic creation of the churches in the Weimar era. As Volkskirche organizations had earlier, the league enlisted members of all church factions in a closed front to the outside.

One could not expect the older, relatively small, and sometimes divisive parents' associations to mobilize the bulk of active church members. Nor could one ignore these associations without leaving a gap in the front and losing their battalions. In the eastern provinces, the Deutscher Bund für christlich-evangelische Erziehung in Haus und Schule, founded in 1876, occupied pride of place, enrolling some 100,000 in its branches shortly before the National Parents' League entered the scene. Its Lutheran and pietist base necessarily limited its appeal. In the western provinces, the largest was the Verband deutscher evangelischer Schulgemeinden und Elternvereinigungen, which sprang to life in 1920 in an attempt to knit together regionally local parents' associations then forming. Also in 1920 it entered into an umbrella association with the largest Evangelical teachers' association, the Verband deutscher evangelischer Lehrer- und Lehrerinnen-Vereine. This loose merger, known by the combined names of the two, boasted a membership of some 200,000 parents and 6,000 teachers shortly after the National Parents' League emerged. Eventually the old and new parents' associations worked out a modus operandi that left the National Parents' League, with its greater resources and official church favor, free to organize parents wherever the others had not struck firm roots—in most congregations of the Old-Prussian church.[37]

The process of fusion had yielded another, larger umbrella association in 1920. The Deutscher Bund and the Verband, along with a number of other smaller parents' and teachers' associations, combined forces to form the Deutsches Evangelisches Schulkartell. Even then the relatively small organizations pulling together in this common front did not loom large on the political horizon, a weakness that the National Parents' League redeemed by way of mass mobilization.

Yet the National Parents' League fell short of comprehending all organized Evangelical parents throughout Germany, and, beyond Prussia, it failed to penetrate several states. Though not quite the exclusive representative of Evangelical parents and not quite national in scope, the League was near enough in both cases, and certainly large enough, to set the tone for all. And this tone sounded unreservedly for fidelity to the official church program, strongly enough to muffle the discordant notes of the Deutscher Bund on the right and of the Reichsbund für Religionsunterricht und religiöse Erziehung on the left. The latter, composed of liberals and religion teachers, sprouted from two older organizations in 1920 to contest the impression that the more orthodox, rallying in the Schulkartell, spoke for the church. Like liberals generally, the Reichsbund militantly combatted any attempt of the churches to parlay Article 149 into a right to inspect religion classes. Inasmuch as this issue eventually erupted within the Old-Prussian church in 1925–27, the Reichsbund grew into a formidable lobby by 1926 of about fifteen thousand members.[38]

The National Parents' League fostered the impression that it was propelled by a spontaneous movement of determined, even irate, parents. Without the responsiveness of parents the league could scarcely have burgeoned; but it is quite as true that without the partially concealed and constant ministration of the church it could hardly have organized on such a vast scale. The EOK and consistories tried to avoid giving the impression that they had converted support of the league into control. If parents' associations looked like nothing more than a concealed tool of the church, their political usefulness would suffer.

Constant church assistance and responsive parents were the two ingredients that combined to produce a strange phenomenon: a National Parents' League almost fully grown at birth. By 1925, two full-time and six part-time officials staffed its central Berlin headquarters, and 160 officials comprised the leadership corps of its seventeen constituent parents' associations, which carried 2 million members and 4,627 local associations (not including their own branches) on membership rolls.[39] Along with the smaller parents' associations, the league sponsored an annual "education week," initiated in the week-long drive in January 1923. Throughout Germany assemblies fired off resolutions to the Reichstag and various levels of government during this week. With the Kirchenausschuss the National Parents' League represented the Protestant cause to federal and state governments and kept in contact with leaders of various party factions. Internally, the league sponsored countless assemblies and courses on school issues. Speakers, specialists, and local leaders were trained and the broad membership reached with an extensive literature prepared with the aid of the Press Association. Above all, member organizations nourished and extended the local parents' associations, without which the National Parents' League could exert little collective influence. At least within the territory of the Old-Prussian church, the league and church officials aspired to monitor every Evangelical school through a local parents' association or some other Evangelical organization, a goal largely realized in the cities but not in the less-threatened countryside.

SHORING UP DEFENSIVE LINES

"Despite many efforts the Reichstag has not passed the federal school law," read a Kirchenausschuss election appeal before the Reichstag elections in May 1924.[40] "The convulsion of Evangelical schools has thereby progressed to an extent no longer tolerable in many German states." The demand for favorable school legislation was also a demand for relief from the perpetual necessity of maintaining certain lines of defense that had buckled under local pressures.

In its election appeal, circulated before both Reichstag elections in May and December 1924, the Kirchenausschuss urged church people to campaign actively for a Reichstag willing to enact the desired legislation. Such a qualification could realistically benefit only the Right parties, though theoretically the Center party as well. "By our ballots on May 4 we must win the Christian and Evangelical confessional school," wrote Josef Gauger, "for if we do not, everything is lost."[41] That a local association dropped out of the Berlin parents' league signaled the danger of disintegration whenever school and partisan politics coalesced. Yet the possible gain seemed well worth the certain risk. Partly because of the school issue, the December elections yielded a favorable constellation in a Reichstag that sat until 1928. The Nationalists entered the new Reichstag as the second strongest party, with more than a fifth of the seats. Together with the Center and Bavarian

People's parties, they could now entertain the possibility of assembling a majority for a bill satisfactory to the churches.

The Reichstag elections in May had also produced a relative victory for the political Right. Alerting provincial consistories to the recurrence of biennial elections to parents' advisory councils in June, the EOK stressed the persisting importance of these elections for school legislation that again seemed possible.[42] It appears that confessional lists improved their margin of success over the 75 percent of all seats captured in Evangelical schools in 1922. In Lower Silesia the percentage rose from 74.41 to 88.12, in metropolitan Berlin from about two-thirds to three-quarters, and in Brandenburg as a whole to even more.

Other signs, however, clearer than in 1922, began to cause church leaders acute anxiety. Parents had not submitted lists in a third of Brandenburg schools, and the total number of parents elected had dropped with the falling-off of elections. In Pomerania, ill-defined "unity" lists, conspicuously unsuccessful before, captured 23 percent of all seats. Despite the vigilance of parents' associations, parents were clearly growing weary of the continuous struggle. Could these elections continue to impress politicians if the Reichstag did not resolve the issue quickly? Consistories complained that school authorities and teachers ignored councils that could give advice only. The effectiveness of these councils as a partial substitute for church supervision of religious instruction was clearly waning.

The more parents' elections exposed these councils as weak reeds and the longer the Reichstag dallied, the more urgent grew the political problem of finding some way to prevent local school committees from subverting confessional education, especially in cities. The ranking Evangelical pastor, Catholic priest, and Jewish rabbi attended local school committees as ex officio members. Did the pastor fully exploit his opportunities? Why not try to form within each committee a pressure group consisting of the pastor and others favorably disposed to confessional schools? Toward the middle of the decade, the EOK and the consistories addressed such questions for the reason that city school committees approved assembled schools, nominated principals and teachers for appointment, assigned them, participated in the supervision of schools and teachers (through city superintendents), and procured texts.

Had the electorate directly chosen school committees, parents' associations could have extended their agitation to assure a favorable composition. Unhappily, roughly three-quarters of the non–ex officio committee members in the cities were political appointees, directly or indirectly. The popularly elected city assembly chose a fourth of the members (from its own ranks); the mayor selected another quarter from his executive committee (both elected by the assembly); and the mayor's appointees, together with the assembly, appointed another fourth. Teachers elected the remaining quarter from their own midst.[43] If the political Right and the Center party lost city elections, the ranking pastor was likely to confront a majority opposed to confessional schools. School committee members, however, also acted as the local administrative arm of the state, responsible to the regional administration for faithfully executing Prussian law. If questionable conditions developed in local schools or school committees took seemingly illegal actions, local parents' associations and church authorities would often lodge protests. If local protests failed to carry the field, consistories would sometimes call upon the EOK to unwrap its ultimate weapon: an energetic protest to the Kultusministerium, accompanied on occasion by barbed questions posed by friendly deputies in the Landtag.

The first line of defense, however, lay with pastors in school committees, the only institutionalized safeguard yet remaining. To exploit this defense, the Education Commission of the Brandenburg consistory organized pastors sitting on Berlin school committees into an association in March 1923.[44] In one instruction sheet, the association emphasized the importance of lobbying city assemblies for a favorable composition of school committees and of cultivating contacts with all component groups. In another sheet, the association developed the theme: Know your friends and enemies well, plan tactics with your friends (parents' associations), and keep your enemy's tactics under close surveillance. From Berlin the systematic attempt to instruct pastors spread throughout the church under the EOK's promotion.

By 1925 the wind blowing against such efforts had begun to shift to the advantage of the church. The radical school movement had subsided for two reasons, the Brandenburg consistory reported: a shift in political mood —increasingly reflected in the composition of city assemblies and school committees as well as in the revival of a "Christian sense"—and the "awakening" and "strengthening" of the Evangelical parents' movement. Here and there parents and children had succeeded in restoring school prayers where previously neglected, and parents' associations had begun to exert a wholesome influence on teachers. The danger hovering over confessional education seemed no longer so much one of overt attack as one of covert subversion.

A glimpse of the Berlin parents' league in action during 1924 illustrates the remaining overt dangers.[45] In June of that year, the league had won an astonishing victory in parents' elections. Well organized it was, but the league's membership had fallen from a reported high of 70,000 in 1922 to 38,000, perhaps because of more stable school conditions and certainly because of a growing weariness. All the same, its member parents' associations had increased from more than 100 to 119, though this number had fallen from a peak of 134 in 1923. Like many other parents' associations, the league was headed by a pastor who could not devote his full energies to its operations. Accordingly, the Brandenburg consistory asked the EOK to subsidize a full-time leader for the purpose of enlivening and expanding the faltering league.

How did the league organize itself? The 119 member associations were usually composite organizations of as many as 12 smaller branches. Through an estimated 1,191 public functions in 1924, they aspired to influence and attract the public. Member associations deputized representatives to monthly city-wide meetings whose attendance ranged from 32 to 110 people representing between 27 and 59 associations at one time. The leader acted as a resource person, sent out a monthly information sheet, and circulated among the associations.

Over what issues did the league join battle in 1924? Member associations, alone or together with the league, successfully protested the following situations to school authorities: the transfer of a Catholic teacher to an Evangelical school; the naming of four Jewish teachers as assistant principals in Evangelical schools; the appointment of an "unsuitable" principal in an Evangelical school and the continued employment of another; the questionable behavior of a superintendent, which resulted in his disciplining; the merger of two schools; and a Christmas play that affronted Christian sensibilities. With mixed success the association in Neukölln fought a series of sharp engagements with its dissident and Socialist superintendent, Kurt Löwenstein. Another association protested the appointment of a teacher in an assembled school as principal in an Evangelical school, an issue left unresolved. Several associations contested the introduction of a primer. Unsuccessful were protests against Catholic classes in an Evangelical school, the conversion of an Evangelical into a Catholic school, the reassigning of another school, and a private exhibit of trashy literature that featured the New Testament as a noteworthy example in an Evangelical school.

The league entered the local school struggle in other ways as well. It took pride in obtaining from the Kultusministerium a seemingly innocuous statement that Evangelical elementary schools might be officially labeled Evangelical, as Catholic schools were labeled Catholic. This statement seemed important, because teachers had sought to have Evangelical schools branded as common schools. Church leaders regarded this attempt as just part of a more general effort of the city teachers' association to undermine confessional schools after having attacked them directly during the struggle over the Schulz bill. The league sponsored public assemblies before parents' elections as well as before the two Reichstag elections. The results of the parents' elections nearly shut out the "nonpartisan" lists that teachers promoted against "Christian nonpartisan" lists, and narrowed the success of secular-school lists. Still the interest of Evangelical parents in their councils flagged. Finally, the league claimed credit for thwarting a drive to collect signatures for assembled schools.

This range of activities largely covered those that engaged other parents' associations throughout Prussia. It is apparent that a variety of sorties against confessional education threw these associations and the church back upon a largely defensive strategy. At what point in their retreat did they resolve to dig in and fight? That point has already been shown with regard to assembled schools. In practice church leaders drew a further line between supervisory officials and teachers, sharply contesting dissident appointments to supervisory positions while indulging wayward teachers. The case of dissident teachers blurred that line.[46] A reporter for the Education Committee at the 1925 General Synod claimed that school administrations had "repeatedly" employed dissident teachers, and the General Synod drew a sharp line against them. This line, however, does not appear to have been followed with much consistency. In 1927 the Church Senate informed the General Synod that the EOK "felt obliged to intervene in especially difficult cases" against dissident teachers. In one case, the EOK protested as late as 1926 one who as early as 1922 had offered his own brand of religious instruction. He had won notoriety in other ways as well—by conducting Socialist youth consecration ceremonies, agitating against church membership, leading a free religious society, and spearheading a school strike. In another case, the EOK contested further employment at the point where a dissident verged on promotion to assistant principal. By "difficult cases" the EOK seems to have meant dissident teachers who behaved conspicuously as dissidents or aspired to a supervisory role. At this point, if not before, the church's toleration snapped.

The proportions of this problem were more apparent than real, for two reasons: Only a relatively small number of teachers contracted out of the church, and dissident teachers could seek refuge in assembled schools. Certainly the EOK would not protest dissident teachers in assembled schools. In one of the two cases cited above, the Kultusministerium obliged the EOK's request for the transfer of a dissident teacher to an assembled school.

Other teachers—still formally church members—had volunteered to staff assembled schools. They began to trickle back into confessional schools, inspiring widespread protests within the church. At the 1925 General Synod one speaker claimed that the assembled schools seen by returning teachers as Marxist party schools had dashed their expectations. If a Saul could convert to a Paul, to deny them readmittance would be unchristian. The General Synod agreed, provided that they certified in writing a willingness to teach according to the intent of confessional schools. The General Synod's position, along with the Berlin example, illustrated yet another line drawn in the strategy of defense: resistance to the penetration of aliens, whether dissidents and others rebounding from assembled schools, roving Catholics, or, one might add, sectarians such as Jehovah's Witnesses.[47]

Perhaps church leaders conducted no general campaign to ferret out dissident teachers because this problem blended into a more important one: the unreliability of a larger number of other teachers. Many seemed to differ little from the few who had contracted out of the church. "The fight against Christian education and the Evangelical school is no longer so openly and brutally conducted as in the first period after the Revolution," the EOK informed the 1925 General Synod, "but rather aims quietly and covertly to undermine the Christian-Evangelical character of the school from the inside out."[48] Church leaders took alarm at the legion of saboteurs within their own camp. The church might well win the battles but lose the war for confessional education.

On this front, the situation dictated a temporary strategic retreat.[49] In 1922 Prussian general superintendents and the EOK emphatically rejected the temptation of attacking the German Teachers' Association with the hope of splitting it. Such a campaign could only offend large numbers of teachers who legally gave religious instruction. The church wielded a strong weapon in Article 149 (guaranteeing confessional religious instruction) but could not use it, for lack of a mechanism. Without firsthand knowledge of school conditions, the church lacked sufficient ammunition as well. In this impasse, church leaders hoped to coax teachers out of their hostility and to await a more favorable time for the implementation of Article 149. As time wore on, the front of teachers opposed to confessional schools broke down under its own strains. After plumping for secular schools in the revolution and then common schools, the association tended to fragment in its attitude toward school type. But teachers retained near unity in their resistance to anything smacking of clerical supervision. Contesting the content of a teacher's religious instruction, except in the most outrageous cases, would confirm teachers in their persisting belief that the church acted to restore clerical supervision.

Unacceptable rather than dissident principals, the Berlin example suggested, constituted the main problem for the church on this level. Carl Becker, who succeeded Otto Boelitz as Prussian Kultusminister in 1925, assured the EOK in May 1926 that the Kultusministerium opposed the appointment of dissident principals and that he knew of no such case since 1922. Accepting this assurance, the EOK regretted that the ministry had not displayed similar vigilance against the employment of dissident teachers. Becker had responded to complaints against dissident principals and Jewish assistant principals lodged by the 1925 General Synod. It, in turn, had reacted to the EOK's contention that both had been illegally appointed. The files of the EOK contain one instance of a freethinker principal who may have left the church, but it appears that, since 1922 at any rate, the church had little cause for complaint. Before then, especially under Kultusminister Haenisch, such cases appear to have developed with the increased employment of dissident teachers in Prussia. As for Jewish assistant principals, Becker agreed in principle against their employment in Evangelical schools. The 1927 General Synod, however, showed little confidence in school supervisory organs. It requested the ministry to accept the procedure of determining church membership before principals, assistant principals, and teachers were considered for appointment.[50]

One reason for this distrust lay in the development of the supervisory policy of the Kultusministerium. Caught between the political Right and the Center party, which wished to freeze the prerevolutionary status quo, and the political Left, which demanded a thaw, the Kultusministerium tried to follow a strict interpretation of the law coupled with political accommodations allowable within the law (assembled schools and dissident supervisors). Church authorities and parents' associations contested the appointment and behavior of supervisors averse to confessional education and the employment of Catholic supervisors in Protestant areas. But these cases seemed less offensive than the provocation of Socialist appointments.[51] The demand of Socialists for their own supervisors paralleled the slow growth of assembled schools. Since the church rejected even a strategic retreat on this front and since strict interpretation afforded no natural defenses, the struggle over the few Socialist appointments became a political one over the spirit of the law.

In the early years probably the most contested Socialist nomination was that of Kurt Löwenstein as school superintendent of metropolitan Berlin. Löwenstein was an Independent Socialist, a dissident Jew, and a partisan of secular schools. In 1920 his nomination by the Socialist-dominated city assembly outraged loyal parishioners and church leaders. Berlin district synods, the Brandenburg consistory, parents' advisory councils, and even teachers' groups flooded the city and provincial government with their protests. The ten Berlin district synods asserted "that the election of Dr. Löwenstein means nothing other than the determined attempt to perse-cute Christians by modern means."[52] In his case, provincial authorities with-held appointment.

Alarmed by a number of Haenisch's appointments, the political Right and the Center party prevailed upon the Landtag on March 10, 1922, to pass a resolution that would nail the Kultusministerium to confessional appointments short of entirely excluding dissident Socialists. It would obli-gate the Kultusministerium to pay more attention to the will of the popu-lation in making supervisory and higher appointments.[53] This resolution placed Otto Boelitz, the new Kultusminister of the People's party, in a quandary. In no supervisory unit did assembled schools and classes enroll anything approximating a majority of pupils. In view of the results of parents' elections, church people could argue that dissident Socialist appointments clearly ignored the will of parents. Boelitz accepted the intent of the motion, only to run afoul of it. Disliking Socialist appoint-ments as much as assembled schools, he conceded both to oblige his Socialist colleagues in the Prussian coalition government.

The case of Ohligs illustrated Boelitz's dilemma. Here he appointed a Socialist as school supervisor in October 1922 and, upon his resignation, another Socialist in the spring of 1923. The local Evangelical parents' association leaped to protest both appointments. On both occasions an assis-tant to Boelitz wrote the chairman of the association, a local pastor, hoping to quash further protests by taking the pastor into his confidence. The necessity of working in harness with Socialists had forced on Boelitz a com-promise by which supervisors of the political Right would be appointed in other supervisory units in exchange for a Socialist in Landkreis Solingen, where Ohligs lay and where many Socialists resided. The assistant assured the pastor that Boelitz would confine Socialist appointments to a bare minimum, and invited him to consider the great difference between the policies of Boelitz and Haenisch. Now that he knew the game plan, the pastor could hardly accept the assistant's later assurance that competence rather than party membership had been decisive in the Ohligs appointment. Nor did the pastor prove sympathetic.[54] He deplored the corrosive effect of partisan politics on schools. The theory of symbiosis, so energetically advanced by Kaftan at the 1921 Church Assembly, should elevate schools above the partisan politics that the Republic so perversely forced on schools.

When the General Synod convened in 1925, the fertile seeds of the largest single school conflict in Prussia had already been sown with the appointment of a dissident Socialist teacher as a supervisor in an East Prussian supervisory unit of exclusively Evangelical schools. The appointment of Schulrat Martin Nischalke and other, less affronting cases prompted the 1925 General Synod to stake out a claim to confessional supervision as a necessary line of defense. The General Synod aspired to win back the de facto confessional supervision that had generally prevailed before the revolution. But it claimed even more. Not only Evangelical church membership but also a firm commitment to Evangelical education should be required of school supervisors employed in supervisory units with a chiefly Evangelical population. Such a position, an opposing speaker noted, went beyond existing law and even beyond traditional practice, by which a supervisor of one confession would supervise schools of the other. The 1925 General Synod even contended that confessional strength in supervisory units at the bottom should determine the composition of supervisory organs at the top—in the regional administration, the province, and the Kultusministerium itself. Of course, confessional supervision was anathema to Socialists, Democrats, most teachers, and Kultusminister Becker (accounted a Democrat, though a nonpartisan appointee).

These resolutions showed that the General Synod hoped to confine the employment of Catholics as well as Socialists in supervisory positions. A representative of the EOK broached the nagging question that was on many lips: Could one possibly imagine the appointment of a dissident in a district of exclusively Catholic schools?[55] The resolutions and this question revealed another side to the Nischalke affair and to the personnel policies of the Kultusministerium: a pervasive feeling that the Prussian Republic discriminated against Protestants. It was widely believed in the Old-Prussian church that the Center and Socialist parties, constant coalition partners in Prussia, cooperated to ensure their school interests at the expense of

Protestantism. Otto Braun, the enduring Socialist minister president, admitted as much in his memoirs: "The Center allowed a certain latitude to prevail in all these questions [employment of dissidents in schools] insofar as they concerned Protestant areas, but resisted any deviation from the 'legal situation' favorable to its Weltanschauung in areas where Catholicism dominated."[56]

In 1925 the General Synod aired complaints that the Kultusministerium had consistently slighted Old-Prussian church authorities before it had issued new instructional guidelines for the various levels of schools. Those for the Grundschule (first four years of the elementary school) had allotted more time for Catholic religious instruction than Evangelical until a cascade of complaint prevailed upon the Landtag and the Kultusministerium to accept parity. The latest affront was the decision of the Kultusministerium to publish its draft of guidelines for higher schools after concluding negotiations with the Catholic church but before consulting Evangelical churches. Earlier neglect had prompted church authorities to conclude, in the words of General Superintendent Dibelius at the General Synod: "It can't continue that the Bishop of Osnabrück [the episcopacy's specialist for school affairs] constructs teaching plans for Catholic instruction (lively hear, hear), while our plans are made in the ministry and our influence on these things is rendered more or less illusory."[57]

In 1925 the EOK reported that preferential hiring of Catholics had helped to shift the confessional ratio to the advantage of Catholics among school administrators, teachers, and certified teacher candidates. The EOK and the 1925 General Synod took particular alarm at the growing confessional imparity of teachers at interdenominational higher schools (Gymnasia and related types) and the inequitable success of Catholics in expanding the number of their higher schools, already more numerous than the Protestant. Evangelical higher schools grew more interdenominational with the appointment of Catholic teachers. The synod recommended the appointment of teachers according to the confessional strength of pupils enrolled in interdenominational schools. The synod also demanded that higher schools founded as Evangelical or traditionally regarded as such retain their identity against Catholic inroads. Soon after the 1925 General Synod, the EOK, following the lead of the Kirchenausschuss, began to collect evidence in support of the allegation that the Kultusministerium and other state agencies pursued personnel policies that ignored Evangelical interests. Finally, the 1925 General Synod demanded the erection of new Evangelical higher schools wherever parents demonstrated a need. Competition with Catholics reinforced Protestant demands for confessional elementary schools as well. If Catholics managed to retain confessional schools in the expected federal law, why should Protestants settle for anything less (common schools) than "their" schools?[58]

In the fall of 1924, Martin Nischalke's appointment as school supervisor in Bartenstein, East Prussia, confirmed suspicions that the Kultusministerium discriminated against Protestants. Boelitz named this dissident Socialist as the provisional successor of a Catholic supervisor in a supervisory unit of exclusively Evangelical schools. Socialists, a colleague asserted, had pressed for the appointment. If trouble arose Boelitz would have revoked the appointment, he later claimed. Soon the executive committee of the district synod complained to the EOK that Nischalke had resumed his earlier agitation against the church, causing much unrest among local Protestants. This information the EOK passed on to the Kultusministerium in a protest that charged neglect of Evangelical interests and predicted conflict if the ministry did not cancel the provisional appointment. Thereupon, local teachers petitioned for Nischalke's permanent appointment, and, in reaction, church people circulated petitions for his removal. Concluding that church complaints had exaggerated, the Kultusministerium made the appointment permanent on April 17, 1925 — in the interlude between Boelitz's and Becker's ministries, though with Becker's full approval.[59]

Outraged church authorities could do little now that Nischalke held the tenure that permanent appointment afforded. Inasmuch as the EOK denounced dissident supervision of Evangelical schools everywhere, it could not recommend a normal transfer. The EOK hoped that mounting pressure would persuade Becker to alter the regional grouping of supervisory units enough to create one of assembled schools for Nischalke. Such a development would carry out for assembled schools and dissident supervisors the confessional principle that the 1925 General Synod espoused. For a year Becker remained intractable. Besieged by protests fired off at every level in the Old-Prussian church, he finally yielded. Rather than realign supervisory units, however, Becker fell back on Boelitz's earlier example of finding units with a strong sprinkling of assembled schools for dissident supervisors.[60]

In Westphalia he settled finally on the unit of Landkreis Dortmund I, where about 21 percent of the pupils attended assembled schools. Nischalke was the only dissident among the thirty-four supervisors in the Arnsberg regional administration. In all of Prussia at the time there were only two other dissident district supervisors, and supervisors of the two confessions inspected most assembled schools and classes. Dissident parents had more reason to complain than either Protestant or Catholic.[61]

Why, then, did Evangelical parents' associations resort to a massive strike in the fall of 1926 after Nischalke's arrival? Dortmund was no Ohligs. For thirty years Landkreis Dortmund had been divided confessionally into four units—two for Catholic schools and two for Evangelical. It was one of the Evangelical units that Becker now claimed for a dissident. In Landkreis Dortmund Protestants already presumably enjoyed the confessional supervision that the General Synod and EOK would extend throughout Prussia in less rigorous form. If it was hard to imagine Becker appointing a dissident over exclusively Catholic schools, it was even harder to imagine him naming one in a unit where Catholics claimed a residual right to confessional supervision. Becker's consistent behavior suggested only one conclusion to Protestant strike leaders: discrimination against Protestants. His allusion to the two other units under dissident district supervisors—Ohlau in Silesia and Ohligs in the Rhineland—hardly helped his case. In both, Protestants outnumbered Catholics two to one, and Protestants enjoyed an overwhelming majority in the Bartenstein unit.

For Becker confessional rivalry appeared as the main cause of an otherwise inexplicable strike. In his view, Protestants in the western provinces resented plummeting to the status of parity with Catholics in a confessionally neutral state. He implied that the strike aimed to restore preference for Protestants. But strike leaders merely hoped to compel the ministry to respect the vital interests of Protestants in the same measure that it allegedly obliged Catholics.

Why would Becker not yield to the strikers? During Landtag debates on December 4, 1926, he pointed out the administrative difficulty of imposing the confessional principle upon the school supervisory apparatus.[62] But accommodating a few dissident supervisors in several supervisory units of assembled schools hardly required a major overhaul, and might offer a promising political solution. Becker professed legal scruples against such a solution, however. Article 174, he contended, ruled out a unit of assembled schools under Nischalke. A Nationalist deputy replied: If the ministry might violate Article 174 by establishing "Evangelical schools without religious instruction," it could certainly appoint an "Evangelical supervisor without religion" over such schools. But surely Becker was quite familiar with rulings of the Federal Court (Reichsgericht) and the State Court (Staatsgerichtshof), which implied that Article 174 left Prussia free to frame supervisory law as it wished. Becker appeared to have avoided the EOK's solution because of aversion to entrenching confessional education. What drove parents' associations to strike was the strong suspicion that this aversion as well as political bias and expediency motivated Becker, rather than fidelity to law. The religionless state now loomed as the oppressor that Kaftan had predicted at the 1921 Church Assembly, and Evangelical parents resorted to the passive resistance that he had endorsed.

Hearing of the impending appointment, near unanimity prevailed among local church leaders, parents' associations, and Evangelical teachers in Landkreis Dortmund. Then the issue of imparity obscured the other issue of confessional supervision. Teachers joined the torrent of protest and even the parade of delegations to Berlin. After Becker ignored these protests by naming Nischalke, the district parents' association proclaimed a strike in Nischalke's unit on November 6 and in the other Evangelical unit three weeks later. From two-thirds to three-quarters of the pupils in the two units boycotted Evangelical schools. At its fullest extent, the strike may have involved as many as thirty thousand pupils.[63]

Strike leaders, who assumed that the unified front of the protest period would endure, had reckoned without the Westphalian Teachers' Association. The association prevailed on its district leaders to disavow the strike and to endorse a strict interpretation of the law, while the Arnsberg regional administration threatened to discipline sympathetic teachers. If it was legal, why had the appointment drawn the fire of the church? The teachers' press answered: The church hoped to shackle teachers by winning confessional supervision through the strike.[64] Its outlay in effort seemed far too extravagant to suppose that the church merely objected to a local appointment. Soon teachers gave battle gladly, for they professed to see in their own intellectual enslavement the true object of the strike.

Once teachers squared off against strikers, both vied to win over parents. Teachers held parents' assemblies to advance their version of the legal question and to discredit strike leaders. The Arnsberg regional administration reinforced these efforts by warning parents that truancy could result in nonpromotion. For their part, strike leaders sponsored substitute instruction and in countless assemblies aired the grievances under which Protestants claimed to suffer. Parents found themselves pressured and intimidated by both sides at once, and escalating charges and countercharges left embitterment and exasperation as the district polarized over the issue. As passions rose, excited statements by strike leaders betrayed their distrust of teachers, who replied in kind with alarming insults against the church.

Both sides came to believe that great stakes rode on the outcome of the protracted strike. The Democratic minister of the interior, Wilhelm Külz, was expected at any moment to publish a proposed school bill that would project the common school as the norm. Earlier that spring the National Parents' League publicly declared such a bill unacceptable, and renewed its demand for parity. "The patience of Evangelical parents has been stretched to the limit by the continual postponement of federal school legislation," the league complained.[65] Protestant leaders had grown exasperated with a Reichstag that, though capable of passing satisfactory school legislation, squandered valuable time instead. The Schiele bill of 1925 — the government's sole offering — had perished when the first coalition of the political Right and the Center party broke down over the Locarno treaties. The thought of resolving the school imbroglio by way of a referendum resurfaced, only to submerge when Külz promised to resume school deliberations, if only with an unsatisfactory bill. Külz had not managed to gain cabinet approval before a second coalition of the political Right and the Center party superseded his own in January 1927.

The strike thus broke out in an agonizing period of flux, when the school issue could shift in one of a number of directions, and strikers as well as their opponents believed that their duel might help set its future course. If strikers managed to win confessional supervision in the largest German state, they might hope, in Becker's words, to preempt the Reichstag decision.[66] They would have demonstrated to the Reichstag that Protestants, no less than Catholics, would settle for nothing short of confessional schools and adequate guarantees for them.

As before, the Old-Prussian church aspired toward the Volkskirche ideal of comprehensive composition and influence. In practice, it relied on a relatively small corps to carry its banner. No longer, however, could one regard it as a mere pastors' church. In the Westphalian school strike, parents' associations filled out the ranks of the Volkskirche fighting for its cause. For what purpose had the church assembled parents' associations in one of the largest provincial organizations, if not to parry the danger that Nischalke posed for confessional schools? Superintendents, pastors and their wives, parish workers and councils, and the gamut of church free associations engaged actively in the conflict. Pastors promoted the strike from the pulpit, and congregational councils gladly welcomed strike meetings into church buildings. By the same token, only parents could give the strike credibility. Despite progress toward the Volkskirche ideal, the combative means chosen to realize it left the Old-Prussian church stranded as an incongruous closed-front Volkskirche. A Volkskirche cannot close fronts against a large number of its own members without damage to its own comprehensive nature.

Earlier theological disputes had eased to facilitate consensus and encourage solidarity. But now dissent from the church's public position largely replaced them as the objects of the church's displeasure. The Saxon consistory reprimanded a pastor in 1926 for carrying his dissent outside the church —into the pages of a teachers' periodical. Within the church, however, public pressure rather than official sanctions weighed heavily on dissentients. When a liberal school principal agitated for common schools at the 1925 General Synod, a representative of the EOK warned against reopening church fronts that the Stuttgart declaration had definitively closed.[67]

The strongest example of internal church intolerance stemmed directly from the Westphalian strike. On October 26, 1926, the district parents' association adopted the following position: "We Evangelical parents of Landkreis Dortmund I have accepted the struggle for our Evangelical school against the dissident supervisor for the sake of conscience and the gospel. Thus we declare that we regard any Evangelical person who works against our cause, no matter who he is, as a Judas who betrays the cause of the gospel." This resolution took direct aim at Pastor Tribukait, a liberal who occupied a pastorate in the Dortmund congregation of St. Reinoldi, outside the initial strike zone. Two days earlier Tribukait had done nothing more than to question whether his congregation, a nonparticipant, had acted wisely in issuing a "sharp public declaration" that "incited striking." If Becker failed to remove Nischalke, the declaration concluded, "we as a church...cannot disapprove of the measures of force [resorted to by] indignant parents, but rather will support them ourselves with holy fire from the pulpit and lecturn."[68]

Whether one welcomed the strike hinged on whether one accepted the necessity of the closed-front Volkskirche. This point was illustrated in the contrasting assumptions of Pastor Tribukait, who abhorred the strike but acquiesced for fear of scandal, and Pastor Richter, who participated without reservation.[69] Religious toleration loomed so high in Tribukait's mind as to commend Christian Simultan schools over confessional and great latitude for teachers. By contrast, Richter feared lest teachers, dissident supervisors, and common schools subvert Christian education. If the church conceded to all three, it would eventually forfeit its Volkskirche status by writing off Christian education. But contesting all three as a closed-front Volkskirche led to unacceptable consequences for Tribukait: a politicization of church membership, suppression of individual conscience, a drive for clerical power to control teachers, and finally the pursuit of power for its own sake because of church pride. Such motives and consequences Richter rejected out of hand. Lust for power had not sullied the motives of strike leaders. They acted in full consciousness of their responsibilities. God had allowed them a last opportunity to regain lost ground before the impending federal law shut the door. For his part, Tribukait laid a finger on the hypocrisy of mobilizing masses, who had already broken inwardly with the church, against one — Nischalke — honest enough to break externally as well. Richter sensed in the same masses, however, a growing loyalty to the church. In seizing this opportunity, Evangelical church people had experienced an exhilarating sense of solidarity that even the greatest optimist could hardly have anticipated. From the beginning of the strike to its end, Richter's views reflected dominant opinion within the Westphalian church. The threatening situation required a combative closed-front Volkskirche.

In the end the closed-front Volkskirche could not prevail against the determined counterattack of teachers allied with the state. The strike's momentum could only flag with time. The political Right tried to redeem the strike by moving Becker, in the Landtag debates on December 4, to negotiate. Becker held his ground. Concession for him meant capitulation to confessional supervision and violation of the state's legal right to sovereignty over schools. While the Landtag debated, the provincial parents' association increased pressure on Becker by proclaiming the strike in the city of Dortmund on December 6 and throughout the entire province on December 8. But teachers and the provincial government managed to confine the strike largely to its originating district.[70] The struggle grew more partisan the longer the strike lasted, the farther it aspired to spread beyond its original base, and the more the issue of confessional supervision surfaced. And the more the struggle developed into a party issue, the less strike leaders could count on a wide political spectrum of parents to rally behind a vital church interest. The strategy of the closed-front Volkskirche could command only diminishing returns at the point that partisan politics overwhelmed the original church cause. The National Parents' League saved the strike from humiliating disaster shortly before Christmas by prevailing on Becker and the federal minister of the interior to submit the dispute to the Federal Court for a ruling. Thereupon the provincial parents' association called off the strike, to everyone's immense relief.

Following earlier court decisions, the Federal Court held on July 11, 1927, that Article 174 shielded state school law from alteration only with respect to school type, not at all with respect to school supervision.[71] Neither the National Parents' League nor Becker could find succor in Article 174—the league to contest Nischalke's appointment, Becker to avoid realigning supervisory units for dissidents. But both parties had surely anticipated this judgment and had resorted to court action primarily as a face-saving device to withdraw from extended political positions. The real question was who won politically. Both parties won something. Becker managed to uphold his position without compromise, but later saw the wisdom of spiriting Nischalke away. Who won politically in a larger sense is hard to say, because the school strike blended into the larger struggle then shaping up over the 1927 Reichstag school bill. Teachers, claiming victory in the strike, found encouragement to march into the next battle. Strike leaders found solace in their spirited demonstration that the state could not ignore Protestant vital interests with impunity and treat Protestants as second-class citizens. The Nischalke affair helped to catalyze sides in Prussia for the next—and again "decisive"—Donnybrook over schools in the Reichstag.

REDEEMING SUPERVISORY RIGHTS

By fighting so tenaciously against the strike, teachers also struggled to hold back the engulfing tide that had turned against their cause since 1924. The Reichstag elected at the close of that year seemed alarmingly disposed to pass a school bill favorable to confessional education. The aborted Schiele bill of 1925 had provided a preview of what teachers thought they might expect in 1927. Martin Schiele, the Nationalist minister of the interior, generated a bill that would entrench confessional to the disadvantage of secular schools and completely rule out common schools as a distinct type. In 1924 the Bavarian government had concluded a concordat with the papacy and corresponding treaties with two Bavarian Evangelical churches. These agreements confirmed existing practices by according churches a wide-ranging influence over normative confessional schools, including the right to supervise religious instruction. Lingering resentment among teachers spread northward to Prussia, where teachers similarly reacted against less threatening attempts by the Old-Prussian church to negotiate a suitable arrangement to supersede its languishing right to supervise religious instruction.

What menaced teachers encouraged most Old-Prussian church leaders, though they would not rival Catholics by claiming direct clerical supervision of religious instruction. In June 1922 Prussian general superintendents, meeting with the EOK, had staked out their position but had refrained from pressing the church for a pronouncement.[72] Broaching the issue of supervision might confirm the suspicion of church liberals and teachers that the church intended to draw on the preamble of its constitution to impose dogmatic standards on religious instruction. The preamble dispute subsided in 1924, but the Schiele bill, which would resolve the issue of supervision, entered and exited before the first General Synod under the new church constitution managed to convene in December 1925. Since the next school bill would likely address the issue of supervision as well, the General Synod hastened to set the stance of the Old-Prussian church.

Article 149 compelled the church to redeem its right to supervision within the context of these words: "Religious instruction shall be given in conformity with the principles of the religious society concerned, without prejudice to the state's right of supervision." At Weimar the Constitution Committee would allow churches to prescribe the content of religion classes but not physically inspect them, lest churches encroach on state supervision. This committee and the Stuttgart Church Assembly concurred in assuming that a religiously neutral state might not determine content. That the present state, no longer Christian, *must* not tamper with content gave the church an emphatic reason for insisting on its constitutional right. Since, in addition, many teachers and school supervisors seemed confessionally unreliable, most church leaders commended observation of religion classes (Einsichtnahme) as a means of assuring the church that teachers actually taught in the spirit of the confession, or at least not contrary to it. These church leaders insisted that observation would fall short of supervision. Deputized visitors would examine content only and not discipline teachers.[73]

Church liberals and religion teachers, of course, saw through this logic. Why visit religion classes at all, if not to exert pressure on teachers and, in the last resort, have them disciplined? If clergymen as well as reliable teachers visited religion classes, as some church leaders advocated, church supervision would yield to clerical supervision. Without observation, the others however insisted, the church could hardly assure itself of its constitutional right that religious instruction conform with its principles. Both sides appealed to Article 149 for support.

But views on constitutionality actually turned on other considerations. Church liberals insisted that a generous trust in teachers was more likely to guarantee content than compulsion. Their opponents also cherished such trust but argued that the church could not forgo a disciplinary remedy where it seemed unwarranted. Out of deference to teachers, neither side wished to secure guarantees beyond those indispensable to the vital interests of the Volkskirche, however defined. It made good sense to co-opt teachers by reaching a compromise that they could accept as well.

The desirability of consulting provincial synods and other Evangelical churches in Prussia eventually persuaded the Education Committee not to press the 1925 General Synod to take a stand. Reluctance to unveil broken fronts publicly in the General Synod probably suggested another solution as well. The General Synod empowered the Church Senate to issue a public statement on behalf of the church after consulting a special study committee. Liberals bridled at the suggestion of reaching an accord behind closed doors, but the Education Committee persuaded the General Synod with the argument that the issue required resolution before the next school bill could emerge. Though they could predict that the Senate would endorse church observation of religion classes, liberals, and especially the Reichsbund für Religionsunterricht und religiöse Erziehung, refused to give up hope. They fought for their cause within the study committee, half of which consisted of teachers, and within the Senate itself, which contained a small liberal minority. Outside they kept up a steady barrage of declarations and appeals on the Senate. After over a year of debate within the church, the Senate published the public declaration that it had finally accepted on January 6, 1927, soon after the Westphalian school strike. Suspicion that the church wished to foist church observation on religious instruction had steeled teachers in their repudiation of confessional supervision during that strike.

The Senate declaration dashed the hopes of liberals and religion teachers by endorsing church observation of religion classes and other "external guarantees."[74] That church observation, the most offensive of the external guarantees, must lead to indirect supervision was apparent in the Senate's assertion that the church, not the state, must ultimately decide what accorded with church principles in contested cases. The Senate, however, circumvented the danger of imposing dogma by accepting the broad definition of doctrinal norms espoused in the Stuttgart declaration.

In one respect liberals and religion teachers could take heart: the Senate would rule out *clerical* observation by entrusting "schoolmen," reliable school supervisors, as the church's investigating agents. This concession struck some pastors as an affront, and clearly crossed the initial position of general superintendents in 1922 and most members of the Senate, who wished to charge general superintendents with primary responsibility for observing religion classes and to employ the clergy in this task as well as schoolmen. In the end the Senate agreed to concede to the extent of vesting primary responsibility in advisory councils (Beiräte) attached to consistories and the EOK as the "organs" commended by the Stuttgart declaration. These councils would nominate school supervisors to the state for confirmation.

In May 1927 the General Synod ratified the Senate's declaration against the votes of twelve delegates. The suggested arrangement was meant to apply to all school levels and to supersede the church's legal right to supervise religious instruction if the Kultusministerium concurred. But it could not be counted on to amend accordingly its supervisory decree of February 18, 1876.[75] Religion teachers, particularly those organized in the Reichsbund, persisted in increasing pressure on the Senate and Kultusministerium alike, even threatening to withdraw from religion classes if the church managed to implement its proposal. The immediate importance of the Senate's declaration lay rather in setting forth the church's position before the dispute over the 1927 school bill burst upon the horizon.

THE FAILING COUNTERATTACK 1927 – 1928

Old-Prussian church leaders must have wondered how much a favorable federal school law was needed to defend confessional education in Prussia. Article 174 slowed the growth of assembled secular schools and shut out common schools. Church leaders could only expect renewed local strife over school type and possibly a loss in the number of confessional schools once school legislation passed. On the other hand, Article 174 seemed a weak guarantee. It had not prevented secular schools or the deterioration of confessional education. Still, the Old-Prussian church hardly needed a federal law to ensure confessional schools as much as a group of other Evangelical churches. In Thuringia and the Hanseatic cities, and in Saxony and several smaller states, Socialist-influenced or -controlled governments had managed to ensconce what amounted to common schools as the prevailing type before the promulgation of the Weimar constitution. In the new common-school states, the influence of churches on religious instruction was either sharply reduced or excluded and its confessionality either deemphasized or effaced. The school civil war in Prussia paled in intensity and importance beside that in the state of Saxony. Through federal legislation the Kirchenausschuss and the National Parents' League hoped to restore the possibility of confessional schools in the new common-school states by way of parents' choice. They also hoped for provisions, earlier contained in the Schiele bill but omitted from the Schulz bill, that would ensure the confessionality of religious instruction and of confessional schools wherever retained or newly established. At this point, the vital interests of the Old-Prussian church blended most clearly with those of other Evangelical churches, as the dispute over observing religion classes illustrated.[76]

Upon entering a federal coalition with the People's party in January 1927, the Nationalist, Center, and Bavarian People's parties aspired to secure the passage of a school law acceptable to Evangelical and Catholic churches alike. It was the coalition government's bill—the Keudell draft —that the General Synod anticipated in May 1927 and commended to the Reichstag with considerable enthusiasm. Unlike the Schulz bill, the Keudell draft accommodated the Old-Prussian church in virtually every respect; and unlike the Schiele bill, it stood a good chance of passage because of the near majority commanded by the coalition's factions. Here at long last was the splendid opportunity that Old-Prussian church leaders had craved since the National Assembly.

In 1925 the General Synod had passed a resolution demanding parity for Evangelical schools and advocating their retention without an initial determination of parents' choice. The Keudell bill, named after the Nationalist minister of the interior responsible for it, obliged the General Synod by placing all school types on a par. Each type, wherever it existed throughout Germany, would retain its character unless parents of two-thirds of its pupils endorsed a switch to another type.[77] The bill's legitimation of existing schools, coupled with the two-thirds bar, would doubtless anchor confessional and secular schools in Prussia, given the preferences of Prussian parents.

That the Old-Prussian church could still count on parent preferences was demonstrated once again in biennial elections of parents' advisory councils in the spring of 1926.[78] Consistories reported that Christian nonpartisan lists had captured 86.7 percent of total council seats in Lower Silesia, a slight drop, and about 85 percent in Pomerania, a sharp gain. In Berlin and in Saxon urban areas, however, Communists and Socialists had contested elections with renewed vigor, whittling down the Evangelical majority. Increasingly consistories complained of parent apathy, and more than ever elections fell off in the countryside. If the Keudell bill suffered shipwreck, could the church sustain the momentum of the Evangelical parents' movement for long? Now as before, the church needed the movement to flaunt the apparent majority will of Evangelical parents before deputies, as well as to fend off local drives to transform confessional schools if the bill passed.

To the great satisfaction of church leaders, the Keudell bill reached beyond the resolution of school type required by Article 146 to settle collateral issues as well. The draft obliged the demand of the 1925 General Synod for a qualified version of confessional supervision. The bill adopted the Church Senate's proposal for observing religion classes without expressly according churches that ultimate right to prevail in contested cases. Out of deference to the Catholic church, however, the bill would permit the clergy as well as commissioned lay educators to visit religion classes without supervising them. Within the parameters of what seemed politically possible, the bill aimed to provide optimum conditions for flourishing confessional schools.

As everyone recognized, the fate of the bill hinged on the uncertain attitude and votes of the moderately conservative People's party. As the successor of the former National-Liberal party's right wing, the People's party might fall back on its anticlerical legacy and liberal preference for Christian Simultan schools. If so, the party was likely to scuttle the bill. By the same token, since the revolution the party had expressed an apparently equal preference for confessional schools, which the bill formally assured. The big question was what balance the party would try to strike in forthcoming deliberations.

Sides for and against the bill formed along earlier lines as each side sought to overawe opponents and to force them to concessions under the weight of an aroused public. This time the primary object was to help fix the stance of the People's party, the key to the legislation. Caught in the vise of growing public pressure by the time of the first Reichstag reading in October, the People's party maneuvered to assume a position between extremes that leaned heavily on its liberal heritage. Clerical observation seemed dangerously akin to clerical supervision. Like the Left, the People's party agreed that the Weimar constitution clearly endorsed common schools as the preferred type; unlike the Left, the party conceived of common schools as Christian Simultan.[79]

Having expressed a strong preference for Simultan schools, the People's party looked askance at the Center's wish for phasing them out by way of parents' choice in the old Simultan territories of Baden, Hesse, and Nassau within Prussia. In the first reading, the People's party would settle for nothing less than exempting the old Simultan areas from the organizing principle of parents' choice, thus perpetuating Simultan schools. Already the new common-school states had sought the same exemption within the Reichsrat (which represented state governments). If these states managed to come under the People's party formula for the old Simultan territories, the hopes of Evangelical as well as Catholic church authorities would miscarry.

Protestant stakes in federal school legislation were considerably greater than Catholic, for the reason that Protestant confessional education had more clearly deteriorated. As a rule, the larger the Catholic population, the more states, prompted by either the Center or the Bavarian People's party, ensured confessional education. The bulk of the Catholic population resided in southern Germany and in the western provinces of Prussia. South German states largely satisfied Catholic confessional demands, even in Baden, where Simultan schools prevailed. Prussia accommodated confessional demands less, but infinitely more than the new common-school states, which were overwhelmingly Protestant. By law in southern Germany and in practice in Prussia, the state required Catholic teachers to obtain the missio canonica (authorization) from diocesan bishops before offering religious instruction.[80] Protestant churches, lacking a comparable guarantee, looked to federal legislation (as well as to varying state arrangements where possible) to ensure the confessionality of religious instruction by other means, such as by observation of religion classes. Comparably more secure with existing state legislation and more effectively protected by Article 174, the Catholic church had less to gain from federal school legislation and less to lose if the Keudell bill failed of passage.

As deliberations in the Reichstag's Education Committee ran their course, the imminent danger hovering above the Kirchenausschuss was that the two Catholic confessional parties would prefer the status quo to a Keudell bill weighted by People's party encumbrances. The status quo seemed all too intolerable to the Kirchenausschuss, and the liberal position of the People's party all too weak, to guarantee Protestant vital interests. At this critical juncture, the Kirchenausschuss concluded that the Evangelical churches had to lobby parties and mobilize public pressure for a promising compromise. Their best hope lay in trying to move the People's party, which, like the Nationalist, catered to Protestant interests. Accordingly, the Kirchenausschuss represented to leaders of both parties the largely affirmative position that it had adopted on the bill on December 8–9. The Kirchenausschuss also orchestrated a large-scale campaign within Evangelical churches that aimed particularly at the People's party.[81] Not since the huge petition drive for religious education in the threatening days of the National Assembly had the churches waged such a concerted and intense campaign to influence lawmakers, at least in the Old-Prussian church. The opportunity was too great to let slip away.

Even before the bill's first reading, the Old-Prussian Church Senate had resolved to mobilize church opinion in a public campaign. To maximize pressure on the Reichstag and thus particularly on the People's party, the Senate agreed to discourage deviations within the church from official positions by asking church officials to monitor expected local resolutions on behalf of the bill.[82] That such pressure to conform would also goad some to bolt the ranks of the closed-front Volkskirche was apparent for the reason that many church liberals shared the reservations of the People's party. The political issue around which the closed-front Volkskirche coalesced had progressively narrowed, from religious instruction as such in 1919 to better terms for confessional education in 1922–23 and finally to outright endorsement of a bill that would, in effect, guarantee confessional education a preferred and secure position in 1927. Room for permissible dissent had correspondingly decreased.

Pastor Tribukait left a vivid account of how the closed-front Volkskirche promoted the bill in Westphalia, where battle-tested parents' associations remained in place to carry the assault, this time under official church leadership. Along with other district pastors, Tribukait had to attend a meeting where the superintendent pressed them to mount a campaign, parish by parish. The superintendent distributed a set of confidential guidelines, which provincial superintendents and the consistory had endorsed, instructing pastors on how to proceed. Tribukait regarded the guidelines as nothing less than a political agitator's manual on how to out maneuver the opposition and turn tight organization to good account. Already considered a turncoat during the strike, Tribukait claimed that his intolerant colleagues unjustly suspected him of leaking the guidelines to the teachers' press. Enemies of the bill promptly exploited the guidelines, now public property, to expose the outpouring of congregational resolutions as the systematic product of a politically scheming church.[83]

The intensity with which anxious church people in Old-Prussian provinces waged the campaign stemmed from their concern for the Volkskirche at this critical hour. The same concern had cemented loyalties to the political Right. "The church must wish a rightist government," insisted *Der Reichsbote* shortly before the bill's coalition took office. "In all German parliaments the Right does the most for the interests of the church." Failure to pass adequate federal school legislation had been a "shocking sin of the

German Republic, unmatched evidence of incompetence."[84] A year later, however, it was clear that one of the major parties of the Right, the People's party, would not sufficiently compromise to ensure the vital interests of Evangelical churches. As early as December 1927 opponents of the bill joined the People's party in the Reichstag's Education Committee to adjust the bill's provisions to square more fully with the announced reservations of the People's party—even to the point of allowing schools in the new common-school states to qualify as Simultan, thus shutting out confessional schools. Concluding that the Keudell bill had miscarried, the Center party insisted on a dissolution of the governing coalition and an end to committee deliberations.[85]

The abrupt and seemingly unnecessary collapse of these deliberations had a shattering effect on most Evangelical churchmen. The modest hope that the Kirchenausschuss's Education Committee had expressed for the bill in early December turned into gloom as the Keudell bill followed its predecessors to the scrap heap of junked legislation. It was frustrating enough that years of systematic efforts, above all in the parents' movement, had come to naught in the federal political arena, though the Kirchenausschuss gamely resolved to carry on.[86] How disgustingly unfair it seemed that the party system should spurn the apparent wish of most parents for confessional schools. What deepened this frustration was the painful realization that the only possible constellation of parties capable of passing such a bill had badly missed an opportunity that might not recur. A future Reichstag majority of Centrists and Nationalists defied the imagination. In fact, the dissolution of the coalition in February 1928 spelled the end of all concerted efforts to resolve the school imbroglio for the duration of the Republic.

In 1924 Pastor Reinhard Mumm accurately assessed the "struggle for the Christian school" as the "greatest struggle" that involved churches under the Republic.[87] What worried Old-Prussian churchmen was the progressive secularization of German life—condemned collectively as materialism—that seemed to eat out the Christian substance of German culture and to impoverish the Volkskirche. Only in confessional schools and confessional religious instruction, it seemed, could the culturally creative force of Christianity leave a desired impact on future generations otherwise exposed to corrosive materialism.[88] Common schools—conceived as secular schools with ad hoc religious instruction—would constrict this creative force, and secular schools would smother it altogether. The religionless state, subject to the same materialist forces as common and secular schools, could hardly defend or restore the vital linkage of Christianity and culture. For that reason, gaps in legislation shielding confessional education appeared all the more threatening than they had under the Christian state, and the prospect of closing them all the more compelling.

Critics of confessional education nettled nationalist churchmen by leveling the charge that confessional schools would perpetuate ideological fissures within the elusive folk community (*Volksgemeinschaft*). Church leaders countered that the gospel engendered a commitment to the folk community that mere physical togetherness in common schools could not match.[89] This frame of reference and its concomitant stress upon the cultural-creative function of Christianity legitimated confessional education as well as the Volkskirche.

Could the folkish nationalism that swept along schoolteachers as well reconcile them to the church under a common cause? By mid-decade various church commentators had begun to express this hope.[90] But most teachers would not recognize the claim of the church to be the guardian of German culture with a right to observe and safeguard religious instruction. Only after the federal government, under Chancellor Papen, had seized the Prussian government on July 20, 1932, did the Kultusministerium implement the wishes of the Old-Prussian Church Senate. One may well question retrospectively whether the church's insistence on observing religion classes had been worth the certain cost of alienating teachers, who had persisted after 1927 in besieging the Senate and Kultusministerium alike with embittered protests. But one must keep the context in sight. Ensuring proper religious instruction would bring some assurance of staying the apparent erosion of Christian culture and the decline of the Volkskirche.[91] The gravity of the situation seemed to justify the undeniable costs of such insistence.

One cannot conclude from the disappointing denouement of the Keudell bill that the churches had lost their "greatest struggle," even though they clearly had not won it. During the Weimar era, Ernst Helmreich rightly observed, "Traditional religious values were no doubt being upheld more by the schools than by German society as a whole."[92] That such a thought could have consoled Old-Prussian church leaders, however, is doubtful.

5

VOLKSKIRCHE ACTIVISM:
Family, Folk, and Economy

IN ITS PATRIOTIC proclamation, the 1927 Church Federation Assembly asserted that the church "cannot neglect to apply, independently and with candor, eternal moral standards to legislation and administration and represent in the whole of public life the demands of the Christian conscience."[1] These words suggested the turn toward activism that the Revolution of 1918 prompted. Clearly the Old-Prussian and other Evangelical churches aspired to become, in the words with which the EOK had disparaged political activism in 1895, "an authoritative cooperating factor in political and social conflicts of the day."

The most provocative conceptualization of the activism that coursed through the Old-Prussian church can be found in two books written by Otto Dibelius, general superintendent of the Kurmark in Brandenburg. *Das Jahrhundert der Kirche,* first published in 1926, advanced Dibelius's thesis, which he rushed to defend against his critics in the second, *Nachspiel,* published in 1928. It was to encourage parishioners to participate responsibly in a church finally freed of the state that Dibelius took up his pen.[2] In *Nachspiel,* he conjured an apocalyptic scenario, already adumbrated in *Jahrhundert,* that suggested the urgency of such participation.[3] The religionless Republic, incapable of generating cultural values, might succumb to the antireligious crusade of world Communism, provoking a showdown between Western Christian culture, then declining, and the ascendant atheism of the East. Only the church, never the state, could engender genuine culture and stay its degeneration. Since moral issues impinged on every area of life, the church, as a Volkskirche, ought to address its message to the whole of German life through a comprehensive program. Especially the Volkskirche must promote love and justice in the interest of social reconciliation.

Like Dibelius, Weimar churchmen often drew their inspiration from Adolf Stoecker. One might call him the apostle to the Weimarians, for the course of events since his death seemed to justify his views. Stoecker perceived that the reality of the Christian state had grown increasingly questionable and drew conclusions that Dibelius advanced as a goal for the Weimar church—a free Volkskirche performing a social and cultural mission within the context of Christian conservative thought. It was no coincidence that the 1925 General Synod commemorated Stoecker's ninetieth birthday with a special ceremony.[4]

Dibelius believed that if by its activism the church awoke to the challenge of secularism, it stood on the promising threshold of a "century of the church," the title of his first book. The optimism that pervaded his writing characterized to a lesser extent much of the Old-Prussian church by mid-decade. The tribulations of this church since 1918 had prompted a sense of church solidarity unknown to prewar church life. The churches had managed to survive the efforts of the revolution (as churchmen viewed them) to enfeeble the Volkskirche as a public force. It seemed that millions of parishioners had expressed their support for church causes, most notably in the Volkskirche movement and in the mobilization of church members for Christian schools. Before and after Dibelius published his summons, churchmen exalted in these efforts of the church to emerge as a force in public life.

Liberals least appreciated this thrust for the internal conformity that it would compel in a Volkskirche that tended to close fronts toward the outside. In *Nachspiel,* Dibelius wrote: "There are finally things in which the church must have a unified will."[5] More than ever the Old-Prussian church—so some church liberals charged—seemed to resemble the Catholic church as a closed-front Volkskirche that sacrificed the church as a purely spiritual force.[6] To this objection, Dibelius replied that the church, unlike the sect, should assert itself in public life because of its sociological nature as a Volkskirche concerned for the folk, not because of a drive for power or any desire to ape Catholicism.

The task that Kaftan assigned Evangelical churches, the same that Dibelius elaborated in his own way, led churchmen to a heightened concern for the perceived breakdown of the orders of creation under the

Republic: the family, the economy, the state, and, beyond Luther's enumeration, the folk. The stress of Lutheranism upon the organic integration of the individual into the orders of creation easily faded into the conservatism that reduced liberalism to an atomist construct, that viewed individualism with suspicion for subverting a sense of community, and that exalted folk above party and individual. Both the Church Assembly social proclamation of 1924 and the patriotic proclamation of 1927 regarded the orders as dissolving under the impact of materialism. Both reaffirmed the classic Lutheran position that morality emanating from faith could restore the orders to their divinely intended functions by rejuvenating communitarian responsibility. Neither impugned the Republic. But the cast of thought that exalted organic wholeness took on an antirepublican coloration when conservative churchmen deplored the Republic for indulging individual and class selfishness.

Typical of this tendency were the systematic ethics of the highly esteemed theologian Reinhold Seeberg, for years chairman of the Church-Social Conference and after 1923 chairman of the Central Committee of the Inner Mission. To Seeberg, the family, the economy, the state, and the folk were orders of creation, or Gemeinschaften, historically evolved involuntary associations. Imbued with love of neighbor, the Christian sought in each order to follow three divinely ordained immanent laws: expediency, freedom, and continuity. Like most churchmen, Seeberg believed that the natural orders suffered from an inordinate emphasis upon freedom, which acted to transform them into voluntary associations, subject to man's will and unresponsive to God's laws: "A state, in which the authority of government has gone over to . . . the broad masses; a family, in which . . . children command parents . . . ; a society, in which the forces of tradition . . . are scorned and destroyed etc., subordinate expediency and continuity and thereby also oppose divine will. These types of perversions destroy their organisms."[7] Like Kaftan and Dibelius, Seeberg believed that the impact of Christianity could only diminish as Christian imponderables, rooted in tradition (continuity), dissolved.

Understandably, in view of its origins, the fledgling Church Federation took on the task of promoting the Volkskirche's activist role. Church leaders generally defined this role as Kaftan understood it—that of preserving Christian society in the absence of a Christian state.[8] Wilhelm Pechmann, president of the Church Assembly, concluded: "We need a Kirchenausschuss that must be ready day and night to watch out for whatever in public life threatens our Evangelical church and to take prompt countermeasures." Reports to the 1921, 1924, and 1927 church assemblies show that the Kirchenausschuss represented the Church Federation on a wide spectrum of issues and took the initiative according to its prerogatives.

This chapter explores the efforts of the churches to help restore the orders of the family, folk, and economy. (Chapters 6 and 7 will examine the political attitudes and activities of churchmen in the political order.) So far, the interplay of conservative churchmen, who dominated the Old-Prussian church, and church liberals has been highlighted. Two other groups of churchmen soon made their presence known: to the political left of Democratic liberals arose the religious-socialist movement that sought to formulate a unitary ethic through an amalgamation of Christianity and socialism; to the political right of the conservative group developed a folkish movement within the Old-Prussian church that would amalgamate folk values and Christianity through racism. Neither extreme group wielded any significant power in the Old-Prussian church before 1927, though each challenged the church to respond to the group's immediate concern.

MORALITY LEGISLATION

In the Weimar period, churchmen commonly perceived an alarming break-down of Christian morality that had destructive consequences for the family. Because materialism in all its forms appeared to deny the individual's responsibility to God's orders, synods passed resolutions urging congregations to fight the corrupting spirit of the Weimar era. The church and its servants also promoted a welter of legislative acts meant to safeguard the moral environment and strengthen family ties.

Concern for morality legislation was nothing new in the churches. New was the context provided by the unhappy ending of the war and the emergence of the Republic. The same self-centered materialism that had helped cause Germany's defeat and had erected a religionless Republic seemed to thwart efforts at folk renewal. Frequently church leaders coupled moral rejuvenation with the nationalist cause of restoring Germany's political prominence in the world. The Kirchenausschuss and church governments followed attentively the progress of morality bills in the legislature and took timely positions on them. The Inner Mission and the large nexus of church free associations joined church organs in promoting these legislative measures and occasionally in organizing petition drives.

In several instances the Weimar constitution made allowance for morality legislation. Article 118 allowed for legislation regulating cinemas, literature, and public entertainment accessible to youth. Supporting regulation in all three areas, the churches saw only part of their suggestions put into law.[9] Reinhard Mumm, chairman of the Reichstag Education Committee, considered himself the "father" of both the cinema and literature laws. In 1920 the Weimar Assembly passed legislation governing the censorship of films and the admission of minors to them. Churchmen and synods deplored the flood of what they perceived as "smutty" literature that engulfed Germany after the revolution. In 1926 the Reichstag passed a law to curtail the circulation of such literature among minors. Despite the urgent plea of the Kirchenausschuss and several Evangelical youth organizations, however, federal legislation to exclude minors from certain places of public entertainment was not enacted, and the church's continual protest against the extension of the "police hour"—the compulsory closing time—was heard but not heeded.

Prostitution was another issue that continually rankled churchmen. Until 1927, state governments regulated prostitution by confining it to bordellos in a specified section of the city. Even before the war a women's "abolitionist" movement agitated to have bordellos, considered hotbeds of venereal diseases, abolished and treatment of infected carriers made mandatory. The large German-Evangelical Women's League and others like it passionately supported the abolitionist cause. The result of Reichstag deliberations was a law passed in 1927 embodying abolitionist demands, though prostitution, to the chagrin of the Kirchenausschuss, was not explicitly declared illegal.[10]

Church assemblies, the Kirchenausschuss, the Inner Mission, and other free associations pressed the federal government to submit a bill that would prohibit the sale of alcoholic beverages to minors and permit voters within each community to determine whether liquor licenses might be issued or denied. Embarrassed churchmen were jolted to discover that Socialists and Communists, not the Nationalists and the People's party, fell in with their plea for local option. Repeated failure to pass the desired legislation stimulated a local-option movement that swelled to sizable proportions under the guidance of the Methodist church leader, Dr. Otto Melle. His committee, encouraged by the Kirchenausschuss, managed to collect nearly half a million signatures on petitions in support of the local-option bill of 1923. This committee again dramatized its accomplishments in May 1926 when it used two trucks to deliver 2 million signatures to the Reichstag. But the government, responding to the Reichstag majority, omitted local option from its bill for stricter controls. The failure of the local-option cause was but one of several issues that persuaded some disillusioned churchmen to consider founding a genuine Evangelical party as an alternative to voting for parties of the Right.[11]

Typical of many churchmen, Johannes Schneider, the church statistician, ascribed the rise in crime after the revolution to the values of the new order. "The masses understand the political slogan of 'freedom,'" wrote Schneider when the "crime wave" peaked, "as doing primarily what one will regardless of any kind of regulation and law."[12] Not since the Thirty Years' War, he continued, had German morality sunk to such low depths. By 1927, however, the crime rate had fallen to a trifle over that of 1910.

Degenerate literature and films, the craze for questionable entertainment, alcoholism, prostitution, and crime betokened to alarmed churchmen a progressive destruction of the German family, the basic cell of the social organism that required renewal for the well-being of state and folk alike. The materialism that caused these social ills also ate at the fabric of the family from within, as the sharp increase in the incidence of divorce, illegitimate births, and abortion suggested. Many indignant churchmen castigated Socialists for introducing Reichstag legislation in 1920 that would weaken existing laws on divorce and abortion. If Socialists had their way, warned *Der Reichsbote,* immorality would be legalized and left unpunished, promiscuity encouraged, and the population reduced.[13] To the 1927 Church Assembly the decline in the birth rate signaled "degeneration and moral decay." Family ties and the willingness to sacrifice for the sake of child rearing no longer seemed strong enough to sustain healthy family life. Some churchmen saw the enfeeblement of the nation as a result, and others contended that Germany required a growing population for her future survival.[14] The housing shortage, especially, seemed to require immediate remedy, for many of the social evils associated with the disintegration of the family could be traced to this basic need. In fact, a 1925 Kirchenausschuss proclamation saw in the problem "our most important social task."[15] Acting as a "public conscience," the Kirchenausschuss appealed to local, state, and federal governments and the public in general to concentrate on the problem's solution.

In no area but public education did the attitude of the public and the government toward a vital church interest change so dramatically as in that of the Sunday blue laws. Here the Old-Prussian church most tangibly sensed the demise of the Christian state, and here the churches fought a losing battle for a Christian Sunday. Before the war federal codes and Prussian laws had enforced "Sunday rest" (Sonntagsruhe). Work was prohibited, or where unavoidable restricted, and public activities that competed with Sunday services were likewise forbidden. The war effort eroded the enforcement of these regulations, and the Prussian republican government perpetuated this laxity. Enforcement of prewar regulations devolved on local authorities, who, in the eyes of churchmen, made little effort to enforce them. An indignant superintendent complained, "When you travel through the countryside for a few hours to conduct church visitations, you see field work where formerly the police and good customs called a halt."[16]

Synods and church assemblies passed resolutions calling for the enforcement of "Sunday rest," and the EOK and Kirchenausschuss continually represented the church's complaint to state and federal governments. Old-Prussian church leaders looked askance when the Republic set political elections permanently on Sundays and when parties chose Sundays, especially at the time of services, for political rallies. In 1920 the General Synod inaugurated the policy of asking congregations to persuade local authorities to enforce "Sunday rest," especially during Sunday services. The 1925 General Synod tried another tactic, recommending that church authorities reach agreements with sports associations, political parties, and other organizations to reduce activities on Sundays and to sponsor nothing during Sunday services. Little came of either initiative.

FOLKISH NATIONALISM

Churchmen invoked nationalism to arouse public concern for morality legislation. This purpose hardly accounts, however, for the inflated folkish nationalism that pervaded church quarters during the war and the Weimar era. Not until World War I, Karl Barth has claimed, did German Protestant theologians begin to regard the folk as an order of creation.[17] The elevation of the folk to such status, however, appears to have signified a change more in degree than in kind. Long before the war, Protestants had claimed that Lutheranism in particular had molded the national ethos (Volkstum), associating closely the distinctive values of Protestantism and Germanness (Deutschtum). No new theological perception, but rather four sets of circumstances, fired folkish nationalism within the church.

The first, the disestablishment crisis, generated a need to justify the endangered Volkskirche in order to secure its privileges and outreach. Kaftan and others argued that the Volkskirche ought to remain the custodian of folk values. This function appeared all the more crucial with the demise of the Christian state. Within Volkskirche theory the amalgamation of Christian and German values inevitably set the face of the church against allegedly antinational ideologies.

The war created a second set of circumstances. Churchmen cherished memories of August 1914, when the German people had set aside internal animosities to respond to the challenge of war as a unified folk.[18] As perceived by war theologians, God had employed the war to bring about a moral and religious renewal of the folk. Since renewal also meant renewal of God-given German values, the war was increasingly perceived as a struggle of values. As the war effort collapsed, war theologians especially concluded that the folk had tragically rejected God's summons for renewal. Could the German folk recover the essence of its values after its defection? For many churchmen, answering this question affirmatively became an act of faith, though they despaired continually.

A third set of circumstances was the establishment of a democratic order following military collapse and revolution. Stahl, Kaftan, and Seeberg, each in his own way, had seen the indispensability of a Christianized national ethos as a makeweight to an amoral individual freedom that gave vent to self-interest and materialism at the expense of the commonweal. The Christian monarchy had presumably tried to check this egoism in public life and to nourish the Christian ethos of the nation. With this check gone, the values of a Christianized national ethos lay more than ever exposed to the infection of materialism; and yet only these values could now cauterize the wound. The divisive operation of parliamentary democracy under the Republic seemed to express the materialism of special group interests and to make a mockery of the national ethos that could bond a national community. Conversion to the folkish ethos, already shaped by Christianity, would presumably orient values toward common goals and thereby undercut individual and group self-interest. A basic folk solidarity also seemed necessary to build a state strong enough to defend the fatherland against the predatory victors of the recent war. Speaking to a Nationalist party convention, Professor Friedrich Brunstäd declared: "Our state is powerless today because our folk is so decomposed and decayed and because it has lost its basis in national values and ideals."[19]

The folkish nationalism that animated the Old-Prussian church, however, did not necessarily undercut the parliamentary system. Nationalism could be viewed as a means of creating the consensus required to mute the discord of political life. Most churchmen certainly had no illusions that a state imbued with a folkish ethos could erect a conflict-free German utopia. But folkish nationalism in the church was at least latently antiparliamentarian for its suspicion of a pluralistic society and the mechanism that expressed this society politically. Many did pit folkish nationalism against parliamentary democracy as a consequence.

In view of the rampant nationalism aroused by the first three sets of circumstances, the fourth appears improbable. As the 1920s wore on, other brands of nationalism gathered strength, collectively known as the "new" nationalism of the "Conservative Revolution."[20] They exhibited an even more intense nationalism than that of conservative churchmen, who found it ironic and affronting to be cast in the role of lesser patriots. More serious, new nationalists appeared to ignore or even reject the notion of a Christianized national ethos. They conceived of nationalism in a competing religious sense that might rule out Christianity as an intrusion of foreign or superfluous values.

The intellectual content of the Conservative Revolution, like that of folkish nationalism in church quarters, is hard to grasp because of its nonrational cast. New nationalists assumed that a member of the folk could only intuit the vital forces of his national ethos, not analyze them rationally. They did not long for a restoration of the recent past, as did the "old" nationalists of the two conservative parties, especially the Nationalist. Rather, the new nationalists sought to penetrate beyond present societal divisions to the metaphysical unity of the folk, which had the potential for spawning a new folk community (Volksgemeinschaft), characterized by common values and an organic structure. Inasmuch as folkish rebirth had to proceed from the metaphysical essence of the nation, liberal democracy appeared totally inappropriate within the desired folk community. For the liberal democracy of the Weimar Republic catered to the pluralistic nature of present German society—to a decadent "civilization." The advocates of the Conservative Revolution divided into three main groups—Young Conservatives, National Revolutionaries, and the "folkish" (völkisch)— each of which aspired to recover the metaphysical unity of the folk in a different way.

Initially grouped around Moeller van den Bruck, Young Conservatives sought unity and authority in the spiritual essence of the folk. This brand of new nationalism accorded better with the folkish nationalism of the church than either of the other two types. A spiritualist conceptualization of folk values need not ignore the contention of nationalist churchmen that Christianity had decisively shaped folk spirit.

For National Revolutionaries the war, stripping away the allegedly false values of a bourgeois civilization, had laid bare the vital forces needed to recreate a folk community and German military power. While one segment fell under the thrall of the war-front experience, another combined nationalism and Bolshevism in a startling farrago that expressed the common desire of new nationalists to engender a social or socialist folk community.

The third group — the "folkish" — aspired to restore a prehistorical German culture that had subsequently been contaminated. In the Weimar era, "völkisch" often meant "racist," connoting a virulent anti-Semitism as well. This book applies the term *folkish* in a considerably broader sense — to old and new nationalism alike, since both revolved around the concept of folk. In this broader sense, the nationalism of conservative churchmen was obviously folkish, often anti-Semitic, but rarely and only tangentially racist. As used here, *racism* means the attribution of inner qualities and attitudes to racial types. If biology determined all values, Christian revelation could determine none. The cast of their theology discouraged orthodox conservative churchmen from subscribing to a racist folkish nationalism, though they were tempted. Theirs was a cultural nationalism that underscored the historical impact of Christianity upon the national ethos. Since the folkish and church leaders differed fundamentally on the content of the national ethos, the church could come to terms less easily with the racist folkish movement than with the other two brands of new nationalism.

Church leaders appreciated the moral effects of the new nationalism and the spiritual longing that seemed to accompany it. Much as they sympathized, they feared the new nationalism for ignoring or rejecting the Christian content of the national ethos and undercutting the spiritual mission of the Volkskirche. The new nationalism penetrated the middle classes, from which the churches drew their greatest support, and caught the imagination of many of the younger generation. The fear arose that, if the churches did not demonstrate ever more conspicuously their deep commitment to the nationalist movement, much of it, like the labor movement decades before, could be lost to the Volkskirche. Quite as important, the churches needed to draw lines consonant with Volkskirche theory even as they strained to accommodate the spirit of the new nationalism.

The Königsberg Church Assembly of 1927 intended to meet both needs. Its patriotic proclamation began by stressing the supranational communion of Christians, warning that no folk could claim God's cause as its own. It then showed the extent to which the churches could oblige the burgeoning nationalist movement. God had ordained the German national ethos and variety among peoples, giving to each a distinctive gift and task within a larger humanity. The patriotic stance of Jesus, Paul, and Luther showed that the churches must reject a cosmopolitanism devoid of folk responsibilities. In one of two keynote speeches at the Church Assembly, Wilhelm Kahl enumerated various patriotic statements made by Evangelical churches to demonstrate that they had practiced what they now preached. Having set forth the churches' commitment to the national ethos, the proclamation proceeded to defend a Christianized national ethos against the new nationalism. For a thousand years Christianity and Germanness had interpenetrated to produce a distinctive German Christianity. "To the gospel . . . our folk owes its deepest and religious convictions and the most precious component of its spiritual education."[21] The word *deepest* contested the right of the new nationalism to cut Germanness loose from its Christian anchor.

These four circumstances — the disestablishment crisis, the war experience, the disintegration of the political order, and the diffusion of the new nationalism — appear to have moved theologians and others formally to rank the folk among the orders of creation. They placed a premium on composing divisions in the folk for the sake of communitarian unity. Conceiving of the folk as an order served their purposes admirably. As an order, the folk received divine ordination. Like other orders, the folk appeared as one of the structural givens of nature, and thus one ordained by God. Primary responsibilities flowed directly from this crucial assumption. As a God-created given, the folk, like other orders, assumed the form of an involuntary association, a community of "fate," into which one was born and by which one acquired responsibilities that could lapse if the folk were merely a voluntary association. Just as the other orders ought to be organically composed to serve the commonweal, so, too, ought the folk, setting a brake on individual and class egoism. Only war theology could have stressed more firmly the ethical responsibilities that Christians owed the folk short of viewing the national ethos as God's revelation itself.

The question whether the "sick" German folk might, like any other organism, "die" was frequently asked by conservative churchmen.[22] Christian nationalism, the prescribed cure, would fortify social sensitivity and entrench a sense of social justice, both needed to control the symptoms of this disease, the discordant life of Weimar Germany. Nursing the folk back to health appeared as the church's most important social responsibility.

One can gauge the intensity of folkish nationalism within church quarters in the attitudes that churchmen showed toward war, folkish religiosity, and Jews. Generally, the more intense the nationalism displayed, the less the ideological readiness to accommodate the Republic.

Attitudes Toward War and Peace

One can find little warrant for folkish nationalism in the New Testament. Especially in the parable of the good Samaritan, Jesus made clear that one's neighbor was not defined by one's ethnicity. Folkish nationalists, however, assumed that love of neighbor meant uniquely love of folk members, and love of folk could therefore mean callous disregard for other peoples. Such a conclusion can be drawn from the writings of Emanuel Hirsch, Reinhold Seeberg, and Paul Althaus. These three respected Protestant theologians had come to an appreciation of war coupled with disdain for political liberalism and the Republic.

In *Deutschlands Schicksal,* published in 1920, Hirsch extolled international anarchy as natural and desirable.[23] In war, an instrument of historical justice, God blessed with victory those who fought with unflagging determination. Obviously, there could be no such thing as the war guilt ascribed to Germany in the Versailles treaty. Likewise, international law and the League of Nations were preposterous, even immoral, conceptions, for they would stifle the growth of nations and thwart historical justice. Because Germany lay prostrate at the feet of its enemies, it was in danger of succumbing to the judgment of God in history. Germans therefore had to cultivate a passionate desire to burst their bonds, suppress internal class and private interests, and find unity in folkish nationalism.

Seeberg's *System der Ethik,* also published in 1920, reflected a similar social-Darwinist orientation.[24] Like Hirsch, Seeberg believed that, as nations waxed strong and grew weak, war might justifiably adjust their holdings. Though perpetual peace seemed impossible, a just but temporary peace could be concluded whenever this adjustment had been reached. Unfortunately, the Versailles settlement had proved unjust, because weaker nations collaborated to deny Germany a peace commensurate with its true strength. They sought to perpetuate this settlement through the League of Nations, supposedly the disinterested guardian of international law. Germany could resume its rightful place in the world only if it found its unity once again in folkish values.

Althaus's *Staatsgedanken und Reich Gottes*, published in 1923, offered a slightly different framework.[25] Each nation had received from God a calling that only a few inspired leaders, steeped in national traditions, could fathom, Althaus wrote. Correctly assessing the mission and potentialities of his folk, the statesman must exploit the opportunities that international affairs afforded for the realization of the national calling. Althaus recognized no static morality that could govern international relations, only a historical justice that determined the rhythmic rise and fall of nations according to their success in following their callings.

The three would assure divine sanction for war against the detested Versailles settlement, since God willed and presided over a world of perpetual conflict. More clearly than Seeberg, Hirsch and Althaus added the corollary that God blessed or condemned peoples, whom He had called into being and endowed, by their response to His challenge in war. Repeated here was a basic assumption of war theology that was now generalized into a theology of history. War was inherent in nature. If so, the conduct of the folk, responding to cosmic necessities, could not be called into account by a morality that gospel could inspire—by the doctrine of the just war or by the command to love one's neighbor. If these war theologians separated Luther's two Regimente in this way, they also fused them with respect to the folkish commitment of the individual. For the domain of law—folkish ethical responsibilities—became an object of God's redemptive actions in history.

War theology colored statements of churchmen even when they did not clearly subscribe to it. But this view of war fell far short of dominating the Old-Prussian church. Religious Socialists and some liberals condemned anything smacking of war theology. Appalled by the unbridled nationalism and carnage of the recent war, they held modern-day "Lutherans" responsible for dissolving the dualist ethic and for sanctioning war without question.[26] War theology, moreover, had unfortunate practical implications for nationalist churchmen most susceptible to it. If they accepted it, they would logically need to accept as well the verdict of Versailles as the just, if temporary, verdict of God in history. Some failed to see this consequence. Seeberg did and, as noted, found a way to avoid it. In any event, the churches pressed in the opposite direction for a revision of an *unjust* verdict on the grounds of a universal sense of justice that foreign churches and other nations could readily acknowledge. Without any elaboration, the patriotic proclamation set the churches against war theology: "As it [the church} seeks peace among peoples, so it promotes freedom and justice for its own people."[27]

Church advocacy of seeking peace while demanding justice for Germany concealed other differences on war within the Old-Prussian church. War resulted from sin, the most prevalent view held, not from creation—and no more than sin could war be eliminated from human affairs. Both were inevitable.[28] Reaction against the Versailles treaty deepened the pessimism of this traditionally Lutheran point of reference. Rarely does one find churchmen directly advocating a just war to burst the bonds of Versailles; but suggestive statements abound urging a moral-religious rebirth of the folk for the sake of defending the fatherland and restoring its role in the world.[29] It is hard to say whether their authors welcomed the prospect of a just war or merely pressed for peaceful treaty revision. Attacks on pacifism in church quarters, the consequence of regarding war as either natural or inevitable, served more directly to strengthen the German will to resist the exactions of the enemy. Pacifism seemed suspect for suggesting that the peace of Versailles could or should be lasting.[30]

In the face of this deep resentment, moderate optimists had difficulty getting a fair hearing in the churches for the positive implications of the traditional Lutheran attitude toward war. If war resulted from sin, Christians and the churches ought to work for peace, just as they sought to curb the effects of sin. War was *not* inevitable. Such was the message carried by moderate nationalists like Otto Dibelius and Theodor Kaftan, the former general superintendent of the Lutheran Landeskirche of Schleswig-Holstein.[31] Both moderate nationalists, like Kaftan, and moderate pacifists, like Martin Rade, could collaborate in the World Alliance for Promoting International Friendship through the Churches, promoted in Germany by Friedrich Siegmund-Schultze. Kaftan's nationalism seemed to differ from Rade's pacifism only in temperament, not in content.

Rade, though no thoroughgoing pacifist, held that Christianity ought to dispose one toward world peace. Christ commanded love of neighbor, praised peacemakers, and rebuked Pharisees, the Jewish "war party." Rade saw no connection whatever between the "convictions of Jesus and any kind of current revenge Christianity." By exhaling fiery nationalism, war theologians alarmed former enemies without deriving any tangible advantages. It was in Germany's interest, Rade argued, to act as an exemplary proponent of peace.[32]

Though liberals breathed nationalism before the war, they more than any other church group split over the issue of pacifism, both during the war and after. Many, like Otto Baumgarten and Martin Rade, held the middle ground between war theology and extreme pacifism. Rade reserved the right "to go with my folk" in case of war.[33] Because many liberals remained extreme nationalists, however, liberals debated the war-peace issue as a matter of vital importance.

At a convention of the Friends of *Die christliche Welt* in October 1923, for example, two pastors, the Nationalist Johannes Kübel and Socialist Georg Shümer, locked horns in heated debate.[34] In countless places, Kübel contended, the Bible viewed war as endemic to society, and distinguished between war and murder. Schümer asserted that the moral predisposition required by Jesus ruled out participation in war. Kübel reasoned that the Sermon on the Mount might not apply to war and that national security should override any appeal to principle. Arguing for the necessity of a unitary ethic, Schümer replied that the exercise of power ought to follow Christian principles even at the risk of courting national disaster. To Kübel, love of neighbor meant, above all, love of countryman; but to Schümer, every man was equally his neighbor. Kübel argued, and Schümer flatly denied, that the national ethos and the state represented God-given values that demanded unlimited obedience. While Kübel foresaw a continual circuit of wars, Schümer looked forward optimistically to a peaceful world order.

Characteristically, nationalist churchmen reasoned that talk of international reconciliation by even moderate pacifists played into the hands of the enemy, since moral commitment to folk seemed to diminish correspondingly. In 1922, President Pechmann of the Church Assembly, for example, lamented "that there are Germans who mean to serve the understanding and reconciliation of peoples by surrendering lightly their own fatherland and its life interests and its inalienable rights. To these Germans, unfortunately, D. Siegmund-Schultze also belongs."[35] But Siegmund-Schultze, a moderate pacifist, often bristled at Allied treatment of Germany.

The war-peace issue hardly lent itself to rational discussion, and little followed the Kübel-Schümer debate. If the relatively close-knit Friends of *Die christliche Welt* found no resolution, there could be little hope of reaching a consensus in the church, where a similar spectrum of views prevailed. Most churchmen found themselves somewhere between extremes, but they generally leaned toward the nationalist pole. In Rade's opinion, the church had grown so nationalistic by 1927 as to jeopardize the Volkskirche: "Already many of our folk—must one not say: half?—believe that our churches, our pastors nurture war instead of peace."[36] The broad democratic masses, wrote Rade, were sick of war and repelled by attacks on pacifism found in church papers and delivered from pulpits.

Types of Extreme Nationalism

If most churchmen leaned toward extreme nationalism, how far could the most extreme church nationalists lean? Several years after the war the new nationalist movement inspired the formation of a racist folkish church party and later an influential group of nonracist Young Conservative theologians. Both new nationalist types challenged the church, already intensely nationalistic, to rise to even higher levels of folkish preoccupation.

The League for a German Church (Bund für deutsche Kirche), the racist church party, went so far as to recast traditional Christianity as a nationalist religion. Nicknamed the German Church (Deutschkirche), the league drew much of its theology from the Germanic Christianity of Houston Stewart Chamberlain, whom it acclaimed as its godfather. After the war, Chamberlain urged his followers to establish a religious society for the cultivation of Germanic Christianity. But those who founded the league in 1921, a small group of folkish enthusiasts at the Arndt Hochschule in Berlin, had far greater ambitions. They believed that they had greater prospects of converting the folk to Germanic Christianity as a church party within the Volkskirche than as an isolated esoteric sect.[37]

The foremost founder, organizer, leader, strategist, and theologian of the German Church was a young and gifted teacher, Dr. Joachim Kurd Niedlich. Reared in a pastor's home that was as politically conservative as it was religiously orthodox, Niedlich, like many of his generation and profession, had responded with enthusiasm to the tug of racist folkish nationalism by 1921. Pastor Bublitz, an obscure country pastor in Brandenburg, edited the league's periodical, *Die Deutschkirche,* which began publishing in 1922. Later Niedlich joined him as coeditor. Until his death in 1928, Niedlich worked at a frenzied pace to organize local groups and to produce the literature that broadcast the synthetic religion of the league.[38]

One can understand German Church theology, as represented chiefly by Niedlich and Bublitz, by reducing it to three propositions.[39] The first was that God revealed Himself through the differing values of the races that He had created. Accordingly, the Aryan or German could experience God in Germanness as revealed in folktales and myths as well as through "prophets" of the folk as varied as Luther and Beethoven.

If it hoped to synthesize Christianity and Germanness, the league needed to accord Jesus a central position in its theology. But Jesus, as a Jew, seemed grievously ill suited for incorporation within a distinctively Germanic religion. Accordingly, the German Church advanced its second proposition: Jesus must have been Aryan, not Jewish. Historical speculation, at least within racist folkish circles, seemed to warrant the conclusion that Jesus's Jewishness was unproven, and that one could believe in the possibility of His Germanness. Aryan tribes had allegedly penetrated the Near East in the remote past. Lingering doubts could largely be laid to rest by showing that Jesus spoke and acted like an Aryan: since Jesus espoused Aryan values, he must have had Aryan blood, which would, of course, account for His Aryan ideals. To be sure, German Church theologians claimed that each folk could only perceive Jesus through its own values. What the league saw in Jesus, however, was nothing more than His Germanness.

Since Germanness determined what was Christian and what was not, German Church theologians denied that the Old Testament, a Jewish folk history revealing an alien mentality, could anticipate and testify to an Aryan Jesus. Accordingly, they put forward a third proposition: the church should deprive the Old Testament of its canonical legitimacy and pare down the New Testament to its Aryan core.

Given these three propositions, the German Church aspired to break down Jewish influences on Christianity, which, in its present form, seemed no more than a Jewish Christianity in an Aryan society. Jewish and Aryan morality, so held the league, clashed as opposites. Concern for reward and punishment and thus calculation for material gain characterized the Jewish mentality; the Aryan sought the good for its own sake. The main reason for this contrast was to show that Germans were not innately materialistic and that Jews were. It then followed that the materialism afflicting the folk came from Jews and that the churches unwittingly promoted value infection by extolling the immorality of the Old Testament as God's revealed will. Germans already had an equivalent Old Testament in the testimony of their Germanness (myths, folktales, prophets). Even parts of the New Testament revealed a questionable Jewish religiosity. St. Paul's theology of law and gospel marked the apostle as a spiritual crossbreed. He had appropriated the gospel of the Aryan Jesus, but, as a Jew, he had retained law, and thus the Jewish morality of reward and punishment, as he formulated a distinctive Jewish Christianity. Even Luther had failed to break the materialist shackles of Jewish Christianity, though his Germanness allowed him to recover the altruism of the Aryan Jesus.[40]

Restoration of the pure Jesus religion, claimed the German Church, would undercut the Jewish materialism of German folk life. Jesus, personifying the highest of Aryan ideals, was no Jewish sacrificial lamb but rather an Aryan hero who fought for his cause to a tragic end without any thought of personal reward or punishment.[41] By emulating an Aryan Jesus, Germans would, in effect, model themselves after their own ideal selves. They would recover the ideals of self-sacrifice and altruistic dedication that the folk required for its integration. By denying any notion of transcendent revelation through a divine Jesus, the German Church managed to confine revelation to the folk, enlarging the Germanic component of a synthetic religion that had little left to synthesize.

Though anti-Semitic, the league assumed in Germanic form certain features of Jewish religious development: a Germanic Old Testament, an Aryan messiah, and a German religious community. Such a scheme compelled a redefinition of the Volkskirche as the German folk community. Accordingly, Bublitz could argue in 1923: "Today the church has only one task: to cooperate in the rebirth of the German people from the inside out. Service to German folk comrades remains even in better times the sole obligation of the pastor."[42] Germanic Christianity seemed to its adherents a more powerful bonding agent of the folk than the prescription of conservative churchmen, for the bonding agent was religion and race and not merely religiously induced ethical responsibility.

By underscoring faith in Germanness as the only major prerequisite for league membership, the German Church tried to steer clear of traditional dogmatic squabbles that its theology might otherwise precipitate. This strategy appears to have guided its efforts to expand and to have attracted nationalist Protestants otherwise repelled by its theology. At least, the German Church claimed to have found adherents in all church parties. In the first elections under the new Old-Prussian church constitution in 1925, the league managed to get twenty on its slate elected to provincial synods —seven to each of the Pomeranian and Silesian, and three to each of the Brandenburg and Saxon. Because of strength in provincial synods, the league placed four members, among them Niedlich, on the General Synod that met in 1925 and 1927. These initial election successes, however, fell considerably short of German Church aspirations. Since only a scant 5 to 10 percent of congregational members voted, its leaders calculated that the German Church ought to reach an eventual majority by mobilizing the 10 percent of the electorate that was most ardently folkish.[43]

A look at the measures that the German Church sponsored at provincial synods and the General Synod reveals its concern for raising racial consciousness and warding off racial dangers. The four provincial synods passed a proposal to convert official church titles into German. Three endorsed folk-rooted adult education in the countryside, and two church-aided genealogical research. One passed a proposal that pastoral candidates receive instruction in folk studies and folk health. As its most notable achievement, the league cited its success in persuading the General Synod to pass a motion favoring the incorporation of German "prophets" earlier and more emphatically in the religion curriculum of elementary schools. On such issues, differing conceptions of the national ethos did not necessarily divide nationalist churchmen. Synods refused to sanction league proposals that seemed inappropriate for the church or counter to its interests: certification of health before church weddings, opposition to clerical (and thus "Jewish Christian") supervision of elementary schools, optional rather than compulsory church collections for Jewish missions, prohibition of Jewish pastors, and avoidance of Jewish banks.[44]

As some proposals suggest, the German Church set high hopes on the potential of education. Here the battle for the folk allegedly raged between German and Jewish ideals. At the close of 1927, the German Church underscored the importance of education by noting the failure of the folkish movement to advance in politics. Folk renewal could more realistically be expected from malleable school children than from their intractable and voting elders. The Germanic Old Testament ought to crowd out the Jewish in elementary schools. Germanness ought to imbue Germanic Christian schools, which, for the sake of folk unity, ought to exist as the only permissible type. If the German Church could yet win control of the church, the influence that the church presently coveted over schools could be put to good use on behalf of Germanic Christianity.[45]

Concern for the political condition of the nation spurred the league's election ambitions as well. *Die Deutschkirche* did not usually heap abuse upon the Republic and its divisive party system. Its editors were persuaded that political criticism or even participation in folkish politics could do little to revitalize the folk. As a consequence, the league faulted the Nazi party for placing political and economic issues on its agenda ahead of religious renewal. Without such a renewal, the folkish state craved by the Nazis—and by the league—could scarcely emerge from the present chaos of values. The German Church claimed political neutrality for itself. But it is clear that the party system had no place in the league's vision of a folk reborn in its ideal image.[46] A folk reborn ought to rule out autonomous churches as well. Bublitz's "secret" ideal was a fusion of church and state as a consequence of mutual devotion to Germanness. Before the political future of the nation could be addressed, however, the folk required the rebirth that a church converted to Germanic Christianity could deliver.

German Church theology prompted the believer to ask how the folk soul could be brought to full consciousness through the ministry of the church. Once aware of its inherent value disposition, the folk would believe and act accordingly, and an appropriate transformation of society should follow. League responses to this question did not seem particularly extreme within the context of Weimar church life. Evangelical churches were inordinately preoccupied with the problem of rooting the church more firmly in the mentality of the folk. From German foreign missionaries around mid-decade the church press began to report a new concept of missions that seemed applicable to German as well as pagan society. Some missionaries had concluded that preaching a generalized Western brand of Christianity had wrongfully suppressed the pagan folk ethos. Pagans could presumably apprehend gospel only through folkish values implanted by God.[47] The German Church relished this insight as confirmation of its own. It experimented, however, with a new style of piety that passed far beyond psychological adjustment to folk peculiarities. It wished to evoke folk consciousness as gospel itself.

Germanic-Christian theology was assumed to reflect a piety of prior religious experience. Thus, the Germanic Old Testament ought to be studied not for the sake of new dogma but for old and abiding attitudes. To evoke the consciousness of his parishioners, the pastor should intuit the values of their—and his—racial souls.[48] Niedlich recommended that a pastor choose a third of his sermon texts from German prophets and folklore and the rest from the Aryan portion of the New Testament. Jewish words ought to be dropped from usage, and the sacraments transformed into folk dedication ceremonies drained of Jewish Christian theology. It made no sense to evoke German awareness with "Oriental" words and values. By 1926 the league had produced some twenty church services, or "masses," for different church occasions, and German Church pastors had begun to conduct such services in their own and neighboring churches.

The league fought along three related fronts. Within the church it fought for Germanness as the basis for unity, and claimed that only its program could breathe new life into a moribund church. Accordingly, the German Church would cherish recognition as the church's shock troops (Stosstrupp) on a second front: against the spirit of Jews and Rome alike.[49] On a third front it wished to combat pagan German religionists in the racist folkish movement and missionize for the church. The league hoped to draw into active church life those church members who likewise purveyed some form of Germanic Christianity, but who despaired of a church proclaiming Jewish Christianity. In 1925 the German Church founded an umbrella association with ten other Germanic Christian groups.[50] Here it worked hard to keep the association from sliding into the camp of pagan religionists. Niedlich, who joined the executive committee, argued that the folkish movement, though balked in the state, could yet conquer the church if the German Church received the movement's support in church elections.

The league sensed that its cause was on the march within the church as well as without. Following election successes in Prussia, it managed to win three seats in the synod of the Thuringian Landeskirche in 1926.[51] Forced to deal with German Church proposals, synod deputies found them less strange over time. Increasingly, however, they sensed the need to resolve the perceived tension between the church and the folkish movement and between Christianity and folk values. An intrachurch discussion of this tension began as the church press and groups of pastors took up the issue. The urgency of the question, however, had begun to dawn on the church before the German Church began to force the issue through elections in 1925. In the preceding year the tones coming out of the conference of the Evangelical League in Munich seemed to welcome the folkish movement as a weapon against ultramontanism.[52] In the fall of that year, a programmatic statement in an Inner Mission periodical showed appreciation for the folkish movement as well as concern for the dangers it might pose. The Church Assembly felt forced to deal with the issue in 1927, though not to the satisfaction of the German Church. This surge of interest within the church was accompanied by a similar preoccupation among patriotic organizations that claimed religious sanction for the national cause.

Taking stock of its competition within the church, the league saw in the dominant church Right, especially the large Positive Union, its foremost opponent. The dominant Right still accentuated the canonical importance of the Old Testament and subscribed to the allegedly Jewish Christianity of St. Paul.[53] But the church Right, the main repository of nationalist conservatism in the church, was caught broadside by German

Church theology.[54] On the one hand, the church Right could appreciate the passionate nationalism displayed by the league. On the other, it could hardly take kindly to the heresy of Germanic Christianity. By and large, the German Church managed to focus church debate on the Old Testament and to avoid confrontation over allegedly Jewish Christianity. Here the league professed toleration of dogmatic differences. These tactics were not altogether successful, because the church Right often linked the two: scuttling the Old Testament amounted to an attack on the New as well. The church Right seemed to view Germanic Christianity as a nationalist excess to be tolerated as well as a theological heresy to be condemned.

Churchmen of the church Right, however, differed in choosing which note to strike. What caught the eyes of Johannes Schneider, Lutheran editor of *Kirchliches Jahrbuch,* and of Reinhard Mumm and Ernst Bunke, both Positive Union leaders, was the heresy of the German Church.[55] But Hans von Lüpke, the founder and leader of the village church movement (Dorfkirchenbewegung), which the church Right dominated, chose to strike the note of toleration. Lüpke assumed that a restoration of the God-given organic village, rooted in the folk ethos, would strengthen the proclamation of gospel. Finding a parallel effort in the German Church, he concluded that it could not, and should not, be preached to death for its deviant theology, since it defended so much of value in the national ethos.[56]

The programmatic statement of the Inner Mission, published but not endorsed by its Central Committee in 1924, tried to strike a balance in judging the folkish movement as a whole. On the one hand, church and Inner Mission could accommodate the folkish movement because God had sanctioned the folk ethos and the fight for the folk's honor and freedom. On the other, the statement indicted tendencies in the folkish movement for contesting essential Christian beliefs. Though biblical Christianity could and ought to be propagated as rooted in the national ethos, the statement admitted that the precise relationship between Christianity and folkish aspirations remained to be clarified. The author proposed a gamble by halfheartedly endorsing a potentially heretical movement even before theological clarity had been reached. The gamble seemed lessened by the argument that cooperation would facilitate attempts to dispatch the moral and religious errors of the movement. On a practical level, the gamble seemed urgently necessary to avoid a tragic split between the church and the movement.[57]

Still, the author had drawn a basic line that dominated church discussion of the folkish movement: endorsement of the movement's nationalist feeling (without much comment on its racism) and rejection of attempts at folkish religion.[58] It was this same line that the 1927 Church Assembly followed in its patriotic proclamation.

In an exceptionally abstruse speech, Paul Althaus, a Lutheran theologian and Young Conservative, made the most publicized attempt to relax the tension between Christianity and the folk ethos within the church Right.[59] As one of two main addresses at the Church Assembly in 1927, his speech hewed to the general church line of distinguishing between nationalism and folkish religiosity. But that line now became thin and wobbly. In rejecting both Germanic pagan religion and the German Church's synthesis, Althaus offered up a folkish theology of history that reaffirmed a basic tenet of war theology: the contention that God judged and acted upon peoples as well as upon individuals. Such a contention fortified a second extreme nationalist position in the church that competed with the first.

Julius Kaftan had elaborated the notion of a Christianized folk ethos to justify the privileges of the Volkskirche. Now Althaus brandished the same notion to strike down the religious pretensions of the folkish movement. A racist folkish religion made no sense for the reason that the national ethos, though originating in race, had developed historically into a spiritual force. A folkish religion taking its values exclusively from the national ethos likewise made no sense, since man's sin had historically contaminated the God-given essence of folk values. Only love for fellow man, inspired by God, could fully bond men in a folk — not the values of the folk ethos at their historically adulterated level. Thus, Althaus contended, a folkish movement that cherished folk rebirth must cherish as well the cleansing and bonding power of gospel.

Althaus invoked Luther's authority against the German Church error of confusing mythology with gospel. Luther had, indeed, rendered gospel understandable to German minds, but not by Germanizing its content. Rather, he had recovered the gospel that St. Paul had rightly understood as something alien to every national ethos. Yet Althaus, like many other churchmen,[60] professed to see Christian gospel and German values bound together by elective affinity, Luther having perceived gospel because his German mentality was so attuned. For the sake of this alien yet congenial gospel, Althaus would leave the Old Testament untouched. God's revelation of salvation was inextricably bound up with the history of an admittedly sinful folk.

Having set up a qualified defense for traditional Christianity, Althaus showed the racist folkish and the larger nationalist movement a more considerate face. Since the essence of folk values was God's gift as creator, the Volkskirche should accept everything that seriously awakened love of the folk ethos. More specifically, the Volkskirche should penetrate with its values the natural involuntary associations that God had created to bind men to a higher responsibility. Althaus assumed that Christian morality and the structure of involuntary associations reinforced each other, since both focused men's strivings on the commonweal. Thus, the natural, divinely ordained organic structure of these associations, including the folk, ought to render them capable of taking on a Christian spirit and of supporting a flourishing church of the folk.

Always keeping Christian and folk values distinct, Althaus related Christianity and the national ethos by pointing out their affinities and moral points of contact. This approach characterized most churchmen in their justification of nationalism and Volkskirche alike. But Althaus pressed further by espousing a theology of history that set a moral concept of folk redemption alongside the Christian conception of individual redemption.

Althaus held fast to the war theology that had loomed large in Protestant churches in the recent war. Specifically, he assumed that God worked through historical events to lead and chasten the folk. In his Church Assembly speech, Althaus claimed that God had assigned the German folk a mission, or a calling, for which He held the folk collectively responsible as history unfolded. God judged the folk by how it responded to His challenge. How Althaus would have specifically defined Germany's mission is unclear, but his emphasis in the speech lay on fidelity to essential values of the German folk ethos.

Althaus contended that the Volkskirche ought to interpret German history for the folk so as to lay bare God's intentions. Since through gospel the church could separate essence from dross in the national ethos, the church could perceive the mission assigned to the German folk and prepare it to respond to His summons. Just as the pastor interpreted God's will for his parishioners, so should the Volkskirche for the folk.

The Volkskirche should see in the contemporary scene a critical stage in the passage of the folk from failure to what could amount to success in pursuing its mission, Althaus thought. He must have assumed that God had judged the German folk and found it wanting in the war and under the Republic. For the German folk stood convicted of self-centered individualism and thus in default of its mission. The growing surge of nationalism by 1927, and stirrings to renew roots in the folk, suggested that the folk had begun to respond to God's scourge. But if the burgeoning nationalist movement would not submit to the purification of folk values that gospel afforded, the desired rebirth of the folk would abort. The present task of the Volkskirche was to read the signs of the times and to elicit the loyalty and respect of the nationalist movement. If the Volkskirche failed, it as well as the folk ethos would suffer.

As noted above in the war-peace debate, other theologians and Althaus himself had earlier articulated versions of a folkish theology of history. But this theology had fallen into partial eclipse with the failing war effort. One wonders why church leaders would want to confer a new aura of legitimacy on it at the Church Assembly, and why the assembled delegates would welcome it with enthusiasm.

Muffled echoes of Althaus's brand of extreme nationalism must have reverberated in the minds of many churchmen. Often they articulated its component parts—the sacredness of the folk ethos, the scourging of Germany, and the necessity of folk renewal—without connecting them within an encompassing theology.[61] The parts must have indicated a consciousness of a larger whole. Certainly they indicated a receptivity to a theology of folk redemption in history. This theology had titilated Protestant consciousness in the war, and would shortly do so again, in the early 1930s. It may be that churchmen despaired of both the folk and the Lord of history (as distinct from the Lord of faith) in the early Republic and regained their confidence only as the nationalist movement flamed into new life.

What is clear is that church leaders wished an assured role for the Volkskirche in the nationalist movement, and that a historical theology of folk redemption abetted their quest. Most clearly in the racist folkish camp, the religious nature of the new nationalism jeopardized such a role. Wishing to remain traditional Christians, leaders of the church Right could hardly compete by following the heresy of the German Church. The theology of folk redemption could avoid this liability and still directly match up the cause of God and the nation in a more theologically acceptable way. The cast of this theology also had a greater galvanizing effect than the more usual conception of nationalism as largely a moral byproduct of gospel. God awaited man's immediate response as He acted in history! Finally, the Volkskirche was assigned a crucial role as the most qualified seer of German history, in addition to its more usual function as the purifier of folk values. The theology of folk redemption appears to have been revived—not, then, invented—to compete with the religiously radical claims of the new nationalism.[62]

Even so, the theology of folk redemption was hardly a conceptual match for German Church nationalism. The German Church's notion of immanent revelation did not hinge on the whim of a transcendent God and the vagaries of historical events. And it did not suffer from the liability of somehow incorporating an alien religion into a conception of nationalism. German Church theology collapsed Christianity and folk values into one system, thereby resolving the tension that continued to agitate other churchmen. In 1924, Niedlich claimed that one stood before a "void" if the religion of Jesus and Germanness could not be synthesized, for otherwise one had to make an abhorrent choice between the two.[63] Althaus thought he could avoid this choice by accommodating folkish religiosity as much as one can imagine short of surrendering Christian revelation. Niedlich and Bublitz condemned the resulting ambiguity, however, and lamented Althaus's performance for talking inspiringly about the folk ethos without drawing necessary consequences for Christianity.[64] A half nationalist was little more than a bogus nationalist.

Such a charge, from within church quarters or without, had an unsettling effect on nationalist churchmen. The more the new nationalism ignored the Volkskirche, questioned its nationalist commitment, or implored a more ardently nationalist response, the more nationalist churchmen worked to prove the indispensability of gospel for the nationalist cause and to raise the claims of the Volkskirche. It is hard to believe, however, that sheer opportunism motivated nationalist churchmen. In their heart of hearts, they thought they knew that Christianity and nationalism must somehow cohere. Their feverish attempts to reconcile differences as much as possible led increasingly to the more xenophobic tone of German Church nationalism, as measures suggested by the German Church and passed by synods indicate.

The felt necessity of reconciling Christianity and folk values explains why the church Right tended to treat Germanic Christianity more as an excessive nationalism to be tolerated than as a heresy to be condemned. Condemnation would drive the folk ethos and Christianity apart at a time when Volkskirche theologians placed a premium upon blending them in a different way. Similarly, they tolerated the German Church for practical reasons. Die Deutschkirche reported no cases of heresy alleged by the church against pastors in the league, though it complained of inquiries.[65] The hospitality shown the German Church by host church parties at synods was likewise an act of toleration. The following of the German Church was much too small to compel this toleration. Rather, the church Right and other church parties as well appeared to fear for the Volkskirche if it contested the religiosity that the new nationalism had spawned in the German Church. The modest though striking success of this small church party in church elections was but one warning that the new nationalism had begun to sweep the Volkskirche. For practical as well as nationalist reasons, therefore, the church Right and other churchmen stood on the theological defensive and shied away from directly attacking German Church theology where it was most vulnerable—its equation of Germanness with gospel.

By 1927 the Old-Prussian church had entered a period of great theological confusion. Debate with the German Church was particularly muddled. It was hard to set argument against argument when the case of the German Church rested so heavily on the compelling feelings of its piety. But the difficulty of the theological task was the main reason for the confusion. Churchmen had to find ways of dovetailing two distinct value systems that circumstances had persuaded them to shove together. By elevating folk into an order of creation, they recognized a second value system that did not easily mesh with traditional Christian social ethics. One could not simply relate faith to folk as an order of creation, as Luther had linked faith and the other orders. The folk was not just a created structure to facilitate orderly social life, but also the generator of its own values. These values presumably penetrated the other orders that were devoid of a similar autonomous ethos. Accordingly, the concept of the national ethos acquired a primary position in Weimar social ethics and confronted churchmen with an unassimilable second system of values.[66] One is amazed by the alacrity with which they accepted the folk as an order. Churchmen who had ransacked the New Testament for proof managed to find but a few quotations that no more than suggested the folk's divine ordination. Most churchmen needed no such proof as they faced up to the theological problem: Since God was alike the creator of the folk and the author of man's salvation, folk values and Christianity must harmonize. The confusing and exasperating question was: How?

The most obvious consequence of exalting the folk as an order of creation was to commit churchmen to nationalism for fundamentally dogmatic reasons within the realm of social ethics. Accordingly, the awakening of folk commitment by the nationalist movement appeared fully in line with God's will for the German nation. The two extreme types of church nationalism appear considerably less extreme when measured against the extreme folkish nationalism that already pulsated through the Old-Prussian church.

Anti-Semitism

"To be German means to be Christian, this saying shall become true *again*."[67] These words of the East Prussian provincial synod in 1920 typically identified "German" and "Christian." Also suggested in the statement was a lapse that Evangelical Christians resolved to correct. Their compatriots had found international or non-German values unpardonably alluring: ultramontane Catholicism, Marxism, Western ideals, Americanization, foreign customs and words. To this extendable list must be added Judentum— Jewishness.

As a rule the intensity of a churchman's anti-Semitism reflected the degree of his commitment to folkish nationalism. Among Democratic liberals such as Martin Rade and Religious Socialists generally, anti-Semitism found little or no response.[68] Among others anti-Semitism was even more pointedly antirepublican than folkish nationalism, since the Republic and the parties of the Left seemed to permit Jews an influence out of proportion to their numbers. Throughout the church, folk renewal and materialism in its many forms were addressed only occasionally by invoking anti-Semitism. When a reader reproached Josef Gauger for displaying his anti-Semitism in *Gotthard-Briefe,* Gauger replied that he did so neither prominently nor frequently.[69] Yet the Jewish problem was clearly a crucial issue for him, and must have been for other nationalist churchmen who wrote or said little about it as well.

Modern anti-Semitism had struck roots in Germany around 1880.[70] It was then that the nationalist historian Heinrich von Treitschke loosed his diatribes against Jews for defying the assimilation that latter-day Jewish emancipation ought to have encouraged. It was then that other anti-Semites found in race a pseudoscientific base for their prejudice and, more logically than cultural anti-Semites, elaborated the traditional charge that Jews acted as incorrigible parasites who fed on the host German folk. It was then that Stoecker and his Christian-Social party shaped cultural and religious anti-Semitism into a political weapon, easing the consciences of many Protestants about the compatibility of anti-Semitism and Christianity. Stoecker's anti-Semitism can be traced back to Luther, medieval Christendom, and the early church.

Thus, anti-Semitism was hardly new to the Weimar church. Stoecker's anti-Semitism was another of his legacies that set the tone for much of the Old-Prussian church in the 1920s. A distinction between racist and Christian anti-Semitism had already been drawn in the 1880s. According to racists, conversion and baptism, Stoecker's basic prescription, could not efface perverse Jewish personality traits that biology had already set and that kept Jews from absorbing German values. Stoecker had grown alarmed at racist anti-Semites who rejected Christianity as Jewish. The distinction between the two types of anti-Semitism, however, had grown muddled when Chamberlain, later followed by the German Church, claimed Jesus as an Aryan and when other attempts at synthesis ensued.[71] What was different in the Weimar church was the broader spread of anti-Semitism, and its greater intensity.

As Christian nationalism intensified, Jews found themselves exposed as aliens more than ethnic Germans who likewise rejected, or simply lacked, a German Protestant heritage. Moreover, Jews had already risen to considerable prominence in manufacturing, commerce, banking, and the professions, and could therefore plausibly be denounced for exploiting the folk from strong economic positions during a time of economic hardship. Traditionally liberal, the bulk of the Jewish electorate threw its political support to the Democrats and the Republic. Some Jews distinguished themselves as leaders in the Socialist Left and took an active role in the revolution that toppled the Christian state.[72] Now Jews could with greater credence be taxed with hostility to Christianity, as well as with treason. Because individual Jews seemed more prominent and influential in the Republic, Jews as a whole became more conspicuous and reprehensible.

Given this set of circumstances, Jews were natural targets of xenophobic nationalism within Protestant churches, as a study by Ino Arndt has demonstrated.[73] Jews were blamed for promoting or causing the revolution, conspiring on an international scale against Germany, spurning patriotism, massively influencing and corrupting government, and shaping public opinion by controlling the press. But most nationalist churchmen rejected racist anti-Semitism and folkish attacks on the Old Testament. Theirs was a "legitimate" Christian anti-Semitism geared to defend the Christian national ethos against Jewish mammonism. Traced here was the Stoecker anti-Semitic tradition, which, as Arndt also demonstrated, was increasingly challenged by racist anti-Semitism.

Pastor Josef Gauger, pietist editor of *Licht und Leben* and *Gotthard-Briefe*, provides a good example of outspoken anti-Semitism within the church Right.[74] An admirer of Stoecker, Gauger charged that the revolution had freed Jews to exploit German society through the republican order. They had schemed for political positions and influence and had grabbed economic power through speculation, especially during the inflation. By controlling much of the press—especially the *Berliner Tageblatt*, the *Vossische Zeitung*, and the *Frankfurter Zeitung*—Jews, to a great extent, had managed to impose their corrupting values upon susceptible Germans and to subvert their nationalist and Christian loyalties.

Jews owed much of their recent ascendancy, Gauger believed, to the Socialist party. Largely led and financed by Jews (in Gauger's view), this party seemed to derive its ideology from Jewish materialism, especially from the perverse doctrines of Ferdinand Lassalle and Karl Marx, both Jews. It seemed no accident that Socialists and Jews alike turned traitor by undermining the war effort and fomenting revolution. Both could gain power only by destroying the Second Empire and the monarchy. The class hatred that Marxism inspired served the interests of Jews in the war and Republic by splitting the folk community and by affording Jews an opportunity to control and exploit. Likewise, Communists seemed the tool of Jews, as did the Democratic party. Only in the antirepublican Right could Gauger find a defense of Christian Germany against the Jewish onslaught.

The Jewish menace in Germany seemed to Gauger the more alarming for shaping the spearhead of an international Jewish conspiracy. He quoted approvingly a Christian conservative who asserted that international Jewish capitalism had conspired with the enemy to crush Germany and promote revolution in order to exploit the nation. The conspiracy reached far beyond economic goals. Gauger quoted a fellow pietist pastor who claimed that international Jewry dominated Communist as well as capitalist states and victorious as well as vanquished nations. The pastor hardly needed to add that such a feat required "incredible flexibility." Susceptible to this argument, Gauger came to see similarities between Jewish world rule and the biblical anti-Christ.

Such extreme conspiracy theories, though they strained the credulity of nationalist churchmen, fell within range of what they thought plausible. Illustrating this credulity were the reactions of the Lutheran editor, Pastor

Wilhelm Laible, to the infamous "Protocols of the Elders of Zion." The "Protocols" took the form of lectures to Jewish "elders," who allegedly conspired for world rule by exploiting tensions among and within Gentile states. Forged (probably by the Russian secret police) around the turn of the century, the "Protocols" were later used by White Russian émigrés to persuade Westerners that the Bolshevik Revolution was only part of a broader Jewish conspiracy threatening all. In Germany, Professor Hermann Strack, a Protestant theologian and leader of the Jewish mission, exposed the "Protocols" as spurious, as did other sources, most notably the London *Times*.[75]

Laible challenged Strack's position. That a document which predicted subsequent catastrophes with such unerring accuracy could be a mere forgery seemed too much to believe. The nations had suffered world war, world revolution, economic ruin, and the destruction of their moral and religious life. Throughout these catastrophes Jews had emerged as winners and leaders. It did not seem implausible to Laible that the incredible events he had witnessed could be explained by an equally incredible conspiracy. If Strack's exposure might tarnish the "Protocols" among churchmen, it could hardly undercut a preexisting and more unspecified belief in a worldwide Jewish conspiracy.

Certain features of Volkskirche theory fortified the cultural anti-Semitism of nationalist churchmen. If Germanness and Christianity had blended to produce a German ethos, it was quite as logical to conclude that the Jews had similarly evolved their own distinctive ethos. Churchmen frequently hailed stereotyped Prussian or German virtues as the imprint of Christianity upon the German character. The collective portrait of Jews appeared colored by the very opposite of these virtues. Furthermore, nationalist churchmen, convinced of the determining impact of values, correlated behavior with the ethos of the received stereotype. Although present-day Germans regrettably lapsed from their ethos, Jews seemed rarely to lapse from theirs. One did not need to prove empirically that Jews exerted a corrosive influence; their very existence, and their prominence, were proof enough. Anti-Semitic charges seemed to confirm what was already suspected. Thus, Hans von Lüpke of the village church movement could roundly condemn the pervasive influence of Jewry, while admitting that he knew no Jews.[76] Finally, if the Volkskirche pledged itself to nourishing Christian-German imponderables, it must quite as logically defend that ethos against all alien values, including Jewishness. Acceptance of the folk as an order of creation underscored this responsibility, entrenching cultural anti-Semitism as an ethical commitment. It is clear that, for some nationalist churchmen, anti-Semitism functioned as part of the Volkskirche's negative identity.[77]

Competition with the racist folkish movement also fortified cultural anti-Semitism within the church, as nationalist churchmen tried to draw lines against their racist compatriots. Increasingly churchmen feared lest hatred for the Old Testament and Christianity burgeon as a consequence of racial hatred for Jews. It made sense to demonstrate that one could legitimately function as a Christian anti-Semite. But how could one castigate present-day Jewish perversity and still spare from attack the ethos of the true Israel from which Jesus had sprung? The most satisfying solution was to argue that the Jewish folk character had degenerated since biblical times.

Late in 1922 Reinhold Seeberg elaborated such a thesis at a conference of the Central Committee of the Inner Mission, which he would soon chair. The ethos of the covenant had hardly kept in check the materialist ethic of Jewishness during Old Testament times, Seeberg explained. Since then secularized Jews had persisted in considering themselves God's elect and therefore entitled to dominate host peoples among whom they were scattered. Uncommitted to the host nation, they sought a position for themselves and control of others by destroying host traditions with such rationalist concepts as individual freedom and equality.[78]

Biblicists such as Gauger drew more directly on scripture to demonstrate the progressive degeneration of the Jewish folk character. In Leviticus 26 and Deuteronomy 28, God threatened to scourge and scatter Jews if they broke His covenant. This the Jewish folk spirit proceeded to do with a vengeance, most grievously when Jews committed deicide. True to His word, God visited His curse upon this rebellious people.[79] The traditional notion of the curse explained Jewish perversity, demonstrated why Jews deserved Christian hostility, and legitimated anti-Semitism biblically. But now the curse met another need—demonstrating to racists and other radical nationalists that Christianity stemmed not from Jewishness but from the promise of the covenant proclaimed by the prophets and rejected by the Jewish folk. Gauger ignored Reformation doctrine by which "Jews" represented the natural tendency of all men to reject God's covenant in Jesus Christ.

The cultural nationalism underlying Volkskirche theory and the need to set it off from racist anti-Semitism spawned what churchmen considered "legitimate" anti-Semitism. Racial hatred wrongly encouraged hatred of persons. The Christian should fight Jewish influence and power out of love for folk, but never out of hatred for Jews as individuals.[80] Such an ethical stance ruled out persecution but allowed banning Jewish emigration from the East and encouraged voting against Jews or political parties influenced by them. Between clearly permissible and impermissible anti-Semitism were other forms that bordered on persecution without ostensibly being motivated by hatred. Some churchmen endorsed measures to limit Jewish access to positions of responsibility and influence. Gauger promoted social ostracism as a defense of Christian Germany.[81] Christians ought not to patronize Jewish businesses and professionals, read Jewish papers, or socialize with Jews. Whoever did, Gauger argued, shared their curse and betrayed German folk values. All cultural anti-Semites seemed to agree that "legitimate" anti-Semitism meant, above all, a struggle for the soul of the folk against Jewish materialism. Accordingly, the most dangerous of Jewish influences was the imprint of the Jewish press upon impressionable German minds.

"Legitimate" anti-Semitism thus justified political defensive measures and fostered a missionary offensive. One may wonder which perception of the Jewish threat—as a political menace or as a pollutant of German values—did more to foster hostility among church people toward the Republic. Jewish participation in an alleged conspiracy to defeat Germany and in the recent revolution highlighted the political threat at first.[82] As the immediate shock of these catastrophes passed, churchmen increasingly focused on the value problem. This shift, however, did not reduce resentment of the Republic, for the reason that Jewish values seemed to shape the ethos of the Weimar Republic and to impede folk renewal.

One can see the consequences of this shifting emphasis in Seeberg's speech.[83] Also Seeberg deplored the political and economic influence of Jews. For him, however, the Jewish problem was more a spiritual and German problem than a narrow political one. Broad sections of the German public already appeared to share the distressingly materialist and rationalist values that Jews propagated. Germans might need to suffer a greater scourge before coming to their proper senses. When the false hopes of the Republic had evaporated and when Germans had seen themselves more clearly as slaves of the enemy, the folk might return to German Christianity and forsake the moral bankruptcy of Jewish values. Seeberg's equation of Jewishness with the alleged ethos of the Republic—with materialism and rationalism—was startling. How could the values of half a million Jews corrupt those of the vast majority? Seeberg considered the Weimar ethos Jewish because, he claimed, secularized Jews most effectively and cleverly nourished it.

In his speech to the 1927 Church Assembly, Althaus conceived of the Jewish problem almost entirely as a value issue. Destructive of the German folk, urban spirituality stemmed primarily from Jewish folk values. Earlier he had seen an affinity between the Jewish ethos and the rationalist individualist spirit of the Enlightenment, which Jews propagated more than others. Like Seeberg, Althaus absolved Jews of exclusive blame for the degeneration of the German folk. Jews could wield no spiritual influence had not Germans defected from their Christian ethos, and folk degeneration resulted from evil which transcended all ethnic groups. Yet "Jewish spirit" and "Jewish power" constituted a value threat for promoting the evil of folk degeneration.[84]

Between Seeberg's lecture in 1922 and Althaus's Church Assembly speech in 1927 the new nationalist movement spread throughout Germany. It seems likely that the increasing emphasis placed by churchmen on the Jewish problem as a value issue at the very center of folk renewal was a sympathetic but defensive response to the stark confrontation that especially the folkish movement posited between Jewish and German values.[85] One could accept this formulation of the Jewish problem by marking off a "legitimate" anti-Semitism that spared Christianity and its ethics. But this formulation presented both Seeberg and Althaus with difficulties. They could not regard Jewish values as merely symptomatic of a general German malaise if they wished to oblige new nationalists. They had to stretch to claim an improbable cause-and-effect relationship, however they might qualify its importance.

Though the folkish movement encouraged hatred for Jews, the most prominent arm of that movement in the Old-Prussian church—the League for a German Church—almost entirely ignored them as it concentrated on the value problem, if one is to judge by *Die Deutschkirche*. True, the Jewish minority appeared all too prominent and influential. But the harm that the small Jewish minority could cause seemed to pale beside the more immense damage that Jewish materialism persisted in inflicting on the German racial soul. Inasmuch as race-conscious Aryans abhorred materialism, Niedlich and Bublitz located the source of materialist contagion outside of the racial soul—above all in Jewish Christianity. The paradox that the German Church faced was that the means by which it sought folk renewal—the Volkskirche—was itself the main agent for propagating Jewishness in Germany. For fear of intermarriage, the German Church deplored German missionary work among Jews, as well as baptizing and ordaining Jews in a German church. Pollution by Jewish blood would contaminate Aryan values at their biological source, entrench Jewish Christianity, and make a mockery of German folk renewal.[86]

A recurring theme in the literature analyzing modern anti-Semitism holds that it historically has aimed at a target much larger than Jews—the quick pace of modernization in all areas.[87] It is true that nationalist churchmen taxed Jews with destroying the Christian state and dominating its modern adversary, the Republic. It is quite as true that churchmen like Seeberg explicitly formulated the value problem to indict the Republic for indulging quintessentially Jewish or modern values. Certainly a folk reborn of Christian nationalism had to shun the broad pluralism and secularism of the Republic or to reconstitute it as a fundamentally different type of state. That they resisted modernity in their attacks on Jewishness, however, would have struck nationalist churchmen as all too negative and pointless. For them, the issue of the Republic and Jews within it was largely secondary to their primary purpose: a Christian renewal of Germany.

THE FLOUNDERING "SOCIAL" VOLKSKIRCHE AND SOCIALISM

The common purpose of renewing a Christian Germany also involved church efforts in the economic order. Many church leaders admitted candidly that Christianity and the churches exerted no noticeable impact on German economic life. Engrained in activist Volkskirche theory was an assumption that they ought to.

When the Church Federation Assembly convened in 1924, it beheld a society that seemed to have progressively dissolved since the relatively stable days before the war. Incipient civil war since the revolution paralleled industrial strife that was politically as well as economically motivated. In November 1923, the value of the German currency plunged to null. The middle classes lost their savings to a catastrophic extent, and unemployment battered the working classes, while speculators with tangible collateral made huge gains by investing borrowed money. In their struggle for existence, individuals and groups appeared to indulge their own material interests to the neglect of each other and of the commonweal. Such was the diagnosis of the assembly's social proclamation.[88]

It was the second part of the social proclamation that captured public attention. While the first part, on the family, centered around Evangelical truisms, the second, on the economy, attempted to stake out a judicious position on the deepening conflict between labor and management, which tore apart the folk community and frustrated German recovery (Gesundung) and resurgence (Aufstieg). The authors of the proclamation were at great pains to profess sympathy with the plight of workers, while reminding them of their responsibilities as equal and valued members of the folk. This sympathetic position was underscored when the proclamation held management, more than labor, morally responsible for its actions, since management wielded greater economic power. Only Christian faith, the proclamation asserted, could generate appropriate social concern and social justice.

Churchmen assessed the significance of the social proclamation in varying ways. For Rade the church sought to redeem the social position that the Old-Prussian church had officially endorsed in 1890 but subsequently spurned.[89] Much of the church saw the historical significance of the proclamation in the same light. For Emil Fuchs, a Socialist pastor, however, the proclamation had arrived twenty years too late to make much of an impact upon workers, who would find in it only ideas spun off by a decadent capitalist order. He urged the church to throw its support to socialism as an order most akin to the spirit of Christ rather than identify itself with a dying capitalism. Some confessional Lutherans provided the counterpoint to Fuchs: they feared lest the church's primary spiritual mission suffer from neglect as the result of a concentration on social problems.[90] But most of the dominant and aggressive church Right conceived of an activist role, also within the economy, as indispensable.

Through social courses, which they subsidized, the churches sought to arouse a greater sense of social responsibility. The 1919 Church Assembly urged member churches to sponsor such courses "to foster the knowledge and understanding of social tasks and of the church's role in solving them."[91] Because of shaky church finances, the main burden of responsibility for social courses fell on the Evangelical-Social School, founded by Ludwig Weber, the national chairman of Protestant workingmen's clubs until 1922. This school had trained leaders for these clubs, as well as Protestant labor secretaries for interconfessional Christian unions. Subsidized by church governments and the Kirchenausschuss, the school moved in 1921 from its original site in Bielefeld to the Inner Mission's Johannesstift in Spandau, where it found adequate facilities to expand its offerings. The school's course offerings grew rapidly. Each year Protestant labor leaders traveled to the Johannesstift for a month-long course. The school obliged the request of the 1921 Church Assembly to widen its offerings. In 1926 it gave twenty-four courses to pastors, teachers, welfare officials, and others.

To oversee the church's social efforts, permanent social committees took shape within the Kirchenausschuss, the Old-Prussian Church Senate, and provincial church governments. Church leaders were painfully aware of their need for expert advice if their efforts were to be taken seriously. Social courses could not satisfy this need, since they focused on imparting a sense of social responsibility. By 1927 Old-Prussian provinces employed seven full-time and seventeen part-time social pastors as specialists. The 1927 General Synod voted to require pastoral candidates to gain experience in some social field and provided funds for the advanced training of theologians in social problems.[92]

What was the thrust of the church's social program? Did it risk taking positions on current issues that might commit the church politically, the point at which the EOK drew back in 1895? Protestant churches did so in the realm of morality legislation and in certain political issues where relatively clear moral principles or church interests intruded. But in economic issues, except for promoting better housing and a revalorization of the currency, the churches found it difficult to press beyond the older approach of stimulating individual social responsibility.

Like most Weimar churchmen, Reinhold Seeberg believed that the church might proffer only moral, not technical, advice on any given social, economic, or political problem.[93] If it made a technical judgment, the church would risk fusing Luther's two Regimente. At the 1924 Church Assembly, Karl Holl, a noted Luther scholar, contended that the church should have Luther's courage to make moral judgments even if they meddled in technical matters.[94] But the social proclamation followed a traditional understanding of Luther, not Holl's counsel. It claimed that the economy ran by its own laws and urged participants in the economic struggle to meliorate resulting hardships by showing due concern for others, for the commonweal, and for social justice. Accordingly, the emphasis fell on individual responsibility, provoking two questions: If the economy ran by internal necessity, what room yet remained for individual moral voluntarism? And where—business leaders especially asked—lay the line demarcating technical from moral decisions?[95]

These questions made churchmen, long aware of their dilemma, even more conscious of difficulties involved in reconciling distinctions drawn in

Lutheran social ethics with the realities of the modern economy. In a speech to Protestant pastors in September 1925, Prälat Schoell, the Württemberg church leader who had helped shape the social proclamation, warned against using outmoded standards by which to judge new industrial conditions. But his resolution of the problem was hardly new. He would revive Luther's concept of the calling as a means of imbuing public life with a Christian spirit. Reliance on such an approach clearly had its drawbacks. Where the producer came into direct personal contact with those whom he served in a relatively simple agricultural economy, the calling seemed more effective than in the modern industrial economy governed by more impersonal forces. Some churchmen readily acknowledged that the church, if it desired an impact, must also judge impersonal economic forces not readily subject to personal moral actions. Even Prälat Schoell sensed the inadequacy of his solution, for he ended his speech with the admission that theologians had yet to produce "a really usable social ethic geared to the present."[96] What deterred them was a combination of theological scruple and practical caution. The Volkskirche would run the risk of prescribing technical solutions for the sake of moral ends and thus embroil itself in damaging partisan controversy.

The same problem confronted social pastors. They met in Eisenach with church officials in June 1925 to produce a statement that would delineate the responsibilities of the social church and the functions of social pastors. Later accepted by the Kirchenausschuss, the statement contended that "the proclamation of the Word from the point of view of social responsibility demands incisive and clear perception of social facts and their connections." But the statement failed to suggest how "facts" and morality might relate, and concluded rather despairingly that much sociological and theological research was yet needed before a modern Evangelical social doctrine could emerge. The conferees saw the church's essential role in sharpening social sensitivity in all areas and advised the church to confine intervention in social conflicts to exceptional cases in order to avoid political involvement.[97]

Perhaps not in theory, but certainly in practice, the Eisenach statement offered contradictory advice. By hoping to match social ethics with a "clear perception" of social reality, and by emphasizing political neutrality, its authors wished to shield Evangelical responses to social questions from ideological answers. Unable to conceptualize such a match with any clarity, however, churchmen fell back on the church's older approach, also commended by the statement, of stimulating individual social responsibility. The folkish nationalism that pervaded the church blended well with this older approach. Since folkish nationalism also placed a premium on proper individual values, it could color Evangelical social ethics and inject the ideological prejudgment that the authors of the Eisenach statement sought to avoid. Evangelical social ethics in the Weimar period and folkish nationalism showed another affinity by orienting the individual's attention toward the national commonweal as the touchstone of what constituted "social" behavior and what not.[98] As a consequence, "social" and "national" sensitivity constituted two sides of the same answer to the question of how social groups might be bonded to form a national community. It was this organic wholeness—and a sense of social justice inferred from it—that nationalist churchmen sought to meld under a religionless state that seemed to cater to a plurality of values and conflict rather than to Christian values and social harmony.

A good example of the preeminent stress that nationalist churchmen placed on proper values as a prerequisite of economic and social renewal can be found in Professor Friedrich Brunstäd's *Deutschland und der Sozialismus,* published in 1927. It deserves comment also because the Nationalist Brunstäd served as director of the Evangelical-Social School, where he lectured on the arguments running through his book to hundreds of pastors, Christian union leaders, and others. His bitter critic, the Religious Socialist Georg Wünsch, wrote that many regarded Brunstäd as a modern Christian social prophet.[99]

But Brunstäd had little to say in his book that was not already commonplace within the church. He argued that Christian morality should apply a countervailing force against man's materialism that had rendered nugatory the immanent pull toward social cooperation that God had built into the economic order. In line with the disdain heaped upon Western liberalism by old and new nationalisms alike, Brunstäd found the cause of economic injustice in antisocial values—in the atomist ideology of the Enlightenment. Since the Enlightenment, man had progressively emancipated himself from a moral commitment to the commonweal through natural-rights theory in the political order and mammonist capitalism and socialism in the economic. The malaise of the present consisted in lack of obligation to the orders and callous neglect of the concept of the calling.[100]

Officially the church professed neutrality toward economic systems, as the 1919 Church Assembly proclaimed: "The gospel is not bound to any one economic form; it fights service to mammon on all levels of the folk and demands that everyone can joyfully perform his work in service to God."[101] Such a statement, reflecting the strictures of the dualist ethic, also tried to strike down Socialist charges that it had fallen in with bourgeois economic interests. But churchmen generally preferred capitalism to socialism. Brunstäd did not condemn capitalism as a system, only its perversion by mammonism. Because God-given instincts seemed to lead to the capitalist form, the latter need not be dismissed as organized selfishness. Similarly, Seeberg justified capitalism with the argument that economic differences arose naturally from varying individual capabilities and an inevitable differentiation of economic function. Both men regarded the acquisition of property as natural. Both, therefore, tarred socialism as unnatural, for it tried to blot out natural differences with artificial means.[102] Such commonplace arguments for the capitalist system, however, were coupled with bitter criticism of capitalist practice during the Weimar period.

Though the church refused to condemn socialism as an economic form, nationalist churchmen often singled out Socialists for special attack with the charge that they fostered the interests of one class at the expense of the folk community. Sometimes, as Gauger's earlier example suggests, socialism and Jewishness appeared as ideological allies. Brunstäd professed great sympathy for the workers' desire for protection from unjust capitalist exploitation, as did the social proclamation. By the same token, one finds a readiness in nationalist church circles to view labor unrest as sufficient evidence that Socialists denied a moral obligation to the commonweal. In Brunstäd's eyes, Marxist socialism drew its substance from the ideology of the Enlightenment and, like degenerate capitalism, substituted the self-sufficient man for the morally committed folkish citizen.

A diagnosis of the economy that traced its malfunction to antisocial values and these to an antisocial ideology can blend well with a political diagnosis. Such was the case with Brunstäd's analysis. It was no accident that German Socialists had agitated for democracy, he contended, since both purveyed an atomist concept of society. Under democracy, materialist forces—be they mammonist capitalist or socialist—subverted the state into a servant of particularist economic interests. For him and the church Right generally, the Republic, which drew this criticism, had failed to harness interest groups. The German folk "must restore its state power, create anew its state," by which Brunstäd doubtless meant a restored monarchy.[103] For constitutional monarchy, rising above economic interests, appeared to him as the most able to advance the commonweal and thus foster social justice.

It is true that economic and political groups agitated for their own interests with singular determination in the Republic and that Protestant criticism found a legitimate, broad target. But the tendency of nationalist churchmen to reduce economic and political problems to a conflict for and against materialism prejudged all issues, tendentiously divided forms of government and economic systems into radically opposed moral alternatives, and failed to come to grips with the intractable problems that plagued postwar Germany. Brunstäd attempted to arouse individual social sensitivity without a "clear perception of social facts and their connections."

Sociologically as well as ideologically a chasm yawned between the church and the working classes. In 1924 an Old-Prussian pastor poignantly depicted the social cleavage that set the churched middle classes off from unchurched workers.[104] The typical "active" church member attended church irregularly, regarded existing social and economic differences as inevitable, and settled easily into a hierarchical society. Politically national-istic, he might contract out of the church if it collided with the political Right on social issues. By contrast, the worker—badly housed and badly fed, and frequently unemployed—refused to accept the social and economic disparities that the churched middle classes took as divinely willed. He protested the conditions of his existence through his speech, his clothing, and his life. Unable to accept God's moral order, he seemed a materialist, and a cynical one at that. The social pronouncements of the church, in short, were unlikely to impress him.

Especially in northern Germany, in the territory of the Old-Prussian church, lower-class hostility toward the church had grown acute. A poll conducted by the Socialist newspaper *Vorwärts* in 1924, for example, revealed that the average worker denounced the organized church for its intense nationalism, its loyalty to the ruling class, and even its mammonism.[105] Disheartened churchmen complained that the disestablishment apparently had not assuaged hatred for the church and often concluded that workers stood aloof because of their inveterate materialism.

If churchmen could have oriented their social ethics to a "clear percep-tion of social facts and their connections," they might have found much agreement with Socialists on practical social problems. Since much of the church's nationalist leadership was resolved to fight the Socialist world view tooth and nail, however, the church could hardly build bridges over the sociological chasm to reach workers, most of whom were already ranged in Socialist and Communist camps. It was rather futile to suppose that the social Volkskirche could wean workers away from Marxist parties by distin-guishing sartorially between Socialist materialism and the justified demands of workers. Understandably, a number of conscience-stricken churchmen groped for approaches that would not immerse the church in bitter struggle with socialism. A church that closed ranks against a large part of its membership could not prosper as a Volkskirche.

Gottfried Naumann, Georg Merz, and Georg Wünsch—three Evangelical pastors—attempted to reassess the relationship of Christianity and socialism in a manner differing from the usual tendentious approach that sharply repudiated socialism for its Marxist orientation. Differing least was Naumann's *Sozialismus und Religion in Deutschland*, published in 1921.[106] Most churchmen lumped socialism and Marxist theory together; Naumann distinguished between the two, pointed out the deep ethical motives of socialism, and professed a preference for socialism over the free economy. In his eyes, a devout Christian could become a Socialist, but presumably not a Marxist. Naumann pointed out a small minority in the Socialist camp that aspired toward a morality deepened by religion, a development that the church might foster by curbing its blanket indictment of socialism. Even more conciliatory was Georg Merz's *Religiöse Ansätze in modernen Sozialismus*, published in 1919.[107] Merz argued that Socialists could be religious despite their Marxist orientation, thereby distinguishing between religious and atheistic Marxists, not merely between Marxism and socialism.

In *Der Zusammenbruch des Luthertums als Sozialgestaltung*, published in 1921, Wünsch made the most extreme of the three attempts to relate amicably to socialism.[108] His views illustrated the difficult shift that Religious Socialists tried to complete from a dualist to a unitary ethic. Scathingly Wünsch denounced the double morality into which, as he saw it, Luther's dualistic ethic had degenerated. Modern Lutherans had upheld legitimate authority without criticizing the use of power and the sins of the existing order. They had marked off a sphere in which the secular ethic (Weltmoral), man's natural animalist egoism, could hold complete sway, and had compounded their error by justifying service to the secular ethic as dedication to the commonweal. In other words, modern Lutherans had sanctified a basically immoral struggle for existence through capitalism and war. Only a unitary ethic could give meaning to the social sensitivity that modern Lutherans advocated, for otherwise capitalism and nationalism forced men into egoism out of self-defense. Wünsch saw in socialism the means to curb the secular ethic in the economic order. Because materialism needlessly skewed present-day socialism, however, a Christian unitary ethic must give socialism the necessary moral stamina to subdue the secular ethic.

After the war the religious-socialist movement grew large enough to excite widespread comment. Concerned pastors and laymen might join the movement to interest alienated Socialist workers in church participation, to encourage religious proclivities within the Socialist camp, to give Socialist theory a religious or moral grounding, and to seek a new unitary ethical approach after the presumed failure of Lutheran social ethics. The last three reasons did not always square with the first, since not all Religious Socialists felt constrained to drive an opening wedge for the church into Socialist ranks.

Following the revolution, religious-socialist groups sprouted in Schlüchtern, Baden, and Berlin. Initially the Schlüchtern group posed as a Democratic association, founded on March 29, 1919, in response to Rade's appeal for Volkskirche councils. Soon it left the Democratic orbit. Some joined the Majority Socialists, while others, disappointed by Socialist parties or influenced by the Swiss theologian Karl Barth, turned away from political activity. At a conference arranged by the Schlüchtern group in September 1919, Barth stressed the absolute quality of faith and castigated any compromise between it and culture—and implicitly between faith and socialism. Soon the residue of the Schlüchtern group cooled its reformist ardor and withdrew to a settlement at Habertshof bei Schlüchtern, in Hesse. Barth's criticism of culture likewise had some effect on the younger generation of German pastors. He condemned the hyphenated Christianity subscribed to by most churchmen—whether Christian-racist, Christian-German, liberal-Democratic, or religious-socialist. According to Mehnert, Barth gave rise on the church's political Left to "theologically based social anarchy," indifferent to political and social problems and hence to the Weimar Republic. [109]

Only in Baden did religious socialism attract a mass following and wield some power within the Landeskirche. In church elections of 1926, Religious Socialists polled twenty-eight thousand votes and captured eight of fifty-seven seats in the synod. Class lines were less tightly drawn in Baden than in northern Germany, industrialism less advanced, workers less hostile to the church, and active church members less suspicious of socialism. [110]

On the turf of the Old-Prussian church, the acute hostility of workers made a large religious-socialist movement friendly to the church impossible. Like other religious-socialist groups, the various Berlin organizations began as part of the radical component of the Volkskirche movement, bent on drawing Socialist workers into the communion of the church. But soon, one by one, Berlin Socialist pastors felt compelled to distance themselves from the church in order to hold the trust of workers.

Pastor Karl Aner founded the first of the Berlin religious-socialist groups—the League "New Church," composed largely of theologians. In 1917 Aner had braved the wrath of his nationalist colleagues by agitating for a peace of reconciliation. A second group, the League of Socialist Friends of the Church, was founded by Pastor Günther Dehn in March 1919. The two leagues merged in December 1919 to form the League of Religious Socialists, with a membership of over a thousand. While the merged league contained as many types of religious socialism as leading personalities, it agreed upon several broad principles: a unitary Christian ethic, pacifism, a democratic Volkskirche, and the necessity of class struggle. It soon established contact with the pacifist Association of Friends of Religion and International Peace, led by the Socialist pastor August Bleier.[111]

Smaller religious-socialist groups struck roots throughout Germany. In 1924 the various organizations established contacts on a national level and in 1926 formed the League of Religious Socialists of Germany, subsequently holding congresses every second year.

Though they often complained about the church's hostile attitude, Religious Socialists could hardly have expected anything else after having accused the church of betraying its mission. In the opinion of nationalist churchmen, Religious Socialists faced a necessary choice between Christianity and the Socialist party. A Christian might not subscribe to Marxist socialism, and membership in the despised Socialist party, permeated by Marxist theory, jeopardized the Christian conscience. The editor of Der Reichsbote advised the church "to leave no doubt that a party that is inherently anti-church and anti-Christian belongs to its enemies."[112]

But much of the church Left, especially Democratic liberals, tended to view the religious-socialist movement with considerable sympathy, largely because liberals and Religious Socialists had much in common. Both favored a democratic Volkskirche, fervently desired the full participation of Socialist workers, deplored the political domination of the conservative church Right, and to some extent agreed on a unitary ethic in regard to such issues as pacifism. Moreover, many Religious Socialists had already traveled through the liberal camp, and liberals reacted more flexibly than the church Right to new approaches to social problems. In time even some of the movement's harshest conservative critics assumed a more conciliatory attitude, arguing that the movement performed a valuable service among workers after the church had so dismally failed.[113] But such an admission came grudgingly, and largely from despair.

Of course, a residue of workers had remained conspicuously loyal to their church, grouped as they were in Evangelical workingmen's clubs (which also enrolled many non-workers) and in interdenominational Christian unions. But the small numbers of these workers, though they were a source of hope, could only underscore the church's limited social appeal. The prospect of finding social justice in a hierarchical community, cemented by nationalism and Christian love, must have struck most workers as illusory and deceptive. Also causing affront was the split in worker solidarity, which Christian workers proposed to widen. Thus, a resolution framed in 1925 by Protestant leaders of Christian unions and workingmen's clubs stated: "An effective dam against the pernicious influence of the anti-Christian, Marxist labor movement can be erected only by fostering an independent Christian labor movement."[114]

Workers oriented toward the political Right exuded an intense folkish nationalism that more pacifistically inclined workers found offensive. The 1921 program of the workingmen's clubs read, in part: "We strive for a Germanness borne on by a strong folk consciousness, since we are entirely committed to our fatherland. We nurture social sensitivity and work toward healthy reform to build up a real folk community."[115] This nationalist tone extended as well to the Evangelical-Social School at which, in addition to Brunstäd, Paul Althaus and leaders of workingmen's clubs, Christian unions, and the Inner Mission lectured, some of them Nationalist politicians. For political as well as ideological reasons, those belonging to Evangelical workingmen's clubs and Christian unions were unlikely to lure their much more numerous comrades.

The church's social program must be judged a considerable success if Christian nationalism properly formed a part of it and if church nationalism legitimately qualified as Christian. Still Christian nationalism failed to penetrate the working classes, and the church acted more the willing follower than the pioneering leader in reaching its 1927 level of nationalist intensity. In the economic order, the "social" Volkskirche floundered for lack of a conceptual orientation that could either express or transcend its nationalist conservatism. That religious-socialist pastors, more than their German Church counterparts, considered themselves pariahs in the church reflected this differential success. In the political order, however, churchmen found greater opportunity to apply both their sense of activism and their nationalism.

6

VOLKSKIRCHE ACTIVISM:
Foreign Affairs

WARTIME DISPUTES over war aims had already exposed the negative attitude that nationalist churchmen would assume toward republican foreign
policy. As many had condemned a concessive negotiated peace in the war,
they now deplored the foreign policy of the Republic as unnecessarily
concessive. They suspected as well the intentions of the growing ecumenical movements that soon bade them welcome. But these movements also
had their allure, not only as a channel of Christian fellowship but also as a
forum in which to contest the peace settlement and to redeem the nation's
honor.

THE ARMISTICE AND THE VERSAILLES TREATY

The consequences attending defeat subjected republican foreign policy to
unusual pressures, from without and from within. The Allied and Associated powers imposed peace terms that the political Right resolved to resist.
Strengthening this resolve was the Right's claim that the invincible German
armies had been tricked into laying down their arms.

Actually, two conspiracies seemed involved, the one foreign, the other
internal. As seen by nationalist churchmen, President Wilson had lured
Germany to an armistice by dangling the prospect of a just peace. But
Germans found their expectations perfidiously denied in a harsh peace treaty
that Germany need not have signed had it "held out" in the fall of 1918,
as the church had advised. Moreover, traitors had allegedly stabbed the
armies in the back, subverted the home front, and sparked a revolution
that made further resistance impossible. Versions of the stab-in-the-back

or Dolchstoss thesis might vary from a real conspiracy to merely a perverse influence on minds and events. But the myth's consistent effect, within the church as well as without, was to discredit the Republic. Nationalist churchmen could plausibly link Socialists, Democrats (Progressives), and Centrists as accomplices in national betrayal. These parties had sponsored the peace resolution of 1917, participated in governments that accepted the Armistice and the Versailles treaty, and formed the first formal republican coalition. But the major targets for attack were Majority and Independent Socialists, who had led or taken control of the revolution and possessed a long record of hostility to the monarchy and the military.[1]

At the time the two conspiratorial theses had a ring of authenticity, owing to the suggestive circumstances of their origins. Yet these indictments have not survived the scrutiny of historians. The truth is that Hindenburg and Ludendorff urged an armistice only when the German armies appeared on the verge of collapse. Prince Max's subsequent correspondence with President Wilson soon made clear to the war-weary German people that a more promising peace could be had on the basis of Wilson's Fourteen Points than by prolonging a now hopeless war. The ensuing revolution was the result rather than the cause of collapse. It had no effect on the armistice terms, which rendered a resumption of war impossible.

Even before the revolution the outlines of the stab-in-the-back myth had begun to etch the minds of Evangelical churchmen. The November Revolution did not so much generate the myth as confirm the already dark suspicions of those sympathetic with the Fatherland party. Thus Wilhelm Philipps could readily endorse the myth after the revolution had presented the last, seemingly conclusive ingredient. In *Die Reformation*, Philipps cited the British major general Sir Frederick Maurice as writing that the civilian population had stabbed the German army in the back.[2] As late as October 6, Philipps believed that Germany could still win the war. Then came the irreversible Armistice. "Unconquered in the fight of weapons," he logically concluded on December 1, "the German people failed in the [Armistice] negotiations." As he had since the previous year, he now scourged Socialists for elevating party above country. "In order to topple the existing Obrigkeit [authority] and militarism," he asserted on December 22, "they [Socialists] had for a long time undermined the basis of our entire folk and state life." To verify his claims, the following week he cited Maurice.

Some Democratic churchmen bridled at the slur that the Dolchstoss myth cast upon the Republic and the German people. As early as November 16, 1918, Ernst Troeltsch traced Germany's collapse to military failure, to the political ineptitude of the old regime, and to the desire of the masses for peace. But such attempts to penetrate beyond circumstantial evidence were not apparent in periodicals of the church Right.[3] Though he too deplored war leadership, Johannes Schneider, the church statistician, concluded that such ineptitude paled beside the immense responsibility that Socialist revolutionaries bore for losing the war.

The Armistice terms also left churchmen traumatized. "We have been forced to accept the most shockingly cruel armistice conditions from our wanton enemies," wrote the EOK to Old-Prussian congregations soon after the revolution.[4] The EOK had especially in mind the continuation of the effective blockade and lack of any guarantee to repatriate German prisoners of war, measures intended to discourage Germany from resuming hostilities. In an appeal to foreign Christians, the Evangelical League asserted: "Eight hundred thousand men, women and especially children have already fallen victim to the hunger blockade, and eight hundred persons die daily of undernourishment."[5] The Kirchenausschuss wrote: "In expectation of a just peace, it [the German people] laid down its weapons; now, however, it is bitterly disappointed, and it is a mockery of all human rights to forbid many thousands of good men, who did nothing other than their duties as soldiers in honest fighting, to return home."[6] The impression that such appeals fell on deaf ears helped to resolve German church leaders upon boycotting ecumenical discussions with foreign churches held the following year.

The wrath of church leaders soon turned into outrage when they confronted the terms of the Versailles treaty. Such elemental feelings, however, were shrouded in a moral and legal argument that made the sense of loss the more intolerable. The terms, charged churchmen, crassly violated the pre-Armistice agreement, Lansing's note of November 5, 1918. In that note the enemy had agreed, as the Germans had originally requested, to conclude a peace based on Wilson's Fourteen Points and "the principles of settlement enunciated in his subsequent addresses," albeit with several qualifications. The general tenor of these principles was a fair peace based on "impartial justice," on "a justice that plays no favourites."[7] The Brandenburg Provincial Synod protested on May 9: "The German folk laid down its weapons and made itself defenseless in the regrettably unjustified trust in the word of President Wilson and in the... promise of the Entente powers to conclude a just peace with the German folk. Now a brutal peace of force is to be imposed on it."[8]

Two provisions of the peace affected German churches directly: cessions of territory and German colonies. Germany ceded 13 percent of its land surface, containing 6 million inhabitants, most of this area lying in the territory of the Old-Prussian church. Mortified, Old-Prussian churchmen discovered a large "indisputably" German population now added to the new Poland that was supposed to consist of "indisputably Polish populations." Likewise, the cession of Danzig appeared as an infringement of Wilson's principle of self-determination. Germany lost its colonies, and the enemy transferred German missionary property in these as well as other areas to non-German boards of trustees of the same faith.

The Kirchenausschuss and the Old-Prussian church took particular alarm at the treatment that might be accorded Germans in ceded areas. To the German peace delegation, the Kirchenausschuss wrote: "In the West our Evangelical brethren would be delivered up to a government that is hostile to churches [France], in the East to a state [Poland] in which aversion, even hatred, for Evangelical Germany will prevail. That may not be!"[9] But the EOK prepared for the worst. To preserve bonds with congregations in ceded areas, the EOK, then and later, espoused the principle that state borders should not divide churches.

Of the economic exactions, churchmen took most exception to reparations. The Lansing note had specified German reparations for civilian damage; but now the treaty included military pensions as well. At a later date a reparations commission would decide how much the enemy demanded of Germany. By signing the treaty, Germany signed a blank check that, churchmen feared, could seal its economic ruin. That Germany could be forced to pay whatever the commission decided seemed assured by the treaty's military stipulations, which reduced the army to one hundred thousand men and deprived the military of offensive weapons. The left bank of the Rhine was to be occupied for up to fifteen years and both banks permanently demilitarized, leaving the western border open to French military pressure. In the future Germany could neither resist enemy attempts to keep the nation enslaved nor maintain order against the insurrectionary Left, churchmen lamented.

Of all the treaty's articles, those dealing with trials of alleged German war criminals and war guilt provoked the strongest reaction in church quarters. In Article 227, the victors "publicly arraign William II of Hohenzollern." Among those similarly accused of war crimes churchmen expected to find Germany's top military and political war leaders. In such trials, which lacked justification in the pre-Armistice agreement, the enemy would take its vengeance by serving as prosecutor and judge alike. The EOK named July 6, a week after German acceptance of the treaty, a day of mourning. Old-Prussian general superintendents had pastors read in church an address that condemned any attempt to extradite the Kaiser and other German leaders "as a deep humiliation that intends to burden us with disloyalty and dishonor."[10] When later the Allies demanded alleged war criminals for trial, the Kirchenausschuss declared it "the holy duty of all Germans to raise their voices loudly before God and the whole world against an unreasonable demand whose fulfillment would turn the injustices of the enemy into a shocking sacrilege."[11] In the end the fears of churchmen proved groundless. The Kaiser escaped the threat unscathed, and Germany seized the opportunity of trying its own war criminals, a proceeding largely barren of tangible results.

Already broached in the affronting indictment of the Kaiser was the charge of German war guilt. This charge persisted in drawing sharp German attacks because of Article 231:

The Allied and Associated Governments affirm *and Germany accepts the responsibility* of Germany and her allies for *causing all the loss and damage* to which the Allied and Associated *Governments and their nationals* have been subjected as a consequence of the *war imposed upon them by the aggression* of Germany and her allies.[12]

Separately, Articles 231 and 232 constituted two parts of the reparations compromise that the victors reached among themselves in Paris. Taken by itself, Article 231 appeared to set forth Germany's legal liability to pay a full war indemnity, and not merely reparations, as stipulated in the Lansing note. The legal basis of such a claim seemed to lie in the charge that Germany and her allies had launched a premeditated war ("aggression").

Such was the way that the German delegation interpreted Article 231 at Versailles, an interpretation broadly echoed throughout Germany and certainly in the Old-Prussian church. What made the war-guilt article all the more intolerable was the perverse success of the enemy in forcing Germany to confess its own guilt—first by the words "and Germany accepts" and second by compelling the German government to sign the treaty or face invasion. In addition to providing a legal base for reparations, the war-guilt charge, ostensibly motivated by sheer vindictiveness, seemed also to build a legal platform for much of the treaty.

The origins of the war-guilt article, however, suggest quite a different interpretation. Article 231 found its way into the treaty because Allied leaders needed some expression of war guilt in order to appease their volatile and vengeful electorates. The article was meant to advance the peacemakers' moral, but not legal, claim to a full indemnity. In Article 232 the second part of the compromise came into focus by repeating the formula of the Lansing note as the legal basis of reparations, which Annex I interpreted to include military pensions as well. Article 231, accordingly, was an affronting political and moral gesture, completely superfluous to the treaty. Its formal deletion could scarcely have altered Germany's obligation to pay reparations or change any other provision of the treaty.

German war guilt grew into a cause célèbre for German Protestants as they locked horns over it with their foreign counterparts in ecumenical movements. That war guilt was a moral issue of the first magnitude and thus preeminently a matter for the churches was sensed by almost all Old-Prussian churchmen. "The demand that we admit to sole [sic] guilt for the war places a lie on our lips that shamelessly affronts our conscience," declared Old-Prussian general superintendents in their address on July 6, 1919.[13] "As Evangelical Christians we ceremoniously raise before God and men the holy protest against the attempt to press this scar on our nation."

That war guilt was also a political issue of prime importance was quite as apparent, for any refutation of the "lie" should entail a revision of the abominable Versailles treaty. In the meantime, many churchmen opposed fulfilling the terms of the treaty, especially reparations, because, in addition to its monstrous terms, the treaty supposedly rested legally on a "lie" extracted under duress. One must recall that this view of German innocence was no invention after the war, but the firm conviction of German churchmen (and most Germans) from the very beginning.

War guilt was equally a moral and political matter because of the historical perception that especially nationalist churchmen framed. The Allies had forced Germany into war, blamed Germany for causing it, showered the globe with lies about German atrocities, and finally compelled Germany to confess a nonexistent guilt in the peace treaty. This vicious defamation seemed to have had political consequences as well as moral. It had turned much of the world against the righteous German cause and had helped persuade the German masses of their nation's iniquity. Both effects had contributed to German collapse, which had left Germany vulnerable to enemy peace terms. Some nationalist churchmen charged, moreover, that left radicals had seized upon German war guilt to justify the revolution and thus the Republic.[14]

Almost to a man, churchmen counseled rejection of the treaty. Acceptance seemed dishonest and dishonorable in view of the imposed war-guilt confession and Germany's patent inability to fulfill stipulated terms. Churchmen weighed the honor of their nation against an invasion and a renewed blockade, and some bluntly stated their preference for "disaster with honor" to a "dishonorable existence." In any event, signing the treaty made no sense it if amounted to national suicide, as some claimed. There was, moreover, the chance that the enemy would yet yield in the face of German solidarity against signing. [15]

It was to restore folk solidarity, so shattered in the months of collapse and revolution, and to bolster the courage of the government to "hold out" in this last hour of extreme peril that a campaign, largely spontaneous, took shape in church quarters against signing the treaty. Though thoroughly disillusioned by foreign Christians, church leaders urgently appealed to them for help in moderating the peace terms. Church groups and prominent churchmen condemned the treaty, and the Kirchenausschuss and Evangelical Press Association collected hundreds of protest petitions, representing several million Protestants, against the treaty, especially against proposed cessions of German territory and the suppression of German missionary work. "Only an unvarnished 'No' can be the answer," read the petition of the Association of Evangelical Women's Organizations. "For German Evangelical women, honor is more important than their own and their children's welfare." [16]

The campaign in the church helped to expand a much larger effort of the German public to vaunt folk solidarity against signing the treaty. To impress peacemakers in Paris, the coalition government of Majority Socialists, Centrists, and Democrats encouraged this display of defiance. But folk solidarity gave way when the Weimar assembly confronted the victors' deadline to accept the treaty or endure invasion. The German government informed its enemies on June 23, 1919, when the deadline expired, that the assembly's majority, largely composed of Socialists and Centrists, had voted to sign the humiliating treaty. These parties reasoned that the German people would not support renewed war and that a defenseless Germany would eventually be forced into a disastrous peace treaty anyway.

The Democrats Rade and Troeltsch argued afterward that Germany had no choice but to sign. [17] Not so forgiving were Protestants who regarded the acceptance of the treaty as another—and potentially fatal—convergence of the external and internal betrayal that had shaped Germany's destiny during and after the war. Now the charge that the revolution bore the onus for the national disaster appeared the more convincing. Now the admonitions of the church to "hold out" in the war appeared fully justified.

An extreme sense of alienation from the outside world settled over churchmen as a result of the war experience and now the peace settlement. The treaty seemed to spell Germany's doom, to brand it a pariah among nations, and to enslave its people. Two years later Friedrich Siegmund-Schultze tried to sum up the consequences of the settlement: "The group of a thousand irreconcilables, which in 1918 still lived on the will to make war, has now grown slowly to an army of hundreds of thousands again." He ascribed this trend, which he deplored as a moderate pacifist, to the "enemies' policy of hatred."[18]

Siegmund-Schultze grew increasingly concerned about "irreconcilables" within German churches. Echoes of war theology still reverberated. In the year of collapse and dictated peace, the church's nationalism of moral and religious renewal gained a fresh start, though inner doubts nagged war theologians. "What has happened is still monstrous, incomprehensible to us," a pastor wrote in the spring of 1919.[19] "We were victors until the end." He raised the question that he claimed thousands of pious people then asked: "Why has God forsaken us so terribly, [the God] who was our warrior for four years, [who] came to our aid in the fields of battle in the East and West?" He could not believe that the Lord of history acted unjustly. Nor would he accept the explanation that the German cause lacked God's favor. God would redeem Germany's present fate in due time, he believed. From the war theologian Emanuel Hirsch sprang the answer that the God who had blessed German arms in 1914 had not failed the German people. They had failed God and thus courted national disaster.[20] Another contended that God had endowed Germany with the Second Empire, but that the materialist folk had allowed it to be snatched away.[21] If Germany was to regain God's favor, the pietist Josef Gauger argued logically, the nation must return to Him.[22] Others elaborated that the outcome of war and the readiness of the folk to accept revolution and a dishonorable treaty seemed to confirm that the folk's materialism had sapped its moral strength.[23] Germany's collapse must be accepted as God's scourge and prod to moral and religious self-renewal.

Wilhelm Philipps redrafted war theology to fit changed circumstances.[24] Inasmuch as Germany no longer possessed the physical means to resist the enemy, the German nation must prepare for the day "when the Lord of history will give our folk the sign for a new fight of liberation." Though enemies might physically disarm the nation, they could not prevent Germans from "arming mentally and spiritually for the new fight of freedom." The war of liberation that Philipps craved presupposed the religious and moral renewal of the German folk. Those who loved the folk, therefore, must nourish Christianity and "Germanness," recapturing the folk person by person. "Then, but also only then, may we hope that sometime a day of liberation from the humiliation and slavery of the present will appear." Such a frank endorsement of a new war was a rarity in church periodicals. But Philipps did point the direction that war theology tended under conditions of defeat.

As Philipps's example showed, one reason for encouraging renewal was to generate the political and military power that war theology romanticized. Reinhold Seeberg's reading of modern German history made this point even clearer.[25] Finally unified, Germany had exuded power that flowed from a spiritual source. As mammonist capitalism and socialism spread, materials soon infected the folk and weakened the spirit that unified it, explaining Germany's collapse in war. Seeberg feared that the materialism of the folk might condemn Germany to perpetual impotence, the prey of its vicious neighbors. But if the Christian national spirit could reconvert the folk, Germany could marshal the power it required to prevail over its predatory enemies. Here the equation of renewal with national power and of materialism with national impotence was clearly expressed.

The prospects of renewal conditioned the reaction of nationalist churchmen to the enemy's behavior and to German foreign policy. They played up the humiliation and misery that resulted from dishonorable conduct in order to goad the folk to renew its Christian and nationalist commitment.[26] Moreover, just as war theologians had spurred the church's summons to hold out in war, nationalist churchmen now tended to condemn the concessive republican foreign policy that had begun with the Armistice and the Versailles treaty. For if the imposed peace amounted to a continuation of war by other means, as many nationalist churchmen chose to believe, the war had not ended and the enemy remained the enemy. The peace resolution of 1917, the pre-Armistice agreement, and the Versailles treaty had already demonstrated the folly of compromise with an immoral enemy bent on Germany's destruction. Concessions would also parry the prod that the treaty gave for renewal. Any internationalist frame of reference or appeal for international cooperation was likewise suspect for spiking the conversion that the nation required for its liberation. Finally, admission of war guilt would sully the German conscience for the wrong reason. Nationalist churchmen sensed that such an admission would challenge the righteousness of the German cause, contest the church's behavior in the war, give the lie to war theology, justify the Versailles treaty and the revolution, and tarnish the good conscience that Germans required for believing that a renewed Germany might ultimately stay the aggression of its enemies.

CONTESTING THE PEACE SETTLEMENT

Caught in this xenophobic atmosphere, German Protestant churches turned a deaf ear to the first foreign attempts to draw them into ecumenical discussions. But once having joined, the German churches gained a worldwide audience for their objections to the war-guilt article through the two ecumenical movements that took shape in the 1920s and that, after the Second World War, merged to form the present World Council of Churches. The Faith and Order movement stemmed from the bold vision of an American Episcopalian bishop, Charles Brent, who since 1910 had inspired American Protestant churches to lay plans for a world conference to examine theological issues separating Christians. By contrast, the Life and Work movement sprang directly from the disheartening realization of Protestant leaders that the churches had failed to dampen the passions of war. As war clouds gathered, a group of concerned Protestants, Siegmund-Schultze among them, convened on August 2, 1914, in Constance, Germany, to assess the contribution that the churches might yet make for the cause of peace. Forced by the outbreak of the war to disband, the group nevertheless constituted itself as the World Alliance for Promoting International Friendship through the Churches and kept alive the hope for an international Christian conference to encourage a peace of reconciliation.[27]

Because of his leadership in trying to arrange a wartime conference, Nathan Söderblom, archbishop of Uppsala, Sweden, became the moving force behind the budding Life and Work movement. As a neutral church leader, he aroused interest throughout the Protestant world for a conference — eventually held in 1925 in Stockholm — to deal not only with the pressing issue of peace but also with the application of Christian ethics to society in general. Inasmuch as the dispute fell within the scope of social ethics, the Life and Work movement felt the full brunt of the war-guilt controversy.

After the conclusion of peace, the war-guilt issue intruded upon ecumenical discussions as "the central and most burning of all the problems debated in post-war years."[28] The issue came immediately to a head at a meeting of the International Committee of the World Alliance, held from September 20 to October 4, 1919, at Oud Wassenaer near The Hague. Only two French Methodists represented the French position, for French Reformed leaders had refused to participate unless German churchmen recognized Germany's guilt. Eventually the German delegates felt constrained to follow the suggestion of Professor Wilfred Monod, a Reformed leader and the president of the French World Alliance committee. In a pointed letter, Monod demanded that German churchmen admit, at least, that German violation of Belgian neutrality in 1914 was unjust, for such a flagrant violation of treaties warped the moral basis of Christian civilization. This the hard-pressed Germans felt obliged to admit, but only for themselves, not for the German churches, which they did not officially represent.

Monod harbored doubts about the sincerity of the declaration. German violation of Belgian neutrality, a prominent German church leader explained to him, while morally reprehensible, could be justified by diplomatic, legal, and military considerations—casuistry, in Monod's opinion, impossible for a Christian. Moreover, the German admission of limited guilt had provoked widespread disgust in German church quarters, even within the German Association of the World Alliance, which Siegmund-Schultze served as secretary. It is little wonder that suspicious French Protestants persisted in their demand that German churches acknowledge Germany's war guilt openly as a prerequisite of French participation in ecumenical meetings. Such was the position of the Protestant Federation of France in convention at Lyons on November 21, 1919.[29]

Unsettled in 1919, the divisive war-guilt issue grew acute in August 1920 when three ecumenical meetings took place, significantly, in "neutral" Switzerland. Two met in Geneva to prepare later world conferences on life and work and on faith and order. A third was a session of the International Committee of the World Alliance, held in St. Beatenberg. German delegates attended in a private capacity without the official endorsement of their churches. For this reason, sensitive French delegates found it easier to take part.

At the first meeting, on life and work, the war-guilt issue clouded prospects for agreement on composing the world conference that Söderblom proposed. In an official letter, the Protestant Federation of France fixed specific responsibility for the war upon Germany and Austria, both guilty of premeditated aggression and of violating recognized principles of international law. Worse still, German and Austrian Christians had, in effect, violated their Christian conscience by refusing to recognize the monstrous guilt of their governments and by willfully promoting an unjust war. As debate on the French letter grew impassioned, A. W. Schreiber, a member of the Kirchenausschuss and a missions director, arose to read a letter that the Kirchenausschuss had sent to the second meeting explaining why German churches had refused to take part in ecumenical discussions. The Kirchenausschuss assailed foreign Christians for not protesting the defamation of German character, the unjust Versailles peace, the hunger blockade, the stationing of black troops in Germany, the destruction of German foreign missions, and the subjection of German minorities in foreign lands. Schreiber personally rejected the Oud Wassenaer confession of limited war guilt. Unable to satisfy one side without affronting the other, the delegates decided to welcome all churches to the projected world conference unconditionally.[30]

French and Belgian delegates again asked for evidence of German contrition at the meeting of the World Alliance in August. Apparently this demand (missing from the minutes) required a German admission beyond the specific case of Belgian neutrality that the Oud Wassenaer confession had addressed. German delegates chose to remain discreetly silent, and the threatening storm passed. But another problem arose when the Management Subcommittee nominated the archbishop of Canterbury as president of the World Alliance. For fear that his election might discredit the World Alliance in Germany, Friedrich Spiecker, the president of the German Association, moved to postpone all elections for a year. Suspicious German Protestants, German delegates reasoned, might consider Anglican domination of the World Alliance an extension of British imperialism under a religious cloak. Already some suspected the Faith and Order movement, which had originated within the Episcopal fold, for precisely that reason. The International Committee nevertheless elected the archbishop and, along with him, Spiecker as one of a number of vice-presidents.[31]

That the meetings of the three ecumenical groups in August had done nothing to draw the poison of the war-guilt issue was apparent in the intransigent stance of President Wilhelm Pechmann of the Church Federation Assembly. Until the "monstrous injustice done to the German people" by the Versailles treaty was reversed, the ecumenical movement would find no positive response from German churches.[32] Such was the message that he conveyed in reply to the Swedish church's greetings to the 1921 Assembly. Indeed, attempts to execute the treaty's provisions until 1925, when the Stockholm conference convened, could only exacerbate ecumenical relations and call down the wrath of nationalist churchmen on the concessive response of German governments. A cascade of issues—the "black disgrace," disarmament, the behavior of the League of Nations, the plebiscite in Upper Silesia, reparations, the Ruhr occupation, and the Dawes plan—showered down on the beleaguered Republic, and all of them, seemingly, sprang from the ultimate question of war guilt.

As its letter on ecumenical participation indicated, the Kirchenausschuss protested the stationing of Senegalese, Madagascan, and Moroccan soldiers in the French occupation zone in the Rhineland. On June 23, 1920, the Kirchenausschuss appealed to Christians throughout the world what it and other irate German Protestants called the "black disgrace," the maltreatment of German civilians and violation of German women and adolescents by "African natives": "No military discipline, however applied, can control the wild instincts of these ten thousand, for years torn from their homes and devoid of Christian education."[33] The Kirchenausschuss vaguely suggested that French occupation policy had intended the humiliation that resulted.

The "black disgrace" paled beside the implications of German disarmament. From 1919 to 1921 the nation endured Allied ultimata to accept the Versailles treaty, disarmament, and a reparations settlement. The division of Upper Silesia by the League Council after the plebiscite in 1921 seemed all too patently a decision mandated by Polish and French national interests. In 1923 Germany could do nothing to prevent French and Belgian occupation of the Ruhr. The lesson that nationalist churchmen purported to learn was that a nation shorn of military power was denied its fair rights and honor. Germany urgently needed a strong army in order to initiate an independent and nonconcessive foreign policy. For these reasons, one chronicler wrote that German foreign policy must aim to remove military restrictions that perpetuated Germany's servitude.[34] The Versailles treaty justified German disarmament as a means of initiating the general disarmament to which Article 8 of the covenant committed members of the League of Nations. Only in 1925 did the league begin to consider general disarmament, and thereafter only falteringly. In February 1925 the Allies refused to vacate the Cologne zone, for the reason that Germany had not sufficiently disarmed. Nationalist churchmen considered such zeal for German disarmament, unmatched by similar zeal for universal disarmament, hypocritical.

The League of Nations seemed as incapable of meting out justice to Germany as of ensuring its military security. Before Germany signed the Versailles treaty, some churchmen welcomed the league as an instrument of peace. More typical before the signing, and certainly afterward, was the view that the league, marshaled behind Germany's enemies, acted to nail the lid on the treaty and in other ways to suppress Germany, while hypocritically mouthing words of peace and justice.[35] Whatever goodwill existed in Germany toward the league dissipated rapidly after the treaty took effect. Vengeful France now appeared as the villain who manipulated the league. Both church liberals and the more orthodox heaped abuse on the league, dubbing it a "syndicate of the victors," a "system of enslavement," an "instrument of French policy."[36]

The line dividing those for and those against the conception of a league, like the line on war, fell between churchmen of extreme and moderate nationalist views. Extreme nationalists tended to regard a commitment to any kind of league as incompatible with their moral commitment to the folk as an order of creation.[37] After all, God had not endowed the created world with an order that transcended the folk and spanned nations. Repeatedly Josef Gauger argued that the League of Nations, like the Tower of Babel, represented an abortive effort of prideful men to secure earthly happiness without God. The most thorough repudiations of the league stemmed from the notion that the Lord of history presided over a chaotic world whose divinely ordained dynamic the league ought not and could not arrest for a peace based on the status quo. Extreme nationalists, accordingly, censured not only radical pacifists but also "organization" pacifists who would apply force through international structures for the sake of peace. Even the moderate nationalist, Otto Dibelius, risked this censure for endorsing a more evenhanded league as one hopeful means of securing world peace.

Almost all churchmen could agree that the status quo of Versailles was intolerable. Siegmund-Schultze even tried to persuade an American friend that world peace required a new peace conference to revise the treaty.[38] Whether Germany ought to join the league turned not only on social-ethical considerations but also on German prospects for revising the treaty through the league. Moderate members of the World Alliance and some liberals—not all of them "organization" pacifists—reasoned that Germany could well succeed by pleading its own case, and in the process help fortify the league as an instrument of justice.[39] But dominant church opinion opposed Germany's entry for practical as well as social-ethical reasons. By subscribing to the covenant, Germany would voluntarily commit itself to fulfill an unrevised treaty and whitewash the "lie" of Versailles. In any event, it seemed highly unlikely that German statesmen could prevail against the entrenched power of Germany's enemies in the league.[40]

Resistance to disarmament and contempt for the league hardened as the enemy proceeded to exact reparations. In January 1921 the Allies accepted a tentative proposal that would demand 226 billion gold marks over a period of forty-two years. The Kirchenausschuss predicted dire consequences. In its protest of February 10, 1921, the Kirchenausschuss declared that the Allies' "intentions—it is no longer possible to doubt them—aim at nothing less than the fearful goal of shattering and irreparably destroying the economic and . . . political existence of our folk in its most elementary conditions."[41] Likewise, the Association of Evangelical Women's Organizations protested that such an enormous reparation burden would enslave "our children and children's children," and recommended rejection of the terms "without regard for the consequences."[42]

The sum finally set by the Reparation Commission on April 27, 1921, proved less onerous—132 billion gold marks. The Allied Supreme Council issued an ultimatum on May 5, 1921, demanding, among other things, that the German government fulfill the new reparations schedule as set forth by the commission. The government that accepted the ultimatum resolved upon a policy of "fulfillment" to demonstrate Germany's good faith as well as the impossibility of complying. It was this policy that subsequent governing coalitions generally attempted to follow. And it was this policy that nationalist churchmen perfervidly condemned. Why jump off the Ulm cathedral, asked *Licht und Leben*, to prove that one can be killed?[43] Lurking behind this question was another, namely, whether Germany should feel obliged to fulfill.

The Kirchenausschuss would no doubt apply the conclusion that it had already drawn in its protest against the higher reparation figure to the lower one as well: "A great Christian cultural folk, rendered defenseless, is to be fatally struck from the ranks of free and viable peoples in the name and pretext of peace and the execution of a 'peace treaty.'"[44] Even the Democrat Ernst Troeltsch charged, as did many other churchmen, that the French intended not merely to exact reparations but also to ruin Germany through occupation when the harsh demands proved impossible to fulfill.[45] Again *Die Reformation* concluded that Germany must reject enemy demands, this time the reparation ultimatum, and wrongly concluded that the Allies had no intention of using force.[46] Then and later nationalist chroniclers traced postwar economic distress to reparations as well as to republican misman-agement of the economy.

Almost from the start, the German government, whose budget showed an incredibly large deficit, defaulted on reparation payments, and the schedule soon could be considered little more than a dead letter. Eventually, Premier Raymond Poincaré, goaded by exasperated French public opinion, resolved to break the reparation impasse by exacting tribute from the mines and industry of the Ruhr basin. On January 11, 1923, the French sent troops and technical experts, joined by Belgian forces, into the Ruhr. Denying that the treaty justified such sanctions, the German government encouraged passive resistance, subsidizing it by further inflating the currency.

Especially nationalist churchmen rejoiced that Germany had finally taken up the strands of an active foreign policy of resistance. Previous govern-ment concessions seemed all the more pointless, since France had occupied the Ruhr anyway. Even Siegmund-Schultze grew exasperated that the French had refused to cooperate with a government that had seriously attempted fulfillment.[47] The previous claim that a defenseless Germany was denied rights and honor also seemed dramatically confirmed. In this vein, the Landeskirche Committee (EOK and GSV) of the Old-Prussian church, declaring that "the enemy has added to the long list of atrocities against a defenseless people a new act of violence that scorns all justice," urged its Ruhr parishioners to "hold out."[48] "If now Germany is finally crushed and deprived of rights," wrote Johannes Schneider, "generations after us will have to bear an existence of slavery."[49]

The Ruhr occupation triggered the first open political clash between French and German Protestants since the 1920 ecumenical meetings. On February 2, 1923, Swedish Lutheran bishops condemned the "methods of violent force" and the "greed for power and short-sighted selfishness" that they saw in the French and Belgian action.[50] On February 27, the Kirchenausschuss appealed to foreign Protestant churches to raise their voices likewise against French injustice. "We were and are now ready to live in peace with our western neighbor within the borders of our national culture," the appeal concluded. "He, however, will not let the German people live and does to us what is not just before God and man. The much acclaimed world conscience is stilled."[51] Replying on February 22, the Protestant Federation of France accused the Swedish bishops of bias.[52] France sought not revenge but reparations, maliciously and unjustly refused by Germany. A heated correspondence between German and French leaders of the World Alliance reiterated the arguments of the two sides. It soon became clear that the Kirchenausschuss had hoped in vain for an outpouring of protest from foreign Protestants. "The world gets excited about atrocities in the Congo," wrote Otto Dibelius, "but when violence is used against Germans, the Anglo-Saxon world wraps itself in icy silence!"[53]

Under a new chancellor, Gustav Stresemann, the coalition government concluded that it could support passive resistance no longer, because of the collapse of the currency and extremist threats to federal unity. On September 26, 1923, without having forced the French to negotiate or retreat, the government called off passive resistance. Nationalist churchmen concluded that the republican coalition parties, now joined by Stresemann's People's party, had returned to the policy of concessions that had caused Germany such grief in the recent past. The specter arose once more of ignominious concessions made by republican parties during 1918 and 1919, and for some a resumption of war with France seemed preferable to subjection to its will.[54]

Recriminations over the end of passive resistance soon blended into the struggle over the Dawes plan, which, accepted by the Reichstag in August 1924, set a more realistic reparations schedule, paving the way for French withdrawal from the Ruhr. The plan would restore the political and economic unity of the nation, obviate a recurrence of the Ruhr occupation, and stabilize the German economy. These advantages appealed to half of the Nationalist Reichstag faction, influenced by industrial and agrarian interests, Christian unions, and complaints from occupied areas. The other half followed Nationalist leaders in denouncing the plan as a second Versailles, for it allowed foreign creditors an abiding influence on the German economy and failed to scale down the sum total of reparations that now Germany voluntarily accepted.[55]

The eruption in the Nationalist faction flowed over into church quarters, where most active churchmen had thrown their political support to Nationalists since elections to the Weimar assembly. Since its founding, party regulars had split over whether to enter a coalition or to remain in permanent and principled opposition in a republic that they detested. By joining, Nationalists could wield greater influence over foreign policy and such matters as school legislation (which churchmen followed with equally rapt attention). Within the party, the Christian Socials around Mumm took this line, as did Friedrich Winckler, who presided over the Old-Prussian General Synod and, after the Dawes crisis, over the Nationalist party as interim chairman. Stresemann, now foreign minister, and the Centrists offered Nationalists a strong inducement to voting for the Dawes legislation: entry into the government and a public refutation of German war guilt. Though coalition negotiations then aborted, the government, redeeming Stresemann's promise, did publicly denounce war guilt and Nationalists did enter a coalition in the following year. In the postmortem of Nationalist behavior, the question debated by Nationalist churchmen was whether expedience or principle ought to prevail in Nationalist politics.

In answering this question, the Lutheran Wilhelm Laible and pietist Josef Gauger, both editors of influential periodicals, found themselves on opposing sides.[56] Both regarded the Republic as a disastrous experiment, and both desired a legal restoration of the monarchy, as did the Nationalist party. Both agreed that the deceptive ideology of Socialists and Democrats, for want of firm nationalist commitment, had generated a weak and concessive foreign policy. Both deplored the multiparty parliamentary Republic for thwarting a consistent foreign policy because of shifting majorities. Finally, both agreed that Germany could not possibly pay the reparations that the Dawes plan required. Despite this agreement, the two editors could not see eye to eye on the Dawes vote. Ever since the Nationalist election victory in May, Laible had urged the Nationalist party to join a coalition for the sake of German foreign policy. He found that, on balance, advantages outweighed disadvantages in the Dawes plan, especially because of the prospects of a Ruhr evacuation and denunciation of war guilt. Not so forgiving of Nationalist deputies who had voted for the Dawes plan, including Christian Socials, Gauger cried, "Our trust is dishonored." Putting principle above all else, he censured these Nationalists for betraying the political convictions of Evangelical Christians to private interests and opportunism. It seemed inconceivable that defecting Nationalist deputies would claim credit for the war-guilt denunciation when the reparations that they now voluntarily approved rested on the very "lie" that the government repudiated. His disillusionment was all the more bitter since without Nationalist defections the total Dawes legislative package could not have passed. For him and his pietist friends, the question of abandoning the Nationalists grew acute.

As manuevering over the Dawes vote suggested, Nationalists had tried to convert alleged German war guilt into a partisan issue. Now that the government in the Dawes debate had publicly rejected German war guilt, the Foreign Office balked at transmitting that declaration to creditor nations, as Stresemann had promised. Not until the eve of the Locarno conference in the following year did Stresemann inform the British and French, but without insisting upon consequences for the Versailles treaty. Everyone—Nationalists, Stresemann, and foreign governments most particularly—knew that an official German assault on war guilt would also amount to a direct assault on the treaty. Nationalists hoped that such an assault would shatter Stresemann's foreign policy of conciliation, begun with the Dawes plan. Also a staunch nationalist who personally rejected German war guilt, Stresemann recognized that because of its impotence Germany could realistically pursue no other policy. Revision of the detested treaty depended on the goodwill of others, which in turn depended upon voluntary German acceptance of treaty obligations and especially upon calming French fears of German resurgence in the future. Stresemann did not dare to press the issue with foreign governments.

If the government vascillated, the German Protestant churches did not. They pressed to "clarify" the war-guilt issue directly through the Life and Work ecumenical movement. One may wonder whether some Nationalist churchmen hoped thereby to aid the attack of the Nationalist party on Stresemann's policy of conciliation. But any demonstration of sympathy for Germany's plight through church channels would serve Stresemann's policy quite as well. Apparently for that reason the German Foreign Office subsidized the German delegation's expenses at the Stockholm conference.[57]

If German Protestant churches took a giant step beyond their government, they likewise had to draw realistic limits on their appeal for redress. It would not do to argue for German exoneration in the interest of German revisionism. Churches in former enemy lands would be on guard against precisely this implication, and the Life and Work movement could well break apart without any gain for either the German or the ecumenical cause. For this reason, German churchmen argued with their ecumenical counterparts as though the moral blemish of war guilt and the dictates of national politics were separable. Eventually the movement took this fiction at face value as the only practicable way of bleeding ecumenism of its poison.

It is clear, however, that German church leaders did fervently hope for political consequences from moral exoneration in ecumenical quarters. Though this point was infrequently stated, it followed implicitly from their tendency to blame war guilt for all ills stemming from the Versailles treaty. "If German war guilt is a lie, then it must be pointed out continuously that the Treaty of Versailles is unjustified morally and legally," wrote Gauger.[58] That being the case, the treaty must somehow lose its force. Such is also the only conclusion that one can draw from the appeal to foreign Christians that the Kirchenausschuss intended to issue in November 1922. "The inhuman treatment of Germany, aimed at complete destruction, is justified with the assertion that Germany bears the blame for the war and should be punished for it," read the appeal. "But this assertion is completely false. . . . One cannot appeal to the guilt confession of Versailles that was extorted . . . from a defenseless people with the most grievous of threats."[59] Once the issue formally entered ecumenical channels for resolution, however, exculpation for the sake of ecumenism, not for German revisionism, had to take pride of place in official German arguments.

Though agreed on the need for a reassessment of the Versailles verdict, opinions divided over the degree of German war guilt and over the results that a reexamination ought to yield. By analyzing the origins of the war and war atrocities, German members of the World Alliance sought at first to convince their foreign brethren that Germany bore no exclusive and probably no primary blame for the dreadful war, and hardly merited the severe peace settlement. Willing to admit Germany's guilt as they understood it, they found it impossible to grant the broad confession demanded by some foreign Protestants, inasmuch as the former enemy appeared far from unblemished and as such an admission might be exploited to justify the hated peace settlement. Rade, Troeltsch, and Siegmund-Schultze upheld Germany's obligation to pay reparations, though all three questioned whether Germany bore any greater responsibility for the war than other belligerents. Rade argued that reparations stemmed from defeat, not from Article 231. No nation could afford to accept such harsh armistice terms, including reparations, unless beaten in the field. What characterized members of the World Alliance and those disposed toward it was a general willingness to distribute guilt in the hope of securing some modus vivendi that could foster international reconciliation.[60]

The general tone of nationalist churchmen was considerably more defiant. Their view of war guilt reflected a determination to assault the treaty more directly. President Pechmann of the Church Federation Assembly likened the enemy to a "guilty wolf" and Germany to an innocent "lamb."[61] The thesis of Germany's essential innocence had greater prospects of sparking national renewal and generating public pressure for a more determined foreign policy. Even as public opinion in Britain and America began to shift against the thesis of sole German guilt, nationalist Germans kept up their drumfire, because treaty terms still stood unaltered. Conceding a measure of guilt might also imply that revolutionaries had justifiably overthrown a guilty government and subverted its army.

German declarations, however resolute, could have little effect unless foreign Protestant churches took up the cry against the war-guilt article. At Oud Wassenaer in 1919, therefore, German delegates had urged the World Alliance to promote an international investigation of the issue. Finally at its convention in September 1924, the German Association of the World Alliance resolved to ask sister branches to honor its request for such an investigation through impartial archival research, a procedure welcomed by the Kirchenausschuss. The church then adopted the argument that it was for moral and ecumenical, rather than for political reasons that the matter required a thorough clarification.[62] But the problem could not be dissected so neatly. If Germans broached it at the Stockholm conference, the French warned, the issue might wreak irreparable damage on the ecumenical movement.[63]

Indeed, the French had much cause to worry about the outcome of the Stockholm conference, held from August 19 through August 30, 1925. They had failed to pry a war-guilt confession out of German churches. Worse yet, German Protestants, encouraged by a Western ground swell of revisionism, had moved to the offensive.

By 1925 German churches had played an active role in the Life and Work movement for several years. Soon after the founding of the Church Federation in May 1922, the Kirchenausschuss had decided to participate despite widespread German distrust of foreign churches. Shortly before the Stockholm conference the Kirchenausschuss took the position that its delegation should not broach war guilt at the conference, lest the attempt backfire and harm the German cause as well as the conference. On national and international issues the delegation should speak with one voice through delegation chairman Hermann Kapler, president of the Kirchenausschuss and the EOK, and thrash out the German position beforehand in closed and confidential discussions of the delegation. Even before the conference began, such an issue arose: the Kirchenausschuss contemplated bolting the conference if the Ruhr were not evacuated as promised by August 15, 1925, four days before the conference convened.[64]

With elaborate ceremony and hospitality, Stockholm welcomed the six hundred delegates who represented Protestant and Eastern Orthodox churches in some thirty-seven countries. Many delegates, particularly from churches in countries neutral or victorious in the recent war, came with high hopes that the churches could help create the moral prerequisites of a durable peace. Their optimism was encouraged by the Dawes plan of 1924 and even more by recent proposals for strengthening the League of Nations. On the horizon loomed the security pacts that would soon be known as the Locarno treaties, which would also facilitate Germany's entry into the League of Nations. Probably a large majority of the eighty German delegates, half of them from the Old-Prussian church, could not share this optimism. The international developments that encouraged others seemed more like an array of mechanisms praised as instruments of peace but calculated to shackle and enslave Germany. It is little wonder that German delegates found it difficult to adjust to repeated expressions of "goodwill" and "international friendship."[65] That German delegates would attend at all is perhaps more surprising than their reservations.

The primary purpose of the conference was to discuss the application of Christian social ethics to the contemporary world, not matters of doctrine. But soon German delegates detected an alien doctrinal assumption regarding the nature of the Kingdom of God in the speeches of their Anglican and American Reformed counterparts—the assumption that the Kingdom of God can be gradually constructed on earth according to distinctly Christian principles and through man's efforts. When the bishop of Winchester spoke of moral progress in international relations since the war, and when the American Presbyterian Charles Wishart linked Calvin, Wilson, and the league with the task of making the earth a suitable threshold for entrance into heaven, the distraught Wilhelm Laible could think only of the unjust humiliations that Germany had endured. Before the outspoken general superintendent of the Rhine province, Karl Klingemann, arose the specter of Versailles and black "angels of peace" (occupation troops) whenever he heard French pacifists extolling peace.[66] German delegates suspected the "Western" concept of an immanent Kingdom of God for invoking divine approval of a peace settlement that suited the national interests of their erstwhile enemies.

So long as no resolutions appeared, the German delegation largely maintained an official silence on issues that touched national concerns. Toward the end of the conference, however, the Third Commission introduced a subcommittee report that contained a series of objectionable resolutions on war and collective security. No thoroughgoing pacifist statements, the resolutions recognized as legitimate a war of defense and patriotism within limits. But they did condemn war as incompatible with Christianity, define an aggressor as that nation which rejected arbitration of disputes, and praise the league as the only organization available to restore international order, commending it to Christians. Bishop Brent expressed the sublime hope of the subcommittee in the most memorable quotation of the conference: "that the Christian Church if it be so minded can, in the name of Christ, rule out war and rule in peace within a generation. I may be a fool, but if so I am God's fool."[67]

Such optimism seemed frightfully naive to most German delegates, of course, perhaps to all. One can understand that praise for the league would raise their hackles, but their reason for opposition to resolutions against war is less obvious. Confronting each other at the conference were two extreme views of how God related to His creation. Brent, like numerous Western churchmen, assumed that one ought to distill static principles from the teachings of Jesus and apply them mechanically and directly to international affairs by way of international organization. By contrast, several German speakers assumed that God had rigged His creation to make war inevitable because of the omnipresence of sin, or that the Lord of history manipulated His creation as He deemed proper. Hence the assertion that efforts to "moralize" international relations arrogantly presupposed human evaluation of divine judgment, which actually invoked force to thwart man's will.[68] One wonders how such a position, repudiating any abstract notion of justice, could square with German demands for redressing the wrongs inflicted on their homeland. Even though the German delegation as a whole did not subscribe to a social-Darwinist appreciation of war, it is clear that the attitudes of moderate nationalists and "organization" pacifists found a much fainter echo in statements of German delegates.

The political motive for rejecting the antiwar resolutions is even more obscure. Again a number of German delegates had gotten the impression that church leaders of victorious nations aimed to perpetuate an unjust peace settlement, this time by their stand on war. The intriguing question is whether at least part of the German delegation regarded as eminently just a war to redress the Versailles settlement, but a war that could run counter to proposed resolutions. Perhaps General Superintendent Klingemann, a Pan-German, entertained such a view when he remarked in plenary discussions: "It has been stated that there may be complications in the life of nations that only war can solve."[69]

Since the resolutions affected national concerns, German delegates assembled in closed and confidential caucuses, as previously agreed, to formulate a united response. The delegation confronted the twofold task of upholding the goals of the conference while eliciting understanding for the German political cause, thereby helping to loosen the shackles that bound Germany. Clearly one proposed declaration, probably submitted by the indignant Wilhelm Laible, expressed well the predominant political sentiment of the delegation, but not its overriding concern for the conference. The declaration would repudiate Germany's alleged war guilt against the wishes of the Kirchenausschuss, graphically describe and condemn the effects of the Versailles treaty, and accuse the league of enforcing an unjust peace.[70]

But the delegation's executive committee turned a deaf ear to the submitted declaration, and, after heated controversy, President Kapler's conciliatory and yet evasive proposal won out. During the morning plenary session on August 25, Kapler rose to read on behalf of his delegation a short statement that astutely avoided a polemic rebuttal. It merely asserted that the resolutions "do not take fully into account the extraordinary difficulties of the problem involved, and their unconditional adoption might, contrary to the intentions of the commission, lead to fatal misconceptions." Finally, the statement revealed the strategy of the German delegation by expressing the hope that no vote on the commission's report would follow.[71] Had the resolutions passed, the stock of the movement would have plummeted among Protestants in Germany. The German delegates staved off the disaster of a positive vote as well as the disaster of contesting war guilt.

Kapler's declaration alarmed the conference, for German reservations spiked collective action and raised doubts about the delegation's moral commitment against war. Sensing the need to clarify the German position, Klingemann, with the consent of his delegation, appealed for the sympathy of the conference. He argued the impossibility of harmonizing existing international conditions and "the present state of the League" with the Kingdom of God. He movingly described Germany's maltreatment at the hands of the Allies.[72] For many German delegates, Klingemann's candid speech represented the high point of the conference, since it discharged their duty of stirring up moral concern for Germany's plight.

Reflecting the deadlock reached in the debate of the proposed resolutions, the Stockholm "Message," which summed up the common mind of the conference, contained only a comparatively weak statement on war: "We summon the Churches to share with us our sense of the horror of war, and of its futility as a means of settling international disputes."[73] That the German delegation bore primary responsibility for such an innocuous statement, as Wilfred Monod subsequently charged, seems confirmed in Kirchenausschuss minutes. Many non-German and even some German delegates found the "Message" and its statement on war too "tame, timid, and thin."[74]

All non-German conferees could at least take satisfaction from the German refusal to broach the explosive war-guilt issue in plenary session. But this refusal did not prevent German delegates from working behind the scenes to air their grievances through a friendly if passionate exchange of views with fellow delegates. German delegates also made a collective attempt to kindle interest in their cause at a German-American luncheon, requested by Germans and arranged by obliging Americans. As the German spokesman, Walter Simons, chief justice of the German Supreme Court, urged Americans to promote an impartial investigation of the guilt charge. For the Americans, Union Seminary professor William Adams Brown replied that until passions subsided each side should take the first step by confessing its own responsibility for the past war. Though Simons agreed, one of the assembled German delegates asked "in a tone which was evidently quite serious, 'Dr. Brown, how can we repent when nothing we have done calls for repentance?' "[75]

The Americans as well as the British and now even the French regarded the divisive issue as a dangerous political matter that they would much prefer to ignore. But the German delegation could not possibly leave for home without showing some progress. Failure to do so would dash the fervent hopes pinned on them and recoil heavily upon the reputation of the church and the Stockholm movement in Germany. Near the end of the conference, therefore, President Kapler addressed a letter to the newly established Continuation Committee. On behalf of the German churches he contended that a clarification of the imputed guilt "is morally a task of paramount importance" for ecumenical cooperation.[76] The letter alluded in no way to political consequences.

Despite the subdued tone of the letter, most delegates returned to Germany happy with the results of the conference. At home, however, two groups of bitter critics soon assailed them. At the moment, the less threatening was the group that deplored the sacrifice of Germany's cause to an international movement. The German delegation had unconscionably ignored its primary duty of fighting for the nation's exoneration in Stockholm. This thesis was most forcibly argued by Landessuperintendent Rische of Wismar, who also doubled as a folkish politician.[77] In time this group would grow in numbers and force Kapler to feel, like Stresemann, hamstrung by the political Right. The second group inverted Rische's argument by charging that the delegation's unwarranted preoccupation with Germany's political interests had regrettably sabotaged the ecumenical cause.

This battery of critics centered around those who had attended the conference as reporters or invited guests but who, with one exception, could not join the delegation in its closed caucusing. They observed from afar and disliked what they saw. The exception was Siegmund-Schultze, who had attended some of the causcuses without participating. But, back in Germany he spoke with abandon—in the pages of *Die Eiche,* which he edited. His report was all the more devastating because he could claim intimate knowledge of caucus debates, which other critics lacked.

Siegmund-Schultze's charges fell into three categories.[78] First, he criticized the composition of the delegation, made up primarily of elderly church worthies of rather orthodox leanings, unskilled in ecumenical affairs. More serious was their personal behavior in Stockholm—their vain boasts about German accomplishments in social relations, their inconsiderate monopolization of discussion time, and their refusal to mix socially with others. Most serious was his third charge that the German delegation had acted not to foster the ecumenical movement but rather to represent the German national political cause. Centered around nine Nationalist deputies in the German delegation, wrote Siegmund-Schultze, was a political clique that tried to guide the delegation's decisions. He claimed that dissenters had been treated rudely: "I cannot express with words how hateful, unbrotherly, and spiteful the conduct of most was toward each other." Through his wide contacts with foreign churchmen he claimed to have learned that German conduct had alienated the sympathy of other delegates for Germany's plight.

To confirm his charges, Siegmund-Schultze pointed to chauvinist commentaries written by participating delegates and to published comments of foreign churchmen. According to the Swiss church leader, Adolf Keller, other delegates viewed Germans in attendance as part of two distinct groups: a small number of congenial men already know in ecumenical circles; and a larger group of suspicious, nationalist churchmen.[79]

Normally long suffering, Siegmund-Schultze had his patience stretched and snapped in Stockholm. If his collective portrait of the German delegation showed what he said it did, however, Siegmund-Schultze was surely wrong in his more extreme conclusions. If delegates so resentful and paranoiac could yet mix socially, pray, and worship with their "enemies" under a common banner and act with such discretion at the critical moment, the spirit of Stockholm must have run a dead heat with the German national spirit. German delegates claimed no more and no less.[80] In their opinion, they had managed to balance two conflicting sets of expectations to the advantage of both causes.

To Siegmund-Schultze any advancement of German political interests seemed an affront to the movement. Such an objection made no sense, because of the nature of the Stockholm conference. All deliberations, to be sure, had to start with Christian principle, not with a secular ethic or narrow political advantage. It was expected and hoped, however, that application of principle would have a political effect. In this sense, Westerners acted more "politically" than the Germans, by introducing the league issue directly into deliberations. If the German delegation had followed suit, it would have asked the conference to clarify the moral principle of war guilt and apply principle by endorsing revisionism. For as Erich Stange, secretary of the movement's European section, pointed out, the political concerns of Germans in Stockholm were also moral problems that belonged on the agenda of a conference claiming to relate ethics to contemporary problems.[81]

Though less overtly "political" than Westerners, Germans did profess to advance German national interests in Stockholm, though for moral reasons. Siegmund-Schultze may well have had the last word, for a peculiarly German reason: what he regarded as political others may have considered supremely moral. One practical consequence of extolling the folk as an order of creation was the pursuit, within vague limits, of national interests as an ethical responsibility. The folkish Christian perspective was certainly incompatible with the spirit of Stockholm for shifting the moral starting point. From what moral base—Christian in general or folkish Christian specifically—did delegates draw their motivation in pleading Germany's cause?

One could probably not sort out the two elements from listening in on the caucuses. Later in the Kirchenausschuss Kapler described them as informal discussions in which delegates felt encouraged to relieve their deepest feelings by the assurance of confidentiality. While Siegmund-Schultze found here his best evidence (and broke confidence by publishing it), Kapler argued that the delegation should rather be judged on the outcome, which showed great sensitivity for the ecumenical cause.[82]

As the controversy gradually subsided, all eyes turned to the fate of Kapler's letter to the Continuation Committee. Meant for consideration by that committee, the letter was mistakenly sent to the American Council of the World Alliance. The council, influenced perhaps by Walter Simons's moving plea at the German-American luncheon, assumed that the Germans demanded a thorough investigation by the churches themselves. But such an investigation the Americans feared to endorse. Lack of access to archives, the distorting passions of war, the inevitable political ramifications of such an inquiry, the injection of this divisive issue into a political atmosphere grown friendlier — all these reasons seemed to rule out an investigation.

In his reply of July 8, 1926, Kapler readily agreed, and set forth the grounds for his request and minimal German demands.[83] Later, at the Old-Prussian General Synod, its moderator, Friedrich Winckler, would exclaim that no German had better put the case against alleged German war guilt. Kapler tried to dispose of the argument heard outside Germany that the authors of the treaty had not meant to indict Germany for war guilt in Article 231. According to Kapler, the article did not merely stipulate a legal responsibility for a war indemnity, but also, as justification, blamed Germany for the war. Any doubts must be dismissed by the victors' reply to the German delegation and Clemenceau's covering letter of June 16, 1919. Both indicted Germany for long desiring war out of base motives, plotting and unleashing it, and deliberately committing barbarities in its course. The Germans, wrote Kapler, wanted agreement merely on the proposition that the war-guilt confession, imposed without previous investigation and out of purely political motivations, should not be recognized as res judicata. The Continuation Committee should encourage, though not sponsor, an investigation.

By this time, ecumenical leaders realized that some resolution of the issue had become imperative. Kapler had reinforced his Stockholm letter by informing Archbishop Söderblom that the German churches would otherwise withdraw from the movement.[84] And yet Kapler's proposal gave pause to wary French leaders who understandably feared lest a restricted moral pronouncement be exploited politically against France and the Versailles settlement. Failing to reach a consensus in May 1926 because of French reservations, the Continuation Committee formed a small subcommittee to draft a reply to the Stockholm letter. For several months the subcommittee, which included Kapler and Monod, struggled in vain to formulate a declaration acceptable to French and German churches. Finally, Monod proposed a short declaration that found thankful German support and acceptance by the Continuation Committee meeting in Bern, Switzerland, on August 28, 1926.

The accepted formulation was disarmingly simple. Its strength lay in moral postulates that no one could contest. At its crux, the statement merely contended "that no final moral judgment is necessarily established in political documents" and "that any confession imposed by force in any domain whatsoever remains without moral value and religious virtue." Finally, the statement advocated a complete investigation of the war-guilt issue and declared the matter settled.[85]

But the rather abstract contents of the declaration, which barely alluded to war guilt and not at all to its specific assessment, found a mixed reception among German Protestants. Both Rische and Siegmund-Schultze voiced their displeasure. Rische would have had the declaration disavow German war guilt specifically. He likened Stockholm and Bern to a second Versailles, for again Germans had given up what they ought to have insisted upon.[86] But more traditional nationalists insisted that the churches had dared to push the war-guilt issue farther and more successfully than the German government, which they considered seriously delinquent.[87] For Siegmund-Schultze, by contrast, the declaration crowned German attempts to exploit the Life and Work movement politically under the guise of moral concern. He held firmly to his former position that the war-guilt issue, essentially a political matter, had no legitimate place in ecumenical discussions.[88]

Despite voices of dissent, German churchmen generally welcomed the Bern declaration with gratitude, and the 1927 Church Federation Assembly and the Old-Prussian General Synod alike declared their satisfaction. Though much preferring a specific ecumenical rejection of the war-guilt charge, church leaders believed that the Bern declaration had achieved as much as they could expect.[89] In this sense, Stockholm ushered in a Christian detente that paralleled the political detente of the same year, associated with the "spirit of Locarno."

As the Weimar period drew to a close, the Kirchenausschuss pressed ecumenical leaders to endorse German revisionism. Exoneration for revisionism's sake had not been Kapler's slogan in Stockholm and Bern. But this note crept back into the official argument when burgeoning radical nationalism pressured church leaders to take new steps. Now the Kirchenausschuss could build on the Bern declaration while arguing for treaty revision. Did changing circumstances account for this departure, or did German church leaders in Bern expect to mount a campaign for revision after luring the French into a trap? It is tempting to accept the latter thesis, for the reason that churchmen predicted a victorious struggle against the Versailles settlement if only its war-guilt base could be shattered. But then they delayed to take up that cross until dissatisfaction with the progress of revisionism grew with the worsening of economic conditions several years later. Even then the Kirchenausschuss refused to wield the threat of bolting the ecumenical movement, as the Old-Prussian Church Senate recommended, if revision did not promptly ensue.[90] No doubt the Kirchenausschuss believed that it had struck a blow for revisionism in Bern without intending to strike any new blows.

In 1925 the attention of churchmen shifted to the frontiers set by the Versailles treaty and the prospect of joining the league. In the Locarno treaties of that year, Stresemann, still foreign minister, sought to offer the French the security that they craved. He hoped that the Western powers might reciprocate eventually by withdrawing from all three occupation zones, by disbanding the Military Control Commission, by scaling down reparations, and even by consenting to border revision. The Locarno treaties provided for a multinational guarantee pact to cover the western (but not the eastern) German frontier and arbitration treaties to govern alterations of either border. On November 27, 1925, the Reichstag passed the Locarno laws, including authorization to apply for league membership.

Once more the counsel of nationalist churchmen against concessions fell in line with arguments of the Nationalists, both of whom scathingly denounced the treaties. They objected that the treaties, like the Dawes plan, amounted to voluntary recognition of the Versailles treaty—this time of the borders that it had set.[91] Democrat Martin Rade lamented that relatively few pastors could appreciate the "spirit of Locarno."[92] But nationalist churchmen found little of this spirit in the enemy, even in the Allied decision to end occupation of the Cologne zone and disband the Military Control Commission despite German failure to disarm to treaty limits.

For much the same reasons, nationalist churchmen regretted that the Locarno treaties obliged Germany to join the League of Nations. Once again the nation would freely consent to shouldering obligations extorted at Versailles and abide by league statutes against German national interests. A shift of attitude occurred, however, when the league opened its doors to Germany in September 1926. Fundamental attitudes changed not so much as tactics. High officials in the Old-Prussian church saw in the league, now joined by Germany on the council, a means of shielding the cultural autonomy of suppressed Evangelical minorities, especially in the East. Indicative of this shift, General Superintendent Dibelius, writing in *Das evangelische Deutschland,* gave both narrowly political and altruistic reasons for his endorsement of the league.[93] Admittedly, the League of Nations had treated Germany shabbily in the past. By now helping to restore the league to its basic purpose, however, Germany and the church had little to lose and something to gain—consideration for Germany and the defense of German Protestant minorities. To furbish the league's image, on February 4, 1927, some 120 clergymen founded a Theologians' Committee in Berlin as part of the German League for the League of Nations, electing Dibelius as chairman.

At the time of Germany's entry, Rade reported that hatred for the league in church quarters had reached a "fanatical" pitch.[94] Whether Dibelius and his committee assuaged this hatred is hard to say. Of course, Rade and his Democratic liberal friends heralded Germany's entrance. For the German Association of the World Alliance, entry complied with its long-standing recommendation. For many nationalists, however, Dibelius's hopes seemed misplaced, since "this wolf will never become a lamb."[95] They nevertheless urged wholehearted participation to get what could be gotten for Germany's cause. Others appeared to make no tactical adjustment whatever to the changed situation.

Looking back on the policy of conciliation in 1927, nationalist chroniclers concluded that Stresemann had led his hapless nation farther into the swamp of bondage and humiliation. Voluntarily Germany had adjusted to the onerous peace settlement by shackling itself with the Dawes plan, Locarno treaties, and league obligations. The "feedback effects" (Rückwirkungen) that Stresemann extolled seemed all too slight to justify such an enormous sacrifice of Germany's future. A successful foreign policy should find a way out of the swamp, not mire the nation without hope of future movement.

This frustration goaded rather than discouraged assaults on the war-guilt allegation, ostensibly the cause of the misery that Stresemann unconscionably abetted. At the dedication of the Tannenburg war memorial in East Prussia on September 18, 1927, President Hindenburg proclaimed Germany's exoneration of all war-guilt charges. The speech delighted nationalist Protestants, who saw in their war hero a defender of German honor again, no matter how much they regretted the impression that Stresemann had him in tow.[96] But the speech alarmed Stresemann and, even more, Western governments, which regarded it as an assault on German treaty commitments.

Following the speech, a field service was held at which an Evangelical army chaplain spoke these words: "We wish to strengthen continually the belief in ourselves and in our children that sometime the day must come when our folk will break its chains and the sun of freedom will rise over German lands."[97] The chaplain, Ludwig Müller, was in the Nazi period to become the notorious Reichsbischof Müller of the reorganized national Protestant church. Were such statements merely the customary rhetoric accompanying resistance to the concessive republican foreign policy? Or did they point beyond to a "just" war bent on reversing the verdict of Versailles? For Siegmund-Schultze the answer was clear. He regretted "that in certain circles of pastors in northern Germany [primarily in the Old-Prussian church] . . . the rejection of any sentiment for peace in the church or in politics is not only annoying, but is an offense to the cause of Christ, thereby betrayed in our generation."[98]

Though others competed to be heard, nationalist churchmen appear to have set the tone of the Old-Prussian church. One can divide the consequences of church nationalism for republican foreign policy into direct and indirect effects.

Directly, nationalists generated disrespect for the Republic by contesting its foreign policy from the dark days of Versailles to the Locarno treaties. They could not, or would not, see that Stresemann, himself a nationalist of the People's party, had begun to dismantle the treaty and set the stage for further advances. Rather than appreciate that national impotence dictated republican foreign policy, nationalists were apt to trace its alleged weakness to the parliamentary system. From their point of view, party rivalry shaped foreign policy rather than national interest (especially until 1923), and parties lacking proper national commitment gained a pernicious influence on foreign policy.

While criticism of republican foreign policy directly linked nationalist churchmen to the antirepublican Right, the indirect consequences of their nationalism for the Republic linked them to the institutional aspirations of the Volkskirche. National renewal, which the church promoted on a Christian basis, required national self-respect and faith in the German cause. For that reason, among others, the church pursued German exoneration of war guilt. Exoneration, however, had more specific political implications. Self-respect should induce a sense of shame for treasonous defeat and revolution as well as reprobation for internationalist and materialist parties judged responsible for both and for the Republic. Clearing Germany's good name of war guilt should help to restore honor to the monarchical Christian order and to stir hope for a redeemed future. Resentment, moral outrage, and hope for treaty revision formed only part of the complex motives of nationalist churchmen. At a more subliminal level, the invidious charge of war guilt struck at the core of their political aspirations within the Republic.

7

VOLKSKIRCHE ACTIVISM:
The State

"THE CONVICTION...of most church Christians is and remains this: They do their duty in the Republic, [but] their heart is inclined toward the Kaiser and the Empire and the [imperial] colors black-white-red. And the Republic, born of the November crime and having taken away the old flag, remains inwardly alien to them." So wrote *Der Reichsbote* at the end of the period under consideration in 1927.[1] This assessment by a daily that catered to nationalist churchmen is demonstrated in the following chapter. The ambiguity of doing "their duty" in a republic that they did not like characterized not only avowed antirepublicans but also pragmatic republicans (Vernunftrepublikaner) who grudgingly made peace with the Republic for lack of an alternative. Wartime attitudes toward domestic politics, like those toward foreign policy, persisted into the republican period. As many had contested political reform in the war, they now deplored the fledgling Republic. Old lines of conflict continued to cut across the church as well, for the liberal minority that had urged a peace of reconciliation and political reform now joined republican ranks.

THE CORRUPTING PARTY STATE

Defeat and revolution bequeathed to the Weimar Republic a legacy of political unrest and a bewildering nexus of problems. Desperately needed was a political consensus that could induce political stability. From its very birth, however, the new state was denied a consensus, for both the extreme Right and Left contested its liberal parliamentary features. Even parties favorably disposed found much to deplore in the political development of this foundling.

As a result of the 1920 election to the Reichstag, the Weimar coalition lost its majority, which eluded it again in the two elections of 1924. The problem of patching together coalitions grew more exacting and exasperating as a result. Twelve times between the revolution and 1927 coalitions were unseated and arduously remade, at times only after lengthy crisis. Also Prussia, spanning two-thirds of Germany, was not spared the divisiveness of coalition government. But here the fateful erosion of the political Middle was less severe, and the Weimar coalition (joined 1921−25 by the People's party) managed to hold together under a resourceful Socialist minister president, Otto Braun. The debilitating nature and frequency of coalition crises brought the party system into disfavor with an increasingly broader segment of the German population, particularly with the middle classes from which German Evangelical churches drew their greatest support. Germany seemed crippled by a political system that evoked odious comparison with the monarchy under which the nation appeared to thrive on strong and decisive leadership that had kept parties in check.

This way of thinking came easily to conservative churchmen because of their ideological predisposition. During the first years of the Republic, they taxed the new government and Socialists in particular with incompetence. Chroniclers pilloried the apparent incapacity or unwillingness of the revolutionary government to impose order on left radicals who had helped catapult Socialists into power.[2] In defense of the Republic, the Democrat Rade contended that disorder stemmed more from collapse than from revolution. He urged his readers to withhold judgment until the Republic had time to elicit respect for its authority.[3] Troeltsch saw the Republic as the only possible defense against chaos, chiding the political Right for its lack of realism.[4] But neither time nor greater realism helped to abate criticism of the Republic among conservative churchmen. They saddled the republican government with political jobbery, feather-bedding, profiteering, prodigal spending, and a general mismanagement of public funds. In 1926 Der Reichsbote cited earlier allegations against Erzberger's probity and the recently exposed Barmat scandal as notorious examples of republican corruption. With considerable exaggeration, the newspaper commented that hardly a day passed without a new public scandal. Earlier the Prussian bureaucracy had won an enviable reputation for its dedication and diligence, Der Reichsbote continued.[5] But under its new masters the bureaucracy had swollen with incompetents of questionable virtue.

The charge that republican parties managed the government incompetently and immorally seemed fully justified in the failure of the state to provide adequate redress for the inevitable shift of wealth in the inflation. Reinforcing this charge was another, namely that the republican government bore the blame for the inflation because of its concessive policy on reparations and general fiscal mismanagement. Inasmuch as inflation, reaching its high point in November 1923, favored debtors at the expense of creditors, the latter hoped to have debts revaluated. Of all debtors, the government stood the most to gain from the inflation's effects, for it had incurred an incredibly large war debt.

The Federal Court (Reichsgericht) abruptly raised the hopes of millions when it held in November 1923 that creditors could claim revaluation of debts (Aufwertung). This judgment opened a Pandora's box of suits, which the minister of finance, Hans Luther, sought to obviate by including revaluation principles in the Third Emergency Tax Ordinance of February 14, 1924. But these principles hardly did justice to a problem for which there were no just solutions. The ordinance, allowing revaluation of merely 15 percent for private debts and none at all for public, met howls of protest, forcing the Reichstag to enact a revaluation law on July 16, 1925. The law raised the revaluation rate to 25 percent for private debts and revaluated the public debt at either 2.5 or 5 percent of its true value.[6]

Largely for four reasons, the revaluation principles drew protests from churchmen and not merely from those of the political Right. First of all, they regarded the stipulated rate of revaluation as egregiously unjust, as indeed it was. Moreover, government regulations had forced the church to make nonspeculative investments, largely in government bonds now practically worthless. Accordingly, the combined investments of the Old-Prussian church all but disappeared. In response to a Kirchenausschuss circular, church governments reported that church assets, ranging from 850 to 900 million gold marks, had been loaned to Reich, state, and local governments. Churchmen also suffered pangs of conscience after having advised parishioners to invest in war bonds, now of little value. One pastor regretted "how I encouraged everyone to give his last mite to the loan, how I most ceremoniously assured everyone that it was absolutely impossible to lose the money."[7] Finally, pressure groups and active church members of the middle classes, whose savings were most heavily hit by inflation, demanded that the church protest inadequate revaluation, reproaching the Kirchenausschuss for its inactivity.

Far from inactive, the Kirchenausschuss espoused the cause of those injured by inflation until the more desirable terms found their way into the revaluation law of 1925. In letters to federal authorities on August 1 and September 27, 1924, and again on February 11, 1925, the Kirchenausschuss urged a more generous revaluation than that afforded by the ordinance principles. It pointed out the plight of pensioners living off investments, the moral dilemma of pastors who had sparked war-bond drives, and the injustice of requiring churches to invest in government bonds, the least revaluated of all debts. The third letter claimed that the experience had caused the aggrieved to lose respect for state authority.[8] By 1927 church officials had concluded that the revaluation law, unchallenged by the Kirchenausschuss, contained as tolerable a settlement as one could expect. Such was the conclusion of President Pechmann of the Church Federation Assembly, a Munich banker, whose views are appended to the 1927 assembly minutes. But many parishioners deplored the law as insufficient and, together with pressure groups, deluged the 1927 assembly with petitions for redress. The Republic appeared not only to deprive its citizens of national honor, but also to rob them of their property.

The dominant church Right traced the political ills under which Germany suffered to parliamentarianism.[9] One might hear occasional praise from the Right for the passage of certain bills, but little for the system as such. The Republic failed to adopt a vigorous foreign policy, secure confessional schools, defend the church adequately wherever threatened, enact desirable social legislation, uphold law and order, and weed out corruption because the machinery of state made government by principle impossible and that by group interest inevitable.

Drawing the brunt of attack were the concept and operation of political parties. Parties aspired to manipulate goverment policy, conservative churchmen charged, and compromised basic issues in order to gain party ends and power. Once in power parties did not scruple at withdrawing from coalitions if their voracious demands remained unfulfilled, bringing on recurrent government crises. Owing to these crises, republican governments proved unable to formulate and carry through consistent policies. Parties, moreover, appealed to the materialist drives of the masses and inevitably failed to elicit a sense of national responsibility. The church Right deplored that a majority, accidentally assembled by self-seeking parties, should arrogate the right of shaping government policy.[10]

Conservative churchmen had, of course, matured under the monarchy. When judging the Weimar "party state," they kept in mind the role played by the monarchy in imposing its countervailing powers on the pretensions of parties. Accustomed to praising past leaders, conservative churchmen lamented that the Republic had not brought forth responsible leaders with an expert knowledge of government.[11] Party hacks seemed all too prominent, mediocrities who had risen through party ranks to attain office thanks to the new system of proportional representation and party lists.

Rightist churchmen sometimes tempered the ideological cast of their thought by conceding that parliamentarianism might suit other countries such as Great Britain. But to impose such a system upon Germany was to do so mechanically, for Germany lacked the prerequisite of such a system, namely political and social cohesion. After enumerating the defects of the Republic, the chronicler of the *Allgemeine evangelisch-lutherische Kirchenzeitung* wrote: "We desire with broad segments of the German people the determined hand that will finally make an end to this specter."[12] He regarded the Republic, "a system worthy of perishing," as only a transitional stage from a more glorious past to a brighter future.

Of course, conservative churchmen were part of the problem that they deplored. Rade hurled precisely this charge at them time and time again. They contributed to the failure of parliamentarianism by denying the Republic the allegiance that it so desperately needed. By participating in the political process without contesting it, Rade argued, Christians could make their weight felt.[13] But conservative churchmen could not endure the broad scope of the secular, pluralist society that was Germany in the 1920s. They wished to narrow the public consensus to the amalgamation of Christianity and nationalism that the Volkskirche extolled as its public justification. Their repeated emphasis on religious and national renewal served this end. Their vision of an authoritarian society cemented by Christian nationalism presupposed a different type of state. Deriving its authority from God, the state must pursue its essential purposes undeterred by the compromising nature of parties. Regrettably the Weimar Republic signaled the momentary victory of a secular, pluralist society over the claim of the Volkskirche to shape the public consensus. For a pluralist society, expressed politically through a party state, relativized the public values that should bond a community.

Still the question of state form, though of great significance, did not loom as nearly as important in the eyes of conservative churchmen as what values ought to sustain German society. One suspects that they could have adjusted much more readily to the Republic if the plurality of public values had not strayed so far from Volkskirche ideals. Parliamentary democracy appeared especially deplorable for allowing Marxist Socialists such great influence in an essentially Christian folk.

THE ILLEGITIMATE REPUBLIC

Should Evangelical consciences feel bound to render loyalty to the Republic, and if so, with or without qualifications? The formal answer to this perplexing question centered around whether revolution could establish legitimate authority. "Let every person be subject to the governing authorities," wrote St. Paul in Romans 13:1–2. "For there is no authority except from God. Therefore, he who resists the authorities resists what God has appointed, and those who resist will incur judgment." Clearly, a Christian cannot condone revolution by New Testament standards. But after revolution had spawned new authorities, must he obey them as the "governing authorities" mentioned by St. Paul, or resist them since their power derived from an act of revolution? This question threw church ranks into disarray and evoked from most churchmen an ambiguous response conditioned by political commitments already made.

One of the first to deal at length with this question was a Lutheran professor of theology, Theodor von Zahn. He argued against those who would accept revolutionary authority on the basis of Romans 13, contending that the passage gave no clear answer. He advised leaving the question to individual conscience and political judgment if one were not already bound by oath to the old order. Seeking to draw clarity from Zahn's argument, Gottfried Traub, a Nationalist and church liberal alike, misconstrued it to deny loyalty to revolutionary authority. To test the legitimacy of governing authority, Traub proposed various ideological standards — its intimate relationship to the folk, its concern for historical forces molding the folk, and its sense of responsibility to God. Such marks of legitimacy, which the Republic purportedly lacked, followed logically from Volkskirche theory and the ideal of a Christian state. Attacking both Zahn and Traub, Professor Adolf Jülicher of Marburg argued the republican version of Romans 13. St. Paul had counseled early Christians to accept Roman rule without inquiring into its origins or intrinsic merit. Likewise, Weimarian Christians ought to accept republican authority simply because it existed.[14]

According to Friedrich Curtius, a Democratic liberal, most churchmen adopted the perplexing middle position of combining aversion for the Republic with passive obedience. As a "religionless" state devoid of Traub's marks and spawned by revolution, the Republic lacked full legitimacy, though Romans 13 compelled its acceptance as legally constituted. Curtius urged his brethren to act realistically by rallying to the Republic. He argued that God had allowed the monarchy to fall, that restoration attempts would plunge Germany into civil war, and that parliamentarianism would doubtless prevail even under a restored monarchy.[15]

The middle position meant accepting the tainted Republic without being loyal to it.[16] On the one hand, *Licht und Leben* considered a counterrevolution quite as evil as the original revolution, but, on the other, made no bones about its disgust with the Republic and desire for a restoration. When Titius proposed at the 1919 Church Assembly that churches accept the new order willingly, most delegates no doubt accepted the authority of the Republic as legal, but could not refrain from showing how offensive Titius's remarks sounded. The Lutheran *Evangelische Kirchenzeitung* actually rejected the Republic as legally legitimate and came close to extolling monarchy as a prerequisite of the Christian state. Titius had, accordingly, shown unforgivable disloyalty to the fallen monarch. Likewise rejecting the Republic, Traub insisted that loyalty to fatherland ruled out any accommodation with the existing state. But others could reverse this argument, reasoning that the new order must be accepted for the sake of fatherland. A few held that not the form but the quality and moral purposes of the new state drew them to it. This reasoning enabled Rade to accept the Republic from its inception.

The question remained whether Christians owed more than passive obedience. Monarchists favoring a legal restoration denied this question, though it nettled them. Republicans, by contrast, bristled at the thought of distinguishing varying levels of obedience, as the idea of passive obedience suggested. For them obedience meant wholehearted commitment that should dismiss any intention of unhinging the Republic, legally or otherwise. Such was the thought behind an advertisement in *Die christliche Welt* on March 16, 1922, placed by Pastor Richard Schmidt of Massow in Pomerania. He summoned his colleagues to found a Republican Pastors' League. "Together we wish to turn to our undecided colleagues," he wrote, "and force the opponents of the Republic among them to come out into the open."[17] A follower of Naumann, Schmidt regretted that 99 percent of all Pomeranian pastors viewed the Republic as a mere temporary arrangement and engaged actively in the monarchist cause. For Schmidt, such conduct could scarcely qualify as obedience.

The heated reaction provoked by the advertisement illuminated the middle position assumed by most churchmen. Typically, *Der Reichsbote* replied that the church must cling to monarchism and point out the sinful spirit of the godless revolution, a spirit that must be repented.[18] *Licht und Leben* argued that pastors qua pastors had no right to take political positions publicly as Schmidt attempted, let alone support the Republic "stemming from oath violations and high treason."[19] Protesting the Pastors' League in *Die christliche Welt,* Pastor Rudolf Schaeffer distinguished between the minimal obedience required by Romans 13 and a basic allegiance to the Republic, for which he had little love.[20] Like *Licht und Leben,* he lamented that the league would violate the church's principle of political neutrality, upheld also by the liberal *Protestantenblatt.*[21] By the same token, the *Protestantenblatt* took pains to point out that this principle also forbade churchmen to work publicly for a restoration, an implication conveniently ignored by *Der Reichsbote.* Though they varied, these arguments all assumed that a public defense of the prevailing system was a partisan political act. Circumstances had pressed their authors into the ambiguous middle, forcing them to qualify what they had formerly taken for granted, namely the legitimacy of the existing political order.

The grudging acceptance of the Republic by most churchmen was accompanied by flickering hopes for a Hohenzollern restoration. Such hopes seemed unrealistic in 1919. Associated with catastrophic defeat, the monarchy had grown highly unpopular. In despair, *Postive Union* concluded that "the monarchical state unfortunately is probably gone forever," and threw its support to the emerging Republic for the sake of preserving order,[22] as did *Die Reformation,* edited by Wilhelm Philipps. But Philipps was more sanguine about the prospects of an eventual restoration. "There is, of course, no possibility of an immediate restoration of the monarchy. No one wants a counterrevolution that would bury everything still standing in blood and destruction," he wrote. "But if we now receive a truly democratic constitution, the majority will of the German people would then be able to express itself. Then would be the time to place the monarchist question on the agenda again."[23] This suggestion struck Ernst Troeltsch as hopelessly naive. Detested as it was, the Republic represented the only form of government that most Germans would accept or tolerate. Troeltsch foresaw civil war if the political Right or Left grew at the expense of the Republic. Unrealistic thoughts of a legal restoration helped to frustrate the growth of a large republican middle-class party and the entrenchment of the Republic. Such a party loomed in his eyes as a prerequisite of an indispensable republic.[24]

But the dominant church Right preferred a monarchical restoration to the Republic.[25] From 1920 to 1924 gratified churchmen greeted the revival of monarchist feeling and took great satisfaction in the election successes of the Nationalist party, which likewise advocated monarchism. They saw in resurgent nationalism a force to attain the desired restoration. Around the middle of the 1920s, however, the groups heralding the "new" nationalism succeeded in dissociating themselves more clearly from the monarchist political Right. Generally the church Right declined to follow them and remained true to monarchist ideals. Those who thought about a folkish dictatorship did so skeptically, deploring rightist disloyalty to the monarchist cause.[26] For other reasons also monarchist zeal waned and prospects dimmed after 1924. Inasmuch as political and economic conditions stabilized, there was less to blame the Republic for, especially since the monarchist Nationalist party joined government coalitions in 1925 and 1927. When Hindenburg scrupulously carried out his presidential duties after his election in 1925, the wind began to leave monarchist sails. As Kaufmann pointed out, Hindenburg "bestowed upon the despised state of Weimar the lustre of national honor and respectability."[27]

Shifting with the movement, some churchmen, still monarchists in principle, no longer viewed the Republic with such jaundiced eyes. One might reason that a restoration appeared less necessary than increasing the powers of the president over the parties in the Reichstag, especially since monarchism had failed to rally a majority of the German people.[28] But the indominable *Der Reichsbote,* though it too saw the need for an authoritarian revision of the constitution, continued to view monarchist prospects optimistically and deplored any compromising of the monarchist cause. "Even if it [the Republic] were good, as in actuality it is bad, we would not stand otherwise; not even if in the future the republican form becomes completely suited to the German people, who today are so politically inept," wrote *Der Reichsbote* on the occasion of the Kaiser's birthday in 1927. "No, our loyalty is biblically based: 'Honor the King!'"[29]

The ambiguous response to the Republic became evident also in the controversy over intercessory prayer (the Fürbitte). In the general prayer at the close of the Old-Prussian church service, the pastor offered, on behalf of the congregation, prayer for those in authority and need. The first of six versions read in part: "May you increasingly favor your servant, Kaiser Wilhelm, our king and ruler, and his entire royal house." Prodded by the Socialist Kultusministerium, the EOK, on December 18, 1918, instructed pastors through provincial consistories to make those changes "that result from altered political conditions."[30] Perhaps few pastors denied that prayer should be said for the existing government to which one was "subject." But how should the Kaiser and his family be remembered in the general prayer? The general solution was to include them in the prayer for the needy.

A reformed royal general prayer used by a Border Mark superintendent contained these words: "Give all authority [Obrigkeit] in Reich and state, in city and country, wisdom, loyalty, and power to rule our folk with justice and to help it out of darkness and need, guilt and humiliation [presumably the Versailles treaty]. Also be close to our dear Kaiser *in his need* and exile and his entire house."[31] The prayer appropriately recognized existing institutions. After a parishioner had contested it, the prayer passed muster with the consistory, which, however, regretted the superintendent's use of "our dear" Kaiser. Repeated for four years, it, like other contested prayers, was eventually dropped.

Republicans, especially Socialists, looked upon the royal general prayer, however reformed, as little more than monarchist agitation. So long as the Republic subsidized clerical salaries, pastors ought to show appropriate respect for the Republic. Certainly republican critics were correct to find a strong monarchist heart beating in the general prayer, but not a crass attempt to agitate for monarchism. When the Landtag considered the annual budget of the Kultusministerium, including church subsidies, Socialists roasted the churches for disloyalty, especially the Protestant. Within the Old-Prussian church, Religious Socialists complained bitterly that the reformed royal general prayer violated the church's political neutrality by challenging the legitimacy of the Republic.[32] This the EOK flatly denied for religious reasons. As the royal intercessory prayer gradually dropped from usage (though it remained a feature of church life), other evidence of clerical political behavior continued to fuel Socialist fires.

Caught between church sentiment and republican charges, the Kultusministerium tried to evade the issue. Its position crystallized after a former Silesian Landtag deputy complained to Haenisch in February 1919 that many pastors said the royal general prayer every Sunday. The chief administrator of the province agreed with the consistory that prohibiting royal intercessory prayer, now tailored to EOK demands, would violate the church's religious freedom. He concluded, as did the EOK, that the crux of the issue was the prayer's format—above all whether it recognized Kaiser or Republic as governing authority. But two Socialists attached to his office responded that "the churchly prayer for the former Kaiser and his house is irreconcilably opposed to the present order of state," even when amended.[33] Haenisch received further advice from Ernst Troeltsch, then parliamentary state secretary in the Kultusministerium. Apparently Troeltsch had been responsible for the ministry's decision to prod the EOK. Advising against state intervention in the issue, Troeltsch contended that the royal general prayer was essentially an internal matter that churches, now more clearly independent, should resolve. His mind boggled at the thought of monitoring church prayers if the state banned an explicitly political general prayer. Since the EOK had acted, such a solution was no longer so pressing. In questionable cases, only two remedies now remained—complaining to the EOK and initiating a suit. Such was the advice that Haenisch gave the Silesian on June 14, 1919.

Two notorious violations of the EOK's instructions, both occurring in Pomerania, found EOK and Kultusministerium on the same side of the issue. In 1922 a Landtag deputy charged that a country pastor had habitually offered a royal prayer remembering not only the Kaiser but also the crown prince and his eldest son, Prince Wilhelm, the pretender to the throne. The deputy complained that many pastors similarly agitated for the monarchy. Called upon by his consistory to explain, the pastor stated that he could not easily switch off his sentiments "as one throws away a worn-out piece of clothing," and he gamely resolved to carry on.[34] After all, his family had been closely associated with the weal and woe of the Hohenzollern since the reign of the Great Elector in the seventeenth century. His was an act of piety that, he claimed, others wrongly took for agitation for monarchism or against the "momentary" form of state. Here one comes across the emotional core of Old-Prussian monarchical loyalty that defied categorization as either religious or political and thus an attitude irreducible to the EOK's pragmatic formula.

The religious and moral rationale of the pastor's emotional response surfaced in the unanimous decision of a Pomeranian district synod in 1921 to ask pastors to retain the old version of royal intercessory prayer. In *Der Reichsbote,* the former Landrat von Bonin, the author of the motion and a noble church patron, defended the decision by questioning whether Romans 13:1 required prayer for republican authority. At the district synod the consistory had unsuccessfully contested the motion and Bonin's thesis. In 1925 Bonin submitted almost the same motion to the Pomeranian provincial synod. In his explanation, Bonin pointed out that the revolution could not create legal authority and thus the Republic. For him, Prince Wilhelm was Prussian king by right. "By omitting intercessory prayer for king and the royal house," he argued, "the wrong impression is unavoidably aroused in those attending church that the Prussian throne is empty, thereby giving aid to the crime of revolution."[35] He denied any partisan motive in broaching his motion. On the contrary, he strongly implied, the church regrettably placed political interests above telling the simple truth when pastors omitted or revised the prescribed general prayer.

That church officials acted politically in their circumspection is certainly correct, though, in their opinion, not at the expense of truth. Since the revolution they had pointedly recognized the legal, if not specifically the moral, legitimacy of existing authority. Such a position could also square with Romans 13. It also enabled them to shield the church from republican attacks without unduly antagonizing strong monarchist sentiment within the church. It would not do to show the church's antirepublican face during the revolution and later when church subsidies came up for annual renewal in the Landtag. Concern for church interests tended to push church officials into the ranks of pragmatic republicans (Vernunftrepublikaner).

The EOK and consistories exerted strong pressure on pastors to conform. Whenever the Kultusministerium brought charges of clerical antirepublican or partisan behavior to the church's attention, they conscientiously investigated, and when necessary called pastors to account. Such charges directly concerned the Kultusministerium, since it needed to defend its budget and thus church subsidies in the Landtag. In the case of the royal general prayer, the EOK, in a report to Kultusminister Boelitz in November 1922, contested the charge that numerous pastors misused their office to agitate for the monarchy and against the Republic. Boelitz tended to confirm the EOK's judgment when in January 1923 he reported to the Landtag that his ministry had not been deluged by many complaints. Later that year, however, he asked the EOK for a conference to discuss more recent complaints about the royal general prayer.[36]

If church officials trained a political eye on the state, they did so on the church as well. Without knowledge of church sentiment, one would have to conclude that the EOK's vague formula was unduly permissive. With the passing of the Kaiser as ruler and summus episcopus, no theological reason—at least by the EOK's logic—could be cited for remembering him in the general prayer. Nor did it make sense repeatedly to single out the former ruler, now a mere church member, as a conspicuous example of need at a time of much greater need among his former subjects. But the EOK had to reckon with church sentiment, particularly with the Pomeranian syndrome and Christian-state theory in which monarchism bulked large. Perhaps for that reason the EOK and the church at large did not hasten to introduce a general, prescribed intercessory prayer that would take account of "altered political conditions."[37] In any event, the vagueness of the EOK's initial instructions left the final judgment in the hands of consistories and the EOK, which could then act circumspectfully to avoid provoking the ire of either monarchists or republicans.

Pastors, church organizations, and synods also offered profuse thanks directly to the fallen monarch, in the first years of the Republic, for his beneficient services to the church. After all, an era spanning almost four hundred years, when the ruler officiated as summus episcopus, had come to an abrupt end. Wilhelm Schubring, always chary of encroachments upon church political neutrality, defended the message of the 1920 General Synod as a "politically unassailable declaration of thanks to the House of Hohenzollern."[38] Yet monarchist sentiment undoubtedly mingled with the thanks, even though such statements were not intended as demonstrations of continuing political loyalty.

The equivocal attitude of many churchmen toward the Republic, an amalgam of passive obedience and hostility, revealed itself in their ambiguous position on the unsuccessful Kapp Putsch in March 1920 and the abortive Hitler-Ludendorff Putsch of November 9, 1923. The *Allgemeine evangelisch-lutherische Kirchenzeitung* and *Licht und Leben* deplored Kapp's attempted overthrow of the Republic; yet *Licht und Leben* sympathized with the conspirators' disgust for the Republic, the aims proclaimed by Kapp, and Kapp's personal qualities.[39] One churchman, the irrascible Gottfried Traub, was amnestied for his peripheral involvement in the Kapp Putsch. His clerical brethren refused to decry his complicity and upheld his patriotic idealism. In view of his antirepublican interpretation of Romans 13, his defense of the conspirators was predictable. Bluntly, he contended that the Republic had no authority to try them and that the Weimar constitution functioned as a mere interim arrangement. Not the staunch patriots who stood trial, but republican revolutionaries were the real traitors.[40]

Traub also witnessed the second famous Putsch of the early Weimar period, this time as spectator. By chance he was present in the Bürgerbräu cellar in Munich when Hitler proclaimed the "national revolution," his ill-fated Putsch. Previously Traub had honored Hitler for his perfervid nationalism. But to Traub's horror, Hitler directed his Putsch against the rightist Bavarian government, against those likewise patriotic. Still Traub continued to honor the idealism that seemed to motivate Hitler, while deploring Nazi excesses and misdirection. Far from condemning the attempted Putsch against the Republic, *Licht und Leben* and *Der Reichsbote* praised the bold display of nationalism made by Hitler and Ludendorff at their trial for treason, regretting that real patriots had to stand trial for their convictions.[41]

The shocking assassinations of Matthias Erzberger and Walter Rathenau by rightist extremists, on August 29, 1921, and June 24, 1922, respectively, elicited the same kind of ambiguous response. Churchmen condemned the murders as sin against God, but sin seemingly mitigated by circumstances. Until his death, Erzberger endured attacks alleging treason and malfeasance in office. Laible could muster little sympathy for the victim upon learning of his death: "The horrible death . . . does not at all alter the fact that he . . . influenced the fate of Germany at decisive moments and that he in his many undertakings did not evince the moral seriousness and strength of character that one expected quite naturally from men of high position under the old regime."[42] *Die Reformation* went so far as to blame the Republic for creating conditions that made recourse to such drastic measures, if not excusable, at least understandable.

Protestants' satisfaction at news of Erzberger's death moved Rade to castigate his brethren for a political course that must lead to civil war. Expressing a similar fear, Troeltsch regarded attacks on Erbzerger as assaults on the Republic. Rade denied Protestants the right to deprive the Republic of their wholehearted allegiance and respect.[43] Characteristically, concern for the Volkskirche loomed uppermost in his mind. He feared lest the church's political bias cut it off from its republican constituency.

The alarming assassination of Rathenau, whose very name recalled the concessive reparations policy of the government, met a similar response in church quarters. Although condemning the murder, Gottfried Traub drew a sharp distinction between common murder and political assassination. *Licht und Leben* proved capable of finding words of appreciation for Rathenau. It contended, nevertheless, that republicans tainted with revolution ought not profess amazement when acts of violence were committed against them. To its credit, the Kirchenausschuss this time minced no words in condemning the Rathenau assassination without qualification: "The way to recovery leads through performance of duty and work, through order and propriety, never through hatred and murder."[44]

The equivocal attitude of most churchmen toward the Republic emerged in sharp relief in comments on President Ebert's death and on the subsequent election of Hindenburg as president. Though churchmen criticized the Republic in the most scathing terms, they sometimes held their Socialist president in high personal regard—some even when the Magdeburg court proceedings in 1924 branded him a traitor.[45]

Not to undermine the front but to end the Berlin munitions strike of January 1918 did Ebert as Majority Socialist leader join the strike committee, a motive clearly established in postwar court suits instigated by Ebert to protect himself from slander and libel. In such a trial in Magdeburg the presiding judge found Ebert's conduct technically treasonable, however justified politically and morally. *Licht und Leben* insinuated that Ebert had acted more from partisan than national interests while professing to appreciate his motives. Appalled by attacks on Ebert's character, the liberal theologian Adolf von Harnack wrote the president, expressing his indignation at the "miscarriage of justice" and pointedly thanking him for his patriotic actions in 1918 and 1919. Thereupon, *Der Reichsbote* condemned Harnack as a turncoat, a scholar much honored under the monarchy but the abettor of revolutionary criminals under the Republic.[46]

Systematic assaults on Ebert's character helped speed his death on February 28, 1925. Grieved by the disrespect at Ebert's death, Martin Rade bluntly reminded Evangelical churches of their responsibility to honor those in authority, a duty seemingly forgotten since the revolution. He deplored the intentional omission of any mention of Ebert's death in church sermons, prayers, and church periodicals. Catholic churches had tolled the funeral day, but Evangelical bells had remained silent. Even the Kirchenausschuss's letter of condolence to the chancellor expended a minimum of words. Despondently, Rade expressed fears that the forces of reaction had enveloped the church, making a Volkskirche containing all political persuasions impossible.[47]

To be sure, a number of periodicals mentioned Ebert's death and commented on his achievements or failings. But such attention was perfunctory, and often politically slanted. Had the Kaiser passed away before the revolution, one can easily imagine how thoroughly the Evangelical press would have rendered obeisance. Perhaps Rade's criticism was as petty as it was annoying, but it did indicate that few churchmen had willingly accepted the Republic. After Archbishop Söderblom praised Ebert in a letter of condolence to his wife, *Der Reichsbote* professed amazement that the archbishop had not heard of the Magdeburg trial or realized how offensive his letter had sounded to his German brethren.[48]

When it became known that a Democratic pastor, Hermann Maas of Heidelberg, had conducted the committal service after republican dignitaries had made farewell speeches, the church press focused abruptly on the Ebert funeral. In particular *Der Reichsbote* took offense that an Evangelical pastor should officiate at the funeral of a dissident, born a Catholic. It sought to discredit Maas by informing its readers that Maas was a pacifist, a Democratic city councillor, an aesthete in the pulpit, a panderer of men, even an apostate. It charged that Maas had misused his text for political purposes, that following the political speeches the committal service functioned as a mere ornament, a mockery of Evangelical funerals.[49] Outraged by these attacks, Maas suspected that *Der Reichsbote's* primary objection was political, not religious, as though the church should brook no traffic with Socialists. Commenting on Maas's explanation, the *Allgemeine evangelisch-lutherische Kirchenzeitung* contended that St. Paul would not have given "an honorable committal talk" for a man under whom the Evangelical churches had experienced what almost amounted to persecution.[50]

The internal political events of 1925 set off a debate that revealed the political streams coursing through the church and the ideologies that fed them. Beginning with Rade's lashing attack on the occasion of Ebert's death, this public airing continued through the subsequent presidential elections. In the first presidential election of March 29, 1925, rightist parties nominated Karl Jarres, the mayor of Duisburg. As an Evangelical Christian and nationalist, Jarres enjoyed the firm support of most churchmen who deemed true morality an effect of religious faith and who therefore postulated the need of electing a Christian subject to conscience, not to party wishes.[51] Since none of the seven candidates received a majority, election law required a runoff election. To marshal a plurality, the republican parties—Socialists, Centrists, and Democrats—disregarded political and ideological differences and agreed upon Centrist Wilhelm Marx, a former chancellor and devout Catholic, as their candidate. To meet this challenge, the political Right persuaded Hindenburg, then seventy-eight years old and living in retirement, to be its candidate.

That most churchmen would support Hindenburg is perfectly understandable. After all, he, like Jarres, was devoutly Evangelical, loyal to the old order, intensely patriotic, and aloof from politics. One could expect him to lend dignity and stability to a state weakened by parliamentarianism. In fact, Hindenburg's unfamiliarity with the miserable parliamentary system could appear as a mark in his favor.[52] What requires more of an explanation is their antipathy for the Catholic Centrist Marx.

By 1925 a tide of antiultramontanism had swept over Evangelical churches, and the alarming prospect of electing a Catholic president to preside over a basically Protestant nation had grown intolerable. One might have expected to find increasing political cooperation between Evangelical and Catholic churches because of common institutional concerns within the Republic. Instead one finds among Protestants a fierce hostility to ultramontanism that was perhaps more widespread in the Weimar era than in any other period of modern German history. Catholic and Protestant church leaders appear to have had little contact even during the revolution and the Weimar assembly when they waged a common battle.

That the balance of power and influence shifted in favor of Catholics under the Republic no Protestant leader would deny. Protestants had commonly regarded the constitutional monarchy of Bismarck's design as a distinctive Protestant contribution to German history. Without the prestige and check of the Protestant monarchy, political Catholicism and the Roman church seemed all too successful in seeking their own at Protestant expense. Here a specifically denominational factor entered calculations for repudiating the Republic, though antiultramontanism extended also into republican ranks.

Particularly nationalist Protestants were apt to argue that the Center had defected from the monarchist cause and joined ideologically incompatible coalitions with Socialists in order to grasp power for Catholics and their church. Nationalist commitment also seemed conspicuously lacking when the Center promoted the acceptance of the peace resolution in 1917, the Armistice, the Versailles treaty, and republican foreign policy. On the national level, the Center participated in every coalition, and, in Prussia, formed with Socialists the core of an enduring coalition. It galled nationalist Protestants that such an improbable alliance of Protestant enemies should rule Protestant Prussia. They were outraged that the Center appeared to conspire with the Socialist party to replace Protestants with Catholics in government and school systems or to find positions for Socialists by edging out loyal Protestants. Soon Protestant officials began to organize themselves in defense leagues. The same sense of discrimination was to fuel the massive Westphalian school strike a year after the presidential elections. In the second election, Socialist support for Marx's candidacy loomed as yet another unprincipled compromise between ultramontanes and Socialists.

Quite as distressing was the success of the Roman church in buying, leasing, or even procuring free of charge former monastic establishments with the aid of the republican state, especially in predominantly Evangelical areas. The increased number of monasteries, convents, and religious was part of what Catholics felicitiously termed a "counter-Reformation," indicating Catholic advances at the expense of a decadent Protestantism. Zealous Catholics encouraged by German bishops founded the Winfried League, with the disturbing goal of restoring Germany to Catholicism. Evangelical churchmen were quick to point out that Protestant conversions far outnumbered Catholic. Yet, by 1925, they had grown thoroughly alarmed at the counter-Reformation and the political support that it had received from the Center party.[53]

The self-serving goals of political Catholicism and the papal curia seemed to blend most conspicuously in their determined pursuit of concordats. To gain foreign diplomatic support after the war, the German government proved receptive to the Holy See's request for negotiations leading to a national concordat. But Socialists in the Prussian government, above all its minister president, Otto Braun, feared a national concordat for pre-empting state control of school affairs. After Prussia thwarted such overtures in 1924, rumors abounded at the time of the presidential elections that Prussia would soon enter negotiations for a concordat, followed perhaps by the national government.

This prospect made Protestants blanch. Liberal Protestants dreaded lest concordats set a general pattern of subjecting schools to undue clerical influence. Others fretted that, having secured school demands in concordats, the Center and Bavarian People's parties might neglect the still unpassed school legislation that Protestants needed for their confessional interests more than Catholics. Concordats might grant the Catholic church a pre-ferred legal position over Evangelical churches. Almost all Protestant church leaders complained that a concordat would rob the state of its sovereignty and preferred treaties between states and the Catholic church like those recently negotiated in Württemberg and Baden.

In response to the threat, the Kirchenausschuss and EOK appear to have followed the prudent advice of their president, Hermann Kapler. Setting forth comparable Protestant demands prematurely might be misconstrued as an endorsement of concordats. Some district and provincial synods and the Evangelical League adopted the opposite tactic of hurling resolutions against concordats. But such a course also had its pitfalls, suggesting that the Old-Prussian church would not demand equal treatment if the curia prevailed. Only if a Prussian concordat appeared imminent, Kapler counseled, should the Old-Prussian church, after protesting the concordat, raise public demands for equal consideration.

The alarm that Protestants felt by 1927, after concordat negotiations began, had already set in before the 1925 presidential elections. In 1927 the General Synod resolved to reassemble in special session if these negotiations matured. By then, the antiultramontane Evangelical League had collected 3 million Protestant signatures against a Prussian concordat. Both regarded concordats as an issue of the first magnitude for Protestants. Already in 1924, the Roman curia had reached its goal of a favorable concordat in Catholic Bavaria. As the presidential campaign began, Protestants correctly assumed that the curia aspired to extend these same arrangements to Protestant Prussia.[54] The march of concordat negotiations was additional evidence that the Center had profitably exploited the evils of parliamentarianism for its confessional cause.

Any Protestant support of Marx, the chancellor who had sanctioned the Bavarian concordat, seemed little short of treason in the estimation of Evangelical church leaders. A vote for Marx appeared as a vote for a Prussian concordat, the disquieting counter-Reformation, and a coalition that discriminated against Protestants. As the candidate of republican parties, Marx seemed to embody everything that most churchmen detested: zealous ultramontanism or Socialist religious indifference, parliamentarianism, and a weak foreign policy. By contrast, the aged field marshal represented everything of value: Evangelical piety, monarchism and authority, devotion to duty and country, and a strong nationalist foreign policy. Even some Democratic liberals, unable to endure the Center's confessional aims, crossed over to Hindenburg. There was no doubt how the church Right would act. In sermons and periodicals aroused pastors reminded parishioners to vote "Evangelical," as though the main issue were religious and not largely political.[55]

When Hindenburg won by a margin of only nine hundred thousand votes, Rade attributed his narrow victory to the effective support marshaled by a politically conscious Evangelical church.[56] Overjoyed by his victory, *Positive Union* took it as "a special gracious gift of God to our German people."[57] Even *Reformirte Kirchenzeitung*, usually hesitant to comment politically, exclaimed: "God's grace preserved us from a plot of the Jesuits for whom everything is all right if only they can assert their power and cunning in the vacancy left by the former Protestant and German Kaisertum."[58]

Clearly, many churchmen expected great things of Hindenburg. Some hoped that he would somehow put an end to the senseless fulfillment policy and bring much needed authority to the German state. Going farther, *Der Reichsbote* welcomed the nationalism stimulated by his election as possibly presaging a monarchical restoration.[59] Above all, the election signified an ideological victory over the enemies of Protestant values and German nationalism. So entwined had Protestantism and nationalism grown in Protestant minds, wrote Rade disparagingly, that most churchmen could scarcely tell the difference between them.[60]

In view of the election's ideological overtones, those Democratic liberals who remained faithful to the republican candidate could expect little mercy from an aroused church. In vain they argued that the election was a political, not an ideological, contest, that ultramontanism was not a basic issue. To the disgust of most churchmen, forty-two republican Evangelical theologians, teachers, and pastors issued an appeal to Protestants endorsing Marx, and Rade, Harnack, and Otto Baumgarten wrote in the Democratic *Frankfurter Zeitung* on his behalf. They pointed to Hindenburg's political inexperience, doubting that in his advanced age he could avoid reactionary advisers. They proclaimed their dedication to the Republic and its constitution, seemingly threatened by those backing Hindenburg. They expressed their trust in republican foreign policy, contested by the Right.[61]

At least 85 percent of the Prussian Evangelical clergy, wrote Baumgarten, took offense at the Democratic-liberal promotion of Marx.[62] Predictably, Gauger referred to it as a public scandal that had brought confusion into church ranks. Like Gauger, the *Allgemeine evangelisch-lutherische Kirchenzeitung* noted that those who contested the Bible also opposed the fatherland. Liberals refuted this easy identification and blanket insinuation, pointing to the large number of liberals who had denied Marx their vote. But only liberals had publicly supported the "Romanist" Marx, Gauger replied.[63]

Like their more orthodox brethren, some liberal leaders censured the actions of Marx's advocates among Democratic liberals. The Nationalist Johannes Kübel warned his friend Rade that the activities of Democratic liberals might lead to a split in the Friends of *Die christliche Welt*. For centuries Protestants had been taught honor of fatherland, loyalty to traditional authority, and aversion for Rome. Now suddenly they were expected to tolerate pacifism and republicanism, and even to respect Catholicism. Unable to shift loyalties so quickly, church people had reacted by frowning on the whole liberal camp. Kübel stressed that his major objection, however, lay not in the political domain, but in the religious. He could not understand why Rade could abet the growing threat of ultramontanism.[64]

To meet such attacks, Rade and other Democratic liberals inverted the argument, maintaining that they had championed Marx for political reasons, not religious. Accordingly, Rade answered, Kübel should not threaten a split, inasmuch as the Friends of *Die christliche Welt* embraced liberals of varying political persuasions. If other Protestants felt threatened by the policies of the Center party, countered Rade and Baumgarten, they had themselves to blame, since such policies could not bear fruit had Protestants rallied to republican parties instead of condemning the Republic as "religionless." To Baumgarten's way of thinking, Marx, if elected, would feel forced to pursue national, not partisan, goals as Ebert had done. At any rate, the confessional threat paled in significance beside the real danger to the Republic that a Hindenburg victory posed. It seemed incredible to Rade that Protestants, obliged by their social ethics to recognize existing authority, could throw their support to a candidate disloyal to the existing republican form of government. He had, therefore, endorsed Marx publicly to foster a more properly Evangelical attitude toward the state.

The confusing issue of allegiance to the Republic came to an indecisive head at the 1927 Church Federation Assembly, held in Königsberg, East Prussia. Here the dual themes of "Church and National Ethos (Volkstum)," on which Paul Althaus spoke, and "Church and Fatherland," treated in a controversial speech by Wilhelm Kahl, focused the assembly's attention on the nation much as the 1924 assembly had concerned itself with the social orders. According to Prälat Schoell of Württemberg, the Kirchenausschuss chose these themes to resolve the tension between the church and the broad folkish movement and between most churchmen and the Republic.[65] Appropriately, far-off East Prussia was selected as the conference site, owing to its national significance. Severed from the German mainland by the intolerable Polish corridor, East Prussia reminded conferees of the "wrong" done the fatherland and of their patriotic responsibility to the beleaguered homeland.

Understandably, the assembly unleashed powerful nationalist sentiments.[66] After a depressing trip through the corridor, delegates paused inside the Prussian border at Marienburg, a former stronghold of the Teutonic Knights, for a special ceremony brimming with nationalist symbolism, including the flying of imperial colors. Later in Königsberg, Ministerial Director Kameke, representing the Nationalist minister of the interior, appropriately connected Christianity and nationalism in his address to the delegates. Conferees were edified to hear such words spoken again in the name of the government. Finally, on the last day, the assembled delegates arose to hear a telegram of greeting to President Hindenburg. Previous assemblies had not sent such "respectful greetings" to President Ebert.

Complete harmony did not prevail in Königsberg, however. Because Kahl had made his peace with the Republic, delegates awaited his speech with some uneasiness. He was a Reichstag deputy of the moderately conservative People's party, which, though preferring initially a monarchical restoration, had gradually come to terms with the Republic under the leadership of Gustav Stresemann, the main architect of republican foreign policy. A close friend of Stresemann, Kahl had minted the term *Vernunftrepublikaner* to describe those who, like himself, had accepted the Republic for pragmatic reasons, not through conviction.[67]

Near the end of his speech, Kahl broached two matters of conscience that aroused many delegates. First, when existing authority demanded obedience that contravened the commands of God, it need not be obeyed. The Republic had not, however, violated Evangelical consciences with such demands. If it had, resistance through constitutional means afforded a proper recourse. Failure to obtain redress left only one alternative open, namely the necessity of suffering injustice. Much more controversial was Kahl's second point. He sought to resolve the conflict between duty to governing authority and loyalty to the old order by asserting that no ruler can claim a residual right to rule. For an omnipotent God can topple the mighty from their thrones. Like Jülicher earlier, he held that St. Paul required acceptance of authority wherever it existed because God had ordained it. Folkish standards to test authenticity Kahl likewise rejected as unbiblical. As a professor of law, Kahl could not doubt that revolution could create legal authority. The gist of Kahl's advice was that Christians could accept the Republic without suffering pangs of conscience.[68]

The "lively, continuous" applause following Kahl's speech concealed a deep-seated difference of opinion regarding the implications of his assumptions. While attending the assembly, Martin Rade wrote an article for a local Königsberg newspaper, asserting that Kahl had professed allegiance to the Republic. Rade recalled that in a major speech at the 1921 assembly Julius Kaftan had branded the Republic as a "religionless" state. With questionable optimism Rade pointed to a change of attitude in the fact that the Kirchenausschuss had assigned Kahl his topic with full knowledge of his republican leanings. "We all have reason to welcome his speech," Rade wrote, "as an important step on the way toward an inner, honest reconciliation between this church and our present state."[69]

As an article by General Superintendent Klingemann of Koblenz showed, Kahl's speech could be interpreted differently and contested in part. Following Traub's earlier lead, Klingemann seemed to reason that only the state permeated by folkish values merited the Christian's full allegiance. This state had tumbled with the monarchy. For the sake of fatherland, one must reject the Republic, not accept it, as Kahl had counseled. Klingemann contended that Kahl had not required complete loyalty to the Republic and had not censured a restoration by constitutional means. This type of reasoning left Klingemann in the characteristic pose of submitting to the Republic formally but most unwillingly. "The voluntary subjection to a given form of state or authority, stemming from Christian faith, does not mean in any way a confession to the Republic," he wrote. "But we must be permitted to have our own opinion regarding the origins of the new state and of the law created for us by the revolution. And the respectful love for that which has been lost to us cannot be contested and taken from us Evangelical Christians."[70]

Klingemann had assessed Kahl's speech more accurately than Rade. For Kahl had found words only to strike down arguments against accepting the Republic as legitimate, not words to inspire loyalty to it. Yet Kahl approached Rade's position by trying to strip the Republic of its divisiveness as a political issue. While Kahl's example did indicate a halfhearted shift in political loyalties toward the Republic among some, Althaus's formulations spotlighted a movement in the opposite direction. His amalgamation of Christianity and Germanness and his stress on national renewal for the sake of Germany's historical mission ruled out the Republic for lacking the folkish qualities that Traub and now Klingemann extolled as marks of proper authority.[71] Goaded by radical nationalists, nationalism and hostility to the Republic had intensified in much of the church.

Kahl showed that Althaus's theology of folk redemption had no corner on interpreting God's intentions in history. Earlier Titius, at the 1919 Church Federation Assembly, and now Kahl emphasized that God had allowed defeat and revolution and that Christians ought to respond by accepting the new order as God's dispensation. This way of interpreting God's will in history ran athwart two assumptions that colored the thought of antirepublican churchmen. First of all, defeat and revolution represented not the clear will of God but His punishment for a moral lapse that only national renewal could redeem along Christian lines. Accordingly, the Republic, continuing evidence of moral lapse, could enjoy God's favor just as little as the revolution. Second, the advice of Titius and Kahl had the alarming effect of sanctioning power no matter how brutally and illegally obtained. Against Kahl's view of revolution as an act of God, *Der Reichsbote* pointed to Old Testament evidence that, though God allowed revolutions to punish evil, they remained sinful acts of rebellion against Him and His creation, incapable of creating authority that stemmed from God.[72] Rather cynically, Troeltsch had viewed this problem in terms of how much time was needed to legitimate revolutionary authority.[73] For many churchmen, however, this was the wrong question. The right question inquired about the marks of Christian authority and the origins of power.

The major question within the church was whether Christians owed the Republic more than passive obedience, not whether republican authority was legally constituted. That the patriotic proclamation of the 1927 Church Assembly omitted mention of the Republic as even legally constituted can be laid to the influence of a significant minority, which would not yet concede this minimal point. Apparently church officials desired a proclamation that affirmed the legal legitimacy of the Republic, perhaps because they faced directly the problem of cooperating with the present state. Such an affirmation was inserted into the two drafts that the Kirchenausschuss discussed.[74] They contained as well the counsel that Christians, because of Romans 13, ought to obey the Republic as a Christian duty and respect its institutions and offices. The two Kirchenausschuss versions hewed to Rade's line, since they required something more than passive obedience. In the committee of the assembly, however, reference to Romans 13, the present state, and respect for its institutions and offices went by the board. Carrying the day, a group within the assembly, including President Pechmann himself, was loathe to recognize the Republic as a legally constituted state on the basis of Romans 13.[75]

What the proclamation did say was that the church must offer intercessory prayer for folk, state, and authority. Following the social responsibility incumbent upon the Volkskirche, the assembly claimed for the church the right to judge the state's legislation and administration as well as to project the Christian conscience into public life without violating political neutrality. To parishioners the declaration commended concern for the commonweal and service and subjection to the state, but no affirmation of the Republic.[76] No discussion followed the proclamation's presentation and the thought-provoking but contradictory speeches of Althaus and Kahl. Klingemann explained that the powerful impact made by the speeches had so overwhelmed their auditors as to immobilize their reactions. Undoubt-edly closer to the truth, another commented that the assembly wished to avoid public dissension in church ranks that debate would inevitably broadcast.

President Pechmann called for a vote on the proclamation, a vote unani-mously given. Yet fourteen members had protested the final and accepted version in committee. They objected that the proclamation could conceiv-ably obligate Christians to obey a government hostile to the churches and Christianity, for the wording would compel obedience to the state in general, if not specifically to the Republic. Here the ideal of the Christian state served as a touchstone of legitimacy. As Scholder noted, their objection took immediate aim at the Weimar Republic and the possibility of a dicta-torship of the political Left.[77] The alarming experience of the Old-Prussian church during the initial Hoffmann era and the persisting strength of left radicalism made this objection still relevant. Later several of the objectors, including Pechmann, acted consistently by applying this touchstone to the Nazi regime as well. One must conclude that antirepublican churchmen such as Pechmann understood more profoundly than Democratic liberals the problematics of Romans 13, however one may judge Pechmann's ideolog-ical reasons. For Romans 13, as interpreted (but not cited) by the proclamation, would require obedience to any state.

If it did not mention the Republic, the proclamation at least referred to the state because, according to Schoell, who headed the drafting com-mittee, "prejudices...are being put about regarding the attitude of the church toward the state and [because] church people are so exceedingly uncertain and needy of guidance in this respect."[78] Clearly Schoell and other church officials wished to assure republicans that the Evangelical churches recognized the Republic as legally constituted and deserving of obedience, an assurance that could still be inferred from the proclamation and cited for the guidance of parishioners. Yet the vague and general phraseology of the proclamation did not address concretely the perplexing problem that troubled Evangelical consciences. A critic of Kahl's speech had written that "the difficult question as to when authority really exists legitimately still needs an answer."[79] He could have made the same point about the proclamation, for it concealed a multiplicity of answers.

By 1927 most churchmen appear to have accepted the Republic, however grudgingly, as legally constituted authority. That such a position does not clearly shine through the patriotic proclamation is explained by the assembly's craving for unanimity. Yet antirepublican sentiment predominated within the church, if sometimes in the compromising figure of the pragmatic republican. One would not expect, however, to find this sentiment enshrined in the proclamation of a Church Assembly bent on accommodating the church to the Republic as far as prevailing church opinion would permit. Yet friends and foes of the Republic within the church testified to the church's antirepublican bias. In 1927, for example, the embattled Rade could claim—surely with some exaggeration—that the prorepublican stance of *Die christliche Welt* distinguished it from almost all of the remaining church press.[80]

POLITICAL NEUTRALITY AND POLITICAL ACTIVISM

Nothing had excited people at church meetings since the revolution as much as politics, wrote General Superintendent Dibelius at the end of the period under consideration. "Political passion dominates everything."[81] Perhaps few Germans could remain untouched by the political turmoil that dogged the Weimar Republic, certainly not churchmen who claimed for the newly independent Volkskirche a social role encompassing society itself. A pastor addressing a Positive Union gathering in 1926 rejoiced that the church "speaks out more than ever in our religiously and morally confused time."[82] He noted with approval the practice of some bishops and general superintendents who plied their pastors and diocese with regular pastoral letters.

If it perceived a mission to the entire folk, the Volkskirche could ill afford to interpret its social message in such a way as to alienate those segments of its constituency drawn to contrary political conclusions. In times of relative political stability the diverging tendencies of the Volkskirche toward both comprehension and activism might be glossed over. But the one tendency clearly counteracted the other in the overstrung political atmosphere of the Weimar Republic. This tension might lessen if the church could adhere to some principle of political neutrality. A line would need to be drawn between Evangelical moral sensitivity (Gesinnung) and political advocacy. The church parties operating in the Old-Prussian church recognized political neutrality as the sine qua non of a Volkskirche straddling a pluralist society. But the parties fell out over the critical question of where the line lay separating Evangelical moral sensitivity from politics.

What appeared to the church Right as a legitimate expression of moral sensitivity struck much of the church Left and observant Democrats and Socialists as camouflage for the ideology of the political Right. Through the spectacles of the conservative and nationalist ideology inspiring most churchmen, one could look upon eminently political questions, such as the alleged stab-in-the-back thesis, the acceptance of the Versailles treaty, parliamentarianism, the Socialist program, pacifism, and even the existence of the Weimar Republic, as moral problems of the first magnitude. While the church Right obscured the line, liberals tended to bring it into sharper focus. They regarded the problem of political neutrality as the "most fatefully difficult" one confronting the Weimar church.[83] One reason for liberal promotion of the direct election (Urwahlen) of synods had been to infuse nonrightist blood into church governance for the sake of political neutrality.

In 1920 the Old-Prussian General Synod adopted a general statement on political neutrality and another on the political activities of clergymen.[84] The first proclaimed the principle of political neutrality without elaborating its concrete implications. The second statement endorsed the political involvement of pastors rather than impose clear limits on their political activity. The net effect was the espousal of political neutrality in such an ambiguous manner as to leave the door wide open for individual interpretation.

The Old-Prussian church had only recently parried the threat of state intervention when the General Synod met in April 1920. In the fall of 1919 the three Prussian ministers for church affairs seemed bent on imposing democratic elections upon an outraged church in order to defuse it politically. It was partly in response to this threat that the General Synod espoused political neutrality. While rejecting state intervention in the first statement, the General Synod recognized its corollary, namely that the church must renounce any intent to intervene, as it were, in the prevailing political and economic systems. The first statement stressed that party membership in no way voided the claim of parishioners on the services of the church. To fulfill its religious mission, the church must function "outside of political party life."

The second statement emerged as the synod's response to a petition that pastors refrain from political activities within their congregations, asking, in effect, that the General Synod recognize as indispensable a line dividing moral sensitivity from politics. One might have expected the synod to oblige, especially since the first statement emphasized that pastors owed a primary responsibility to their office. But the synod was prepared to believe, according to the second statement, that politically gifted and tactful clergymen could engage in political activity without alienating parishioners. By the same token, it balked at imposing restrictions on the less gifted and the less tactful.

Urging acceptance of the second statement, two speakers cited examples of clergymen who had successfully promoted church interests in both the Prussian Constituent assembly and the Weimar assembly. One of them noted that a political pastor would have brought scandal upon himself under the monarchy. But now the church needed political pastors to foster church political interests in regard to such issues as school legislation. In view of the importance of this argument and previous reluctance to tolerate political pastors, the second major argument, that pastors were also entitled to participate in politics as citizens, seems far less compelling. The second statement suggests that actual church political interests overrode concern for a precise definition of political neutrality. By the same token, differences of opinion over political neutrality and the difficulty of drawing any clear line suggest that no formula could be precise. Much depended on the circumspection of the EOK and consistories, which after the revolution, as before, held the right to discipline the clergy.

Both to affirm political neutrality and to extricate the church from the flag issue that brought the fall of Chancellor Luther's government in May 1926, the Evangelical churches went so far as to adopt their own flag. The flag was meant to symbolize church independence from the state as well as Protestant unity. Since many churchmen regarded the Republic itself as a political issue, the display of republican colors at church functions could be regarded as a violation of the church's political neutrality. Of course, displaying the former imperial colors was quite as much as infringement —therefore the need for a politically neutral flag. Such a flag would spare the reproach of republican authorities and avoid dissension in local church boards.[85]

Political neutrality broke down most easily in pastoral sermons. It was widely agreed in the Old-Prussian church that the sermon must come to grips with current moral issues, but how to implement this intent without breaching political neutrality caused disagreement. Concern for the comprehensive nature of the Volkskirche generally moved the church Left to conclude that the sermon and church pronouncements could grapple with political issues only in the abstract by pointing out relevant moral principles.

Even though a conscientious pastor claimed to speak from an Evangelical moral sensitivity, he should shy away from divisive political issues lest he cast dust in the eyes of his parishioners.[86] Liberal periodicals continually took offense at "political sermons" preached by rightist clergymen. It seemed incredible that a rural pastor would dare to review from the pulpit so complicated and controversial a problem as Germany's foreign policy. A prayer for the election of a Christian president in 1925 would have appeared politically innocent had not everyone regarded it as an endorsement of Hindenburg. As the years wore on, many liberals grew alarmed that the Volkskirche and its servants seemed to act as though the Volkskirche must close fronts against the political Left. Liberals had traditionally bucked a church pronouncing on dogma; now they deplored one pronouncing on politics. In both cases, the Volkskirche seemed to strike against freedom of conscience.

More than liberals, other church parties tended to emphasize the necessity of an activist church. The periodical of the Middle party, *Preussische Kirchenzeitung,* favored a more direct treatment of political issues than liberal standards would allow.[87] As a whole, the church Right went much farther in this direction. A pastor of the Positive Union party advised his colleagues that the sermon must "on the one hand work out clearly and distinctly Christian principles and apply them to the burning question so that the listener does not remain uncertain regarding the practical demands of the gospel on the conscience." No wonder liberals complained. The Right position would allow for partisan commentary on almost any issue under the guise of Evangelical moral sensitivity. The pastor did, however, recognize limits: "On the other hand, spicy insinuations [and] the naming of names and parties are to be omitted completely."[88]

During the summer of 1919, *Der Reichsbote* published an exchange of views on "political sermons" that illustrated the liberal complaint. The exchange began with a letter from an irate reader, who wrote: "Every Sunday when I sit in...church, I sense that I am in a German-Nationalist People's assembly. One is reminded of the church of God through nothing but the cross on the altar, so emphatically denied in this way."[89] Outraged by the writer's disparaging remarks, Pastor Roggisch of Eichfier in the Border Mark replied:

May the sermon leave unmentioned—perhaps out of fear of mispleasing the red rulers or some mad republican—the insane crime of the November Revolution, the breaking of oath, which has had such terrible results for our fatherland and surrendered us defenseless into the hands of our merciless enemies? Should it not be the duty of the sermon to brand the Judas act of those navy brigades who betrayed their poor fatherland for foreign money and—according to the opinion of a decent and honorably thinking enemy admiral—together with the red revolutionaries shoved the dagger into the backs of the furiously fighting, brave German army? Must the sermon keep quiet when a government cut off from God attempts to take religious instruction from the school, i.e., to lay hold on the ... authority of God after destroying the Kaiser's authority? Should the sermon quietly settle for the grotesque farce of transferring the authority of the summus episcopus of the Evangelical Landeskirche to the hands of a, to say the least, completely indifferent triumvirate? ... Should the sermon ignore that the accursed Revolution has dissolved all bonds of propriety and order, of piety and fear of God? Should it never speak of the rotten fruit of fifty years of Socialist agitation, of the Spartacists?[90]

To show how one might judge political events with Christian principles, Pastor Johannes Mueller of Annen, Westphalia, published a sermon in *Der Reichsbote,* flaying the alleged national betrayal and the new government, "cut off from God" and therefore incapable of rebuilding the German state. Germany's political guilt lay in deviating from the path blazed by Bismarck. To Pastor Diestelkamp of Schmoelln, Mueller's sermon seemed too obviously political in emphasis, and Superintendent Dittrich of Lesum contended that God's Word shed no light on whether Bismarck had trod the right path. To this criticism, Mueller replied that as a work of patriotism Bismarck's contribution to the German state had indeed been a work of God and that guilt might be assessed from a religious point of view for its destruction. Characteristically, he denied that he had ventured onto political ground, since he had not named parties responsible for Germany's collapse. And most of those writing to him concurred. Someone from Posnania confirmed that the sermon possessed "no political character at all" and squared also with his "religious feelings."[91] But then Mueller did not need to supply names if everyone already knew the identity of the assumed culprits. It is apparent that the Evangelical moral sensitivity of conservative churchmen blended imperceptively with their political views. By political neutrality, the church Right tended to mean neutrality toward parties but not toward moral (political) issues that parties provoked.

If one agrees with the church Right that the Republic constituted a genuine political issue, Democratic liberals more openly breached the principle of political neutrality. At services on Constitution Day (August 11) especially, Democratic liberal pastors upheld the Republic on the basis of Romans 13 and sometimes had part of the Weimar constitution read.[92] They, however, recognized no breach inasmuch as the Republic, in their opinion, lacked the status of a legitimate political issue.

Like the church Right, the small band of Socialist pastors did not balk at applying an Evangelical moral sensitivity to concrete political questions. The big difference was that Socialist pastors made little pretense of hewing to political neutrality, as the example of Günther Dehn illustrated. On May 1, 1919, a national holiday, Dehn officiated at services held by the League of Socialist Friends of the Church in Berlin. In his sermon he sought to infuse socialist thinking with Christian content. A disgruntled woman in the congregation told *Der Reichsbote* that Dehn had performed more as an abusive Socialist agitator than as a proper Evangelical minister, defiling the house of God with his rabid political views. Similarly, *Der Reichsbote* condemned Dehn for selling out Christianity to socialism. Dehn answered: "Just as most of my colleagues claim the right—and no one denies them this—to give really political talks often on the basis of their German-Nationalist or German-Democratic moral sensitivity, so, too, have I given a Christian sermon on the basis of Socialist moral sensitivity." In effect, Dehn argued that all politically interested churchmen began with an ideology, not with Evangelical moral sensitivity, and he claimed the right to do likewise.[93] Dehn must have expressed his views on the sermon only polemically or with great reservation. Soon to turn his back on religious socialism, he was already receptive to Karl Barth's condemnation of "hyphenated Christianity."

On May 1, 1919, the church had opportunity to demonstrate its vaunted political neutrality by holding services as it had formerly done to commemorate national holidays. Such services on the holiday of international socialism would indicate that the church could abide Socialists—at least, so argued a small minority of concerned liberal churchmen and leaders of Christian unions. But many clergymen viewed the day not as a national, but as a class, holiday, commemorating materialist values and the recent revolution. Rather than conduct services, one pastor wrote that he preferred to quit the ministry. For the most part, apparently, Evangelical churches remained closed.[94]

Much of the church press also reflected the conflicting interpretations of political neutrality that often shaped the sermon. Here the EOK and consistories did not have any direct authority to exercise control. For the sake of political neutrality, the liberal editors of *Die christliche Welt* and *Protestantenblatt* counseled other church editors to refrain from commenting on divisive political issues. Liberals deplored attempts of the large Evangelical Sunday press to pass judgment on the week's news from the perspective of the political Right, ostensibly from that of an Evangelical moral sensitivity.[95] The church Right, however, remained unmoved by the pragmatic counsel of liberals, who appeared more derelict in their duties than judicious in their advice. "We live at a time when the state assimilates one cultural area after another (school, youth, welfare, art, public morality), and also at a time when the state increasingly loses its Christian orientation," a pastor of the Positive Union party charged in 1926. "The Christian church may not quietly accept this development into an unchristian state of compulsory culture, achieved in Bolshevist Russia."[96] The Volkskirche's response must match its challenge by criticizing the unchristian state, by voicing the demands of Christians on the state, and by influencing elections.

With this threefold obligation in mind, periodicals of the church Right—for example, *Die Reformation* and the *Allgemeine evangelisch-lutherische Kirchenzeitung*—offered their readers a fairly extensive review of current political events from the vantage ground of Evangelical social sensitivity. A religious newspaper and at the same time a political one, *Der Reichsbote* presented quite a problem to liberals, whose definition of political neutrality required a pragmatic separation of these two spheres. By the same token, the newspaper, widely read by the Old-Prussian clergy and closely monitored by the church press, never let such considerations trouble it. Intent upon imposing the dictates of faith on all areas of life, pietist journals reviewed recent political developments in the same vein. Failure to inform the public or abandoning it to the indoctrination of Christian enemies struck Josef Gauger, the editor of *Licht und Leben*, as a "sin of omission."[97] He nevertheless grew so disturbed at the politicizing of religion in political commentaries that beginning in December 1922, he published a separate monthly, *Gotthard-Briefe*, that pietists could order for their political guidance.

In view of the political allegiance of Old-Prussian churchmen, it would have been extremely difficult to maintain a semblance of political neutrality even if the church Right accepted the constricting liberal definition. It was no secret among Weimar politicians that an overwhelming proportion of active Evangelical members favored and voted for the political Right. Observant journalists of the political Left occasionally reproached the church for its political bias and suspected that reactionary pastors manipulated congregations as a rallying point against republican parties.[98] Seemingly as a bloc, the dominant church Right endorsed the political Right.[99] By contrast, the church Left divided its political loyalties, one segment adhering to the political Right, the other to the Democratic and, to a lesser extent, Socialist parties.

Many in the church Right agreed with liberals that the Volkskirche must accommodate parishioners belonging to various contending parties. But such agreement was often theoretical, tactical, and strongly qualified. Certainly one could not take kindly to avowedly anti-Christian parties. The Communist party should lie well beyond the limits of serious consideration for any devout Christian. It was highly questionable whether Socialists approached these limits. Even the Center and Democratic parties fell under a cloud of suspicion owing to their cooperation with Socialists in Weimar governments and their democratic or ultramontane commitments. The church Right regarded conservatism as an outgrowth of Christian social ethics and tended to assume that those moving beyond also moved beyond the pale of recognizably Christian social ethics. It was the prospect of realizing an Evangelical world view that drew churchmen toward the political Right. This affinity and the church Right's questionable definition of political neutrality accounted for the saying that the Evangelical church voted Nationalist but was politically neutral. But this saying exaggerated the hold of Nationalists on the church Right. Notably pietists deplored compromises that Nationalists seemed to make with principle and increasingly looked for other means of projecting an Evangelical world view at elections.[100]

Liberal hopes that the church could separate Evangelical moral sensitivity from its concrete political application mostly collapsed in the presidential elections of 1925 and the referendum a year later over confiscating the former princes' property. In both cases, the church came closest to acting as a closed-front Volkskirche. Still, theoretically at least, churchmen could claim to have eschewed partisan behavior by emphasizing confessional loyalty in the first case and God's commandments in the second.

In the presidential elections that aroused political passions to fever pitch, much of the church press and various church associations advised their readers and members to remain confessionally loyal by voting for Hindenburg. According to Wilhelm Schubring, editor of *Protestantenblatt,* superintendents reprimanded dissenting pastors and aroused church authorities denounced theology professors who dared to advocate the election of a Catholic republican.[101] Liberals feared that the Volkskirche might break up under the strain of campaigning against the republican Left. In part their fears materialized in 1926 when over 180,000 members, nearly three times the 1924 total, contracted out of Evangelical churches. Church political involvement also put a crimp in the success of Christian nonpartisan lists in urban elections to parents' advisory councils in the spring of 1926. These elections, as well as the numbers contracting out, suggested again that the more they turned into political issues,the less well church causes fared.

On the confiscation issue, church authorities took an unambiguous stand for the first time on a major controversial political issue that had nothing directly to do with their own immediate interests. It seemed as though the enterprising Volkskirche had entered a daring new stage in its aspiration to pose as the conscience of the wayward folk. Talk about such a role was cheap unless the church was prepared to brave controversy at the critical moment. But the consequence was exposure to political attack on an issue that had whipped up public passions more than any other since the revolution. Except for the Democratic party, which officially remained neutral, the parties of the Right and Center condemned the proposal of the two Marxist parties to have the former princes' property confiscated without compensation. Intervention in this issue, therefore, set the churches, Protestant and Catholic alike, squarely against the Marxist parties. Most churchmen viewed the Marxist proposal as nothing short of legalized theft.

The Marxist solution failed to receive legal sanction, but not without luring non-Marxist voters, among them loyal church people. After the Reichstag had turned a deaf ear to the initial Communist proposal, Communists resorted to the popular initiative, provided by Article 73. Because this maneuver seemed likely to win over embittered workers, Socialists joined the initiative drive for signatures during the period March 4-17, 1926. After the Reichstag on May 6 rejected the bill forced on it by the initiative, the measure was submitted to the electorate in a referendum held on June 20. As many as 15.5 million voted in favor of the measure, but not enough to carry it. [102] Along with the combined strength of Communists and Socialists, a large segment of the middle classes had signed the initiative petition and voted affirmatively in the referendum. Among them were those whom inflation had hurt or ruined. If the state refused payment on war loans devalued by inflation, they asked, why should the property of princes escape the same fate?

Within the Old-Prussian church, pressure first mounted in Pomerania for a church initiative. On April 4, after the signature drive, the rural congregation of Wendisch-Silkow issued the first call that was later endorsed by the executive committee of the provincial synod and by provincial confessional Lutherans. The local church patron, Gustav Graf von Schwerin, prevailed upon the boards of Wendisch-Silkow to accept the resolution that he had framed, and he energetically took the lead in persuading other congregations to follow suit. "For the first time since the humiliating days of the November Revolution," the resolution read, a large part of the folk "is preparing to commit a crime and an intentional and unconcealed insurrection against God's commandments."[103] Specifically, the seventh, ninth, and tenth commandments, against stealing and covetousness, lay in obvious jeopardy. The resolution implored President Kapler of the EOK for a pronouncement that would be published in church papers and read from all pulpits before the projected referendum vote. All who gave aid to the immoral cause of uncompensated expropriation, the resolution counseled, should be treated as notorious sinners and excluded from the communion table.

Urged on by a wave of such resolutions (which, however, omitted mention of sacramental compulsion) as well as by requests from prominent churchmen, the Old-Prussian Church Senate obliged with a resolution on May 20 and the Kirchenausschuss with another on June 4. Both statements highlighted the moral issue and professed political disinterest. To Old-Prussian congregations, the Church Senate proclaimed:

We are not concerned with parties or politics—the Evangelical church stands above parties and refrains from taking any political stand—but we are concerned with the demands of the Christian conscience and the Word of God. In this case as often in our political life these demands appear to us to be most grievously endangered. . . . Loyalty and faith are shattered, the bases of an ordered state existence undermined, if individual citizens [Volksgenossen] are to have all of their property taken away without any compensation.[104]

More succinct and emphatic was the declaration of the Kirchenausschuss: "The proposed confiscation without compensation means depriving German citizens [Volksgenossen] of their rights and contradicts clear and unambiguous principles of the gospel."[105]

Predictably, the church's Cassandran statements were caught up in the swirl of public controversy. The rightist press exploited them; the Marxist press denounced them. Predictably also, churchmen of the political and church Right deplored the evident ingratitude of the masses toward former princes and the beguiling demagoguery of the Marxists.[106] That the intrusion of the church into the issue could alienate parishioners on both sides was evident in the plea of the administrative council of the Anhalt Landeskirche to the EOK for advice. In Anhalt three Religious Socialist pastors had publicly assailed the Kirchenausschuss for its position and commended a vote for the Marxist proposal as a Christian duty.[107] Thereupon Marxists had lauded the dissenting pastors, while patriotic organizations and rightist parties had declared their lack of interest in a church that could tolerate such disgraceful behavior. For the most part, church liberals concluded that church leadership had blundered badly by having subjected the Volkskirche to such a strain. They chastized the church for not remaining politically neutral.

Foremost among liberal critics was Johannes Kübel, who had bitterly denounced his friend Martin Rade in the recent presidential elections. But this time the Nationalist Kübel and the Democrat Rade saw eye to eye on the question of political neutrality. In *Die christliche Welt,* Kübel published a censorious speech, one that he would have liked to give to the Church Senate before it issued its unfortunate declaration.[108] To be sure, Kübel agreed that the contemplated expropriation amounted to theft. But as a liberal pastor, he held that the church violated its political neutrality when it applied principle to concrete reality. The consequences had become painfully apparent in the current controversy; for the church could be branded with inconsistency and thus with acting politically on behalf of the princes. Never before had the church taken an official stand on a burning issue, Kübel charged, nor had it ever defended the rights of the propertyless. By defending dynastic property now, the church set a dangerous precedent and created the unfortunate impression that it was politically biased and two-faced.

As the charge of inconsistency and bias circulated within and beyond the church, discussion of political neutrality reached a new level of urgency. The crucial question was whether previous church pronouncements were different in kind from declarations on dynastic property. If there was no difference, the churches could legitimately claim to have acted consistently and with no political bias. Such was the position that the Kirchenausschuss apparently took. It collected pronouncements of member churches to neutralize the contention that because it had not raised its voice on other public issues, it ought to have remained silent now.[109]

Previous church pronouncements and political lobbying fell into three main categories. Under national concern could be grouped declarations on such matters as the postwar blockade, the plight of German war prisoners, the Upper Silesian settlement, black occupation troops, the Rathenau assassination, the Ruhr occupation, and the war-guilt issue. In a second category—social and morality legislation—clearly definable moral principles seemed at stake and the political obligation of the churches obvious. Finally, it seemed understandable that the churches would claim a right (in a third category) to lobby for their own immediate interests, such as favorable disestablishment terms and confessional education.

To Kübel and other critics, however, the precedent set in the confiscation issue heralded the entry of the churches into a highly dangerous fourth category of political activity—all remaining political issues that found parties at loggerheads. Though he exaggerated, Kübel was largely correct. Never before had Weimar churches applied moral principles to a major controversial issue that found the German public hopelessly divided and that lay beyond immediate church institutional concerns. Hoping to dissuade the Kirchenausschuss, the Landskirche of Frankfurt a/M. had already raised the question of inconsistency.[110] If the Kirchenausschuss acted, it would enter "new land" with dire consequences for the comprehensive structure of the Volkskirche. The churches would lose a sense of proportion for what political issues they could address publicly and what they should not.

Though intensified, debate over political neutrality flowed in the same channels as before. Gauger admitted that church statements on confiscation were inconsistent with past practice. At fault, however, were not these statements but past practice. He regretted, for example, that the churches had not condemned the revolution or pressed more vigorously for revaluation.[111] Taking aim at Kübel, Pastor Erich Meyer restated the case for the social Volkskirche. Like Gauger, he maintained that the churches should take a forthright stand on every political question that was at the same time an important moral issue. He considered Kübel's distinction between proclaiming principles and applying them meaningless in practice. The Volkskirche must indicate to the confused mind of the common man the moral principles involved in political decisions.

Rade's reaction to the contrasting arguments of Meyer and Kübel revealed the pragmatism with which many liberals approached the problem of political neutrality. He agreed in theory with Meyer, in practice with Kübel. Like Kübel, Rade criticized church authorities for bias and for constraining conscience. Unlike Kübel, Rade charged the Kirchenausschuss with misusing religion for political ends. He saw in the issue, as he had in Marx's candidature, a testing of the Republic. Once more Rade grieved that the church's political stand had aggravated republican disrespect for the church.[112]

Rade had good reason to suspect that antirepublicanism motivated the

churches' response. How much is impossible to determine. Antirepublicanism also stemmed from moral considerations. How, then, can one sort
out the political element from the moral in the calculations of churchmen?
Graf von Schwerin might profess purely moral motivations, but surely he
felt his way of life threatened for reasons that cannot clearly be reduced to
either category.

The tight knit of moral and political considerations can be sensed in the
more specific reasons for the intervention of the Evangelical churches. Only
after the initiative signature drive did pressure build for an official church
position. The drive had revealed that well over 2 million non-Marxist voters
would endorse uncompensated expropriation. The Marxist bill would apply
this windfall not only to the economic relief of the working class but also
to disabled war veterans, survivors of the war dead, small farmers, and
victims of inflation. By pandering to the economic resentments of the
lower middle class especially, Marxists appeared to make inroads into a
traditional church constituency. This group, the "confused," was the specific
target of church statements. (Bias toward princes appeared to be an unjust
charge, since the churches had already endorsed revaluation for the inflation's
victims.) Some churchmen feared that the Marxist campaign against the
property of a single small class could well turn out to be a first step in a
concerted Bolshevist attack upon the property of all. Whether or not this
scare galvanized most churchmen, they believed that the dispute over property had crystallized the current ideological struggle between Christian and
Marxist values. To some, moreover, the projected confiscation was but a
continuation of the Marxist revolutionary assault on the political authority
of the princes, as the resolution of Wendisch-Silkow suggests.[113]

Evangelical churches would probably not have intervened, however, if
the Marxist framing of the question had not made the moral issue of theft
so obviously clear cut. Had the question centered around the compromise
bill of the coalition parties, the moral principle would have seemed much
less obvious and the temptation to intervene more remote. The complexity
of political issues and traditional Lutheran scruples against prescribing technical political solutions by moral principle deterred churchmen. Given these
barriers, the church's penetration into the "new land" could be repeated
only upon rare occasions.

Other practical considerations gave church authorities pause. If the
Volkskirche entered the "new land" of escalating political controversy,
church leaders were likely to discover that they could not speak as authori-

tatively for the church. Here and there enough pastors had contested both pronouncements to tarnish the moral credibility of the Church Senate and the Kirchenausschuss.[114] Confused about their responsibilities, church authorities were tempted to discipline the dissenters. One church government instituted such proceedings, only to dismiss them. Rade reported that church officials had summoned other pastors to explain their public dissent.[115] Discipline was unlikely to cow pastors who had already mustered courage to defy prevailing church opinion, however. Discipline also stirred the protest of liberals, who deplored the tendency of the closed-front Volkskirche to bind individual conscience. At the 1927 General Synod of the Old-Prussian church, Friedrich Winckler, chairman of the Church Senate, regretted that its declaration had been wrongly interpreted as binding on pastors and congregations.[116] But in liberal eyes the mere act of issuing a declaration bound conscience. Finally, the confiscation issue confirmed the previous lobbying experience of the Old-Prussian church. The more church causes became political issues, the more gaps opened in the closed front of the Volkskirche as these issues pitted church allegiance against party loyalty or political preference. Both fought out in 1926, the Westphalian school strike and the confiscation issue provided dramatic examples of this tendency. Those who would press on into the "new land" confronted the discouraging reality that a significant minority of loyal parishioners and church leaders would defect rather than follow.

In the confiscation dispute, Religious Socialists drove the biggest wedge into the Volkskirche's closed front. The executive committee of the League of Religious Socialists even launched an attack on the churches in its public appeal for dispossessing princes: "Christ the Lord . . . as he saw the poor of his folk in their poverty fights on our side, even when the leaders of the 'Christian' churches present themselves to the princes and their 'holy property.'"[117] One wonders how Religious Socialists could prize political neutrality while deploring the reformed royal general prayer, and yet ignore this principle in support of confiscation.

Generally liberals undertook to defend Religious Socialists from the angered church Right for the sake of the Volkskirche. Yet liberal toleration snapped when Religious Socialists egregiously breached political neutrality. Outraged by the misuse of the pulpit by the Socialist pastor August Bleier while the confiscation issue raged, liberals submitted a resolution of censure to a Berlin district synod lamenting that Bleier "conducts his spiritual office in such a way that hatred and dissension arise from his demagogic behavior, unbecoming to the spiritual office. We regret that such a man is in our midst."[118]

Because Religious Socialists were a small minority, however, liberals saw in the political activism of nationalist and conservative churchmen the main threat to the principle of strict political neutrality. But this threat could not develop its full potential. The complexity of most political issues, theological scruples, and internal dissent placed natural limits on the extent that the Volkskirche could breach its own political neutrality, as liberals interpreted this principle.

The question remains of how the EOK tried to enforce political neutrality by exercising its right to oversee and discipline the clergy. A collateral question is how seriously the EOK judged this principle breached by the Old-Prussian clergy. Only through the complaint of others could the EOK and consistories learn of potential abuses, since the administrative apparatus did not monitor sermons or clerical political activities. The EOK responded to complaints by admonishing the clergy when found delinquent by investigating consistories. Consistories settled most complaints before they could reach the EOK. But the EOK did try to set the parameters of proper conduct.

As noted already, the EOK believed that political pursuit of the church's institutional interests ought not be construed as breaching political neutrality. Encouraged by the EOK and the Kirchenausschuss, churchmen advised parishioners to vote for parties that fostered these interests—church privileges in elections to constituent assemblies in 1919 and confessional schools in national elections thereafter.[119] That this advice favored the political Right was clear to all. Before the January elections in 1919, a Berlin general superintendent and the president of the Brandenburg Consistory counseled Berlin clergy against voting for the Christian People's party (the rechristened Center). The party still served specifically Catholic purposes, they pointed out. Two Brandenburg general superintendents commended the Nationalist party to their clergy as the best means of securing church interests. Both pairs of administrators appeared to believe that they had pounded home the nail that the EOK had already driven. But the EOK disavowed both recommendations.[120] At this point the EOK established the basic principle that would guide it: Even in the interests of the church, clergymen may not attack or advocate any party in the course of their pastoral duties. The same was true of forms of government or economic systems, toward which the church had proclaimed its neutrality in the revolutionary period. It appears that, with notable exceptions, the clergy cleaved to this line. It was the same line, after all, that the dominant church Right generally recognized.

More than the church Right, however, the EOK acknowledged that much could be said and insinuated in a sermon or upon other occasions that might be interpreted as an infraction of neutrality short of praising or condemning a party, form of government, or economic system. From this gray area complaints flowed into consistories and the EOK. Inasmuch as Evangelical moral sensitivity and partisan politics could not easily be sorted out in this area, the EOK applied several pragmatic tests: In the given situation, had the actions of the clergyman affronted others besides the complainant? A sermon redolent of nationalism or conservatism could cause widespread offense in Berlin but not in rural Pomerania or in special services for former officers. Even apart from the circumstances, was the pastor's point of departure religious and moral and not conspicuously political?[121] In passing such judgments, the EOK and consistories became entangled in a casuistic thicket that defies clear generalization about standards applied. The impossibility of formulating a code of political behavior for Old-Prussian pastors is quite as apparent.

Liberals regretted that the EOK and consistories failed to draw a sharper line, and Democratic liberals and Religious Socialists complained that only the political Right had freedom for its views in the church.[122] In reality they chafed less at restrictions imposed on them by church authorities than at the hostility of the church public.

In the Weimar period a two-way traffic of complaint developed between the EOK and the Kultusministerium, the EOK deploring infractions of school law, the Kultusministerium forwarding complaints of the political Left about church political neutrality. Complaints about the reformed royal intercessory prayer dwindled as it was gradually dropped from usage. Other complaints about alleged infractions of political neutrality grew apace, as the Old-Prussian church became politically involved in the presidential elections and the confiscation issue. Socialists and Communists raised specific complaints during Landtag discussions of church subsidies. Apparently they sought to neutralize the voice of the Evangelical church, or to strike back at it while their agitation collided with the church's. Either the EOK sanctioned the promotion of Hindenburg's election as a confessional concern or it was powerless to prevent church agitation. In either case churchmen breached the EOK's basic definition of political neutrality by endorsing one candidate. Even though the church's position on confiscation did not run afoul of this basic definition, President Kapler and the EOK resisted official church action and felt forced to swim with the current of church opinion.[123] Among their concerns were state subsidies. In 1928 an EOK official highlighted the importance of church political neutrality by informing general superintendents that the indiscretions of a minority of the clergy had jeopardized state contributions in the Landtag.

Given this situation, the EOK proved receptive to the polite but firm suggestion of a number of Evangelical Landtag deputies, ranging from members of the People's party to Socialists, including Carl Severing, Socialist minister of the interior. On March 6, 1926—after the presidential elections but before the confiscation referendum—the deputies recommended that the EOK remind the church's servants of its political neutrality "in view of unfortunate events of recent time."[124] As the referendum neared, the EOK sent consistories such a reminder, on April 17, 1926. As the cause of its concern, the EOK cited "repeated events and observations of the past years."[125] In their discussions of this prod in Silesia, General Superintendent Schian and his superintendents once again stumbled over the main problem. On the one hand, they agreed on the need to illuminate the moral and religious aspects of current conditions, while on the other they stressed the necessity of refraining from any partisan position. Again it was the gray area in between that presented the problem.

President Kapler believed that church officials had loyally served church and Republic alike by cautioning the clergy against breaching political neutrality and by calling violators to account.[126] He found this task complicated by the necessity of mediating between two extremes. At one pole, in his opinion, was a fairly small minority of clergymen whom official pressure could hardly influence. Nettlesome also were relatively innocent indiscretions that cropped up unexpectedly. Upon the 250th anniversary of his congregation in 1926, for example, a Rhenish pastor had solicited and published greetings from the exiled Kaiser. The greetings seemed appropriate to the occasion because the Hohenzollern had protected the Protestant diaspora in the Rhineland over the centuries. But a Democratic newspaper and a Socialist one as well charged the pastor with misusing the festive occasion for monarchist and Nationalist propaganda. Exonerating the pastor of this charge, the consistory faulted the pastor, a monarchist, not for soliciting the greetings but for publishing them, because of the affront that they had caused.

At the other extreme, Kapler believed that Democrats and Socialists wrongly generalized from scattered cases to picture most of the clergy as remiss in political neutrality and hostile to the Republic. The EOK had a case against the repeated claim of the political Left. After the confiscation referendum, the Kultusministerium asked the EOK to respond to charges of Socialists and Communists in recent Landtag budgetary discussions as well as to several reports of leftist newspapers. After consistories had diligently investigated each case, the EOK replied in January 1927 that all charges rested on a deplorable fabrication of facts. Thus, a Socialist deputy had taxed a certain pastor for agitating against the Republic, republican colors, and pacifism in a talk, charges that the pastor flatly denied. In the EOK's opinion, no charge was weighty except possibly one on which opinions might legitimately differ. [127]

Whether the Left's attacks were legitimate or not, the EOK had practical political reasons for drawing the reins more tightly on the clergy. Not only was the Landtag's granting of subsidies at stake, but possibly also parity with the Catholic church should the curia reach its goal of a Prussian concordat. That seems to have been President Kapler's worry in 1928, when he observed to general superintendents that the Democratic and Socialist press had systematically represented the Catholic church as loyal to the Republic and the Evangelical as disloyal. [128]

Perhaps the EOK minimized the frequency of cases breaching political neutrality and the political Left exaggerated because the two drew the line between Evangelical moral sensitivity and partisan politics at different places in the troublesome gray area. If a contested sermon had a nationalistic point that was not overtly political, the EOK was not likely to fault it. Against charges relayed by the Kultusministerium, the EOK claimed that the Evangelical clergy warranted protection from unjust attack because it devoted itself to the renewal of the nation. [129] For the EOK, as for most of the clergy, nationalist commentary could hardly be regarded as partisan, since it emphasized individual ethical responsibility to the whole. But republicans were apt to see partisan consequences in the church's folkish nationalism for the reason that the political Right claimed a corner on nationalism and directed nationalist barbs against the Republic. Some of the cases that the EOK exposed as fraudulent were nationalist sermons or talks that appeared to fall into the gray area. Apparently the complainants made explicit what they thought the pastors meant implicitly.

On Memorial Sunday each year, nationalist sermons commemorating the war dead were most apt to skirt the EOK's limits and antagonize the political Left. Members of local rightist veterans' organizations often marched into these services as a group, in uniform and bearing flags. In 1927 the Brandenburg consistory reported that their republican counterpart, the Reichsbanner, attended as well. The policy of consistories was to welcome all such organizations. Yet the participation of the Reichsbanner, composed largely of Socialists, must have been exceptional. Its leadership regarded the Evangelical church as a tool of the reaction.[130] The pastor tried to strike the right tone at such services. In one contested sermon, the pastor equated the sacrifice of Germany's war dead with the sacrificial death of Jesus, the model and source of power for all those prepared to deny themselves for the nation. Though this sermon glorified war and sanctified nationalism, it passed muster with the consistory.[131] Such sermons and the parade of rightist veterans' organizations into church on Memorial Sunday helped shape the image of the Evangelical church as the spiritual companion of the nationalist Right.

The Stahlhelm, the largest of the rightist veterans' organizations at mid-decade, requested Evangelical pastors to consecrate flags and standards in oath-taking ceremonies and to conduct special services. Founded in 1918 as a veterans' organization, the Stahlhelm developed after 1924 into a political combat league that assailed the Republic and lobbied against Stresemann's foreign policy. If pastors consented to Stahlhelm requests, would they not breach the church's political neutrality? An EOK decree of 1890, still in effect, denied pastors permission to take part in such oath-taking ceremonies. The Saxon consistory blunted the impact of this decree, however, by ruling in 1924 that it did not prohibit a display of Stahlhelm flags in church and mention of the Stahlhelm in church prayers whenever its members attended in a body. Still, the church would not sanction oath-taking to the Stahlhelm as it did to the army.[132]

Despite clear regulations, some pastors could not refuse the Stahlhelm's request for illicit church ceremonies. A former chaplain described their moral appeal in *Die Dorfkirche*.[133] Hundreds of determined young men stand before the altar, desiring the church's dedication of their noblest aspirations and willingness to sacrifice all for country. The oath is intoned, the flag is dipped, hands are placed on the shaft. Finally, the pastor consecrates the flag to God as a holy symbol. Certainly the church should not deny these idealists its pastoral services as they reached to it for meaning in life. Gottfried Traub likewise deplored the church's regulations against such ceremonies, arguing that a church neglecting nationalism dug its own grave in this "revolution state."[134] But other nationalist pastors nursed reservations about clerical participation in the activities of the Stahlhelm and similar organizations. Political neutrality seemed in jeopardy, and the presence of pastors seemed to be more of a religious ornament than a commitment of religious renewal.[135] More emphatically, the *Protestantenblatt* denounced clerical participation for exposing the church to political censure and imperiling its political neutrality.[136] Such was also the position that the EOK began to consider after the Stahlhelm veered into a more explicitly antirepublican course. Whereas the EOK still distinguished between nationalist commitment and its political consequences, the liberal periodicals *Die christliche Welt* and *Protestantenblatt* had reached the conclusion that the nationalism pervading church quarters threatened any pretense of political neutrality.[137]

It is apparent that there could be no satisfactory way of defining political neutrality in the Old-Prussian church so long as its dominant elements insisted on an activist role that was ideologically attuned to only part of the Volkskirche's constituency. To them, neglect of this role for the sake of social comprehension meant abandonment of the folk to secularism and materialism. Only partly responsible for breaches of political neutrality was the political complexion of the Old-Prussian church. The basic problem was that the glue of political neutrality, however strong, could not hold together two incompatible elements of Volkskirche ideology—political activism and social comprehension. Such was the dilemma of an incipient closed-front Volkskirche.

CONCEPTUALIZING ANTIREPUBLICANISM

By 1927, the terminal year of this book's scope, most Old-Prussian churchmen had hardly begun to accommodate themselves ideologically to the Republic. Those who did so publicly were very much the minority —Democratic liberals and Religious Socialists. Those committed ideologically to monarchism but pragmatically to the Republic—the so-called Vernunftrepublikaner—usually kept their silence; accordingly, their indeterminate number could not alter the impression that antirepublicanism suffused the church at large.

By the same token, the large majority did not crusade actively and conspicuously against the Republic, and the EOK acted diligently and prudently to reduce the level of friction with the new state. Volkskirche ideology, which inspired criticism of the republican political order, also drew limits on its expression for the sake of the comprehensive nature of the Volkskirche and political neutrality. The more church causes grew into partisan issues, the more even active parishioners withdrew their political support, throwing up clear warning signals against the tendency of the Volkskirche to close political and ideological fronts.

Lack of ideological accommodation has been demonstrated in a number of ways. Most political loyalties still remained tied to the political Right, especially (though with decreasing enthusiasm) to the antirepublican Nationalist party. More than in the Empire, the church needed to rely on parties to ensure its interests in the Republic, and the obliging Nationalists acted as the church's most dependable political ally. The active involvement of churchmen in the presidential elections of 1925 and in the confiscation issue of 1926 entrenched an alliance that earlier had revolved more directly around securing church institutional interests. That the patriotic proclamation of the 1927 Church Assembly could not clearly recognize the Republic as legitimate in any sense, despite the intentions of some church leaders, suggests a mere pro forma acceptance of the Republic long after the revolution. The touchstone of the authoritarian "Christian" state and the theory of symbiosis still remained in place to judge and censure the behavior of the Republic and even its legitimacy. Though the federal constitution guaranteed the status of the Volkskirche, the Republic left confessional education—a vital church interest—exposed to attack and corruption. The Old-Prussian church had to struggle before and even after the promulgation of the federal constitution for a status and independence that rightist churchmen claimed for the church as its due. Socialist parties appeared as the chief enemy in this struggle as well as ideologically in general, but the Democratic party—a possible bridge to the Republic—shared this opprobrium by seemingly holding the church in bondage to the "religionless" state. It was questionable whether the Republic could take credit for the status secured by the constitution, since parties and not the "state" as such made basic decisions in a mere party state. Moreover, Volkskirche structure was considered a means to an end that reflected poorly on the "religionless" Republic: the preservation or recovery of a Christian society.

The most convincing evidence for the inability of most churchmen to appreciate the Republic by 1927 was their extreme nationalism, which contested the Republic's broadly pluralist society and the parliamentarian democracy that expressed it politically. Christian nationalism would narrow the national political and ideological consensus to a Christian base and help win back the alienated to their Christian heritage. Christian nationalism lay at the very core of Volkskirche ideology. Inasmuch as the Volkskirche and Protestant Christianity had allegedly generated and molded German values, the Volkskirche should properly function as their custodian. Accordingly, other value systems could be denounced as non-German or unchristian: democracy, ultramontane Catholicism, pacifism, Jewishness, and above all, Marxism. The parties that reflected these values— a collection of more or less Protestant ideological enemies—dominated Weimar coalitions after supposedly helping to topple the "Christian" state.

Another indicator of the church's extreme nationalism was its toleration of a heretical racist (and antirepublican) movement in its own midst and of the new nationalism that seemed to slight Christianity. Conceiving of the folk as an order of creation, nationalist churchmen could appreciate other nationalist movements for cultivating dedication to the same ethical end while hoping to win them for Christian nationalism. With this prospect in mind, some recovered the theology of the national calling, which during the war had matched up the cause of the nation with God's purposes.

The Old-Prussian church's nationalism, in fact, was its most striking political feature. Directly or indirectly, Christian nationalism motivated or justified a series of political causes, most notably: Volkskirche privileges, confessional schools, morality legislation, support for rightist parties, a more aggressive foreign policy, and rejection of war guilt. Christian nationalism allowed Old-Prussian churchmen to address the political mentalities of the nation and thus indirectly other political issues as well. Significantly, it was Christian nationalism that was most likely to breach the church's political neutrality in the gray area. Christian nationalism, accordingly, is the most basic category and Volkskirche ideology the broadest context for interpreting the political attitudes of Old-Prussian churchmen.

Nationalist churchmen called ardently for a Christian renewal of Germany in the shape of a folk community (Volksgemeinschaft) without spelling out the practical implications of such a concept. From their nationalism and negative comments on the Republic one can surmise what they so vaguely projected. The involuntary authoritarian orders of creation (state, family, folk, economy) had decayed under the Republic (and earlier under the Second Empire) into seemingly voluntary associations responsive to the masses and no longer to God's purposes. Christian nationalism could cement a more authoritarian society by encouraging the mutuality of love and respect—between superiors and inferiors—that St. Paul urged on Christians. It appears that churchmen, theologically speaking, invoked nationalism from the world of the created orders to aid faith in producing the bonding agent for such a society. Not an egalitarian society grounded in a supposed mutuality of selfish interests, but only an authoritarian one animated by a transcending moral purpose could generate the desired tightly knit folk community. Accordingly, it seems appropriate to regard Christian nationalism as a form of nationalist conservatism. A community bonded by Christian nationalism could ensure social justice as well as generate the social cohesion and unity of purpose required for the defense of the nation against its predatory enemies. This vision of society linked rightist churchmen to the nationalist ideology of the political Right. Concretely, the intoxicating experience of national and religious renewal during the first months of the war provided an approximate example of what such a society could be like. Since then, and more particularly in the Weimar period, nationalist churchmen reacted against what they regarded as a debilitating chaos of values, and they did so in terms of the social ethics that had developed in the long history of the Old-Prussian church.

Like the others, the political order had degenerated into the form of a voluntary association, responsive to the materialist masses through parliamentary democracy. Likewise here, Christian nationalism should bond unequal members in a common folk so that a more authoritarian state, released from the pressure of special interests, could govern for the commonweal as God intended. It is apparent that, conceptually at least, nationalist churchmen saw in parliamentary democracy, not in the Republic as such, the main evil besetting the Weimar political order. If they regretted parliamentary democracy in the state, they were certain to restrain it in the church, though ecclesiastical principles also came to their aid. If the prospects of a monarchist restoration seemed dim, the Republic could at least be restructured to curtail parliamentary democracy. But then, nationalist churchmen rarely addressed how their government ought to constitute itself in the future. They may have assumed that this question made little sense until the cause of national renewal had progressed, or that it was too perplexing to answer, given the current stalemate between the political Right, Left, and Center. In any event, the question seemed to be a secondary concern, since nationalist churchmen understood politics as primarily a struggle over values. Democratic liberals such as Troeltsch, however, had no trouble fielding the question: the democratic Republic was a necessity, since it was the only form of government that most Germans would accept or tolerate.

It may seem obvious that Christian nationalism would set the response of rightist churchmen after 1927 to the national renewal that the political Right, entering a more radical phase, proclaimed against the Republic. What is not so obvious is that this response was an ambiguous one already shaped to a considerable extent before 1927. On the one hand, churchmen could find other brands of nationalism compatible with Christian nationalism in accord with their own conception of the folk as a created order. On the other hand, their attitudes toward war, racist Christianity and Germanic paganism, anti-Semitism, and the ecumenical movements, however extreme, showed an awareness that Christianity must impose limits, however vague, upon the excessive claims of nationalism. Finally, institutional independence, which the Old-Prussian church had learned to prize, could not be forgotten even as the Nazis tried to include the Old-Prussian church among the victims of tyrannical "coordination" (Gleichschaltung). When the 1920 General Synod resolved its thanks to the Hohenzollern, it also bade farewell to the heritage of the summus episcopus.

ABBREVIATIONS

AELK	*Allgemeine evangelisch-lutherische Kirchenzeitung*
CEH	*Central European History*
CW	*Die christliche Welt*
DK	*Die Deutschkirche*
Dorfk.	*Die Dorfkirche*
DP	*Deutsches Pfarrerblatt*
EB	*Eiserne Blätter*
ED	*Das evangelische Deutschland*
EK	*Evangelische Kirchen-Zeitung*
EOK	Evangelischer Oberkirchenrat
GB	*Gotthard-Briefe*
Gen.	*Generalia* (EOK files), followed by division in Roman numerals, section in Arabic figures, and volume in Roman numerals. Thus: *Gen.* XIV 37 II.
GG	*Geisteskampf der Gegenwart*
GSV	Generalsynodalvorstand
HZ	*Historische Zeitschrift*
IM	*Die Innere Mission im evangelischen Deutschland*
JCEA	*Journal of Central European Affairs*
JHI	*Journal of the History of Ideas*
KJ	*Kirchliches Jahrbuch für die evangelischen Landeskirchen Deutschlands*
LL	*Licht und Leben*
NkZ	*Neue kirchliche Zeitschrift*

PK	*Preussische Kirchenzeitung*
PM	*Protestantische Monatshefte*
PP	*Preussisches Pfarrarchiv*
Protb.	*Protestantenblatt*
PU	*Positive Union*
Rb	*Der Reichsbote*
Ref.	*Die Reformation*
RGG	*Die Religion in Geschichte und Gegenwart*
RK	*Reformirte Kirchenzeitung*
VfZ	*Vierteljahrshefte für Zeitgeschichte*
VGS	*Verhandlungen der . . . Generalsynode* (transcripts of the General Synod), followed by volume and year of the General Synod.
VKt	*Verhandlungen des . . . Kirchentages* (transcripts of the Church Federation Assembly), followed by the year of the Assembly.
Wb	*Die Wartburg*
Zs	*Der Zusammenschluss*
Zw	*Zeitwende*

NOTES

PREFACE

[1] J[ohannes] Schneider, *Die Konfessionsschichtung der Bevölkerung Deutschlands nach den Ergebnissen der Volkszählung vom 16. Juni 1925* (Berlin, 1928), p. 24.

[2] Karl Dietrich Erdmann, "Die Geschichte der Weimarer Republik als Problem der Wissenschaft," *Vierteljahrshefte für Zeitgeschichte {VfZ}*, 3 (1955), 8, 18–19.

[3] Claus Motschmann, *Evangelische Kirche und preussischer Staat in den Anfängen der Weimarer Republik* (Lübeck, 1969); J.R.C. Wright, *'Above Parties.' The Political Attitudes of the German Protestant Church Leadership 1918–1933* (London, 1974). In "The Evangelical Churches and the Weimar Republic, 1918–1933" (diss. University of Colorado, 1977), Frank Joseph Gordon surveys church political attitudes throughout the Weimar period. Following Motschmann, Gordon placed primary blame on the Republic for the hostile attitudes of Evangelical churches.

[4] Gottfried Mehnert, *Evangelische Kirche und Politick, 1917–1919* (Düsseldorf, 1959); Herbert Christ, *Der politische Protestantismus in der Weimarer Republik* (diss. University of Bonn, 1967); Kurt Nowak, *Evangelische Kirche und Weimarer Republik* (Göttingen, 1981); Karl-Wilhelm Dahm, *Pfarrer und Politik* (Cologne, 1965); Jochen Jacke, *Kirche zwischen Monarchie und Republik* (Hamburg, 1976).

[5] See, e.g., Frederic Spotts, *The Churches and Politics in Germany* (Middletown, Conn., 1973), pp. 9–12, 119–48, 237–71.

[6] On the Barmen synod and its background, see Arthur C. Cochrane, *The Church's Confession under Hitler* (Philadelphia, 1962) and Klaus Scholder, *Die Kirchen und das Dritte Reich, 1* (Frankfurt/M., 1977).

[7] Spotts, *Churches and Politics,* should be read along with Hans Gerhard Fischer, *Evangelische Kirche und Demokratie nach 1945* (Lübeck, 1970), for the conflict between Barthians and Lutherans over political ethics.

[8] The six in order of size in 1925: Evangelical Lutheran Landeskirche of Hannover (2,375,047), Evangelical Lutheran Landeskirche of Schleswig-Holstein (1,416,305), Evangelical Landeskirche in Hesse-Cassel (911,954), Evangelical Landeskirche in Nassau (477,381), Evangelical Reformed Landeskirche of the Province of Hannover (228,835), and Evangelical Landeskirche of Frankfurt a.M. (215,560). (Schneider, *Konfessionsschichtung,* p. 24).

[9] Spotts, *Churches and Politics,* pp. 17–20.

[10] Confessional statistics from Schneider, *Konfessionsschichtung,* pp. 19–25.

INTRODUCTION: FROM POLITICAL QUIETISM TO ACTIVISM

[1] Martin Luther to the Saxon elector (Oct. 31, 1525), *Dr. Martin Luthers Briefwechsel, 3* (Weimar, 1933), 595.

[2] Numbers of those who contracted out of Evangelical churches:

	1909	1913	1915–18	1919	1920	1921
Old-Prussian church	14,833*	17,854*	2,754	132,441	163,819*	99,658
In Berlin	8,997*	6,031*	1,553	41,341	48,663*	33,548
German Evg. churches	17,754*	22,996*	3,494	229,778	305,245*	246,302

	1922	1923	1924	1925	1926	1927
Old-Prussian church	48,843	48,299	27,528	61,815	94,811*	81,376
In Berlin	27,031	30,378	7,947	23,901	38,237*	35,146
German Evg. churches	149,709	111,866	68,341	131,793	180,772*	165,219

*Indicates peak years of the four waves.

(In *Kirchliches Jahrbuch, ed. J. Schneider {Gütersloh,* 1913–29] (*KJ*): 40 [1913], 542; 42 [1915], 463; 44 [1917], 141; 49 [1922], 101; 52 [1925], 121; 55 [1928], 129; 56 [1929], 93.)

[3] See Kirchner, *Die christliche Welt* [*CW*] (Feb. 12, 1920), 98–101; *Das evangelische Deutschland* [*ED*] (May 24, 1925), 160; *ED* (Apr. 18, 1926), 128; and Staeglich, *ED* (Aug. 8, 1926), 249, and (Aug. 15, 1926), 258–59.

[4] Friedrich Thimme, "Das Verhältnis der revolutionären Gewalten zur Religion und den Kirchen," in *Revolution und Kirche,* ed. Friedrich Thimme and Ernst Rolffs (Berlin, 1919), pp. 1–19; *Die Religion in Geschichte und Gegenwart* (2nd ed., 5 vols. Tübingen, 1927–31) [*RGG*], 5 (1931), 620–22.

[5] *RGG, 3* (1929), 827–30; Evangelischer Oberkirchenrat (EOK) report to General Synod, *Verhandlungen der . . . Generalsynode* (2 vols. Berlin, 1926) [*VGS*], 2 (1925), 371–74.

[6] See Gerhard Jacobi, *Tagebuch eines Grossstadtpfarrers* (9th ed. Berlin, 1930), pp. 172–73, and Günther Dehn, *Die alte Zeit, die vorigen Jahre* (Munich, 1962), pp. 164–85; *KJ, 56* (1929), 91.

[7] Percentage of Protestants who married in church ceremonies in given years:

	1910	1920	1922	1925	1927
Old-Prussian church	87.24	84.28	81.59	80.58	79.38
In Berlin	54.60	47.62	47.43	44.49	41.74
German Evg. churches	91.06		85.56	84.17	82.56

(In *KJ:* 50 [1923], 56; 53 [1926], 99; 56 [1929], 61.)

[8] Baptism-birth percentages in given years:

	1910	1920	1922	1925	1927
Old-Prussian church	96.41	95.75	97.56	94.79	95.81
In Berlin	91.45	89.02	99.39	88.36	94.47
German Evg. churches	96.85	96.48	97.69	95.15	95.76

(In *KJ:* 53 [1926], 82–83; 56 [1929], 42–43.)

[9] Numbers confirmed in given years:

	1910	1920	1922	1925	1927
Old-Prussian church	385,244	385,308	382,782	343,474	345,407
In Berlin		31,304	49,284	44,531	43,240

(In *KJ:* 42 [1915], 450; 50 [1923], 71; 53 [1926], 113; 56 [1929], 73.)

[10] *KJ,* 41 (1914), 109; Dehn, *Die alte Zeit,* pp. 174–75; *ED* (Nov. 7, 1926), p. 357; *Die Deutschkirche* [*DK*] 7 (1928), 38.

[11] See the sociological profile drawn by P. Gabriel, "Das evangelische Kirchenvolk," in *Evangelische Kirchenkunde,* ed. Wilhelm Heienbrok (Bielefeld, 1929), pp. 109–85. Also see Wilhelm Bousset, "Die Stellung der evangelischen Kirchen im öffentlichen Leben bei Ausbruch der Revolution," in *Revolution und Kirche,* ed. Thimme and Rolffs, pp. 59–66; Jacobi, *Tagebuch,* pp. 11–12, 67, 83–84, 92–93, 107, 150–51, 172–73, 178–79; Erich Foerster, "Die Stellung der Evangelischen Kirche," in *Geistige und sittliche Wirkungen des Krieges in Deutschland* (Stuttgart, 1927), pp. 100–103.

[12] Otto Dibelius, *Das Jahrhundert der Kirche* (Berlin, 1927), p. 199; *VGS, 1* (1925), 93–94.

[13] Reinhard, *VGS, 1* (1920), 419; Haendler, *VGS, 1* (1927), 492.

[14] Supply of pastors in the Old-Prussian church:

	1890	1900	1910	1920	1923	1925	1927
Passed final exam	447	170	158	229	193	197	176
Ordained	329	295	150	207	170	231	182
Available for ordination		1,014	224	60	119	73	56

Most of those "available for ordination" from 1920 to 1927 did not represent a surplus, since they were still in training. (In *KJ:* 50 [1923], 101; 53 [1926], 145; 56 [1929], 98–99.)

[15] Loycke, *VGS, 1* (1925), 535–36; *VGS, 2* (1925), 188.

[16] *Verhandlungen des . . . Kirchentages* [*VKt*] (1921), pp. 125–31, 137.

[17] Karl Holl, "Luther und das landesherrliche Kirchenregiment," *Gesammelte*

Aufsätze zur Kirchengeschichte, 1 (Tübingen, 1932), 327–36; Otto Hintze, "Die Epochen des evangelischen Kirchenregiments in Preussen," *Regierung und Verwaltung, 3* (Göttingen, 1967), 56–84; Johannes Victor Bredt, *Neues evangelisches Kirchenrecht für Preussen* (3 vols. Berlin, 1921–28), *1,* 157–82, 190–202, 319–23; Karl Rieker, *Die rechtliche Stellung der evangelischen Kirche Deutschlands* (Leipzig, 1893), pp. 320–22; Robert M. Bigler, *The Politics of German Protestantism* (Berkeley, 1972), pp. 4–11, 20–24.

[18] Walter Elliger et al., *Die evangelische Kirche der Union* (Witten, 1967), pp. 14–65; Hintze, "Die Epochen," 75, 87; Bredt, *Kirchenrecht, 1,* 141–56, 247, 377–79; Rieker, *Die rechtliche Stellung,* pp. 308–16; Bigler, *Politics,* pp. 37–38.

[19] Bredt, *Kirchenrecht, 1,* 181–90, 321–34, 344–46; Rieker, *Die rechtliche Stellung,* pp. 310–16, 351–61, 393–97; Hintze, "Die Epochen," 72–74, 90–93; Elliger et al., *Kirche der Union,* pp. 76–79; Foerster, *CW* (Feb. 20, 1919), 115–16. See Martin Heckel, "Zur Entwicklung des deutschen Staatskirchenrechts von der Reformation bis zur Schwelle der Weimarer Verfassung," *Zeitschrift für evangelisches Kirchenrecht, 12* (1966), 1–39, on the shifting legal relationship between church and state since the Reformation.

[20] Bredt, *Kirchenrecht, 1,* 257–311, 335–76, 385–437; *2,* 259, 707, 727–34; Rieker, *Die rechtliche Stellung,* pp. 398–407, 467–75; Hintze, "Die Epochen," 85–96; Elliger et al., *Kirche der Union,* pp. 96–99; Bigler, *Politics,* pp. 38–41; Klaus Erich Pollmann, *Landesherrliches Kirchenregiment und soziale Frage* (Berlin, 1973), pp. 9–53.

[21] Spaeth, *Protestantenblatt* [*Protb.*] (March 15, 1919), 123; Hans Götz Oxenius, *Die Entstehung der Verfassung der evangelischen Kirche der altpreussische Union von 1922* (diss. University of Cologne, 1959), p. 19; Pollmann, *Kirchenregiment,* pp. 15–16, 46–53.

[22] Rade, *CW* (Feb. 13, 1919), p. 107; Bousset, "Die Stellung," p. 51.

[23] Bredt, *Kirchenrecht, 1,* 438–42, 549–52, 561–62, 575–78; Hintze, "Die Epochen," 95; Rieker, *Die rechtliche Stellung,* pp. 399–400, 473; von Soden, *Protb.* (Apr. 15, 1923), pp. 60–61; De Weerth, *Reformirte Kirchenzeitung* [*RK*] (Dec. 28, 1924), 307.

[24] For the following analysis of Luther's social ethics, I have relied on F. Edward Cranz, *An Essay on the Development of Luther's Thought on Justice, Law and Society* (Cambridge, Mass., 1959), pp. 116–78; Gunnar Hillerdal, *Gehorsam gegen Gott und Menschen* (Göttingen, 1955), pp. 17–119; Gustaf Wingren, *Luther on Vocation,* trans. Carl C. Rasmussen (Philadelphia, 1957), passim; John M. Headley, *Luther's View of Church History* (New Haven, 1963), pp. 1–18.

[25] H. Richard Niebuhr, *Christ and Culture* (New York, 1956), pp. 175–77.

[26] Ernst Troeltsch, *The Social Teaching of the Christian Churches,* trans. Olive Wyon (4th Eng. ed., 2 vols. London, 1956), *2,* 465–576, 808.

[27] Wingren, *Luther,* p. 37; Hillerdal, *Gehorsam,* pp. 98, 107–12; Otto A. Piper, "The Church and Political Form," in *God and Caesar,* ed. Warren Quanbeck (Minneapolis, 1959), pp. 11, 20.

[28] Franz Schnabel, *Deutsche Geschichte im neunzehnten Jahrhundert*, 2 (2nd. ed. Freiburg, 1949), 19, 25–26, 32–34, 37–39; William O. Shanahan, *German Protestants Face the Social Question*, 1 (Notre Dame, 1954), 99–100, 110. In *The Politics of German Protestantism*, Bigler shows that conservatives and the orthodox suppressed religious and political liberalism within the Old-Prussian church during the first half of the nineteenth century. On the Protestant churches in the early nineteenth century, see Schnabel, *Deutsche Geschichte*, 4 (3rd. ed. Freiburg, 1955), 379–529. On the whole century, see John E. Groh, *Nineteenth Century German Protestantism* (Washington, D.C., 1982).

[29] Henning von Arnim, ed., *Friedrich Julius Stahl: Die Philosophie des Rechts* (Tübingen, 1926), passim; J. F. Stahl, *Das monarchische Princip* (Heidelberg, 1845), passim; Shanahan, *German Protestants*, 1, 241–54; Schnabel, *Deutsche Geschichte*, 4, 539–47. See Stahl's description of the "Christian" state in Wilhelm Mommsen, ed., *Parteiprogramme von Vormärz bis zur Gegenwart* (Munich, 1951), pp. 17–18. After German unification, the term *Christian state* became popular among Conservatives as a slogan. (Arnold Horowitz, "Prussian State and Protestant Church in the Reign of Wilhelm II" [diss. Yale, 1976], pp. 135–36, 327, 366–67, 377; Uriel Tal, *Christians and Jews in Germany* [Ithaca, 1975], pp. 120–59, 291–92.)

[30] Fritz Fischer, "Der deutsche Protestantismus und die Politik im 19. Jahrhundert," *Historiche Zeitschrift* [HZ], *171* (1951), 475–518.

[31] Bousset, "Die Stellung," 57–62; Vernon L. Lidtke, "August Bebel and German Social Democracy's Relation to the Christian Churches," *Journal of the History of Ideas* [JHI], 27 (1966), 245–64; Karl Kupisch, *Zwischen Idealismus und Massendemokratie* (Berlin, 1955), pp. 69–70; Fischer, "Protestantismus," 485, 489, 492; Shanahan, *German Protestants*, 1, 193–94, 301, 307; Schnabel, *Deutsche Geschichte*, 4, 564.

[32] Karl Buchheim, *Geschichte der christlichen Parteien in Deutschland* (Munich, 1953), pp. 122–23, 139, 175–77, 183; Shanahan, *German Protestants*, 1, 100–101, 198–200, 229, 233–34, 272–82, 297, 301–22; Fischer, "Protestantismus," 493–95, 497–99.

[33] According to Fischer, "Protestantismus," 496, a "cult of monarchism" steeped the Old-Prussian church and "almost equated Christianity with monarchism." See, e.g., Ernst von Dryander, *Erinnerungen* (Bielefeld, 1922), p. 208.

[34] *VKt* (1921), 124–25, 128–31, 142–46, 150–51, 155. Also see Dibelius, *Jahrhundert*, p. 237.

[35] *VKt* (1921), 121, 125, 139, 144; *VGS*, *1* (1920), 440, 447, 451–57; *VGS*, *1* (1925), 381; Dibelius, *Jahrhundert*, p. 67 and passim; Bredt, *Kirchenrecht*, 2, 111.

[36] Philipps, *Die Reformation* [Ref.] (Feb. 17, 1918), p. 53.

[37] Friedrich Brunstäd, *Die Staatsideen der politischen Parteien* (Berlin, 1920), pp. 5–9.

[38] *VKt* (1921), pp. 122–23, 129–30.

[39] Ibid., p. 130.

[40] See, e.g., Brunstäd, *Staatsideen*, pp. 12–30; Pfannkuche, *Eiserne Blätter [EB]* (Aug. 1, 1920), 65 ff., and (Oct. 10, 1920), 255 ff.; Günther Holstein, *Luther und die deutsche Staatsidee* (Tübingen, 1926). Of the periodicals examined, the *Gotthard-Briefe [GB]*, edited and largely written by the pietist pastor Josef Gauger, commented most comprehensively on the passing political scene. Appalled by partisan self-seeking in the Republic, Gauger sought a restoration of the monarchy by constitutional means, yet he could appreciate Swiss republican and British parliamentary government. In his estimation, Germany lacked the social cohesion of these two nations and needed the firm grasp of a monarchy not beholden to selfish party rule. Even so, he accounted himself a stern critic of Wilhelm II and his regime. Gauger's was a pragmatic monarchism, not a doctrinaire and blind glorification of the fallen monarchy. (See *GB*, 1 [1922–24], 55, 68, 135, 140, 242, 252, 254, 257, 342; 3 [1926], 256; 4 [1927], 93–94, 142; 5 [1928], 105, 236–38.)

[41] Shanahan, *German Protestants*, 1, passim; Heinrich Hermelink, *Das Christentum in der Menschheitsgeschichte von der französischen Revolution bis zur Gegenwart*, 3 (Tübingen, 1955), 60–68; Fischer, "Protestantismus," pp. 502–507; Kupisch, *Massendemokratie*, pp. 91–92, 96. By 1925 the Inner Mission comprised 3,855 charitable institutions and enrolled in its services 22,571 deaconesses and 3,434 deacons (1926 figure) as well as other professionals and hundreds of thousands of lay volunteers. (See *Die Religion in Geschichte und Gegenwart [RGG]*, 3 [1929], 271–80.)

[42] Walter Frank, *Hofprediger Adolf Stoecker und die christlich-soziale Bewegung* (Berlin, 1928), pp. 31, 47–80, 197–204; Buchheim, *Parteien*, pp. 192–95, 239–80; Pollmann, *Kirchenregiment*, pp. 140–46.

[43] Frank, *Stoecker*, p. 85; *Positive Union [PU]* (Nov.–Dec. 1926), 101; Pollmann, *Kirchenregiment*, 79–80, 205–206; Fischer, "Protestantismus," 509–12. See the 1879 decree in Karl Kupisch, ed., *Quellen zur Geschichte des deutschen Protestantismus 1871–1945* (Munich, 1960), pp. 74–75.

[44] Pollmann, *Kirchenregiment*, pp. 82–84, 107–16; Hans Eger, *Der evangelisch-soziale Kongress* (diss. University of Heidelberg, 1930), pp. 13–24, 71–78; Karl Kupisch, *Friedrich Naumann und die evangelisch-soziale Bewegung* (Berlin, 1937), pp. 52–54. See the 1890 circular in Kupisch, ed., *Quellen*, pp. 78–79.

[45] Pollmann, *Kirchenregiment*, pp. 112–16, 159, 300; Eger, *Kongress*, p. 43; Kupisch, *Naumann*, 59–66; Theodor Heuss, *Friedrich Naumann* (2nd. ed. Stuttgart, 1949), pp. 71–99. Evangelical workingmen's clubs soon cooperated with similar Catholic clubs against Socialist unions by supporting interconfessional Christian unions, organized around the turn of the century. Membership in the Evangelical clubs rose to nearly 200,000 by 1914, only to drop to 93,318 by 1927. In 1890 Weber also took the lead in founding a national association of Evangelical clubs, which he chaired until his death in 1922. (See Pollmann, *Kirchenregiment*,

93–96; *RGG, 2* [1928], 1163; *Der Reichsbote [Rb]* [Dec. 4, 1925]; *KJ, 54* [1927], 390.)

[46] Pollmann, *Kirchenregiment,* pp. 9, 12–13, 18–25, 29–33, 39–40, 43–48, 54–64, 137–56.

[47] Pollmann, *Kirchenregiment,* pp. 25–26, 40, 49, 93–101, 117–23, 151–56, 158–207, 294–302; Kupisch, *Naumann,* pp. 61–68; Heuss, *Naumann,* pp. 91–94; Frank, *Stoecker,* pp. 321–25. Note that the EOK, not synods, claimed authority to set the church's social course by virtue of church government's right to supervise the clergy.

[48] Pollmann, *Kirchenregiment,* pp. 75–78; Frank, *Stoecker,* pp. 346–47. See the 1895 decree in Kupisch, ed., *Quellen,* pp. 88–91.

[49] Frank, *Stoecker,* pp. 326–36, 352–58; Pollmann, *Kirchenregiment,* pp. 172–76, 186–88, 258–70.

[50] Frank, *Stoecker,* pp. 362–71; Heuss, *Naumann,* pp. 98–155; Kupisch, *Naumann,* pp. 72–93.

[51] Eger, *Kongress,* pp. 81–84; Pollmann, *Kirchenregiment,* pp. 270–85; Gottfried Mehnert, *Evangelische Kirche und Politik, 1917–1919* (Düsseldorf, 1959), pp. 27–28.

[52] Pollmann, *Kirchenregiment,* p. 301; Heuss, *Naumann,* p. 108.

[53] Pollmann, *Kirchenregiment,* pp. 36–39, 65–70, 153; Horowitz, "Prussian State," pp. 279–332, 365–72; Fritz von der Heydt, *Gute Wehr* (Berlin, 1936), pp. 102–22; *RGG, 2* (1928), 447–51.

[54] *VKt* (1921), pp. 126–27, 130–38.

[55] Ibid., pp. 131–40.

[56] Following chapters demonstrate the representative quality of Kaftan's formulations as well as their prevailing influence. Kirchenausschuss minutes suggest and Kaftan in his address notes, however, that some Kirchenausschuss members objected to his argument for political involvement. (Kirchenausschuss minutes [June 23–25, 1920], p. 16, and [Feb. 8–10, 1921], pp. 19–20, both in *Generalia [Gen.]* XII 102 V; *Vkt* [1921], p. 127.)

[57] *VKt* (1921), pp. 127, 131–34, 140, 144, 150–51.

THE WAR

[1] On the political structure of Prussia and the Empire, see Fritz Hartung, *Deutsche Verfassungsgeschichte* (6th ed. Stuttgart, 1950), pp. 259–86, 297–302. On the major parties, see Ludwig Bergsträsser, *Geschichte der politischen Parteien in Deutschland* (11th ed. Munich, 1965); Hans Booms, *Die Deutschkonservative Partei* (Düsseldorf, 1954); Ellen Lovell Evans, *The German Center Party 1970–1933* (Carbondale, Ill., 1981); Carl E. Schorske, *German Social Democracy, 1905–1917* (New York, 1965); Koppel S. Pinson, *Modern Germany* (New York, 1966), pp. 163–218; John L. Snell, *The Democratic Movement in Germany, 1789–1914* (Chapel Hill, N.C., 1976).

[2] Hans Götz Oxenius, *Die Entstehung der Verfassung der evangelischen Kirche der altpreussischen Union von 1922* (diss. University of Cologne, 1959), pp. 18–19, 23–27; Klaus Erich Pollmann, *Landesherrliches Kirchenregiment und soziale Frage* (Berlin, 1973), pp. 58–60.

[3] *Prot.* (Sept. 6, 1919). On church liberalism and heresy trials, see Oxenius, *Union,* pp. 29–36; Pollmann, *Kirchenregiment,* pp. 55–57; Johannes Victor Bredt, *Neues evangelisches Kirchenrecht für Preussen* (3 vols. Berlin, 1921–28), 2, 329, 355–58, 363; Walter Elliger et al., *Die evangelische Kirche der Union* (Witten, 1967), pp. 105–7, 111–15; Gottfried Mehnert, *Evangelische Kirche und Politik, 1917–1919* (Düsseldorf, 1959), pp. 15–18; Johannes Rathje, *Die Welt des freien Protestantismus* (Stuttgart, 1952), pp. 147–54, 179–94. Also *RGG: 1* (1927), 1589–92; *3* (1929), 1626–28; *4* (1930), 1580–82. On how heresy trials involved political parties and threatened church unity, see Arnold Horowitz, "Prussian State and Protestant Church in the Reign of Wilhelm II" (diss. Yale, 1976), pp. 179–262.

[4] On these two parties, see Von der Goltz, *Preussische Kirchenzeitung {PK}* (two March issues, 1925); Oxenius, *Union,* pp. 17–20, 40–47; Pollmann, *Kirchenregiment,* pp. 60–64; and *RGG: 2* (1928), 446–47, and *4* (1930), 1358–59.

[5] *RGG, 2* (1928), 446, 998–1006; Bredt, *Kirchenrecht, 2,* 640–41.

[6] Erich Foerster, "Die Stellung der Evangelischen Kirche," in *Geistige und sittliche Wirkungen des Krieges in Deutschland* (Stuttgart, 1927), pp. 97–100; Bredt, *Kirchenrecht, 2,* 677–83.

[7] Kübel, *Der Zusammenschluss {Zs}* (Jan. 1927), pp. 32–33; Günther Dehn, *Die alte Zeit, die vorigen Jahre* (Munich, 1962), pp. 76, 100, 108, 165, 180, 184.

[8] Mehnert, *Kirche und Politik,* pp. 27–30.

[9] Booms, *Deutschkonservative Partei,* pp. 34–58; Hartung, *Verfassungsgeschichte,* pp. 291–96; Schorske, *Social Democracy,* pp. 29–32, 224–84; Andreas Dorpalen, "The German Conservatives and the Parliamentarization of Imperial Germany," *Journal of Central European Affairs {JCEA}, 11* (1951), 187–96; Andreas Dorpalen, "Wilhelmian Germany—A House Divided against Itself," *JCEA, 15* (1955), 240–47; Beverly Heckart, *From Bassermann to Bebel* (New Haven, 1974), pp. 3–15 and passim.

[10] Reinhard Patemann, *Der Kampf um die preussische Wahlreform im Ersten Weltkrieg* (Düsseldorf, 1964), pp. 9–17. A law of 1849 divided voters into three direct-tax classes. The bulk of voters, assessed the lowest taxes, fell into the third class. Thus, the great majority controlled only a third of the votes in second-stage elections that decided on deputies by majority vote.

[11] Reinhard Wittram, *Das Nationale als europäisches Problem* (Göttingen, 1954), pp. 109–148.

[12] As quoted in *KJ, 42* (1915), 186–87.

[13] *VKt* (1924), p. 217. See Martin Schian, *Die deutsche evangelische Kirche im Weltkriege* (2 vols. Berlin, 1921–25), 2, 24.

[14] Schian, *Kirche,* *1,* 218–23, and *2,* 23–26, 108, 134–51, 265–69, 354.

[15] *PU* (Sept. 1917), pp. 186–87.

[16] Wilhelm Pressel, *Die Kriegspredigt 1914–1918* (Göttingen, 1967), passim. Pressel is reluctant to draw so certain a conclusion, since he could make no systematic study of nonpublished sermons.

[17] In, e.g., *KJ,* see: *42* (1915), 219–20; *44* (1917), 473, 481–82; *45* (1918), 344–50.

[18] Schian, *Kirche, 2,* 295. In addition to Schian's two volumes, see in *KJ: 42* (1915), 188–212; *43* (1916), 77, 80, 103–7; *44* (1917), 491–95; *45* (1918), 419–39. In a letter to the Generalsynodalvorstand [GSV] (May 10, 1918), the EOK claimed: "We have regarded it as our patriotic duty during the war to invest all liquid capital, insofar as it is not needed to meet urgent needs, in war loans." (*VGS, 2* [1920], 107.) Two thousand one hundred twenty-eight pastors and pastoral candidates, belonging to the Old-Prussian church, served in the war as chaplains, soldiers, or aides in military hospitals. Of these, 201 lost their lives, and 1,179 won decorations. (Ibid., p. 249.)

[19] Schian, *Kirche, 2,* 28–31, 154–63. In *KJ: 42* (1915), 137–48; *45* (1918), 420, 496.

[20] On the political crisis during the war, see Fritz Fischer, *Germany's Aims in the First World War* (New York, 1967), pp. 95ff.; Hans W. Gatzke, *Germany's Drive to the West* (Baltimore, 1950); Patemann, *Wahlreform,* pp. 44, 161, 235–57; Schorske, *Social Democracy,* pp. 283–321; Arthur Rosenberg, *Imperial Germany* (Boston, 1964), pp. 73ff.

[21] See, e.g., Philipps, *Ref.* (Jan. 28, 1917), p. 38.

[22] In *CW:* (Aug. 3, 1916), pp. 597–99; (Dec. 28, 1916), pp. 993–94; (May 31, 1917), p. 426; (June 21, 1917), pp. 484–85; (July 26, 1917), p. 554. Also see Laun, *Die Eiche* (3rd quarter, 1927), pp. 225–27; Roger Chickering, *Imperial Germany and a World without War* (Princeton, 1975), pp. 192–217; Foerster, "Die Stellung," pp. 133–35.

[23] Albert Marrin, *The Last Crusade* (Durham, N.C., 1974), pp. 82–142, 217–40.

[24] In *CW* (July 26, 1917), pp. 560–62; (Oct. 17, 1917), p. 756; (Dec. 6, 1917), pp. 843–44; (Jan. 17, 1918), p. 47. Also Mehnert, *Kirche und Politik,* pp. 54–55.

[25] Schian, *Kirche, 2,* 23, 151.

[26] Pressel, *Kriegspredigt,* p. 270.

[27] *PU* (Dec. 1917), p. 248. See, e.g., *RK* (Oct. 21, 1917), pp. 330–31; Pfennigsdorf, *Geisteskampf der Gegenwart {GG}* (Feb. 1918), p. 34.

[28] *Ref.* (Jan. 7, 1917), p. 9.

[29] *Ref.* (June 10, 1917), p. 273.

[30] *CW* (Sept. 26, 1918), p. 364. Silesian church authorities forbade the pastor to preach on such a theme. (Silesian Consistory to EOK [Sept. 3, 1918], *Gen.* VI

2 I.) Correspondence in *Gen.* XV 2 I shows that the government and the EOK discouraged pastors from promoting the Fatherland party in church services. See *CW* (Feb. 28, 1918), p. 110; Schian, *Kirche, 2,* 27; Mehnert, *Kirche und Politik,* pp. 57–63.

[31] Dehn, *Die alte Zeit,* pp. 208–9, 314–16.

[32] Pressel, *Kriegspredigt,* pp. 65–66, 149–51, 205–6, 211–19, 268–76, 301, 321–24, 355–57.

[33] *PU* (Dec. 1917), p. 247.

[34] In *Prot.,* see, e.g., (Aug. 25, 1917), p. 518; (Sept. 8, 1917), p. 543; (Sept. 15, 1917), pp. 546–47. See also Mehnert, *Kirche und Politik,* pp. 43–48.

[35] Schian, *Kirche, 2,* 26. See *CW* (March 28, 1918), pp. 135–39. Karl Aner claimed that a theology faculty had intended to award an honorary doctorate to Friedrich Rittelmeyer, one of the five who issued the Aner appeal. But the faculty refused to do so once he signed the peace appeal. The appeal eventually attracted the signatures of 2,000 men and women. Aner claimed that this number did not represent the true strength of the Protestant peace movement for the reason that the military and the censors worked effectively to suppress the movement. (Aner, *Das neue Deutschland* [Dec. 15, 1918], pp. 109–12, clipping in *Gen.* II 27 II.)

[36] *Ref.* (Jan. 20, 1918), p. 23.

[37] *CW* (Dec. 13, 1917), pp. 858–59; *Prot.* (Nov. 10, 1917), p. 656.

[38] *CW* (Jan. 17, 1918), p. 47.

[39] Schian, *Kirche, 2,* 157. Pressel ascribed unqualified support of the Fatherland party to a traditionally false understanding of the doctrine of the two Regimente. (Pressel, *Kriegspredigt,* pp. 202, 221, 268–83, 353–60.) Nationalism aimed an ethical — not political — appeal at the individual. By contrast, the demand for a negotiated peace aimed at influencing the state, the domain of law in which the church presumably had no license to intrude. Behind this dichotomy lay a double morality that imposed ethical responsibilities upon the individual but not upon the state. Agitation for the Fatherland party, accordingly, could be regarded as ethical rather than as political behavior. War theology, in turn, wreaked havoc on the two Regimente doctrine. The charge of fusing the two Regimente ought to have settled on war theologians instead of on Aner and his colleagues. War theology transformed ethical responsibility to the folk — the domain of law — into a gospel of folkish redemption.

[40] On the suffrage crisis, see Patemann, *Wahlreform,* pp. 18–96, 127–260; Fischer, *Germany's Aims,* pp. 333–41, 393–401.

[41] *Ref.* (July 22, 1917), p. 334, and (Dec. 30, 1917), p. 522.

[42] Emil Karow, "Der Evangelische Oberkirchenrat und der Pfarrerstand," in *Hundert Jahre Evangelischer Oberkirchenrat der Altpreussischen Union 1850–1950,* ed. Oskar Söhngen (Berlin-Spandau, 1950), pp. 76–79; *VGS, 2* (1925), 308.

[43] *VGS, 2* (1925), 310–12; *VGS, 2* (1927), 46.

[44] *VGS, 2* (1927), 49; Bredt, *Kirchenrecht, 1,* 553, 560–62, and 2, 178–91,

205–10, 224–41; Georg Burghart, "Der Evangelische Oberkirchenrat in den Jahren 1900–1950," in *Hundert Jahre,* ed. Söhngen, pp. 28–29. The percentages are only approximately accurate, since they compare the per capita church tax of 1914 with the per capita total tax load of 1913.

[45] The church's legal claims are elaborated in [Johannes Duske], *Denkschrift über den Umfang der Staatsleistungen der deutschen Länder an die evangelischen Kirche bis zur Ablösung* (Berlin-Charlottenburg, 1928); Johannes Duske, *Die Dotationspflicht des preussischen Staates für die allgemeine Verwaltung der evangelischen Kirche der altpreussischen Union* (Berlin, 1929).

[46] Ernst Christian Helmreich, *Religious Education in German Schools* (Cambridge, Mass., 1959), pp. 39–44, 59–68, 85–87; Thomas Alexander, *The Prussian Elementary Schools* (New York, 1918), pp. 79–90, 93, 95, 176, 229–30, 286–303, 507.

[47] Helmreich, *Religious Education,* pp. 40, 44, 55, 62, 66–79, 85–100; Alexander, *Elementary Schools,* pp. 62–74, 286–89, 293, 394–400, 413–14; Friedrich Kreppel, "Der Lehrer in der Zeitgeschichte," in *Das Wilhelminische Zeitalter,* in *Zeitgeist im Wandel,* ed. Hans Joachim Schoeps, *1* (Stuttgart, 1967), 199–218.

[48] *Ref.* (July 22, 1917), p. 334, and (Feb. 17, 1918), p. 53; *PU* (April/May 1918), pp. 64–67.

[49] *Proth.* (July 28, 1917), p. 471; *Ref.* (May 25, 1918), pp. 251–52, and (Aug. 3, 1918), pp. 368–70.

[50] Foerster, "Die Stellung," pp. 120–28.

[51] *Ref.* (April 21, 1918), pp. 126–27; *Proth.* (March 23, 1918), p. 140.

[52] *Proth.* (May 25, 1918), pp. 251–52; *Proth.* (Aug. 31, 1918), pp. 413–14; *CW* (June 13, 1918), p. 235; *CW* (Oct. 3, 1918), p. 384; *Ref.* (Feb. 17, 1918), p. 53; *Ref.* (Oct. 20, 1918), pp. 331–32; *PU* (July/Aug. 1918), p. 110.

[53] *VGS, 2* (1920), 37. See Horowitz, "Prussian State," pp. 270–73.

[54] *PU* (Sept. 1918), p. 133; *PU* (Nov./Dec. 1918), p. 182; *Ref.* (July 29, 1917), p. 338; *Ref.* (March 24, 1918), p. 95; *Ref.* (April 14, 1918), p. 119; *Proth.* (April 27, 1918), p. 204; *CW* (June 13, 1918), p. 234.

[55] *Ref.* (May 6, 1917), p. 213. See Schian, *Kirche, 2,* 32–36; Fritz von der Heydt, *Gute Wehr* (Berlin, 1936), pp. 111, 126–29.

[56] *PU* (Sept. 1917), pp. 186–89; *PU* (Jan./Feb. 1918), pp. 19–20; *Ref.* (June 17, 1917), p. 286; *Ref.* (Dec. 30, 1917), p. 527; *Ref.* (Feb. 24, 1918), pp. 58–59; Kirchenausschuss minutes (June 5, 1917), *Gen.* XII 102 IV, pp. 2–4; *VGS, 2* (1920), 244–47.

[57] *Ref.* (April 14, 1918), p. 119.

[58] Walter Delius, "Altpreussische Kirche und kirchliche Einheit des deutschen Protestantismus," in *Hundert Jahre,* pp. 93–112; Schreiber, *Die Eiche, 13* (1925), 315–19.

[59] *Ref.* (Oct. 6, 1918), p. 316; Kirchenausschuss minutes, *Gen.* XII 102 IV, pp. 14–15.

[60] As quoted in Mehnert, *Kirche und Politik,* p. 84. See Mehnert, pp. 37–38, 70–73, 79–92; *CW* (July 26, 1917), pp. 353–55; *Ref.* (Sept. 2, 1917), p. 382.

[61] *Allgemeine evangelisch-lutherische Kirchenzeitung {AELK}* (Dec. 28, 1917), p. 1216.

[62] Pressel, *Kriegspredigt,* pp. 22–28, 151, 186–87, 218–19, 275–78, 283, 294–312, 348; Mehnert, *Kirche und Politik,* pp. 67–70.

[63] In *Ref.,* see (May 6, 1917), p. 213; (May 13, 1917), p. 226; (Sept. 9, 1917), p. 389; (Sept. 30, 1917), p. 418. Also see *RK* (Oct. 21, 1917), p. 331; *Protestantische Monatshefte {PM}* (Nov. 1917), p. 323; *Prot.* (Nov. 17, 1917), p. 668.

[64] As quoted in Pressel, *Kriegspredigt,* pp. 305–6.

[65] As quoted in Mehnert, *Kirche und Politik,* pp. 85–86.

[66] John L. Snell, "Die Republik aus Versäumnissen," *Die Welt als Geschichte, 15* (1955), 196–219.

[67] As quoted in *KJ, 45* (1918), 297.

RECONSTRUCTING THE VOLKSKIRCHE

[1] *VKt* (1919), pp. 57–58.

[2] Gottfried Mehnert, *Evangelische Kirche und Politik, 1917–1919 (Düsseldorf,* 1959), pp. 96–97.

[3] *Preussisches Pfarrarchiv (PP), 10* (1918), 269.

[4] Ibid., pp. 290–91. See above, pp. 48–49, on the status of confessional education before the Revolution.

[5] Ibid., pp. 266–67.

[6] Ibid., pp. 277–78.

[7] Ibid., p. 284; Hermann Giesecke, "Zur Schulpolitik der Sozialdemokraten in Preussen und im Reich 1918/19," *Vierteljahrshefte für Zeitgeschichte {VfZ}, 13* (1965), 164; Günter Köhler, *Die Auswirkungen der Novemberrevolution von 1918 auf die altpreussische evangelische Landeskirche* (diss. Kirchliche Hochschule, Berlin, 1967), p. 122.

[8] *Prot.* (Jan. 4, 1919), pp. 4–5; *KJ, 46* (1919), 355; Köhler, *Die Auswirkungen,* pp. 21–22, 120–21; Giesecke, "Schulpolitik," p. 166; Claus Motschmann, *Evangelische Kirche und preussischer Staat in den Anfängen der Weimarer Republik* (Lübeck, 1969), pp. 28–29, 103; Jochen Jacke, *Kirche zwischen Monarchie und Republik* (Hamburg, 1976), pp. 44–47, 62–65; Friedrich Thimme, "Das Verhältnis der revolutionären Gewalten zur Religion und den Kirchen," in *Revolution und Kirche,* ed. Thimme and Ernst Rolffs (Berlin, 1919), pp. 24, 28–39; Wolfgang Stribrny, "Evangelische Kirche und Staat in der Weimarer Republik," in *Zeitgeist der Weimarer Republik,* in *Zeitgeist im Wandel,* ed. Hans Joachim Schoeps, *2* (Stuttgart, 1968), 163. Later Haenisch commented: "Hoffmann wanted to resolve the separation issue

immediately within two days; he believed that he had mastered this program within several days" (Eberhard Kolb, ed., *Der Zentralrat der deutschen sozialistischen Republik* [Leiden, 1968] p. 613.)

[9] *CW* (Dec. 12, 1918), p. 484; Thimme, "Das Verhältnis," pp. 38–39; Hans Müller, "Der deutsche Katholizismus 1918–19," *Geschichte in Wissenschaft und Unterricht*, *17* (1966), 528–31; Rudolf Morsey, *Die Deutsche Zentrumspartei, 1917–1923* (Düsseldorf, 1966), pp. 112–15.

[10] *PP, 10* (1918), 268–70; Köhler, *Die Auswirkungen*, pp. 35–37; Motschmann, *Evangelische Kirche*, pp. 41–44; Jacke, *Monarchie und Republik*, pp. 47–50.

[11] Morsey, *Zentrumspartei*, pp. 117–28; Kolb, *Zentralrat*, pp. 139–40.

[12] *RK* (Dec. 22, 1918), p. 277; *RK* (Jan. 5, 1919), p. 5; *KJ, 46* (1919), 325; *AELK* (Jan. 10, 1919), p. 36; Köhler, *Die Auswirkungen*, pp. 69–70; Jacke, *Monarchie und Republik*, pp. 96–97.

[13] *Proth.* (Dec. 14, 1918), pp. 578–79; Köhler, *Die Auswirkungen*, pp. 73, 130; Volkskirchendienst to EOK (Dec. 1918), *Gen.* XIV 37 I; Herbert Christ, *Der politische Protestantismus in der Weimarer Republik* (diss. University of Bonn, 1967), p. 72.

[14] *CW* (Dec. 16, 1919), p. 44; *Ref.* (Dec. 8, 1918), p. 389; *Ref.* (Dec. 22, 1918), pp. 406–7; *Ref.* (Jan. 19, 1919), p. 23; *AELK* (Feb. 21, 1919), p. 163; *PP, 10* (1918), 292; Motschmann, *Evangelische Kirche*, pp. 29, 50–51, 105–10; Morsey, *Zentrumspartei*, p. 115; Jacke, *Monarchie und Republik*, pp. 72–73; Köhler, *Die Auswirkungen*, pp. 33, 128–30, 172–81; Thimme, "Das Verhältnis," pp. 36–37. In his letter to Hoffmann on Dec. 31, 1918, Haenisch wrote: "You will recall that I predicted from the beginning that this entire hasty school and church policy will have the heaviest political consequences and that I finally went along only after you had again threatened to appeal to the workers and soldiers council" (Kolb, *Zentralrat*, p. 139).

[15] *Germania* Clipping (Jan. 15, 1919) in *Gen.* XIV 20 V; *PP, 11* (1919), 20; Morsey, *Zentrumspartei*, p. 116; Motschmann, *Evangelische Kirche*, p. 53.

[16] Köhler, *Die Auswirkungen*, p. 135; *PP, 10* (1918), 292.

[17] In *Gen.* XIV 37 I. Haenisch could hardly yield the principle of optional religious instruction without alienating teachers and socialists.

[18] *PP, 11* (1919), 16–17; minutes of EOK, GSV, and Vertrauensrat (April 10, 1919), *Gen.* II 27 II, pp. 14, 17–18.

[19] Köhler, *Die Auswirkungen*, pp. 140–45; Friedrich Kreppel, "Der Lehrer in der Zeitgeschichte," in *Das Wilhelminische Zeitalter*, in *Zeitgeist im Wandel*, ed. Schoeps, *1*, p. 218, fn. 29. Its program, adopted at this convention, would, nevertheless, permit religious instruction as a "special subject" (apparently outside of the regular curriculum) within schools if churches took over responsibility for giving it. (Karl-Heinz Günther et al., eds., *Quellen zur Geschichte der Erziehung* [Berlin, 1959], p. 284.) Such was also the compromise solution that Haenisch favored. (*RK* [March 2, 1919], p. 58.)

[20] As quoted in *Ref.* (Jan. 19, 1919), p. 23.

[21] *RK* (Jan. 19, 1919), p. 15.

[22] Ibid.; *Protb.* (Jan. 4, 1919), pp. 4–5; *Ref.* (Jan. 26, 1919), p. 31; *AELK* (Jan. 10, 1919), pp. 36–37; *AELK* (April 4, 1919), pp. 293–94; Karl-Wilhelm Dahm, *Pfarrer und Politik* (Cologne, 1965), pp. 134–37; Christ, *Protestantismus*, pp. 67–73.

[23] As quoted in Motschmann, *Evangelische Kirche*, p. 51.

[24] Kolb, *Zentralrat*, pp. 139–41. See *AELK* (Jan. 10, 1919), pp. 36–37; *Ref.* (Feb. 23, 1919), pp. 62–63; Köhler, *Die Auswirkungen*, p. 131.

[25] *PP*, *10* (1918), 227; *PP*, *11* (1919), 20; Friedrich Koch, "Die rechtliche Lage des Kirchenregiments in der altpreussischen Landeskirche nach dem Wegfall des Königtums," *PP*, *11* (1919), 167–68; Jacke, *Monarchie und Republik*, pp. 59–62; Köhler, *Die Auswirkungen*, pp. 43–53; Motschmann, *Evangelische Kirche*, pp. 30–31.

[26] *AELK* (Jan. 24, 1919), p. 84.

[27] Martin Rade, "Die gemeinsamen Interessen der katholischen und der evangelischen Kirche angesichts der Trennungsfrage," in *Revolution und Kirche*, p. 113; Koch, "Die rechtliche Lage," pp. 165–66; Jacke, *Monarchie und Republik*, pp. 53–54, 97.

[28] In *Protb.* (Dec. 7, 1918), p. 565; (Dec. 14, 1918), pp. 580–81; (Dec. 21, 1918), p. 596; (Jan. 4, 1919), pp. 4–5. Mehnert, *Kirche und Politik*, pp. 125–27.

[29] *CW* (Feb. 13, 1919), p. 109; Mehnert, *Kirche und Politik*, p. 128. On Rade's efforts, see: *CW* (Nov. 28, 1918), p. 466; *CW* (Dec. 26, 1918), pp. 499–501; Otto Dibelius, "Volkskirchenräte, Volkskirchenbund, Volkskirchendienst," in *Revolution und Kirche*, p. 209; Jacke, *Monarchie und Republik*, pp. 56–58, 152–55; Mehnert, *Kirche und Politik*, pp. 115–21.

[30] *Licht und Leben {LL}* (Feb. 16, 1919), pp. 83–84; (Feb. 2, 1919), pp. 57–61; Karl Heim, "Die Bedeutung der Gemeinschaftsbewegung für eine staatsfreie Volkskirche," in *Revolution und Kirche*, pp. 255–73; *Neue kirchliche Zeitschrift {NkZ}*, *32* (1921), 271–72, 275–79; *CW* (March 6, 1919), pp. 147–49; *RK* (March 9, 1919), pp. 62–63; *KJ*, *46* (1919), 366; *Ref.* (Dec. 1, 1918), p. 378.

[31] Köhler, *Die Auswirkungen*, pp. 76–84; Jacke, *Monarchie und Republik*, pp. 158–165. Here and elsewhere Jacke argues that the church Right fought for an authoritarian church in order to retain the power in the church that conservatives had lost in the state. He leaves the impression that the church Right—and the EOK, for that matter—craved power for power's sake. Both church Right and Left claimed altruistic intentions. It is not clear why the church Right should be denied an altruistic motivation and the church Left spared.

[32] In *RK* (Feb. 9, 1919), pp. 34–35; (March 23, 1919), p. 79; (April 20, 1919), p. 110.

[33] *AELK* (Feb. 7, 1919), pp. 131–32. See Hans Götz Oxenius, *Die Entstehung der Verfassung der evangelischen Kirche der altpreussischen Union von 1922* (diss. University of Cologne, 1959), pp. 27–28, 117–18; *Protb.* (Dec. 28, 1918), p. 606.

[34] Oxenius, *Union,* pp. 28, 118, 137; *Ref.* (Feb. 9, 1919), p. 42; *RK* (Dec. 1, 1918), pp. 211−12; *Proth.* (Dec. 28, 1918), p. 606.

[35] *PK* (Jan. 1920), pp. 1−15.

[36] *LL* (March 16, 1919), pp. 142−43; *Ref.* (May 25, 1919), p. 167; *Ref.* (Aug. 31, 1919), p. 278.

[37] Dibelius, "Volkskirchenräte," p. 208.

[38] *Ref.* (June 29, 1919), p. 205.

[39] *KJ, 48* (1921), 352.

[40] *Ref.* (March 30, 1919), p. 98.

[41] *CW* (Nov. 28, 1918), p. 466; *Proth.* (Dec. 21, 1918), p. 596; *Proth.* (Dec. 28, 1918), p. 606; *Ref.* (March 2, 1919), p. 66; "Kirche und Schule" (supplement), *Rb* (April 13, 1919); Mehnert, *Kirche und Politik,* pp. 214−61; Oxenius, *Union,* p. 118.

[42] *Ref.* (March 30, 1919), pp. 98−99; Kirchenausschuss minutes (June 17−18, 1919), *Gen.* XII 102 IV, pp. 12−13, 20−22; *VGS, 2* (1920), 219−23; Tilemann, *VKt* (1921), p. 105.

[43] In *CW* (March 27, 1919), pp. 195−96; (April 3, 1919), p. 226; (June 26, 1919), p. 422. Johannes Rathje, *Die Welt des freien Protestantismus* (Stuttgart, 1952), pp. 268−69.

[44] *VKt* (1919), p. 152.

[45] Ibid., p. 222.

[46] Ibid., p. 219. See also pp. 220, 223, 227, 237.

[47] Otto Baumgarten, *Meine Lebensgeschichte* (Tübingen, 1929), pp. 403−4.

[48] As quoted in Mehnert, *Kirche und Politik,* p. 233.

[49] *VKt* (1919), p. 227.

[50] *Evangelische Kirchen-Zeitung {EK}* (Feb. 23, 1919), p. 94.

[51] *Ref.* (Sept. 14, 1919), p. 293.

[52] Minutes of joint EOK-GSV meetings in *Gen.* XII 154 I: (April 27−29, 1921), p. 1; (Jan. 12, 1922), p. 8. See also *VGS 1* (1920), 77.

[53] *Rb* (Aug. 23, 1919). See the Kirchenbund constitution in *VKt* (1921), pp. 30−37, and Boehme's commentary in *Gen.* XII 154 I. Representing the twenty eight church governments, the Church Federation Council held a veto over Church Assembly decisions. Of the Assembly's 210 members, 150 were elected from the highest synods of member churches and 25 were appointed by the Kirchenausschuss. Subject to the Kirchenausschuss's confirmation, theology faculties nominated 8 delegates; religion teachers, 12; and free associations, 15. As the executive, the Kirchenausschuss consisted of 36 members—18 elected by the assembly and 18 by the council. As before, the EOK president served ex officio as Kirchenausschuss president. Church Federation competence was "indirect" over traditional functions of member churches and "direct" in matters of external common concern.

[54] *LL* (Oct. 16, 1921), p. 592.

[55] See, e.g., *Deutsches Pfarrerblatt {DP}* (June 1924), p. 137.

[56] Mehnert, *Kirche und Politik,* pp. 130–39; *LL* (Jan. 12, 1919), p. 23; *LL* (Jan. 26, 1919), pp. 49–51; *Proth. (Dec.* 28, 1919), pp. 606–7; *GB, 2* (1925), 69–76; Günter Opitz, *Der Christlich-Soziale Volksdienst* (Düsseldorf, 1969), pp. 35–133.

[57] As quoted in Mehnert, *Kirche und Politik,* p. 168. See Mehnert, pp. 164–73; John K. Zeender, "German Catholics and the Concept of an Interconfessional Party 1900–1922," *JCEA, 23* (1964), 424–39.

[58] Mehnert, *Kirche und Politik,* pp. 139–49, 237–39; Werner Liebe, *Die Deutschnationale Volkspartei 1918–1924* (Düsseldorf, 1956), pp. 7–25, 111, 116.

[59] Mehnert, *Kirche und Politik,* pp. 149–51, 238; Wolfgang Hartenstein, *Die Anfänge der Deutschen Volkspartei 1918–1920* (Düsseldorf, 1962), pp. 7–73; Wolfgang Treue, *Deutsche Parteiprogramme 1861–1956* (2nd ed. Göttingen, 1956), pp. 120–21.

[60] *Proth.* (Dec. 6, 1919), p. 618; *ED* (Feb. 28, 1926), p. 71; *AELK* (Aug. 13, 1920), pp. 650–51; Mehnert, *Kirche und Politik,* pp. 183–84.

[61] As quoted in Mehnert, *Kirche und Politik,* p. 153. Also see Theodor Heuss, *Friedrich Naumann* (2nd. ed. Stuttgart, 1949), pp. 452–57.

[62] Treue, *Parteiprogramme,* pp. 127–28.

[63] Mehnert, *Kirche und Politik,* pp. 173–74.

[64] Ibid., pp. 174–78; supplement to *Proth.* (Jan. 18, 1919); Motschmann, *Evangelische Kirche,* pp. 45–46; Jacke, *Monarchie und Republik,* pp. 103–4, 110–15. As Jacke illustrated, some church leaders also tried to close fronts against the Democrats, despite their favorable responses.

[65] *CW* (Feb. 13, 1919), pp. 108–9; *CW* (Feb. 27, 1919), pp. 137–38; *RK* (Jan. 5, 1919), p. 6; *NkZ, 31* (1920), 483; Motschmann, *Evangelische Kirche,* pp. 45–47; Jacke, *Monarchie und Republik,* pp. 94–103.

[66] Mehnert, *Kirche und Politik,* pp. 180–82, 236–39.

[67] Ibid., pp. 178–79; Jacke, *Monarchie und Republik,* pp. 115–18.

[68] Kirchenausschuss to member church governments (Jan. 31, 1919), *Gen.* XIV 37 I.

[69] In *Gen.* XIV 37 I. A comparison of signatures with votes—of soft data with hard—undoubtedly exaggerates the percentage.

[70] Reinhard Mumm, *Der christlich-soziale Gedanke* (Berlin, 1933), pp. 96, 99, 110.

[71] *PP, 11* (1919), 12–15; Carl Israël, *Geschichte des Reichskirchenrechts* (Berlin, 1922), pp. 9–10; Jacke, *Monarchie und Republik,* pp. 88–93, 120–22. Church leaders saw the Socialist program looming behind such proposals. See, e.g., Kaftan, *Ref.* (March 2, 1919), pp. 66–67.

[72] *Ref.* (March 30, 1919), p. 102. See Israël, *Geschichte des Reichskirchenrechts,* pp. 10–12.

[73] *PP, 11* (1919), 17–19. The Kirchenausschuss demanded constitutional provisions ensuring public corporation status, church taxation, compensation for state

subsidies, protection of church property, church administrative independence, legal recognition of Sundays and church holidays, retention of theological faculties, chaplaincy work in public institutions, and Christian public education. Similar demands were voiced by synods and church organizations while the assembly met. See Israël, *Geschichte des Reichskirchenrechts,* pp. 13–20.

[74]Israël, *Geschichte des Reichskirchenrechts,* pp. 20–29, 33–39, 53; Heuss, *Naumann,* p. 478.

[75] (June 17, 1919), *Gen.* XII 102 IV, p. 18. For a commentary on the religion and education articles of the Weimar constitution, see Gerhard Anschütz, *Die Verfassung des Deutschen Reichs vom 11. August 1919, Ein Kommentar für Wissenschaft und Praxis* (4th ed. Berlin, 1933), pp. 618–96.

[76] Erich Foerster, *Kirche und Schule in der Weimarer Verfassung* (Gotha, 1925), pp. 12–24; Heinrich Schulz, *Der Leidensweg des Reichsschulgesetzes* (Berlin, 1925), pp. 33–41; Agnes von Zahn-Harnack, *Adolf von Harnack* (2nd ed. Berlin, 1951), pp. 387–88; Heuss, *Naumann,* p. 480.

[77] *PP, 11* (1919), 16–17; minutes of Vertrauensrat, EOK, and GSV (April 10, 1919), *Gen.* II 27 II, pp. 13–14, 18; Köhler, *Die Auswirkungen,* pp. 145–51, 215–17; Burghart, *VKt* (1919), pp. 265–66, and *VGS, 1* (1920), 565.

[78] Herbert Kraus, *The Crisis of German Democracy* (Princeton, 1932), p. 210.

[79] Foerster, *Kirche und Schule,* pp. 8–11.

[80] Ibid., pp. 5–8, 26–39; Schulz, *Der Leidensweg,* pp. 37–70; Giesecke, "Schulpolitik," pp. 172–75; Günther Grünthal, *Reichsschulgesetz und Zentrumspartei in der Weimarer Republik* (Düsseldorf, 1968), pp. 53–67.

[81] Kraus, *The Crisis,* p. 209. I have altered Kraus's English rendition for clarity. My italics.

[82] Schulz, *Der Leidensweg,* pp. 61–63. See decisions of the Federal Court (Reichsgericht) of Nov. 4, 1920, *Gen.* XIV 37 II, and of June 11, 1927, *Gen.* XIV 37 VI, *Beiheft A.*

[83] Schulz, *Der Leidensweg,* pp. 45–46, 51–52, 57, 76; Foerster, *Kirche und Schule,* pp. 33–34, 39–40.

[84] Mumm, *Der christlich-soziale Gedanke,* p. 99.

[85] *Ref.* (March 30, 1919), p. 102; *Rb* (Aug. 1, 1919).

[86] See, e.g., decree of the Magdeburg Consistory of Dec. 6, 1919, *PP, 12* (1919), 297; Foerster, *Kirche und Schule,* pp. 41–42.

[87] Thus Mumm, *Rb* (Aug. 2, 1919), and *Rb* (Dec. 31, 1920). Grünthal, *Reichsschulgesetz* (pp. 60–61), offers a different interpretation: Most of the Nationalist faction voted against the "first" school compromise out of concern for retaining class-discriminatory preparatory schools and out of pique at the cooperation of Centrists and Majority Socialists. Also see Schulz, *Der Leidensweg,* pp. 52, 65–66; Foerster, *Kirche und Schule,* p. 37.

[88] See, e.g., decree of Magdeburg Consistory of Dec. 6, 1919, *PP, 12* (1919), 297–98.

⁸⁹ Mumm to Burghart (Aug. 6, 1919), *Gen.* XIV 37 I. See also Mumm, *Rb* (Aug. 2, 1919).

⁹⁰ Kraus, *The Crisis,* p. 215.

⁹¹ Ibid., p. 207.

⁹² Johannes Niedner, "Die rechtliche Stellung und finanzielle Lage der evangelischen Landeskirchen nach ihrer Trennung vom Staat," in *Revolution und Kirche,* p. 174; Paul Mikat, *Das Verhältnis von Kirche und Staat in der Bundesrepublik* (Berlin, 1964), pp. 2–7.

⁹³ This thesis, advanced by Socialists in the Weimar period, had a polemical point. Jacke, *Monarchie und Republik* (pp. 145–49), deplored the financial privileges that the Weimar assembly accorded churches for the reason that the Protestant allegedly misused its newly gained freedom from the state to undermine the Republic. Suppose that the assembly had withheld these traditional privileges. One can speculate that antirepublicanism would have deepened all the more among loyal Protestants, to say nothing of Catholics.

⁹⁴ Schiller, *Rb* (Sept. 22, 1920).

⁹⁵ *Ref.* (Sept. 14, 1919), p. 295.

⁹⁶ *Ref.* (Oct. 26, 1919), p. 342.

⁹⁷ Jacke, *Monarchie und Republik,* pp. 171–74, 177, 400 (fn. 192); Motschmann, *Evangelische Kirche,* pp. 55–62; Oxenius, *Union,* pp. 57, 140; *CW* (April 3, 1919), p. 225; *CW* (April 17, 1919), p. 250; *CW* (May 15, 1919), pp. 317–19. Jacke speculated (pp. 178–79) that the government had not meant to absorb these prerogatives, in which case the Nationalists inadvertently saddled the church with the three ministers. In this section, I am indebted to Jacke and Motschmann for information on the motives of the EOK and GSV. The two gave widely diverging interpretations of the constitutional dispute. Jacke argued that the church Right craved confrontation with the Republic and ecclesiastical power for political reasons. Neither my evidence nor his, in my opinion, warrants such extreme conclusions. Motschmann, on the other hand, contended that liberals and Democrats bore the main responsibility for the dispute and for poisoning church-state relations.

⁹⁸ *PP,* 11 (1919), 19–20; Koch, "Die rechtliche Lage," pp. 60–62; Jacke, *Monarchie und Republik,* pp. 174–76. Also see protest of GSV (April 2, 1919) in *VGS, 1* (1920), 68–72.

⁹⁹ Jacke, *Monarchie und Republik,* pp. 177–80; Oxenius, *Union,* p. 61; *CW* (July 3, 1919), p. 438.

¹⁰⁰ As quoted in *CW* (Jan. 8, 1925), p. 38. See, e.g., *Ref.* (April 20, 1919), pp. 125–26; *Ref.* (Sept. 14, 1919), p. 295; *GG* (May 1919), pp. 98–100; supplement to *Rb* (May 25, 1919); *Rb* (April 7, 1919); *AELK* (Sept. 26, 1919), pp. 846–48; Meyer, *VGS, 1* (1920), 54–55.

¹⁰¹ In *Protb.* (April 5, 1919), pp. 155–56; (July 19, 1919), p. 342; (Aug. 23, 1919), p. 405. In *CW* (May 1, 1919), pp. 286–87; (July 24, 1919), pp. 479–81; (Aug. 14, 1919), pp. 522–25.

[102] *VGS*, 2 (1920), 127–40; *GG* (May 1919), p. 100; *Ref.* (June 22, 1919), p. 194; *RK* (May 25, 1919), pp. 147–48; *Rb* (Aug. 20, 1919); *Protb.* (Aug. 23, 1919), pp. 400–3; Jacke, *Monarchie und Republik*, pp. 165–70, 183–93; Motschmann, *Evangelische Kirche*, pp. 62–84; Oxenius, *Union*, pp. 50–53, 56; Köhler, *Die Auswirkungen*, pp. 77–84.

[103] Jacke, *Monarchie und Republik*, pp. 194–99; Köhler, *Die Auswirkungen*, pp. 85–91; Motschmann, *Evangelische Kirche*, pp. 84–86; Oxenius, *Union*, pp. 60–63.

[104] Jacke, *Monarchie und Republik*, pp. 199–200; *Protb.* (Aug. 2, 1919), pp. 361–62.

[105] Fischer, *Protb.* (Aug. 23, 1919), p. 403; *CW* (Sept. 11, 1919), p. 390; *CW* (Oct. 30, 1919), p. 710; *CW* (Jan. 29, 1920), p. 78.

[106] See, e.g., Graue, *CW* (Dec. 25, 1919), p. 829; Schubring, *Protb.* (March 8, 1919), p. 115; Philipps, *Ref.* (April 13, 1919), p. 115, and (July 13, 1919), p. 221; Baarts, *Rb* (Sept. 2, 1919).

[107] See, e.g., Ebert, *AELK* (June 6, 1919), p. 491; Mumm, *Rb* (April 4, 1919); Philipps, *Rb* (June 7, 1919); supplement to *Rb* (June 8, 1919); Dunkel, *Rb* (June 29, 1919); *Ref.* (April 13, 1919), pp. 116–17; Eckert, *Ref.* (July 20, 1919), p. 227.

[108] *Die Hilfe* (Oct. 9, 1919), p. 566

[109] *CW* (May 1, 1919), p. 287; *Ref.* (April 13, 1919), p. 116.

[110] Jacke, *Monarchie und Republik*, pp. 200–2.

[111] Ibid., pp. 180–82, 202–9; Motschmann, *Evangelische Kirche*, pp. 86–91, 115–30; Oxenius, *Union*, pp. 61–64; *CW* (Nov. 20, 1919), p. 756, and (Dec. 11, 1919), p. 804; *Protb.* (Nov. 29, 1919), p. 606.

[112] *Ref.* (Nov. 30, 1919), p. 383, and (Dec. 28, 1919), pp. 414–15; Jacke, *Monarchie und Kirche*, pp. 210–15; Motschmann, *Evangelische Kirche*, pp. 95–105.

[113] *Ref.* (Dec. 7, 1919), p. 386, and (Dec. 28, 1919), p. 415; Jacke, *Monarchie und Republik*, pp. 215–28; Köhler, *Die Auswirkungen*, pp. 106–10.

[114] As quoted in Oxenius, *Union*, p. 65.

[115] As quoted in *AELK* (Nov. 28, 1919), p. 1052.

[116] *Protb.* (Aug. 2, 1919), p. 363. See Schubring, *Protb.* (Nov. 29, 1919), p. 600; *Protb.* (Jan. 3, 1920), pp. 13–14; *Protb.* (Jan. 24, 1920), p. 44; *AELK* (Dec. 12, 1919), p. 1099; *Ref.* (April 4, 1920), p. 94.

[117] Schubring, *Protb.* (Dec. 6, 1919), pp. 616, 618; Rade, *CW* (Jan. 1, 1920), pp. 6–8; *CW* (Jan. 29, 1920), p. 77; *CW* (April 1, 1920), p. 219.

[118] See, e.g., Pfannschmidt, *EK* (Nov. 30, 1919), pp. 570–73; *Ref.* (Dec. 7, 1919), p. 389; Laible, *AELK* (Jan. 23, 1920), pp. 91–92; Goetz, *CW* (Jan. 1, 1920), pp. 9–10; Rade, *CW* (Jan. 1, 1920), pp. 6, 8; Schubring, *Protb.* (Nov. 29, 1919), p. 599; *Protb.* (Jan. 24, 1920), p. 44.

[119] *CW* (Jan. 28, 1920), pp. 22–25, and (Jan. 29, 1920), p. 77. On prewar

church liberal views, see Arnold Horowitz, "Prussian State and Protestant Church in the Reign of Wilhelm II" (diss. Yale, 1976), pp. 27–31, 208, 244–46, 257–60.

[120] *AELK* (Jan. 23, 1920), p. 92.

[121] *Protb.* (Nov. 29, 1919), p. 600. See *Protb.* (Jan. 24, 1920), p. 43; Philipps, *Ref.* (Jan. 11, 1920), p. 11; *PK* (Feb. 1920), p. 19.

[122] As quoted in *Protb.* (Dec. 6, 1919), p. 618. See *Ref.* (Dec. 7, 1919), p. 386, and (Dec. 14, 1919), p. 396; *EK* (Jan. 18, 1920), pp. 35–36; *Protb.* (April 24, 1920), p. 175.

[123] *PK* (Jan. 1920), pp. 7–8; Jacke, *Monarchie und Republik,* pp. 228–31; Oxenius, *Union,* pp. 66–67.

[124] Jacke, *Monarchie und Republik,* pp. 231–39; Motschmann, *Evangelische Kirche,* pp. 91–93; Oxenius, *Union,* pp. 67–69.

[125] *Protb.* (May 8, 1920), pp. 186–87. For the drafts and their official justification and explanation, see *VGS, 2* (1920), 146–92, 292–93; for the debate, *VGS, 1* (1920), 408–87, 527–30. Also see Jacke, *Monarchie und Republik,* pp. 239–45; Motschmann, *Evangelische Kirche,* pp. 111–13; *Protb.* (May 15, 1920), p. 195, and (July 24, 1920), p. 263; Rade, *CW* (Sept. 9, 1920), p. 580.

[126] Jacke, *Monarchie und Republik,* pp. 246–51, 257–58; Oxenius, *Union,* pp. 69–72; Mann, *PK* (July 1921), pp. 82–83; Hein, *PK* (Aug. 1921), pp. 94–95. For the first time a Socialist, the liberal Henneberg, attended a high church assembly in Prussia. Liberals won nineteen seats, compared to the one that they held in the General Synod.

[127] Jacke, *Monarchie und Republik,* pp. 251–303; Oxenius, *Union,* pp. 74–110; Gerhard Niemöller, "Die Verfassung der evangelischen Kirchen in Preussen von 1919 bis 1933" (research essay Münster, 1953), pp. 31–66; Johannes Victor Bredt, *Neues evangelisches Kirchenrecht für Preussen*(3 vols. Berlin, 1921–28), 3, passim.

[128] *Bericht über die Verhandlungen der ausserordentlichen Kirchenversammlung zur Feststellung der Verfassung für die evangelische Landeskirche der älteren Provinzen Preussens vom 24. bis 30. September 1921 und vom 29. August bis 29. September 1922* (2 vols. Berlin, 1923), *1,* 831. On these compromises and arguments, see *Kirchenversammlung, 1,* 167–77, 183–84, 781–848, 826–31, 1296–303, 1403–4, 1411.

[129] On preamble discussions, see *Kirchenversammlung, 1,* 178–85, 224–32, 245–384, 1341–44, 1350–54; the EOK's stand in *Anlage A, Kirchenversammlung, 2,* 61–64; Jacke, *Monarchie und Republik,* pp. 286–94.

[130] See *Kirchenversammlung, 1,* 191, 296, 313, 348–49.

[131] Jacke, *Monarchie und Republik,* pp. 280–83, 296.

[132] *Protb.* (Nov. 5, 1922), p. 141; *Protb.* (July 8, 1923), pp. 84–86; *Protb.* (March 23, 1924), p. 40; *Protb.* (Oct. 12, 1924), p. 169; *CW* (April 5, 1923), p. 233; Raack, *PK* (Jan. 1923), p. 9; Jacke, *Monarchie und Republik,* pp. 294–97; Oxenius, *Union,* p. 110. Two liberal petitions against the preamble—one by thirty-seven professors of theology and the other by about 2,500 religion teachers—asked

the state to shield religious and academic freedom. A third, submitted by the recently organized League of Religious Socialists, petitioned the Socialist faction to reject the church's constitution.

133 Raack, *PK* (Nov. 1923), p. 87; Raack, *PK* (Feb. 1924), p. 21; Kahl, *PK* (Jan. 1924), pp. 3–5; Schubring, *Proth.* (April 27, 1924), pp. 58–60; Schäfer, *DP, 28*(1924), 27–28, 48–49, 62–63, 78–80, 95–96; Oxenius, *Union*, p. 111; Jacke, *Monarchie und Republik*, pp. 197–98; Bredt, *Kirchenrecht*, 3, 358–64. The text of the law is found in Bredt, 3, 49–58.

134 Hallensleben, *Proth.* (Nov. 2, 1924), pp. 217–20; *DP, 28*(1924), 121–23, 202–3, 244–45; *VGS, 2* (1925), 13–14.

135 (July 15, 1924), p. 108.

136 *VGS, 1* (1927), 628–33.

137 See [Johannes Duske], *Denkschrift über den Umfang der Staatsleistungen der deutschen Länder an die evangelishen Kirche bis zur Ablösung* (Berlin-Charlottenburg, 1928) pp. 7–30. See pp. 46–48 above for a description of the system of finance.

138 *VGS, 2* (1925), 311–15, 318; *VGS, 2* (1927), 46; Doden, *DP* (Aug. 12, 1924), p. 208; Schäfer, *DP* (Sept. 2, 1924), pp. 244–45; Schäfer, *DP* (March 24, 1925), pp. 208–9.

139 Koch, *DP* (March 24, 1925), pp. 207–9; Schäfer, *DP* (July 21, 1925), pp. 494–95; Schäfer, *DP* (Nov. 10, 1925), p. 802; Schäfer, *DP* (March 23, 1926), pp. 225–26; *VGS, 2* (1927), 52–53, 106–7.

140 *VGS, 1* (1927), 249–57, 540–46; Hoffmann, *DP* (April 5, 1927), pp. 288–89; Mühlichen, *DP* (April 19, 1927), p. 324.

141 *VGS, 1* (1925), 199–203, 401; *VGS, 2* (1925), 72–90, 310–11, 317; *VGS, 2* (1927), 46; Appendix 9a to Church Senate minutes (Nov. 3–4, 1930), *Gen.* III 48 II, p. 2.

142 *VGS, 2*(1925), 308–9, 323–30; *VGS, 2*(1927), 48–50, 108–15; [Duske], *Denkschrift*, pp. 74–79. Kirchenausschuss minutes (July 24–25, 1925), *Gen.* XII 102 VI, reported that Evangelical Landeskirchen had loaned 850–900 million gold marks to federal, state, and community governments. Churchmen could justify increased church taxes and state contributions for the reason that the churches had lost vast amounts of capital to the obvious advantage of the state—a "third" secularization of church property in the eyes of some.

143 *VGS, 1* (1925), 398–406; *VGS, 2* (1925), 76–77, 84, 91–98, 188, 309, 312–14, 319–22; *VGS, 1* (1927), 25–26, 489–501, 570–77; *VGS, 2* (1927), 45, 48–49, 54–57; [Duske], *Denkschrift*, pp. 62–63.

144 [Duske], *Denkschrift*, pp. 78–81; *VGS, 1* (1927), 496; *VGS, 2* (1927), 48–50, 52.

145 *VGS, 1* (1925), 405; *VGS, 2* (1927), 49.

146 *VGS, 1*(1925), 398–403; *VGS, 2*(1925), 79–80, 312–14; *VGS, 1*(1927), 579–80; *VGS, 2* (1927), 49; [Duske], *Denkschrift*, pp. 81–82; Schäfer, *DP* (March

23, 1926), pp. 225–27. According to Schäfer, who investigated the tax rate in 423 Rhenish congregations, the mean tax rate was assessed at about 20 per cent of the Reich income tax in 1925, though it might mount as high as 83 percent in some congregations.

[147] *VGS, 1* (1927), 578–82; *VGS, 2* (1927), 50–52.

[148] *VGS, 1* (1927), 576–77. See *VGS, 2* (1925), 310, 315; *VGS, 1* (1927), 544, 578.

[149] Bredt, *Kirchenrecht, 2,* 86. In the Prussian Landtag, the Center party, which Socialists dared not affront for the sake of their coalition, formed with the political Right a *"Corpus Ecclesiae"* (Bredt's term) that catered to church interests.

THE SCHOOL CIVIL WAR

[1] Decisions of the Federal Court on Nov. 4, 1920, *Gen.* XIV 37 I, and on July 11, 1927, *Beiheft* A to *Gen.* XIV 37 VI. See pp. 48–49 above on the Prussian school system and pp. 88–96 above on the school issue at the National Assembly.

[2] Herbert Springer, *Protestantische Kirche und Volksschule in Deutschland* (Leipzig, 1929), pp. 72–73.

[3] Decision on July 11, 1927, *Beiheft A* to *Gen.* XIV 37 VI.

[4] Henselmann, *VGS, 1* (1925), 456; Kultusminister Becker, *Sitzungsberichte des Preussischen Landtags, 2. Wahlperiode, 11* (Berlin, 1927), 15699–700.

[5] Thomas Alexander, *The Prussian Elementary Schools* (New York, 1918), pp. 54–78; Otto Boelitz, *The Reorganization of Education in Prussia,* trans. I.L. Kandel and Thomas Alexander (New York, 1927), pp. xix-xxiii.

[6] Hermann Giesecke, "Zur Schulpolitik der Sozialdemokraten in Preussen und im Reich 1918/19," *VfZ, 13* (1965), 170–71, 175; Günther Grünthal, *Reichsschulgesetz und Zentrumspartei in der Weimarer Republik* (Düsseldorf, 1968), pp. 108–9.

[7] Zoellner, Stolte, and Adams, *VGS, 1* (1920), 546–48, 556–60; *VKt* (1921), p. 235; *VGS, 1* (1925), 559; *VGS, 2* (1927), 126.

[8] Saxon Consistory to EOK (May 7, 1919), *Gen.* XIV 37 I; *VGS, 2* (1920), 263; Brandenburg Consistory to EOK (March 25, 1924), *Gen.* XIV 37 V; EOK to Brandenburg Consistory (June 10, 1924), *Gen.* XIV 37 V.

[9] Meinhold, *VGS, 1* (1920), 539–41; *VGS, 2* (1925), 165–66; *VGS, 2* (1927), 66–67; *VKt* (1919), pp. 243–44; Ritter, *DP* (Oct. 25, 1927), pp. 789–90; Friedrich Kreppel, "Der Lehrer in den zwanziger Jahren," in *Zeitgeist der Weimarer Republik,* in *Zeitgeist im Wandel,* ed. Hans Joachim Schoeps, *2* (Stuttgart, 1968), pp. 131, 138; Ernst Christian Helmreich, *Religious Education in German Schools* (Cambridge, Mass., 1959), p. 134.

[10] *VKt* (1919), pp. 239–93; *VGS, 2* (1920), 260–62; *VKt* (1921), pp. 160–79, 234–42.

[11] Schlüter, *VGS, 1* (1920), 537; *Ref.* (Apr. 17, 1921), pp. 29–30; Laible, *AELK* (April 29, 1921), p. 268; *LL* (Sept. 25, 1921), p. 543.

[12] Kirchenausschuss minutes (June 30-July 2, 1921), *Gen.* XII 102 V, p. 34; Barth, *Protb.* (Nov. 1, 1919), pp. 538–41.

[13] (Nov. 26, 1921), p. 409. See also *Protb.* (July 24, 1927), p. 423, and (Nov. 13, 1927), pp. 643–44.

[14] Pfarrer Tribukait, *Der Kirchen-Schulkampf in Westfalen* (1928?), pp. 46–52.

[15] EOK to general superintendents (Nov. 27, 1919), *Gen.* XIV 37 I; *Protb.* (Dec. 24, 1919), p. 654; Dibelius, *Tägliche Rundschau* (March 9, 1920), clipping in *Gen.* XIV 37 I; *Sitzungsberichte des Preussischen Landtags, 2. Wahlperiode, 11* (Berlin, 1927), 15723.

[16] EOK to consistories (Oct. 29 and Nov. 11, 1919), and EOK to general superintendents (Nov. 27, 1919), *Gen.* XIV 37 I.

[17] (Dec. 7, 1919), p. 391.

[18] Silesian Consistory to EOK (Dec. 4, 1919), Brandenburg Consistory to EOK (April 6, 1920), and Saxon Consistory to EOK (March 31, 1920), *Gen.* XIV 37 I.

[19] Dibelius, *Tägliche Rundschau* (Mar. 9, 1920); *RK* (June 27, 1920), p. 195; *KJ, 47* (1920), 453; Saxon Consistory to EOK (March 31, 1920), *Gen.* XIV 37 I; Tillich and Moeller, *VGS, 1* (1920), 551–52; *VGS, 2* (1920), 262–63.

[20] Brandenburg Consistory to EOK (July 3, Oct. 15, and Oct. 29, 1920), *Gen.* XIV 37 II; *Sitzungsberichte der verfassunggebenden Preussischen Landesversammlung, Tagung 1919/21, 9* (Berlin, 1921), 11548.

[21] Letters in *Gen.* XIV 37 II: EOK to Kultusministerium (Nov. 18, 1920), Harnack to Burghardt (Nov. 27, 1920), Burghart to Harnack (Nov. 30, 1920), EOK to Steinhausen (Dec. 3, 1920), Brandenburg Consistory to EOK (Oct. 29, 1920). See also *PK, 16* (Dec. 1920), 142; *Rb* (Dec. 1, 1920).

[22] Brandenburg Consistory to EOK (Oct. 29, 1920), and EOK to Steinhausen (Dec. 3, 1920), *Gen.* XIV 37 II.

[23] Rhenish Consistory to EOK (June 26, 1922), *Gen.* XIV 37 IV.

[24] Helmreich, *Religious Education,* pp. 135–37.

[25] *KJ, 50* (1923), 345; Heilmann, *Die Innere Mission im evangelischen Deutschland {IM}, 18* (1923), p. 63; *Rb* (April 6, 1927); Kreppel, "Der Lehrer," p. 137; Brandenburg Consistory to EOK (Jan. 25, 1922), *Gen.* XIV 37 III; Westphalian Consistory to EOK (Sept. 5, 1922), *Gen.* XIV 37 IV; Brandenburg Consistory to EOK (Feb. 24, 1925), *Gen.* XIV 37 V; Schulz to Reichstag (Aug. 24, 1921), in *Verhandlungen des Reichstags, I. Wahlperiode 1920, Anlagen zu den Stenographischen Berichte, 368,* Nr. 2624, pp. 2598–99.

[26] Heinrich Schulz, *Der Leidensweg des Reichsschulgesetzes* (Berlin, 1925), p. 100. See *RK* (Dec. 5, 1920), p. 343; (March 5, 1922), p. 55; (April 30, 1922), p. 102; (May 7, 1922), p. 107; (May 27, 1923), p. 123; (June 12, 1927), p. 190. Also see *AELK* (Oct. 14, 1921), p. 651; *AELK* (April 28, 1922), p. 269; *AELK* (May 12, 1922), p. 302; Giesecke, "Zur Schulpolitik," pp. 176–77.

[27] Schulz, *Leidensweg,* pp. 71–112.

[28] Grünthal, *Reichsschulgesetz*, pp. 70–79; Jung, *DP* (Aug. 16, 1927), pp. 598–601, and (Sept. 6, 1927), pp. 106–8.

[29] EOK to consistories (Nov. 26, 1921), Saxon Consistory to EOK (Nov. 21, 1921), Silesian Consistory to EOK (Nov. 21, 1921), *Gen.* XIV 37 III.

[30] Silesian Consistory to EOK (Nov. 21 and 22, 1921), *Gen.* XIV 37 III.

[31] In *Gen.* XIV 37 III. See Kirchenausschuss to member church governments (Feb. 28, 1922), *Gen.* XIV 37 IV. The formal name of the National Parents' League: Reichsverband evangelischer Eltern- und Volksbünde.

[32] Letters in *Gen.* XIV 37 III: Westphalian Consistory to EOK (Jan. 14, 1922); Rhenish Consistory to EOK (Feb. 4, 1922); Brandenburg Consistory to EOK (Feb. 21, 1922); Pomeranian Consistory to EOK (March 17, 1922); East Prussian Consistory to EOK (May 26, 1922); Saxon Consistory to EOK (June 26, 1922). See also Brandenburg Consistory to EOK (April 6, 1920), *Gen.* XIV 37 I; Brandenburg Consistory to EOK (Nov. 22, 1920), *Gen.* XIV 37 II.

[33] Schulz, *Leidensweg*, pp. 112–14; Grünthal, *Reichsschulgesetz*, pp. 65–70, 78–92, 114–32, 245–56.

[34] Saxon Consistory to EOK (Oct. 2, 1922, and March 12 and April 27, 1923), Brandenburg Consistory to EOK (Oct. 27, 1922), EOK to consistories (Jan. 29, 1923), *Gen.* XIV 37 IV.

[35] Petition, Reichselternbund and Schulkartell to Reichstag (March 6, 1922), *Gen.* XIV 37 III; Kirchenausschuss to member church governments (Dec. 20, 1922), *Gen.* XIV 37 IV; Kirchenausschuss minutes (Nov. 16–18, 1922), *Gen.* XII 102 V, p. 42, and (March 4–5, 1926), *Gen.* XII 102 VI, p. 22; *PK, 18* (May 1922), 59; clipping of article in *Die Schulfrage*, *Gen.* XIV 37 IV; Grünthal, *Reichsschulgesetz*, pp. 101–2, 139, 145–49; Schulz, *Leidensweg*, pp. 151–54.

[36] Grünthal, *Reichsschulgesetz*, pp. 79, 114–43, 150–55, 292; Schulz, *Leidensweg*, pp. 112–35.

[37] *KJ, 47* (1920), 455–65; *KJ, 49* (1922), 316–17, 376–77; *KJ, 50* (1923), 342; *KJ, 51* (1924), 400–2; *AELK* (Sept. 12, 1919), p. 810; *AELK* (July 22, 1921), pp. 461–62; *RK* (April 4, 1920), p. 107; *Ref.* (April 17, 1921), pp. 29–30; *Ref.* (July 17, 1921), pp. 54–55; *Proth.* (Nov. 7, 1926), pp. 641–42.

[38] *AELK* (Nov. 3, 1922), p. 701; *KJ, 49* (1922), 370–71; *KJ, 52* (1925), 469–70; *Proth.* (June 4, 1921), p. 226; *Proth.* (Nov. 9, 1924), pp. 234–35; *Proth.* (Sept. 5, 1926), pp. 516–17.

[39] Letters in *Gen.* XIV 37 IV: Kirchenausschuss to member church governments (Feb. 28, 1922), Reichselternbund to EOK (Dec. 21, 1922), Hinderer to EOK (May 29, 1923), EOK to Hinderer (June 12, 1923), Saxon Consistory to EOK (April 27, 1923). See also EOK to consistories (May 14, 1924), *Gen.* XIV 37 V; *RK* (May 14, 1922), p. 114; *RK* (Jan. 17, 1926), p. 22; *RK* (Feb. 14, 1926), p. 55; *CW* (May 24, 1923), p. 327.

[40] Brochure enclosed in Kirchenausschuss to member church governments (Nov. 15, 1924), *Gen.* XIV 37 V.

[41] *GB, 1* (1922–24), 241.

[42] EOK to consistories (May 14, 1924), *Gen.* XIV 37 V. This file contains consistory reports on these elections. See also *VGS, 2* (1925), 161–62.

[43] Boelitz, *Reorganization,* p. xxii.

[44] Brandenburg Consistory to EOK (Feb. 24 and May 19, 1925), and EOK to consistories (July 10, 1925), *Gen.* XIV 37 V; Pomeranian Consistory to EOK (Nov. 12, 1926), *Gen.* XIV 37 VI; Gennrich, *VGS, 1* (1925), 453–54; *VGS, 2* (1925), 164; Kockelte, *DP* (March 22, 1927), p. 243.

[45] 1924 annual report attached to letter, Ev. Gesamt-Elternbund Gross-Berlin to EOK (June 10, 1925), *Gen.* XIV 37 V; Brandenburg Consistory to EOK (Feb. 24, 1925), *Gen.* XIV 37 V.

[46] *VGS, 1* (1920), 537, 573; *VGS, 1* (1925), 451–54; *VGS, 2* (1925), 162; *VGS, 2* (1927), 68; Brandenburg Consistory to EOK (Aug. 14, 1920), *Gen.* XIV 37 II; Brandenburg Consistory to EOK (Feb. 24, 1925), *Gen.* XIV 37 V; Saxon Consistory to EOK (July 5, 1926), *Gen.* XIV 37 VI; Pomeranian Consistory to EOK (Nov. 12, 1926), *Gen.* XIV 37 VI; Silesian Consistory to EOK (Nov. 24, 1926), *Gen.* XIV 37 VI. Otto Braun, Prussian Minister President, in his memoirs: "Dissident {konfessionslose] teachers were employed; difficulties resulted only in their appointment as principals" (Braun, *Von Weimar zu Hitler {New York,* 1940], p. 230).

[47] *VGS, 1* (1925), 444–50; *VGS, 2* (1925), 163; Westphalian Consistory to EOK (March 25, 1925), Rhenish Consistory to EOK (July 16, 1925), and Reichselternbund to EOK (July 29, 1925), *Gen.* XIV 37 V.

[48] *VGS, 2* (1925), 153.

[49] Minutes of meeting of general superintendents and EOK (June 1–2, 1922), *Gen.* XIV 37 IV; Brandenburg Consistory to EOK (Feb. 24, 1925), *Gen.* XIV 37 V; *KJ, 52* (1925), 423–27; *KJ, 54* (1927), 460.

[50] *VGS, 1* (1925), 451–52; *VGS, 2* (1925), 162–64; *VGS, 1* (1927), 598, 619; *VGS, 2* (1927), 67–68; Brandenburg Consistory to EOK (Feb. 24 and Sept. 21, 1925), *Gen.* XIV 37 V; Kultusministerium to EOK (May 10, 1926), *Gen.* XIV 37 VI.

[51] Church objections do not appear centered on Socialist party membership as such but on the assumed hostility of Socialists to Christianity and confessional schools. (See, e.g., Westphalian Consistory to EOK [Feb. 27, 1924], *Gen.* XIV 20 V.) In 1925 the later Socialist Kultusminister, Adolf Grimme, accepted an appointment in the Saxon provincial agency for higher schools. The provincial parents' association decided not to contest his appointment for the reason that he was a religious socialist, though hardly a Christian acceptable to the church. (See Saxon Consistory to EOK [Sept. 15, 1925], *Gen.* XIV 37 V.)

[52] As quoted in *Rb* (Sept. 30, 1920). See *AELK* (Sept. 17, 1920), p. 731; *Rb* (Sept. 25, 1920); *RK* (Oct. 10, 1920), p. 296.

[53] *Sitzungsberichte des Preussischen Landtags, 1. Wahlperiode, 6* (Berlin, 1927), 7822, 8015; *Sitzungsberichte, 2. Wahlperiode, 11* (Berlin, 1927), 15723.

[54] Rhenish Consistory to EOK (Oct. 8, 1923), *Gen.* XIV 20 V.

[55] *VGS, 1* (1925), 451–57; Becker to EOK (May 10, 1926), *Gen.* XIV 37 VI.

[56] Braun, *Weimar,* p. 230.

[57] *VGS, 1* (1925), 192. See ibid., pp. 163–98; *VGS, 2* (1925), 155–57, 160; Kirchenausschuss minutes (March 24–25, 1925), *Gen.* XII 102 VI, pp. 20–21; *KJ, 49* (1922), 375; *AELK* (Feb. 23, 1923), pp. 124–25; *GB, 1* (1922–24), 217–18, 260.

[58] *VGS, 1* (1925), 452, 587–94; *VGS, 1* (1927), 598, 602–5; *VGS, 2* (1927), 42, 68–69, 75; Kirchenausschuss minutes (March 24–25, 1925), *Gen.* XII 102 VI, pp. 20–21; Kirchenausschuss to member church governments (Nov. 15, 1924), *Gen.* XIV 37 V; Church Senate minutes (Nov. 2–3, 1926), *Gen.* III 48 I, pp. 6–7; Schmidt, *GG* (April 1925), pp. 124–26; Jung, *DP* (Sept. 13, 1927), pp. 671–74; Plath, *Proth.* (Oct. 2, 1927), p. 553; Tribukait, *Kirchen-Schulkampf,* p. 49; Erich Wende, *C.H. Becker* (Stuttgart, 1959), pp. 204–5.

[59] Letters in *Gen.* XIV 20 V: East Prussian Consistory to EOK (Nov. 13, 1924), EOK to Kultusminister (Nov. 29, 1924), Superintendent Nietzki to Kultusminister (Feb. 24, 1925), Kaestner to EOK (March 2, 1925), Becker to Superintendent Nietzki (March 9, 1925). See *Sitzungsberichte, 2. Wahlperiode, 11,* 15683, 15719–20.

[60] On Nischalke's transfer, see correspondence in *Gen.* XIV 20 V, and *VGS, 1* (1925), 451–53.

[61] On the origins and issues of the strike, see correspondence in *Gen.* XIV 37 VI; clippings in *Beiheft A* to *Gen.* XIV 37 VI; *Sitzungsberichte, 2. Wahlperiode, 11,* 15680–746; Tribukait, *Kirchen-Schulkampf,* pp. 7–32; Richter, *DP* (Dec. 14, 1926), pp. 1000–2, and (Jan. 25, 1927), pp. 62–63.

[62] *Sitzungsberichte, 2. Wahlperiode, 11,* 15698–705.

[63] According to Richter, *DP* (Jan. 25, 1927), p. 62, the total came to "more than 30,000 children."

[64] *Preussische Lehrer-Zeitung* (Nov. 25, 1926), clipping in *Beiheft A* to *Gen.* XIV 37 VI; Tribukait, *Kirchen-Schulkampf,* pp. 15–19; Richter, *DP* (Dec. 14, 1926), p. 1001, and (Jan. 25, 1927), pp. 62–63; Winckler, *DP* (April 5, 1927), pp. 287–88; Flemming, *DP* (Nov. 29, 1927), pp. 868–71.

[65] *ED* (April 18, 1926), p. 127. Kirchenausschuss minutes (March 4–5, 1926), *Gen.* XII 102 VI, p. 22; *Führerblatt* (Nov. 3, 1926), p. 2, in *Gen.* XIV 37 VI; Richter, *DP* (Dec. 14, 1926), p. 1001; *KJ, 53* (1926), 449–51; *KJ, 54* (1927), 404–7; Tribukait, *Kirchen-Schulkampf,* pp. 13–14; Grünthal, *Reichsschulgesetz,* 186–96, 276–81.

[66] *Sitzungsberichte, 2. Wahlperiode, 11,* 15703.

[67] Saxon Consistory to Pfarrer Müller (March 12, 1926), *Gen.* XIV 37 VI; Stolle

and Henselmann, *VGS, 1* (1925), 567–70, 573; Scheffler, *Protb.* (June 26, 1927), pp. 367–69; Schubring, *Protb.* (Dec. 18, 1927), pp. 718–19.

[68] Both quotations cited in Tribukait, *Kirchen-Schulkampf*, pp. 24–28.

[69] Ibid., pp. 22–24, 29–31, 48–62; Richter, *DP* (Dec. 14, 1926), pp. 1000–2, and (Jan. 25, 1927), pp. 62–63.

[70] *Sitzungsberichte, 2. Wahlperiode, 11*, 15702–703, 15726; *Allgemeine Deutsche Lehrerzeitung* (Jan. 6, 1927), clipping in *Beiheft A* to *Gen.* XIV 37 VI; Richter, *DP* (Jan. 25, 1927), pp. 62–63; Tribukait, *Kirchen-Schulkampf*, pp. 14, 19–20, 31–32.

[71] See decision in *Beiheft A* to *Gen.* XIV 37 VI.

[72] Minutes of meeting of general superintendents with EOK (June 1–2, 1922), *Gen.* XIV 37 IV, pp. 5–7, 11–13.

[73] See the debate in *VGS, 1* (1925), 558–87. See also *KJ, 49* (1922), 370; *KJ, 50* (1923), 342–43; *KJ, 51* (1924), 402; *Protb.* (Nov. 9, 1924), pp. 234–35; *Protb.* (Oct. 17, 1926), pp. 596–97; *Protb.* (July 24, 1927), p. 423; Heine, *Rb* (Feb. 15, 1925).

[74] In *VGS, 2* (1927), see the text on pp. 125–27 and the Senate report on pp. 66–67. Church Senate minutes in *Gen.* III 48 1 (May 20–21, 1926), pp. 9–10; (Aug. 18, 1926), pp. 5–6, 11–12; (Nov. 2–3, 1926), pp. 6, 9; (Jan. 4–6, 1927), pp. 11–12. See also *Protb.* (Aug. 1, 1926), pp. 452–53; *Protb.* (Sept. 5, 1926), pp. 516–17; *Protb.* (March 6, 1927), pp. 133–34; *Rb* (March 15, 1927); *Rb* (April 15, 1927); *KJ, 54* (1927), 71–72, 468–70.

[75] Church Senate minutes in *Gen.* III 48 I: (May 22, 1928), p. 12, and (Aug. 17, 1928), p. 10.

[76] Helmreich, *Religious Education*, pp. 106–8, 120, 132–45; *VKt* (1921), pp. 245–47; *KJ, 50* (1923), 346; *KJ, 52* (1925), 463–64; *Rb* (May 4, 1924); Mumm, *Das Vaterland* (July 25, 1925), clipping in *Gen.* XIV 37 V; *Führerblatt* (Nov. 3, 1926) in *Gen.* XIV 37 VI; *Rb* (July 20, 1927). The Stuttgart declaration did not contest Christian Simultan schools in Baden, Hesse, and Nassau. In all three areas, as well as in the new common-school state of Thuringia, Evangelical churches had declared for Christian Simultan schools. (See Raack, *PK, 24* [1928], 73.)

[77] *VGS, 1* (1925), 559; *VGS, 1* (1927), 597–98; Grünthal, *Reichsschulgesetz*, pp. 186–246. See text of the bill (Nr. 3650) and explanation in *Verhandlungen des Reichstags, III. Wahlperiode 1924, Anlagen zu den Stenographischen Berichten, 419* (Berlin, 1927).

[78] Consistory reports in *Gen.* XIV 37 VI.

[79] *Verhandlungen des Reichstags, III. Wahlperiode 1924, 394* (Berlin, 1928), 11505–523, 11531–613.

[80] Grünthal, *Reichsschulgesetz*, pp. 213–15, 226–28; Helmreich, *Religious Education*, pp. 80–82, 139–40; Mulert, *Protb.* (Sept. 25, 1927), p. 543.

[81] In *Gen.* XII 102 VI, see Kirchenausschuss minutes (March 4–5, 1926),

p. 22; (Dec. 8–9, 1927), pp. 11–17; (March 15–16, 1928), pp. 6–7. Also Church Senate minutes (Feb. 22–23, 1928), *Gen.* III 48 I, p. 12; Tribukait, *Kirchen-Schulkampf,* pp. 4–5.

[82] In *Gen.* III 48 I, see Church Senate minutes (Oct. 6–7, 1927), p. 9; (Nov. 11, 1927), p. 6; (Jan. 6, 1928), p. 6. In *Protb.,* see (July 24, 1927), p. 423; (Oct. 9, 1927), pp. 568–70; (Nov. 13, 1927), pp. 643–44.

[83] Tribukait, *Kirchen-Schulkampf,* pp. 33–68.

[84] *Rb* (Jan. 9, 1927).

[85] Grünthal, *Reichsschulgesetz,* pp. 230–46; *GB,* 5 (1928), 128–33.

[86] Kirchenausschuss minutes (March 15–16, 1928), *Gen.* XII 102 VI, pp. 6–7. *Der Reichsbote* (July 20, 1927) had predicted "chaos in the area of schools if nothing comes of it [the Keudell bill]."

[87] *DP, 28* (1924), 27.

[88] See, e.g., Lütgert and Adams, *VGS, 1* (1925), 169–70, 562; Buntzel, *DP* (Dec. 14, 1926), pp. 997–1000. Liberals could resort to the same argument for Christian Simultan schools. (In *Protb.,* see, e.g., [Sept. 10, 1921], pp. 311–13; [Oct. 9, 1927], p. 569.)

[89] See, e.g., *VGS, 1* (1925), 559, 562, 567–68, 574–77; *LL* (Sept. 18, 1927), pp. 600–2.

[90] *DP* (Feb. 24, 1925), pp. 122–23; Buntzel, *DP* (Dec. 14, 1926), pp. 997–1000; Kreppel, "Der Lehrer," pp. 134–51.

[91] Church Senate minutes in *Gen.* III 48 II: (April 28–29, 1932), pp. 30–31; (Aug. 3, 1932), pp. 41–42; (Oct. 13, 1932), pp. 47–49. See also Church Senate minutes (May 22, 1928), *Gen.* III 48 I, p. 12; *Preussische Lehrer-Zeitung* (Nov. 13, 1930), clipping in *Gen.* XIV 20 V. Commenting on the 1927 Church Senate declaration, General Superintendent Zoellner even claimed: "The question of life or death is at stake here for the Evangelical church as a Volkskirche" (*Rb* [March 15, 1927]).

[92] Helmreich, *Religious Education,* p. 150.

VOLKSKIRCHE ACTIVISM: FAMILY, FOLK, AND ECONOMY

[1] *VKt* (1927), pp. 338–40.

[2] Otto Dibelius, *Das Jahrhundert der Kirche* (Berlin, 1927), passim; idem, *Nachspiel* (Berlin, 1928), passim.

[3] Dibelius, *Nachspiel,* pp. 21–26.

[4] *Rb* (Sept. 17, 1925); *Rb* (Dec. 12, 1926); *VGS, 1* (1925), 272.

[5] Dibelius, *Nachspiel,* 94.

[6] Pfarrer Tribukait, *Der Kirchen-Schulkampf in Westfalen* (1928?), pp. 54–56; Dibelius, *Nachspiel,* pp. 34–39. Hermann Schafft, *Vom Kampf gegen die Kirche für die Kirche* (Habertshof bei Schlüchtern, 1925) offered a counterpoint to Dibelius's theme. Renewal of congregations, not church organization, provided the ultimate means of affecting society. The gospel should judge all culture, even the Christian,

for all culture had but a relative value. No doubt Dibelius agreed in theory. But he wondered how such a view could allow the churches to advance Christian values in public life (See *Nachspiel*, p. 39, fn. 12).

[7] *System der Ethik* (Leipzig, 1920), p. 135. Also see pp. 97, 130–44.

[8] *VKt* (1921), pp. 36, 77–81, 252.

[9] On these areas, see *VKt* (1921), pp. 184–85; *VKt* (1927), pp. 30, 96; *VGS*, *1* (1920), 290–98, 505–8; *VGS*, *2* (1925), 367; *VGS*, *1* (1927), 20–22, 589–90; *VGS*, *2* (1927), 61–63; Mumm, *KJ*, *53* (1926), 518–19; Mumm, *Rb* (Oct. 28, 1926); *Rb* (Nov. 27, 1926); Roecker, *ED* (Jan. 18, 1925), p. 17; Matz, *ED* (Oct. 25, 1925), p. 336; ibid. (Sept. 19, 1926), pp. 300–301; ibid. (Dec. 12, 1926), p. 396; *ED* (Sept. 19, 1926), p. 303; *ED* (May 22, 1927), pp. 167–68; *LL* (Jan. 30, 1927), pp. 70–72; *IM* (Jan. 1927), p. 36; *IM* (May 1928), p. 214; Reinhard Mumm, *Der christlich-soziale Gedanke* (Berlin, 1933), pp. 125–26.

[10] *VKt* (1921), pp. 23, 220; *VKt* (1924), pp. 21, 252; *VKt* (1927), p. 31; Kirchenausschuss minutes (May 26–27, 1922), *Gen.* XII 102 V, pp. 22–29, 43–45; ibid. (Nov. 16–18, 1922), p. 31, Anlage 6; H. W., *Rb* (Feb. 3, 1927); Bohn, *IM* (March 1927), pp. 119–21. See Richard J. Evans, *The Feminist Movement in Germany 1894-1933* (London, 1976), pp. 16–17, 43, 53–54, 163–64, 167–68, 237.

[11] *VKt* (1921), pp. 183–84; *VKt* (1927), pp. 71–73; *VGS*, *1* (1925), 416–17; Weymann, *ED* (Nov. 30, 1924), pp. 177–78; *ED* (March 29, 1925), p. 103; *LL* (March 14, 1926), pp. 169–71; *RK* (June 6, 1926), p. 182; Strathmann, *Rb* (Jan. 27, 1926); *GB*, *2* (1925), 140–57; Mumm, *KJ*, *53* (1926), 524–25; ibid., *54* (1927), 397. For Gauger's criticism of the political Right, see *LL* (Aug. 23, 1925), pp. 546–49.

[12] *KJ*, *51* (1924), 229–30. For statistics, see *KJ*, *56* (1929), 101.

[13] Ruhkopf, *Rb* (Aug. 12, 1920). On these issues, see Kirchenausschuss minutes (Feb. 8–10, 1921), *Gen.* XII 102 V, pp. 22–23; ibid. (May 26–27, 192), pp. 6–8; *VKt* (1921), pp. 23, 192; *VKt* (1924), pp. 20, 88; *RK* (July 24, 1921), p. 179; Schweitzer, *IM* (April 1923), pp. 66–69; Harmsen, *IM* (Aug. 1926), pp. 239–44; *ED* (May 3, 1925), p. 141.

[14] *KJ*, *56* (1929), 31; *VGS*, *1* (1920), 282–90; *VKt* (1924), pp. 215–19; *VKt* (1927), pp. 276, 358–59; Schiller, *Rb* (July 8, 1925).

[15] *VKt* (1927), pp. 77–79; Mahling, *IM* (April 1925), p. 90; *IM* (May 1926), p. 163.

[16] Schowalter, *ED* (April 15, 1925), p. 82. See *RGG*, *5* (1931), 608–9; *VKt* (1924), pp. 252–53; *VKt* (1927), pp. 84–86; *VGS*, *1* (1920), 85–87; *VGS*, *1* (1925), 259–70; *VGS*, *2* (1925), 147–52; *VGS*, *1* (1927), 590–91; *VGS*, *2* (1927), 63–64.

[17] Barth, *Die Lehre von der Schöpfung* in *Die Kirchliche Dogmatik*, *3* (2nd ed. Zürich, 1957), 345–48. See Wolfgang Tilgner, *Volksnomostheologie und Schöpfungsglaube* (Göttingen, 1966), for a history of folkish theology from Herder to the German Christians of the early 1930s.

[18] See, e.g., *DP* (Oct. 21, 1924), p. 343.

[19] Friedrich Brunstäd, *Völkisch-nationale Erneuerung* (Berlin, 1921), p. 10.

[20] In the description of the "new" nationalism that follows, I have largely kept to the analysis of Kurt Sontheimer, *Antidemokratisches Denken in der Weimarer Republik* (Munich, 1962). I have found it impossible, however, to classify many nationalist churchmen as clearly either "new" or "old" nationalists.

[21] *VKt* (1927), p. 339.

[22] See, e.g., Kittel, *AELK* (Aug. 5, 1921), p. 484, and Eisenhart, *Rb* (Dec. 4, 1926).

[23] Emanuel Hirsch, *Deutschlands Schicksal* (Göttingen, 1920), passim.

[24] Reinhold Seeberg, *System der Ethik* (Leipzig, 1920), pp. 228–37, 256–68.

[25] Paul Althaus, *Staatsgedanken und Reich Gottes* (Langensalza, 1923), pp. 37–51, 61–65.

[26] See, e.g., Georg Wünsch, *Der Zusammenbruch des Luthertums als Sozialgestaltung* (Tübingen, 1921), pp. 30–34.

[27] *VKt* (1927), p. 339.

[28] See, e.g., Hützen, *Ref.* (July 11, 1920), pp. 171–72; *LL* (Oct. 23, 1921), pp. 602–4; Kuhlmann, *LL* (March 14, 1926), p. 168; Laible, *AELK* (Jan. 8, 1926), pp. 25–26; Schier, *DP* (Sept. 6, 1927), pp. 651–52.

[29] Thus in *Rb:* Bunke, (June 7, 1919); Pfeiffer, (Aug. 31, 1919); Ruhkopf, (Sept. 3, 1925); Loeff, (June 11, 1927). Examples of those favoring a just war: Ralk, *Rb* (Feb. 16, 1924), and Limprecht, *DP* (Aug. 30, 1927), p. 636.

[30] The moderate pacifist, Günther Dehn, in his memoirs: "To a great extent ... the present [after 1919] appeared to pastors in the light of the time after 1806/7. Then the badly defeated folk found its way to freedom by renewing its will to defend itself not without the energetic assistance of the church (one often talked in pastors' circles of Schleiermacher's patriotic effectiveness). In the same way, so one thought, it is also now the task of the church to help so that Germany becomes a free land again." (*Die alte Zeit, die vorigen Jahren* [Munich, 1962], p. 209.)

[31] Kaftan, *AELK* (June 5, 1925), pp. 403–5. Later Dibelius was moved to defend his position in *Friede auf Erden?* (Berlin, 1930).

[32] Martin Rade, *Christentum und Frieden* (Tübingen, 1922), passim.

[33] Ibid., p. 35; Baumgarten, *CW* (June 5, 1919), p. 368.

[34] Kübel and Schümer, *CW* (Sept. 20, 1923), pp. 588–89; ibid. (Oct. 25, 1923), pp. 631–51.

[35] As quoted by Siegmund-Schultze, *Die Eiche, 10* (1922), 177. Siegmund-Schultze explained his pacifism in *Die Eiche, 15* (1927), 238–49.

[36] *Die Eiche, 15* (1927), 261.

[37] *Dk* (Nebelung 1922); Bublitz, *Dk, 4* (1925), 112. (For *Dk* vols. before 1925, I shall cite the issue, since these vols. lack pagination. I shall also follow the *Dk* practice of citing Germanic months. Nebelung, e.g., is Nov.) See Jean Réal, "The

Religious Conception of Race: Houston Stewart Chamberlain and Germanic Christianity," in *The Third Reich,* ed. Maurice Baumont, et al. (New York, 1955), pp. 243–86. Pastor Friedrich Andersen of Flensburg, the league's Bundeswart (nominal head) and a prewar convert to Germanic Christianity, elaborated on Chamberlain's religious conceptions in *Anticlericus,* revised and republished as *Der deutsche Heiland* (Munich, 1921). The book is a good introduction to the ideological world of the German Church. On Andersen, see *Dk* (5. i. Nebelung 1924) and *Dk,* 7 (1928), 164.

[38] On Niedlich, see Niedlich, *Dk, 4* (1925), 12; Bublitz, *Dk, 7* (1928), 188. Also see Hans Buchheim, *Glaubenskrise im dritten Reich* (Stuttgart, 1953), pp. 43–47.

[39] On German Church theology in *Dk,* see: Vogel, (5. i. Oster 1925); Niedlich, (20. i. Oster 1924), (5. i. Ernting 1924), and *4* (1925), 18–19, 112–14; Bublitz, (20. i. Oster 1924), (5. i. Mai 1924), *4* (1925), 31–32, and *6* (1927), 380. Also see Niedlich, *DP* (Mar. 24, 1925), pp. 206–7.

[40] In *Dk:* Niedlich, (20. i. Oster 1924) and (5. i. Ernting 1924); Bublitz, *4* (1925), 31–32.

[41] In *Dk:* Niedlich, (20. i. Jul 1924), and *5* (1926), 27–28; Bublitz, *4* (1925), 31–32.

[42] *Dk* (Hartung/Hornung 1923).

[43] In *Dk:* (5. i. Jul 1923); *4* (1925), 57, 75–76, 109; Niedlich, *5* (1926), 28, 141; appeal appended to (20. i. Jul 1927).

[44] In *Dk:* *4* (1925), 114–15, 133, 145; *5* (1926), 8; *6* (1927), 108–9, 116–18, 133–34, 180–81, 189–91, 197–98, 206–8; 7 (1928), 22–24, 37. Also see *VGS, 1* (1925), 27, 277–84, and *VGS, 1* (1927), 161–63.

[45] In *Dk:* Niedlich, *5* (1926), 3–4, 100–1; *6* (1927), 165–67; appeal appended to (20. i. Jul 1927).

[46] In *Dk:* Niedlich, (5. i. Ernting 1924), *4* (1925), 63–65, and 7 (1928), 34, 141; Bublitz, (5. i. Scheiding 1924).

[47] In *Dk, 6* (1927): 66; Witte, 73–75; Niedlich, 189.

[48] In *Dk:* Niedlich, (Oster and Mai 1923), and *5* (1926), 147–48.

[49] In *Dk:* Niedlich, *4* (1925), 83; *5* (1926), 5.

[50] In *Dk:* Vogel, (5. i. Oster 1925); Niedlich, *4* (1925), 107–8; Andersen, ibid., 138; Bublitz, *5* (1926), 32–33, 134–35, and *6* (1927), 199; 7 (1928), 192. For an overview of religious streams in the folkish movement, see Weinel, *RGG, 5* (1931), 1617–23.

[51] *Dk, 6* (1927), 81.

[52] *Dk* (5. i. Gilbhart 1924). See Klaus Scholder, *Die Kirchen und das Dritte Reich, 1* (1977), 134–37.

[53] In *Dk, 4* (1925): Bublitz, 31–32; Niedlich, 112–13.

[54] See, e.g., Laible, *AELK* (Sept. 23, 1921), p. 600; Kittel, *LL* (April 28, 1922), pp. 258–60; Schneidemesser, *PU, 21* (1925), 48–51, 59–63; Eberlein, *GB, 3* (1926), 122–26; Bunke, *PU, 23* (1927), 168–75; Müller, *Rb* (Sept. 20,

1927). Liberals as well responded ambiguously. See, e.g., Schubring, *Protb.* (Dec. 24, 1922), pp. 162–64; Weinel, *CW* (Oct. 1, 1925), p. 913.

[55] Schneider in *KJ: 52* (1925), 556–57; *53* (1926), 585–88. Niedlich in *Dk:* (5. i. Gilbhart 1924); *4* (1925), 20, 131–32; *5* (1926), 27–28; *6* (1927), 12–15. Bunke, *PU, 23* (1927), 126–27, 168–75. Reinhard Mumm and especially Johannes Schneider carried on a well-publicized feud with Niedlich and the German Church.

[56] Lüpke in *Die Dorfkirche* [Dorfk.], *18* (1924–25), 1–6, 105–7, 193–98; *Dk, 5* (1926), 140; *DP* (Nov. 30, 1926), pp. 955–57.

[57] *Dk, 4* (1925), 5–6; Tiling, ibid., pp. 10–11. See ibid., pp. 11–12, for Andersen's cutting response to the Tiling theses. Apparently Magdalene von Tiling's theses were the same as those that some contemporaries thought had the endorsement of the Central Committee. (See *DP* [Dec. 23, 1924], p. 491.) She was a leader in Evangelical women's groups and a Nationalist politician.

[58] This line persisted through the Kirchenkampf of the 1930s. (See Scholder, *Die Kirchen,* pp. 149–50.)

[59] *VKt* (1927), pp. 204–24.

[60] See, e.g., Kirmss, *PM, 24* (1920), 137–47; Schubring, *Protb.* (Oct. 30, 1920), p. 362; and Seeberg, *GG, 60* (1924), 217–19. Liberals as well as the orthodox commonly subscribed to such a notion of elective affinity. In *DP* (March 10, 1925), pp. 161–63, see dispute over elective affinity, Pastor Herrfurth deploring that equating Evangelical and German absolutized Germanness, General Superintendent Klingemann replying that an affinity nonetheless existed.

[61] Thus the patriotic proclamation spoke of each folk's "special gift and task" without elaborating a theology of history. (*VKt* [1927], p. 339.)

[62] Scholder argued (*Die Kirchen,* p. 133) that "political theology," by which he referred to the theology of historical redemption, was "the answer of German Protestantism to the folkish movement"—the most important answer until well into the Kirchenkampf. He did not, however, make clear that "political theology" continued the thema of war theology. Rather, in his view, "political theology" suddenly intruded upon Protestant consciousness in the mid-1920s.

[63] *Dk* (5. i. Ernting 1924).

[64] Niedlich, *Dk, 6* (1927), 132–33; Bublitz and Niedlich, ibid., 176–77.

[65] Niedlich in *Dk:* (20. i. Jul 1924); *4* (1925), 132. *Dk, 5* (1926), 169: Because of Deutschkirche election successes, "church authorities have since behaved toward us in a completely loyal fashion."

[66] See Scholder, *Die Kirchen,* p. 139.

[67] *Rb* (Dec. 11, 1920). My italics.

[68] *CW* (April 10, 1924), p. 249.

[69] *GB, 1* (1922–24), 95.

[70] On anti-Semitism in the Second Empire, see: Alexander Bien, "Der moderne Antisemitismus und seine Bedeutung für die Judenfrage," *VfZ, 6* (1966), pp.

340–60; Paul W. Massing, *Rehearsal for Destruction* (New York, 1949); and Uriel Tal, *Christians and Jews in Germany* (Ithaca, N.Y., 1975).

[71] Tal, *Christians and Jews*, 223–305; Richard Gutteridge, *The German Evangelical Church and the Jews 1879–1950* (New York, 1976), pp. 4–12.

[72] See Werner E. Mosse, ed., *Deutsches Judentum in Krieg und Revolution 1916–1923* (Tübingen, 1971), and Mosse, ed., *Entscheidungsjahr 1932* (Tübingen, 1965).

[73] See unpubl. diss. (Tübingen, 1960) by Ino Arndt, "Die Judenfrage im Licht der evangelischen Sonntagsblätter von 1918–1933," pp. 1–128, 210–17. See also Gutteridge, *Church and the Jews*, pp. 35–68.

[74] In *LL* (July 20, 1919), p. 394; (July 27, 1919), p. 410; (Aug. 3, 1919), p. 420; (Aug. 31, 1919), p. 477; (Jan. 11, 1920), pp. 29–31; (Oct. 17, 1920), p. 532. In *GB, 1* (1922–24), 38–39, 53, 126–28, 131, 140, 197, 225, 228–32, 274, 279, 315, 319, 345. In *GB, 2* (1925), 21, 112, 288, 378–79. In *GB, 3* (1926), 117. In *GB, 4* (1927), 252. In *GB, 5* (1928), 109.

[75] Norman Cohn, *Warrant for Genocide* (London, 1967), pp. 15–148, 169–93. On Laible, see Arndt, "Die Judenfrage," pp. 23–25, and, for other examples, pp. 110–13, 210.

[76] *Dorfk.*, *15* (1921), 33–38.

[77] In *AELK*, see (Aug. 5, 1921), p. 664; (Oct. 28, 1921), pp. 678–79; (Nov. 4, 1921), pp. 694–95; (June 1, 1923), pp. 341–42. Also see *Protb.* (Sept. 6, 1919), pp. 435–36; Beutel, *IM, 17* (1922), 187–89; Loeff, *Rb* (April 23, 1924); *ED* (June 14, 1925), p. 190.

[78] Seeberg, "Antisemitismus, Judentum und Kirche," in *Zum Verständnis der gegenwärtigen Krisis in der europäischen Geisteskultur* (Leipzig, 1923), pp. 103–17, 134–35. Also see Lüpke, *Dorfk.*, *15* (1921), 35–38; Procksch, *AELK* (May 25, 1923), pp. 322–27; Boeck, *EB* (Feb. 28, 1925), pp. 671–73.

[79] In *LL* (June 20, 1920), pp. 315–16; (June 27, 1920), p. 326.. In *GB, 1* (1922–24), 126, 131–32, 225, 346.

[80] Arndt, "Die Judenfrage," pp. 31–38, 42–49, 55, 60, 87, 211; Seeberg, "Antisemitismus," pp. 101, 126–27, 130–32. Compared to the folkish goals of the Nationalist party, adopted in 1924, the anti-Semitism of most nationalist churchmen appears moderate. Nationalists, to whom large numbers of churchmen rallied, would strip Jews of German citizenship and isolate them from the rest of German society. (See *Rb* [March 4, 1924].) See George L. Mosse, "Die deutsche Rechte und die Juden," in Werner E. Mosse, ed., *Entscheidungsjahr*, pp. 183–246.

[81] In *GB, 1* (1922–24), 131, 197, 225, 229. In *GB, 3* (1926), 94.

[82] Arndt, "Die Judenfrage," pp. 14–38, 210.

[83] Seeberg, "Antisemitismus," pp. 101–6, 117–36.

[84] *VKt* (1927), pp. 208, 216; Althaus, *Staatsgedanken*, pp. 54–55.

[85] Arndt demonstrated the tug of the folkish formulation but not clearly its consequence: Now the Jewish problem lay at the center of folk renewal and not merely at its periphery as a political threat. (See Arndt, "Die Judenfrage," pp. 39–46, 59–70, 212–13, 217.)

[86] Bublitz, *Dk* (20. i. Oster 1924). In *Dk, 4* (1925), 63–65; Baltzer, 12; Niedlich, 51, 113, 145. In *Dk, 6* (1927), Niedlich, 189; Bublitz, 206. *Proth.* (Dec. 6, 1925), p. 777.

[87] Arndt duly noted the antirepublican impact of anti-Semitism. See "Die Judenfrage," pp. 118–21, 211, 216, 220. On antimodernity as a motivation, see, e.g., Cohn, *Warrant,* pp. 169–70, 255–60.

[88] *VKt* (1924), pp. 215–19.

[89] Ibid., p. 230; *CW* (July 17, 1924), pp. 563–65; Fuchs, ibid., pp. 559–63.

[90] Laible, *AELK* (Jan. 8, 1926), pp. 27–31.

[91] *VKt* (1919), p. 314. See *VKt* (1921), pp. 187–88; *VKt* (1927), pp. 82–83; Mumm, *IM* (Dec. 1921), pp. 196–200; Mumm, *KJ, 54* (1927), 392.

[92] *VKt* (1919), p. 315; *VKt* (1924), pp. 198–99, 203; *AELK* (May 20, 1927), p. 476. See reports on social efforts within the Old-Prussian church in *VGS, 2* (1925), 220–32, and *2* (1927), 120–24.

[93] *System der Ethik,* p. 144.

[94] *VKt* (1924), p. 234.

[95] *RK* (July 5, 1925), p. 167; *Zeitwende {Zw}* (Feb. 1925), p. 209.

[96] *DP* (July 13, 1926), pp. 542–43; *VKt* (1924), pp. 112–15.

[97] *VKt* (1927), pp. 75–76.

[98] See extreme examples of this equation in Hützen, *Ref.* (July 11, 1920), pp. 171–72; Rüffer, *Rb* (March 12, 1924, and Dec. 21, 1926); Heine, *Rb* (March 29, 1925); Fresenius, *EB* (Jan. 18, 1925), pp. 531–33; Krüger, *DP* (May 25, 1926), pp. 369–74.

[99] *CW* (June 1, 1925), p. 488.

[100] Friedrich Brunstäd, *Deutschland und der Sozialismus* (Berlin, 1927), pp. 303–43.

[101] *VKt* (1919), pp. 306–7.

[102] Brunstäd, *Sozialismus,* pp. 303–11, 328–35; Seeberg, *System der Ethik,* pp. 202–11.

[103] Brunstäd, *Sozialismus,* pp. 318, 340–43. For attitudes of church nationalists toward Socialists, see, e.g., Eisenhart, *Rb* (May 24, 1919); Ruhkopf, *Rb* (Aug. 5, 1920); Heine, *Rb* (Feb. 28, 1924); Schiller, *GG (Dec.* 1919), pp. 218–20; Pfennigsdorf, *GG* (April 1922), pp. 73–74; Engel, *RK* (Oct. 31, 1920), pp. 310–12; Kirmss, *Proth.* (Feb. 28, 1920), pp. 92–93; Schaeder, *AELK* (Jan. 7, 1921), pp. 7–8; Kaftan, *AELK* (June 5, 1925), p. 392; *NkZ* (1925), pp. 731–33.

[104] Jacobi, *GG* (Nov. 1924), pp. 254–61.

[105] As reported by Ostertag, *EB* (June 15, 1924), p. 935. See the appeal to workers in the Church Assembly's social proclamation, *VKt* (1924), pp. 218–19.

[106] Gottfried Naumann, *Sozialismus und Religion in Deutschland* (Leipzig, 1921), pp. 66–105.

[107] In *Christentum und soziale Frage, 1* (Munich, 1919), passim.

[108] Georg Wünsch, *Der Zusammenbruch des Luthertums als Sozialgestaltung* (Tübingen, 1921), passim.

[109] Gottfried Mehnert, *Evangelische Kirche und Politik, 1917–1919* (Düsseldorf, 1959), pp. 188–202; Gerda Soecknick, *Religiöser Sozialismus der neueren Zeit unter besonderer Berücksichtigung Deutschlands* (Jena, 1926), 80–95; Dehn, *Die alte Zeit,* pp. 217–22; Scholder, *Die Kirchen, 1* (1977), 49–64.

[110] Mehnert, *Evangelische Kirche,* pp. 207–9; Soecknick, *Religiöser Sozialismus,* pp. 96–99; *AELK* (Aug. 20, 1926), pp. 807–8; Dietrich, *CW* (Sept. 9, 1926), pp. 856–57.

[111] Mehnert, *Evangelische Kirche,* pp. 204–6; Soecknick, *Religiöser Sozialismus,* pp. 96–100; Dehn, *Die alte Zeit,* pp. 213–17; Wünsch, *CW* (Sept. 4, 1924), pp. 714–17. On the movement, see also Kurt Nowak, *Evangelische Kirche und Weimarer Republik* (Göttingen, 1981), pp. 46–50, 89–93, 137–39.

[112] *Rb* (Jan. 7, 1927). On attitudes of the church Right toward religious socialism, see Schoell, *VKt* (1924), p. 113; *Rb* (Dec. 1, 1920; Sept. 5, 1920; Dec. 15, 1926; Feb. 2, 1927); Schreiner, *IM* (Sept. 1922), pp. 166–68; Bunke, *PU* (March 1927), pp. 32–38; Laible, *AELK* (Oct. 24, 1919).

[113] See, e.g., Bunke, *PU* (March 1927), pp. 34, 38. Also see Kahl's appeal for toleration at the Church Assembly, *VKt* (1927), p. 247.

[114] As quoted in *PU* (Sept. 1925), p. 83.

[115] As quoted in *RK* (July 24, 1921), p. 179. Like unions in general, workingmen's clubs lost members in the Weimar period. In 1914 they had numbered nearly 200,000, but in 1927, only 93,318. See *Rb* (Dec. 4, 1925); Mumm, *KJ, 54* (1927), 390.

VOLKSKIRCHE ACTIVISM: FOREIGN AFFAIRS

[1] On the Dolchstoss charge at the end of the war, see above, pp. 54–55. Many references to the Dolchstoss explanation may be cited in nationalist publications. See, e.g., Seitz and Rothardt, *LL* (April 13, 1919), p. 193; von Hennigs, *PU, 16* (1919), 1; Mueller, *Rb* (June 24, 1919); *EK* (June 15, 1919), p. 285; Pauli, *EK* (Aug. 17 and 24, 1919), pp. 386–88, 399–402; Laible, *AELK* (June 27, 1919), pp. 560–61; Pechmann, *NkZ, 31* (1920), 36–38; *Ref.* (July 17, 1921), p. 53. See Harry R. Rudin, *Armistice 1918* (New Haven, 1944), pp. 392–99; and Siegfried A. Kaehler, *Studien zur Deutschen Geschichte des 19. und 20. Jahrhunderts* (Göttingen, 1961), pp. 303–4, 315–23. On the intersection of internal politics and foreign policy, see Ludwig Zimmermann, *Deutsche Aussenpolitik in der Ära der Weimarer Republik* (Göttingen, 1958); Henry Ashby Turner, Jr., *Stresemann and the Politics of the Weimar Republic* (Princeton, N.J., 1963); Erich Eyck, *A History of the Weimar Republic,* trans. Harlan P. Hanson and Robert G.L. Waite (2 vols. Cambridge, Mass., 1962–63).

[2] Pp. 316, 324–25, 357, 381, 405, 411.

[3] Ernst Troeltsch, *Spektator-Briefe,* ed. H. Baron (Tübingen, 1924), pp. 1–17, 21; *KJ, 46* (1919), 314–18; *KJ, 47* (1920), 302–7.

[4] As quoted in *CW* (Dec. 12, 1918), p. 484.

[5] As quoted in *RK* (Feb. 16, 1919), p. 40.

[6] As quoted in *RK* (March 9, 1919), p. 66.

[7] See in Rudin, *Armistice,* pp. 321–22, 400–3, the Lansing note and Wilson's proclamations.

[8] As quoted in *Rb* (May 9, 1919). See protest of the Kirchenausschuss in *AELK* (May 9, 1919), p. 404, and protest of the Evangelical League in *RK* (May 25, 1919), p. 149.

[9] As quoted in *AELK* (May 9, 1919), p. 404. See *RGG,* 5 (1931), 1553–56; Alma Luckau, ed., "Document 42" in *The German Delegation at the Paris Peace Conference* (New York, 1941), pp. 250–52.

[10] As quoted in *RK* (July 20, 1919), p. 214.

[11] Kirchenausschuss minutes (Jan. 29–31, 1920), *Gen.* XII 102 V, pp. 18–19.

[12] *The German Treaty Text* (London, 1920), p. 116. My italics. For the most part, I have followed the interpretation of Fritz Dickmann, "Die Kriegsschuldfrage auf der Friedenskonferenz von Paris 1919," *HZ, 197* (1963), 43–99.

[13] As quoted in *RK* (July 20, 1919), p. 214.

[14] See, e.g., *Ref.* (June 1, 1919), p. 171; *Ref.* (June 8, 1919), p. 181; Laible, *AELK* (June 27, 1919), p. 561.

[15] *LL* (June 29, 1919), pp. 248–51; Rade, *CW* (June 26, 1919), p. 422; *Ref.* (April 27, 1919), p. 133; *Ref.* (May 25, 1919), p. 166; *Ref.* (June 29, 1919), p. 205; *Rb* (May 8, 1919); *Rb* (June 23, 1919).

[16] As quoted in *RK* (June 1, 1919), p. 158. *RK* (May 25, 1919), pp. 149–50; *RK* (June 15, 1919), p. 174; *CW* (July 17, 1919), p. 467; Laible, *AELK* (May 23, 1919), p. 450; *Rb* (May 13, 1919); *Rb* (May 17, 1919); *Rb* (May 26, 1919); Axenfeld, *Rb* (June 5, 1919); *Rb* (July 3, 1919); *Ref.* (May 18, 1919), pp. 157–58; *Ref.* (April 27, 1919), p. 135; Arno J. Mayer, *Politics and Diplomacy of Peacemaking* (New York, 1967), pp. 764–67.

[17] Troeltsch, *Spektator-Briefe,* p. 70; *CW* (July 3, 1919), p. 438. See *LL* (June 22, 1919), p. 330; *LL* (July 6, 1919), pp. 366–68; Laible, *AELK* (June 6, 1919), p. 496; *AELK* (June 27, 1919), pp. 560–61; *Rb* (April 19, 1919); *Rb* (April 29, 1919); *Rb* (May 17, 1919); *Ref.* (March 2, 1919), p. 69; *Ref.* (Aug. 10, 1919), p. 252; *Ref.* (Dec. 14, 1919), p. 395; *Ref.* (Jan. 18, 1920), p. 20; *EK* (June 15, 1919), p. 285.

[18] *Die Eiche,* 9 (1921), 291.

[19] Ludwig, *AELK* (March 14, 1919), pp. 202–7.

[20] *GG, 66* (1919), 40–42.

[21] Pfeiffer, supplement to *Rb* (April 13, 1919).

[22] *LL* (July 6, 1919), pp. 369–70.

[23] See, e.g., Bunke, *Rb* (April 17, 1919); *LL* (June 15, 1919), pp. 310–13; Michaelis, *LL* (July 20, 1919), pp. 393–94; *Ref.* (July 6, 1919), p. 213; *IM, 15* (1920), 28.

[24] In *Ref.* (July 6, 1919), p. 214; (July 20, 1919), p. 228; (July 27, 1919), p. 236.

[25] "Die geistige Strömungen im Zeitalter Wilhelms II." in *Zum Verständnis der gegenwärtigen Krisis in der europäischen Geisteskultur* (Leipzig, 1923), pp. 1–55.

[26] See, e.g., *EK* (June 15, 1919), pp. 285–86; *EK* (June 28, 1919), p. 309; Hirsch, *GG, 66* (1919), 42; Seeberg, *Rb* (Sept. 24, 1920); Schiller, *Rb* (Dec. 28, 1920).

[27] Tissington Tatlow, "The World Conference on Faith and Order" in *A History of the Ecumenical Movement,* ed. Ruth Rouse and Stephen Charles Neill (London, 1954), pp. 407–25; Nils Karlström, "Movements for International Friendship and Life and Work, 1910–1925" in *Ecumenical Movement,* pp. 509–30.

[28] Karlström, "Life and Work," *Ecumenical Movement,* pp. 530–32; Siegmund-Schultze, *Die Eiche,* 7 (1919), 240–46; Wilfred Monod, *Après la journée 1867–1937* (Paris, 1938), p. 250–51.

[29] Schreiber, *AELK* (Dec. 17, 1920), p. 936.

[30] *Records of the Preliminary Meeting to Consider a Universal Conference of the Church of Christ, on Life and Work* (Geneva, Switzerland, 1920); Karlström, "Life and Work," *Ecumenical Movement,* pp. 533–39; Schreiber, *AELK* (Dec. 24, 1920), pp. 961–64; Siegmund-Schultze, *Die Eiche,* 9 (1921), 100–18; *CW* (Aug. 26, 1920), p. 557; Charles Macfarland, *Steps Toward the World Council* (New York, 1938), p. 59. On German missions, see Kenneth Scott Latourette, "Ecumenical Bearings of the Missionary Movement and the International Missionary Council," in *Ecumenical Movement,* pp. 365–67. Allied nations, which received German colonies as mandates, forced most German missionaries to return home. On the minority problem, see Adolf Keller and George Stewart, *Protestant Europe* (New York, 1927), pp. 177–86.

[31] *Minutes of the Meeting of the International Committee Held at St. Beatenberg, August 26th, 27th and 28th, 1920* (London, n.d.), pp. 11, 22–23, 42; Tatlow, "Faith and Order," *Ecumenical Movement,* p. 417; Schreiber, *AELK* (Dec. 24, 1920), p. 969; Siegmund-Schultze, *Die Eiche,* 9 (1921), 23–37.

[32] *VKt* (1921), p. 266.

[33] Kirchenausschuss minutes (June 23–25, 1920), *Gen.* XII 102 V, p. 6, *Anlage A.* See also *Ref.* (May 23, 1920), pp. 150–51; *KJ, 49* (1922), 398–99; *CW* (April 28, 1921), pp. 297–301.

[34] *AELK* (Aug. 5, 1927), p. 789. Also see, e.g., Pechmann, *AELK* (Oct. 14, 1921), p. 650; *AELK* (June 19, 1925), pp. 425–26; Kuhlmann, *LL* (June 3, 1923), p. 197; *Rb* (Nov. 27, 1925); Pflister, *Rb* (Feb. 18, 1926).

[35] Rade, *CW* (Nov. 14, 1918), p. 436; *Rb* (April 23, 1919); Siegmund-Schultze, *Die Eiche* (Dec. 1919), pp. 247–48; ibid. (Jan. 1921), p. 37; *Ref.* (April 27, 1919), p. 133; *LL* (Sept. 27, 1925), pp. 626–27.

[36] Troeltsch, *Spektator-Briefe,* p. 223; *LL* (July 6, 1919), p. 368; Rüffer, *Rb* (Dec. 24, 1925).

[37] See, e.g., *EK* (Aug. 24, 1919), p. 406; Boeck, *EB* (April 25, 1920), pp. 733–35; Haarbeck, *RK* (Feb. 15, 1920), p. 51; Burkhardt, *GB, 1* (1922–

24), 201–3; *LL* (June 8, 1924), pp. 331–33; *LL* (Aug. 30, 1925), p. 564; *LL* (Jan. 2, 1927), p. 9; Dibelius, *ED* (Sept. 26, 1926), pp. 305–6.

[38] *CW* (May 24, 1923), pp. 307–11.

[39] Rade, *CW* (Dec. 25, 1919), p. 834; Devaranne, *Proth.* (April 17, 1920), pp. 164–66; Siegmund-Schultze, *Die Eiche* (Oct. 1924), pp. 491–98.

[40] See, e.g., Traub, *EB* (Sept. 14, 1924), p. 201; *LL* (Oct. 5, 1924), pp. 602–3.

[41] Kirchenausschuss minutes (Feb. 8–10, 1921), *Gen.* XII 102 V, *Anlage B*.

[42] *RK* (March 13, 1921), pp. 62–63.

[43] *LL* (Dec. 3, 1922), p. 620. In *Central European History {CEH}*, see: Sally Marks, "Reparations Reconsidered: A Reminder," *2* (1969), 356–65, and "The Myths of Reparations," *11* (1978), 231–55; David Felix, "Reparations Reconsidered with a Vengeance," *4* (1971), 171–79.

[44] Kirchenausschuss minutes (Feb. 8–10, 1921), *Gen.* XII 102 V, *Anlage B*.

[45] Troeltsch, *Spektator-Briefe*, p. 177. Also see *AELK* (Feb. 4, 1921), p. 76, and (May 20, 1921), p. 315.

[46] *Ref.* (Feb. 13, 1921), p. 13, and (May 15, 1921), p. 37. Also see *AELK* (March 31, 1922), pp. 204–5; *LL* (March 26, 1922), pp. 172–74.

[47] *Die Eiche* (Jan. 1924), p. 4; *LL* (April 1, 1923), p. 115; Traub, *EB* (Feb. 11, 1923), p. 504; *AELK* (Feb. 2, 1923), p. 76; *GB*, *1* (1922–24), 39.

[48] As quoted in *KJ*, *50* (1923), 357–61.

[49] *KJ*, *51* (1924), 19.

[50] *CW* (Feb. 8, 1923), p. 94.

[51] Kirchenausschuss minutes (Feb. 27–28, 1923), *Gen.* XII 102 V, *Anlage I*.

[52] *CW* (May 24, 1923), pp. 317–18).

[53] *Die Eiche* (July/Oct. 1923), p. 140. See pp. 207–11, 220–24.

[54] See, e.g., *EB* (April 22, 1923), pp. 662–63; *LL* (April 29, 1923), pp. 150–52; *AELK* (Oct. 5, 1923), p. 644; *AELK* (Jan. 25, 1924), pp. 59–60; Rade, *CW* (Dec. 6, 1923), p. 749; *GB*, *1* (1922–24), 146, 161–62, 166, 209.

[55] Werner Liebe, *Die Deutschnationale Volkspartei 1918–1924* (Düsseldorf, 1956), pp. 18, 21–22, 51, 61, 74–79, 104–5.

[56] For Laible's views in *AELK*, see: (May 30, 1924), pp. 346–47; (June 6, 1924), p. 363; (July 18, 1924), p. 459; (Sept. 5, 1924), pp. 571–72; (Sept. 19, 1924), p. 619. For Gauger's views in *LL*, see: (May 4, 1924), pp. 250–51; (July 13, 1924), pp. 406–7; (Sept. 21, 1924), pp. 569–71. Also see *GB*, *1* (1922–24), 271–83, 304–15; 317–18, 324–27, 338–53.

[57] Kirchenausschuss minutes (Nov. 4–5, 1925), *Gen.* XII 102 VI, p. 11.

[58] *LL* (Sept. 21, 1924), p. 571. Also see, e.g., *IM* (Jan. 1923), pp. 1–2; *AELK* (Nov. 28, 1924), p. 67; Wilhelm Zoellner, *Die ökumenische Arbeit des Deutschen Evangelischen Kirchenausschuss und die Kriegsschuldfrage* (Berlin, 1931), pp. 19–20, 46, in *Gen.* IX 67 I.

[59] Kirchenausschuss minutes (Nov. 16–18, 1922), *Gen.* XII 102 V, *Anlage 5*. The appeal was not sent.

[60] Siegmund-Schultze, *Die Eiche, 8* (1920), 73–119; T. Kaftan, *Die Eiche, 9* (1921), 200–212; Siegmund-Schultze, *Die Eiche, 12* (1924), 2–3; Rade, *CW* (May 22, 1919), pp. 326–28; Rade, *CW* (Oct. 13, 1921), p. 746; Rade, *CW* (Nov. 20, 1924), pp. 966–67.

[61] *AELK* (Oct. 14, 1921), pp. 648–51. See T. Kaftan's comments on extreme German views of war guilt in *Die Eiche, 10* (1922), 249.

[62] Siegmund-Schultze, *Die Eiche, 12* (1924), 563–66; *Die Eiche, 13* (1925), 157–59. Respect for the German Association, heretofore suspect for its pacifism, grew among churchmen because of this request.

[63] *Die Eiche, 13* (1925), 191–93.

[64] Kirchenausschuss minutes (June 24–25, 1925), *Gen.* XII 102 VI, pp. 15–19.

[65] Klingemann, *EB* (Dec. 6, 1925), p. 404; Adolf Deissmann, *Die Stockholmer Bewegung* (Berlin, 1927), pp. 17–18.

[66] G. K. A. Bell, ed., *The Stockholm Conference 1925* (London, 1926), pp. 41, 82; Deissmann, *Die Stockholmer Bewegung,* p. 87; *AELK* (Sept. 13, 1925), pp. 686–88; *EB* (Dec. 6, 1925), p. 404.

[67] Bell, ed., *The Stockholm Conference 1925,* p. 446. Also see Adolf Deissmann, ed., *Die Stockholmer Weltkirchenkonferenz* (Berlin, 1926), 75–78.

[68] In Bell, ed., *The Stockholm Conference 1925,* see speeches by Klingemann (p. 451) and Wolff (pp. 536–37). Also see Staehlin, *Zeitwende, 2* (1925), 491, and Brunstäd's speech in Herring, *DP* (Dec. 29, 1925), p. 939.

[69] Bell, ed., *The Stockholm Conference 1925,* p. 452. Also see Klingemann, *EB* (Dec. 6, 1925), p. 404; Laible, *AELK* (Sept. 25, 1925), p. 711.

[70] Laible, *AELK* (Sept. 25, 1925), pp. 711–13.

[71] Bell, ed., *The Stockholm Conference 1925,* p. 450. On caucus debates over war guilt, see Kirchenausschuss minutes (Nov. 4–5, 1925), *Gen.* XII 102 VI, p. 8; Simons, *DP* (Jan. 26, 1926), p. 60; Deissmann, *VGS, 1* (1927), 624; Zoellner, *Die ökumenische Arbeit,* pp. 22–23.

[72] Bell, ed., *The Stockholm Conference 1925,* pp. 450–52. President Pechmann later corrected the misunderstanding that Klingemann's speech had been as official as the Kapler declaration (p. 716). But he added "that among many friends both within and without the German delegation, for whom Dr. Klingemann has spoken from the heart and the conscience, there is none who would side with him more joyfully and more thankfully than I do." See Deissmann's criticism of the speech in *Die Stockholmer Bewegung,* pp. 98–101.

[73] Bell, ed., *The Stockholm Conference 1925,* p. 712.

[74] Charles Henry Brent, *Understanding* (New York, 1926), p. 11. See Deissmann, *Die Stockholmer Bewegung,* pp. 137–39; Kirchenausschuss minutes (Nov. 4–5, 1925), *Gen.* XII 102 VI, p. 9.

[75] Brown, *Toward a United Church* (New York, 1946), p. 85. See Alfred E. Garvie, *Memories and Meanings of My Life* (London, 1938), p. 196.

[76] *Minutes of the Meeting of the Continuation Committee August 26–30th, 1926,*

Berne, Switzerland (London, n.d.), pp. 20–21. See Hadorn, *Die Eiche, 14* (1926), 72.

[77] Rische, *DP* (May 12, 1925), pp. 330–31; Rische, *DP* (Nov. 24, 1925), pp. 838–40; Rische, *Rb* (Nov. 4, 1925). Also see Pfannkuche, *EB* (Sept. 27, 1925), p. 222; Füllkrug, *IM* (Oct. 1925), pp. 289–90; *AELK* (Oct. 23, 1925), pp. 802–3.

[78] *Die Eiche, 13* (1925), 350–76. Other critics: Hermelink, *CW* (Oct. 15, 1925), pp. 925–35; Heiler, *CW* (Nov. 5, 1925), pp. 991–97; Laun, *DP* (Nov. 3, 1925), pp. 775–77; Herring, *DP* (Jan. 5, 1926), pp. 1–3; Gaertner, *Die Eiche, 14* (1926), 56–69.

[79] *Die Eiche, 14* (1926), 72–88; Keller, *CW* (Dec. 17, 1925), 1184–85. Offensive commentaries in *AELK:* (Sept. 11, 1925), pp. 663–66; (Sept. 18, 1925), pp. 686–89; (Sept. 25, 1925), pp. 707–13; (Oct. 2, 1925), pp. 724–27.

[80] See, e.g., Kirchenausschuss minutes (Nov. 4–5, 1925), *Gen.* XII 102 VI, p. 8; Klingemann, *EB* (Dec. 6, 1925), pp. 402–8.

[81] *Die Eiche, 14* (1926), 186–89.

[82] Kirchenausschuss minutes (March 4–5, 1926), *Gen.* XII 102 VI, pp. 10–16. The Kirchenausschuss was outraged by Siegmund-Schultze's breach of confidentiality. It was also worried lest his charges damage relations with foreign churches because he could claim to know the delegation's inner mind. Bishop Ludwig Ihmels of the Saxon Landeskirche agreed to publish an article (*ED* [April 11, 1926], pp. 115–16) in the delegation's defense.

[83] *VKt* (1927), pp. 122–26, 136–42; *VGS, 1* (1927), 12.

[84] Raack, *PK* (March 1926), pp. 69–70.

[85] *Minutes of the Meeting of the Continuation Committee, 1926*, pp. 21–23. Also see Garvie, *Memories*, pp. 198–99; Monod, *Après la journée*, p. 263; Siegmund-Schultze, *Die Eiche, 14* (1926), 397–98; Zoellner, *Die ökumenische Arbeit*, pp. 33–41; Nils Ehrenström, "Movements for International Friendship and Life and Work, 1925–1948," in *Ecumenical Movement*, p. 566.

[86] Rische, *Neue Preussische (Kreuz-) Zeitung* (June 16, 1927) in *Beiheft* to *Gen.* IX 67 I; Rische, *Rb* (July 20, 1927).

[87] See, e.g., Philipps, *Rb* (Dec. 6, 1927).

[88] *Die Eiche, 14* (1926), 399–400. Siegmund-Schulze also reasoned that German churches, by settling for a moral declaration, missed their chance for an investigation of war origins—outside of the ecumenical movement.

[89] Kirchenausschuss minutes (Dec. 8–9, 1926), *Gen.* XII 102 VI, p. 32; *VGS, 1* (1927), 625–28.

[90] In its proclamation of June 1, 1929, upon the tenth anniversary of the Versailles treaty, the Kirchenausschuss traced the injustices of the peace to war guilt. Taking up the thread left at Bern, the proclamation urged an investigation of war guilt. (Zoellner, *Die ökumenische Arbeit*, pp. 44–45.) The Kirchenausschauss did not, however, notify foreign churches of the proclamation. In June 1931, Paul

Althaus and Emanuel Hirsch launched a public attack on any official ecumenical ties whatever. Communion with those whose governments suppressed the German folk, they charged, seemed all too fraudulent to defend. (Klaus Scholder, *Die Kirchen und das Dritte Reich,* 1 [Frankfurt/M. 1977], 212–14.) Apparently to demonstrate the national value of such ties, Kapler began cautiously to press the cause of revisionism with foreign churches. (See correspondence attached to letter, Kapler to church governments [June 20, 1931], *Gen.* IX 67 I.) He took sharp exception, however, to the Old-Prussian Church Senate's request of October 10, 1931, whose critical amendment, passed by a mere 18 to 15, urged withdrawal from the movement if revisionism failed to carry the day. A policy of threat, Kapler believed, would destroy personal relations with foreign churchmen and thus dim prospects for revision and damage the ecumenical cause. Such a threat the Kirchen-ausschuss declined to include in its proclamation to foreign churches of October 23, 1931, which, however, plumped for revision by coupling injustices and war guilt. (Church Senate minutes [Oct. 9–10, 1931], *Gen.* II 48 II, pp. 53–57, 59. Church Senate request and Kirchenausschuss proclamation in *Gen.* IX 67 I. See also J.R.C. Wright, *'Above Parties'* [London, 1974], pp. 70–73.)

[91] *Rb* (Sept. 2, 1925); *Rb* (Oct. 21, 1925); *Rb* (Nov. 28, 1925); *Rb* (Dec. 29, 1925); *Rb* (Nov. 16, 1926); *LL* (Nov. 29, 1925), pp. 765–67; *LL* (Dec. 13, 1925), pp. 796–97; *GB, 2* (1925), 323–40, 369–70; *AELK* (June 26, 1925), p. 451; *AELK* (Oct. 30, 1925), pp. 819–20; *AELK* (Nov. 6, 1925), pp. 841–42; *AELK* (Nov. 27, 1925), pp. 914–15.

Old-Prussian churchmen had good reason to resent the new eastern boundary. Of the two Evangelical churches affected by territorial cessions, the Old-Prussian church lost the lion's share by far, almost entirely in the East. Still church leaders refused to join the cause of German Irrendentism, for fear of provoking Eastern governments (particularly Poland) and cutting church ties to over a million parishioners.

Congregations and synods that found themselves in ceded areas remained tenaciously loyal to the Old-Prussian church, and the mother church managed to keep them within her fold to an extent that varied with each area. The ethnically German Free City of Danzig allowed its Protestant constituency (207, 286) to reorganize as an Old-Prussian church province. In 1925, two years after Lithuania had seized Memel, the Old-Prussian church reached an accord with the new Lithuanian state by which Protestants in Memel territory (133,330) formed an autonomous church province. The Memel accord amounted to an Evangelical concordat that obliged the principle of self-determination proclaimed by the Old-Prussian church since the war: congregations themselves, not the new states in the East, should determine church affiliation. Such a principle the new Polish state (as well as French authorities in the Saar in 1919 and Lithuania in 1924) refused to recognize. Church ties with the homeland might cultivate an undesirable sense of German identity. Because agreement with Poland eluded the Old-Prussian church throughout the 1920s, the mother church's ties with her largest diaspora church, the United Evangelical Church in Poland (concentrated largely in the former provinces of West Prussia and Posnania), were not assured internationally, though the Polish church deputized delegates to the Old-Prussian General Synod. Especially until 1926, Poland consciously discriminated against its German minority and its new Evangelical church. Between the end of the war and 1925, the German Evangelical population in this area dwindled from upwards of 900,000 to possibly as low as 300,000, German Protestants returning to the fatherland either voluntarily or under duress. By contrast, the small United Evangelical Church in Polish Upper Silesia (55,372), after the plebiscite and partition, came under the protection of a German-Polish agreement in 1922 that allowed this diaspora church, while formally independent, close relations with the mother church. In the West, congregations and synods in the Prussian Saar remained in the Rhine province of the Old-Prussian church. (EOK report to the General Synod, *VGS, 2* [1925], 287–304; Gotthold Rhode, "Das Deutschtum in Posen und Pommerellen in der Zeit der Weimarer Republik" in *Die deutschen Ostgebiete zur Zeit der Weimarer Republik* [Cologne, 1966], pp. 92–124; Kurt Nowak, *Evangelische Kirche und Weimarer Republik* [Göttingen, 1981], pp. 109–16. Figures in parentheses are from the 1910 census. The EOK report sets the dwindling German Evangelical population at 300,000 [p. 298], perhaps too low [see Rhode, p. 99].)

[92] *CW* (Nov. 5, 1925), p. 970.

[93] Dibelius, *ED* (Sept. 26, 1926), pp. 305–6; Jordan, *Die Eiche, 15* (1927), 313–14.

[94] *CW* (Sept. 23, 1926), pp. 881–82.

[95] *AELK* (Feb. 11, 1927), p. 140. Also see *AELK* (Sept. 17, 1926), p. 906; *Rb* (Jan. 23, 1927); *Rb* (Feb. 6, 1927); *LL* (Jan. 3, 1926), p. 8; *LL* (Aug. 15, 1926), p. 518; *LL* (Sept. 26, 1926), pp. 616–19.

[96] See, e.g., *LL* (Sept. 27, 1927), pp. 634–35; *RK* (Oct. 2, 1927), pp. 318–19.

[97] Quoted in *Rb* (Sept. 20, 1927).

[98] *Die Eiche, 16* (1928), 9.

VOLKSKIRCHE ACTIVISM: THE STATE

[1] *Rb* (June 26, 1927).

[2] See, e.g., *AELK* (Jan. 24, 1919), pp. 79–80; *LL* (Feb. 16, 1919), p. 87; *EK* (June 22, 1919), p. 298; *Ref.* (Aug. 10, 1919), p. 252.

[3] *CW* (May 20, 1920), pp. 328–30.

[4] Ernst Troeltsch, *Spektator-Briefe,* ed. H. Baron (Tübingen, 1924), p. 56.

[5] Loesen, *Rb* (Feb. 26, 1926). See, e.g., *EK* (March 2, 1919), pp. 105–6; *EK* (Dec. 21, 1919), p. 612; *Ref.* (Oct. 17, 1920), pp. 198–99; *GB, 1* (1922–24), 19–23, 160; *GB, 4* (1927), 142; *LL* (Oct. 31, 1926), pp. 698–99. Prussian coalition governments, which excluded Nationalists, purged top "political" administrative posts of monarchists, divided these positions among themselves in

proportion to their party strength, and opened up the civil service to republicans. Conservative Protestants reacted angrily to a politicization of the bureaucracy that tended to exclude them. (Hans-Peter Ehni, "Zum Parteienverhältnis in Preussen 1918–1932," *Archiv für Sozialgeschichte, 11* [1971], 246–55; Gotthard Jasper, *Der Schutz der Republik* [Tübingen, 1963], pp. 224–27.) The Barmat scandal aroused public indignation in the years 1924–27. Nationalists accused Socialists of colluding with a Jewish entrepreneur to defraud the government.

[6] Erich Eyck, *A History of the Weimar Republic,* trans. Harlan P. Hanson and Robert G.L. Waite (2 vols. Cambridge, Mass., 1962–63), *1,* 286–89; Larry Eugene Jones, "Inflation, Revaluation, and the Crisis of Middle-Class Politics," *CEH, 12* (1979), 143–68.

[7] *LL* (Nov. 15, 1925), p. 735. Not all church governments responded to the circular. See Kirchenausschuss minutes (June 24–25, 1925), *Gen.* XII 102 VI, pp. 9–11.

[8] *PP* (1925), pp. 347–48; *VKt* (1927), pp. 34–36, 360–65. See also *ED* (July 19, 1925), p. 245; *AELK* (July 24, 1925), pp. 530–31; Kirchenausschuss minutes, *Gen.* XII 102 VI (June 24–25, 1925), pp. 9–11; (Nov. 4–5, 1925), p. 27; (March 23–24, 1927), p. 17 and *Anlage 5*; (Dec. 8–9, 1927), pp. 10–11, 19.

[9] See, e.g., *LL* (Feb. 22, 1920), p. 101; *Ref.* (April 16, 1922), p. 22; *Die Wartburg* [*Wb*] (July 1923), p. 79; *AELK* (Dec. 19, 1924), pp. 828–29; *AELK* (May 28, 1926), pp. 522–23; *Rb* (April 1, 1927); *Rb* (April 30, 1927); *GB, 1* (1922–24), 162–63, 256–57, 342–43; *GB, 2* (1925), 12; *GB, 5* (1928), 105–6.

[10] See, e.g., attitude of President Pechmann of the Church Federation Assembly in Raack, *PK* (Jan. 1927), p. 31.

[11] See, e.g., *LL* (May 16, 1920), pp. 243–44; *LL* (Nov. 18, 1923), p. 365; *AELK* (Nov. 30, 1923), p. 764; *AELK* (Dec. 7, 1923), pp. 779–80; *Rb* (Feb. 7, 1926).

[12] (Nov. 23, 1923), pp. 748–49; (Jan. 25, 1924), p. 58; (May 14, 1926), p. 473; (May 28, 1926), p. 523. See also Ruhkopf, *Rb* (Dec. 22, 1920); *LL* (Nov. 16, 1924), p. 698; Kuhlmann, *GB, 4* (1927), 98–101; *GB, 5* (1928), 236–38.

[13] Rade, *CW* (July 12, 1923), pp. 430–31; Troeltsch, *Spektator-Briefe,* pp. 79, 81, 93. See, e.g., Heimbach, *Ref.* (Dec. 8, 1918), p. 386; *LL* (May 2, 1920), pp. 218–19; Schiller, *Rb* (July 15, 1925); *AELK* (Aug. 19, 1927), pp. 786–87.

[14] *NkZ, 30* (1919), 309–57; *CW* (May 8, 1924), pp. 340–43.

[15] *Die Eiche* (April 1922), pp. 118–20.

[16] *LL* (Sept. 18, 1921), pp. 529–30, and (Oct. 22, 1922), pp. 571–73; *EK* (March 9, 1919), p. 117; *EK* (March 23, 1919), pp. 133–37; *EK* (Nov. 2, 1919), p. 531; *Rb* (July 14, 1919); *CW* (Oct. 30, 1919), pp. 697–99; *ED* (Oct. 24, 1926), pp. 339–40.

[17] *CW* (March 23, 1922), p. 212.

[18] As cited in *Proth.* (April 1, 1922), p. 54.

[19] (March 12, 1922), p. 143.

[20] (March 23, 1922), p. 210.

[21] (April 1, 1922), p. 54.

[22] (Jan./March 1919), pp. 14–15.

[23] (Jan. 19, 1919), p. 22.

[24] *Spektator-Briefe,* pp. 56, 90, 93, 94, 96.

[25] See, e.g., *Rb* (Sept. 17, 1919); *Rb* (Jan. 26, 1924); *Rb* (July 13, 1925); Philipps, *Rb* (Jan. 25, 1927); *Ref.* (Dec. 12, 1920), p. 213; *LL* (Jan. 26, 1919), p. 42; *GB,* 5 (1928), 236–39.

[26] See, e.g., Probst, *Rb* (March 21, 1924); *Rb* (Feb. 3, 1927); Traub, *EB* (Jan. 31, 1926), p. 84.

[27] Walter H. Kaufmann, *Monarchism in the Weimar Republic* (New York, 1953), p. 232.

[28] See, e.g., *AELK* (Oct. 29, 1926), p. 1050; *AELK* (Aug. 12, 1927), pp. 762–63; Boeck, *EB* (Aug. 29, 1927), pp. 564–66.

[29] (Jan. 23, 1927).

[30] In *Gen.* IX 2 II. See *RK* (Nov. 24, 1918), p. 207; Gauger, *LL* (Oct. 22, 1922), p. 572; *AELK* (Jan. 1, 1926), p. 20.

[31] Grenzmark Consistory to EOK (Jan. 11, 1923), *Gen.* IX 2 III. My italics.

[32] Bund religiöser Sozialisten Deutschlands to EOK (Aug. 18, 1922), *Gen.* IX 2 III.

[33] See in *Gen.* IX 2 II correspondence that resulted from the complaint of Hugo Wenke.

[34] Grützmacher to Pomeranian Consistory (Oct. 23, 1922), and Pomeranian Consistory to EOK (Nov. 1, 1922), *Gen.* IX 2 III.

[35] As quoted in *Rb* (Sept. 20, 1925). See *Proth.* (Sept. 3, 1921), p. 305; Pomeranian Consistory to EOK (Oct. 11, 1921), *Gen.* IX 2 III; Hesse, *PK* (Dec. 22, 1918), p. 227; *Rb* (Dec. 5, 1918); *Rb* (Feb. 3, 1927).

[36] In *Gen.* IX 2 III, see EOK to Kultusministerium (Nov. 10, 1922); Boelitz's "answer" to Landtag president (Jan. 13, 1923); Boelitz to EOK (Sept. 3, 1923). Above judgments on the EOK and Kultusministerium are based on their correspondence concerning specific cases found in *Gen.* VI 16 II, IX 2 II, and IX 2 III.

[37] But the EOK did urge the 1925 General Synod to create a new order of service, since, among other reasons, "certain components are no longer usable in the present form because of the transformation of the church constitution and state conditions." (*VGS,* 2 [1925], 190.)

[38] *Proth.* (May 1, 1920), p. 183. See *VGS,* 1 (1920), 6–7, 529–30; *Rb* (May 20, 1919); *CW* (Oct. 28, 1920), p. 700.

[39] *LL* (April 18, 1920), p. 191; *LL* (July 11, 1920), pp. 311–13; Laible, *AELK* (Sept. 30, 1921), p. 619.

[40] In *EB* (Jan. 1, 1922), pp. 437–40; (Jan. 22, 1922), pp. 480–88; (Feb. 11, 1923), pp. 501–5; (Nov. 18, 1923), pp. 332–35; (March 8, 1925), p. 686.

[41] *LL* (April 13, 1924), pp. 202–3; Ruhkopf, *Rb* (Feb. 29, 1924).

[42] *AELK* (Sept. 2, 1921), p. 555; *Ref.* (Sept. 25, 1921), p. 61.

[43] Troeltsch, *Spektator-Briefe*, pp. 112–13, 205–9; *CW* (Sept. 8, 1921), p. 662.

[44] Raack, *PK* (July 1922), p. 83. See *EB* (Oct. 22, 1922), p. 246; *LL* (July 9, 1922), p. 391, and (Aug. 6, 1922), pp. 451–53.

[45] See, e.g., *Ref.* (Aug. 31, 1919), p. 277; *AELK* (June 6, 1924), p. 363; *GB*, 2 (1925), 85–92.

[46] *LL* (Jan. 11, 1925), p. 32; Agnes von Zahn-Harnack, *Adolf von Harnack* (Berlin, 1951), pp. 411–12; *Rb* (Jan. 11, July 31, and Sept. 24, 1927).

[47] *CW* (March 19, 1925), pp. 280–82.

[48] *Rb* (March 10, 1925).

[49] *Rb* (March 17, 1925); *CW* (April 2, 1925), pp. 324–26.

[50] (April 24, 1925), p. 299.

[51] Loess, *Rb* (March 13, 1925); *PU* (March 1925), pp. 22–23; *AELK* (March 27, 1925), p. 218; *LL* (March 29, 1925), p. 210; *GB*, 2 (1925), 82–85, 94.

[52] See, e.g., *AELK* (April 17, 1925), p. 283; *LL* (May 10, 1925), p. 304.

[53] *GB*, 1 (1922–24), 213, 217–18, 240, 244–48, 345–46; *GB*, 2 (1925), 53, 117–23, 127–28, 133–34; *KJ*, 50 (1923), 418–34; *KJ*, 51 (1924), 498–518; *KJ*, 52 (1925), 569–70; *VGS*, 1 (1925), 125, 361; *VGS*, 2 (1925), 334–35; Fritz von der Heydt, *Gute Wehr* (Berlin, 1936), pp. 127–28, 136–39, 145–48. On Catholic aspirations and Protestant reactions, see Heinrich Hermelink, *Katholizismus und Protestantismus in der Gegenwart* (Gotha, 1924). On alleged discrimination against Protestants in school systems, see pp. 150–52 above. As a permanent coalition partner, the Center party managed to increase the Catholic percentage of the bureaucracy by arguing that the monarchy had discriminated against Catholics. (Ehni, "Zum Parteienverhältnis in Preussen," pp. 252–54.)

[54] *CW* (May 1, 1925), pp. 421–22; *ED* (May 2, 1926), p. 143; *Wb* (April 1925), p. 28; Kirchenausschuss minutes in *Gen.* XII 102 VI (March 23–24, 1927), pp. 17–18, and (June 14–15, 1927), p. 8; *VGS*, 1 (1925), 538–47; *VGS*, 1 (1927), 633–36, 651–56; von der Heydt, *Gute Wehr*, pp. 148–49; Klaus Scholder, *Die Kirchen und das Dritte Reich*, 1 (Frankfurt/M, 1977) 65–91.

[55] *LL* (April 12, 1925), pp. 238–42; *CW* (June 1, 1925), pp. 505–10, 512; Mulert, *CW* (July 2, 1925), p. 610; Otto Baumgarten, *Meine Lebensgeschichte* (Tübingen, 1929), p. 465.

[56] *CW* (June 1, 1925), p. 505. Conservative Bavarian Catholics also helped Hindenburg to his narrow victory, refusing to vote for Marx.

[57] *PU* (May 1925), p. 53.

[58] *RK* (May 3, 1925), p. 107.

[59] *Rb* (July 13, 1925); *AELK* (May 1, 1925), p. 315; *AELK* (May 15, 1925), pp. 346–47; *AELK* (May 29, 1925), pp. 378–79; Traub, *EB* (June 21, 1925),

p. 950; *PU* (March 1925), p. 22; *Wb* (May 1925), p. 37; *LL* (May 3, 1925), p. 288; *GB*, 2 (1925), 129–35.

[60] *CW* (June 1, 1925), p. 509.

[61] See Gauger, *GB*, 2 (1925), 175–86; Karl Holl, "Konfessionalität, Konfessionalismus und demokratische Republik," *VfZ*, 17 (1969), 254–75; Baumgarten, *Lebensgeschichte*, pp. 464–66.

[62] Baumgarten, *Lebensgeschichte*, p. 473.

[63] *AELK* (May 15, 1925), p. 347; *LL* (May 10, 1925), pp. 305–7; *GB*, 2 (1925), 175–78, 186; Haun, *PK* (2nd July issue, 1925), p. 165.

[64] *CW* (June 1, 1925), pp. 505–13; *CW* (June 18, 1925), pp. 564–66; Baumgarten, *Lebensgeschichte*, pp. 464–66.

[65] *RK* (June 19, 1927), p. 198.

[66] *VKt* (1927), pp. 340–42; Laible, *AELK* (June 30, 1927), pp. 612–13, and (July 8, 1927), p. 636.

[67] Henry Ashby Turner, Jr., *Stresemann and the Politics of the Weimar Republic* (Princeton, 1963), p. 112.

[68] Kahl's speech, *VKt* (1927), pp. 234–50.

[69] *CW* (July 21, 1927), pp. 653–57.

[70] *Rb* (June 24, 1927).

[71] See pp. 190–92 above. That Althaus's formulations implied a rejection of the Republic is shown by his own example. In his *Leitsätze zur Ethik* (Erlangen, 1928), pp. 60–63, Althaus postulated, as marks of legitimacy, the state's folkish bondedness and sense of responsibility to God untrammeled by majority will. On this basis, in October 1933, he justified his enthusiastic support of the Nazi state, which, consonant with his theology of history, Althaus extolled as God's gift to the German folk. (*Die deutsche Stunde der Kirchen* [Göttingen, 1934], pp. 5–8, 19.)

[72] *Rb* (June 28, 1927).

[73] Troeltsch, *Spektator-Briefe*, p. 221.

[74] J.R.C. Wright, 'Above Parties' (London, 1974), p. 60; Kirchenausschuss minutes (June 14–15), *Gen.* XII 102 VI, pp. 12, 18–19, *Anlagen 3* and 6.

[75] Scholder, *Die Kirchen*, 1, 24, 143. See also Fischer, *Proth.* (July 3, 1927), p. 380; Schoell, *ED* (July 3, 1927), p. 215; Laible, *AELK* (July 8, 1927), pp. 636–37.

[76] *VKt* (1927), pp. 338–40; Füllkrug, *IM* (Aug. 1927), p. 322; Brinckmann, *PU* (Sept. 1927), p. 115.

[77] Scholder, *Die Kirchen*, 1, 143. In "Römer 13, 1–7 in unserer Generation," *Zeitschrift für Theologie und Kirche*, 56 (1959), 316–76, Ernst Käsemann analyzed the difficulties of German theologians in interpreting Romans 13.

[78] *ED* (July 3, 1927), p. 214.

[79] Füllkrug, *IM* (Aug. 1927), p. 322. Nowak and Wright saw a political shift among high church officials toward pragmatic republicanism with Hermann

Kapler's appointment as EOK president in 1925. (Kurt Nowak, *Evangelische Kirche und Weimarer Republik* [Göttingen, 1981], pp. 171–73; Wright, *Above Parties,'* pp 25–26, 50, 58–61.) But ever since the revolution Old-Prussian church officials had acted as Vernunftrepublikaner in releasing tensions between church and state, as this study has illustrated in a variety of ways.

[80] *RGG*, *1* (1927), 1591.

[81] Dibelius, *Nachspiel* (Berlin, 1928), pp. 91–93.

[82] *PU* (Sept. 1926), p. 75.

[83] *Proth.* (May 1, 1920), p. 183, and (Nov. 27, 1920), p. 394.

[84] *VGS*, *1* (1920), 270–77, 530–31.

[85] In Kirchenausschuss minutes, *Gen.* XII 102 VI (June 3–5, 1926), p. 28; (Dec. 8–9, 1926), pp. 39–41; (June 14–15, 1927), pp. 3–4. Also see EOK to Pomeranian Consistory (Aug. 9, 1926), *Gen.* VI 16 II.

[86] In *Proth.* (Nov. 12, 1921), p. 388; (Aug. 15, 1924), pp. 119–22; (May 10, 1925), p. 301; (Oct. 30, 1927), pp. 604–5. Also see Mahling, *Zs* (Oct. 1926), pp. 64–67; Kübel, *Zs* (Jan. 1927), pp. 34–39.

[87] Violet, *PK* (April 1920), p. 38.

[88] *PU* (Sept. 1926), p. 74.

[89] *Rb* (June 12, 1919).

[90] *Rb* (June 19, 1919).

[91] *Rb* (July 9, 23, and 31, 1919; Aug. 8 and 21, 1919).

[92] *CW* (June 28, 1923), pp. 366–68, and (Sept. 20, 1923), p. 576.

[93] *Rb* (May 23, 1919); Günther Dehn, *Die alte Zeit, die vorigen Jahre* (Munich, 1962), pp. 215–21.

[94] *Rb* (April 26, 1919); Knieschke, *Rb* (April 30, 1919); Jentzsch, *Rb* (May 18, 1919); *CW* (May 15, 1919), p. 320; Martin, *CW* (May 29, 1919), p. 356.

[95] See, e.g., Rosenkranz, *CW* (June 28, 1923), pp. 366–67.

[96] *PU* (Sept. 1926), p. 74.

[97] *LL* (Feb. 3, 1924), p. 69.

[98] See, e.g., Baumgarten, *CW* (March 17, 1921), pp. 201–9; *Rb* (May 1, 1924); *ED* (Nov. 8, 1925), p. 357; *LL* (May 6, 1928), pp. 299–300.

[99] Karl-Wilhelm Dahm, *Pfarrer und Politik* (Cologne, 1965) estimated (pp. 25, 148) that 70–80 percent of German Protestant pastors were "conservative-nationalists" and that at most 5–8 percent belonged to each of three other types at their most successful stage: "religious-socialist" in the mid-1920s, "folkish-German faith (deutschgläubig)" at the end of the Republic, and "democratic-liberal." These estimates, drawn from interviews and periodic literature, are necessarily impressionistic. In *Zs* (Jan. 1927), see Mulert, pp. 19–31, and Kübel, pp. 31–38. Also see Herbert Christ, *Der politische Protestantismus in der Weimarer Republik* (diss. University of Bonn, 1967), pp. 273–324.

[100] Representative election calculations of nationalist churchmen can be followed in Josef Gauger's long articles in *GB*, *1* (1922–24), 237–59 and 341–46, before

the two Reichstag elections of 1924. By a process of elimination he settled on the Nationalists in the first election and added the folkish party in the second because of his disillusionment with the Nationalists. Around mid-decade, Christian-Social pietists began to consider independent means of gaining political influence, including the formation of Evangelical parties as an alternative to voting Nationalist. (See Günter Opitz, *Der Christlich-Soziale Volksdienst* [Düsseldorf, 1969], pp. 35–108.)

[101] *Proth.* (July 5, 1925), pp. 418–21. See *CW* (June 18, 1925), pp. 558–60; Mulert, *CW* (July 2, 1925), pp. 605–12; Baumgarten, *Lebensgeschichte,* pp. 464–70.

[102] Eyck, *Weimar Republic, 2,* 62–66; Kaufmann, *Monarchism,* pp. 160–63.

[103] In *Beiheft* to *Gen.* II 32 I: congregation of Wendisch-Silkow to Kapler (April 4, 1926); Winckler to Kapler (April 5, 1926); Schwerin to Kapler (April 9, 1926); Kapler to Winckler (April 14, 1926); Pomeranian Provinzialkirchenrat to Church Senate (April 26, 1926). Also resolution of confessional Lutherans in *Rb* (May 5, 1926).

[104] Church Senate minutes (May 20–21, 1926), *Gen.* III 48 I, pp. 5–6. Also see Kapler to Kirchenausschuss (May 22, 1926), *Beiheft* to *Gen.* II 32 I.

[105] Kirchenausschuss minutes (June 3–5, 1926), *Gen.* XII 102 VI, pp. 10–12 and 15–16, *Anlage* 3. A minority of the Kirchenausschuss opposed any declaration for fear of alienating parishioners in a moral issue that had already stirred political passions. Also see Kapler to Kirchenausschuss (April 21, 1926), *Beiheft* to *Gen.* II 32 I.

[106] Kuhlmann, *LL* (April 11, 1926), p. 234; Michaelis, *LL* (May 30, 1926), pp. 347–49; *LL* (June 13, 1926), pp. 375–77; Loess, *Rb* (Jan. 22, 1926); Ruhkopf, *Rb* (March 6, 1926); Behm, *Rb* (March 30, 1926); *RK* (June 13, 1926), p. 190; *AELK* (April 23, 1926), pp. 401–2. See Gauger's survey of the church press in *GB, 3* (1926), 226–31, 246–54.

[107] Anhalt Landeskirchenrat to EOK (June 21, 1926), *Beiheft* to *Gen.* II 32 I.

[108] *CW* (June 10, 1926), pp. 564–65.

[109] Kirchenausschuss to church governments (July 7, 1926), *Beiheft* to *Gen.* II 32 I.

[110] Frankfurt Landeskirchenrat to Kirchenausschuss (May 14, 1926), *Beiheft* to *Gen.* II 32 I.

[111] *GB, 3* (1926), 224–25; *CW* (July 8, 1926), pp. 642–43.

[112] In *CW* (April 8, 1926), pp. 345–46; (June 24, 1926), pp. 600–1; (July 8, 1926), pp. 643, 647–49.

[113] Pechmann's position, Kirchenausschuss minutes (June 3–5, 1926), *Gen.* XII 102 VI, p. 11; declaration of Evangelical League, *Rb* (April 18, 1926); Schlawe Kirchenrat (congregation in Pomerania) to EOK (May 3, 1926), *Beiheft* to *Gen.* II 32 I; *GB, 3* (1926), 152–55, 175–76, 228–30, 246–51, 260.

[114] *GB, 3* (1926), 252–53; *CW* (July 8, 1926), p. 658; *CW* (Oct. 7, 1926),

pp. 961–62; Schubring, *Protb.* (July 11, 1926), pp. 419–20; *Protb.* (Oct. 31, 1926), pp. 629–31.

[115] *CW* (May 27, 1926), p. 18; Rhenish Consistory to EOK (July 3, 1926), and Pomeranian Consistory to EOK (Nov. 9, 1926), *Beiheft* to *Gen.* II 32 I.

[116] *VGS, 1* (1927), 50.

[117] As quoted in *ED* (June 20, 1926), p. 199. Also see *CW* (June 10, 1926), p. 566; Rade, *CW* (July 8, 1926), pp. 647–48.

[118] As quoted in Schubring, *Protb.* (July 11, 1926), p. 420.

[119] Thus the Kirchenausschuss declarations before the two 1924 Reichstag elections. (In *AELK:* [April 11, 1924], p. 236; [Nov. 21, 1924], p. 748.)

[120] In *Gen.* VI 16 II: President of Brandenburg Consistory to EOK (Jan. 14, 1919); EOK to Kultusministerium (May 6, 1919).

[121] These seem to have been the questions asked in cases found in *Gen.* VI 16 II.

[122] In *Protb.*, see, e.g., (July 10, 1920), pp. 358–59; (Oct. 4, 1925), pp. 635–36; (Oct. 11, 1925), p. 649; (Dec. 13, 1925), p. 785. Also *CW* (Dec. 16, 1926), p. 1272. I have come across no case in which Old-Prussian church authorities clearly berated republican pastors for affirming the Republic in sermons. Martin Rade cited the case of Pastor Walter Rust to demonstrate the antirepublican bias of church authorities. But the facts of the case do not warrant his conclusion. In his rural Pomeranian congregation, Rust praised President Ebert upon his death for keeping Germany "from sinking into Bolshevism" during the revolution. Rust regretted that Ebert had died before he could clear his name of treason. Thereupon, the patron of the congregation complained that, according to Rade, Rust had advocated socialism and communism. Having examined the sermon, the consistory concluded that Rust had failed two pragmatic tests: he had not couched his remarks in a religious context, and he must have known that his political opinion would affront many in his congregation. Rade also charged that church officials had often failed to take similar steps against rightist sermons. Whether the EOK's efforts matched the problem in the gray area depended, however, on how one defined political neutrality. Rade cited the example of a superintendent who, without apparent reprimand, had compared the hated Republic to the barren fig tree mentioned in Luke 13:6–9. The mere citing of scripture or articulation of Evangelical social sensitivity offered no adequate safeguard against political sermons. Without contesting Rade's point, the EOK would argue that his criticism affected the application of its test, not the test itself. (Rade, *CW* [July 7, 1927], pp. 624–28.)

[123] Kapler to Winckler (April 14, 1926), *Beiheft* to *Gen.* II 32 I; minutes of meeting of EOK with general superintendents (Sept. 28, 1928), *Gen.* VI 16 II, p. 3.

[124] Graue to EOK (March 8, 1926), *Gen.* VI 16 II.

[125] EOK to consistories (April 17, 1926), *Gen.* VI 16 II; Schian to EOK (Dec. 1, 1926), *Gen.* VI 16 II.

[126] Minutes of meeting of EOK with general superintendents (Sept. 28, 1928), *Gen.* VI 16 II, p. 2; Rhenish Consistory to EOK (Feb. 5, 1927), *Gen.* VI 16 II.

[127] In *Gen.* VI 16 II: Trendelenburg to EOK (Nov. 2, 1926); EOK to Kultusministerium (Jan. 31, 1927).

[128] Minutes of meeting of EOK with general superintendents (Sept. 28, 1928), *Gen.* VI 16 II, pp. 1–2.

[129] EOK to Kultusministerium (Jan. 31, 1927), *Gen.* VI 16 II.

[130] Brandenburg Consistory to EOK (Feb. 5, 1927), *Gen.* VI 16 II; *CW* (Oct. 7, 1926), p. 980.

[131] In *Gen.* VI 16 II: E. Pr. Consistory to Sembill (Dec. 7, 1926); Sembill to EOK (Dec. 11, 1926).

[132] *EB* (March 22, 1925), pp. 728–29; James M. Diehl, *Paramilitary Politics in Weimar Germany* (Bloomington, Ind., 1977), pp. 169–75, 190–243.

[133] Traue, (Jan. 1925), pp. 174–75, and (July 1925), pp. 463–64.

[134] *EB* (March 8, 1925), p. 700, and (March 22, 1925), p. 729.

[135] See, e.g., *GB, 4* (1927), 128–34, and *DP:* (Nov. 3, 1925), pp. 784–85; (Nov. 17, 1925), p. 824; (May 11, 1926), pp. 369–74; (June 15, 1926), pp. 475–76.

[136] (Nov. 30, 1924), p. 286; minutes of meeting of EOK with general superintendents (Sept. 28, 1928), *Gen.* VI 16 II, p. 3.

[137] Rade, *CW* (July 7, 1927), p. 623; *Proth.* (Nov. 27, 1920), p. 394.

GLOSSARY

Consistory	central administrative bureau in each church province
Deutscher Evangelischer Kirchenausschuss	German Evangelical Church Committee, the executive committee of the Church Federation
Deutschtum	"Germanness," the Germanic ethos
Evangelischer Oberkirchenrat (EOK)	Evangelical High (Supreme) Council, the central administrative bureau of the Old-Prussian church, located in Berlin-Charlottenburg (West Berlin)
General Superintendent	highest clerical official in a church province
General Synod	highest representative church assembly in the Old-Prussian church
Generalsynodalvorstand (GSV)	Executive Committee of the General Synod
Kirchenbund	Church Federation
Kirchentag	Church Assembly of the Church Federation
Kulturkampf	"conflict of cultures," state persecution of the Catholic church in the 1870s, connoting thereafter any state persecution of organized religion
Kultusministerium	State Ministry of Culture; full Prussian name as decreed on November 15, 1918: Ministerium für Wissenschaft, Kunst, und Volksbildung (Ministry for Science, Art, and Public Education)
Land	territorial state
Landeskirche	territorial church, a traditionally established church

summus episcopus	supreme bishop, a position held by the Prussian king in the Old-Prussian church until the Revolution of 1918
Superintendent	highest clerical and administrative official of each church district (Kreis)
Vertrauensrat	Council of Confidants
völkisch	adjective referring to the values of the folk
Volksschule	folk school, elementary school
Volkstum	folk ethos

SOURCES AND BIBLIOGRAPHY

MANUSCRIPT COLLECTIONS (EOK FILES) AT THE ARCHIV DER
EVANGELISCHEN KIRCHE DER UNION, WEST BERLIN

Generalia:	II	27	II	On separation of church and state.
	II	32	I	On dispossessing princes.
			(Beiheft)	
	III	48	I	Church Senate minutes.
	VI	2	I	On participation of pastors and church officials in political organizations.
	VI	16	II	On political conduct of church and pastors.
	IX	2	II	On royal intercessory prayer.
	IX	67	I	On war guilt.
	XII	102	IV–VI	Kirchenausschuss minutes.
	XII	154	I	On forming a church federation.
	XIV	20	V	On school supervision.
	XIV	37	I–VI	On religious instruction and parents' councils.
	XIV	37	VI	On the Dortmund school strike.
			(Beiheft A)	

TRANSCRIPTS

Bericht über die Verhandlungen der ausserordentlichen Kirchenversammlung zur Feststellung der Verfassung für die evangelische Landeskirche der älteren Provinzen Preussens von 24. bis 30. September 1921 und vom 29. August bis 29. September 1922, 2 vols. Berlin, 1923.

Verhandlungen der ausserordentlichen Versammlung der siebten Generalsynode der evangelischen Landeskirche Preussens, 2 vols. Berlin, Wiegandt & Grieben, 1920.

Verhandlungen der achten Generalsynode der evangelischen Kirche der altpreussischen Union in ihrer ordentlichen Tagung eröffnet am 5. Dezember 1925, geschlossen am 15. Dezember 1925, 2 vols. Berlin, Martin Warneck, 1926.

Verhandlungen der achten Generalsynode der Evangelischen Kirche der altpreussischen Union in ihrer ausserordentlichen Tagung eröffnet am 23. April 1927, geschlossen am 12. Mai 1927, 2 vols. Berlin, Martin Warneck, 1927.

Verhandlungen des 1. deutschen evangelischen Kirchentages 1919, Berlin-Steglitz, Kirchenausschuss & Evangelischer Pressverband, 1919.

Verhandlungen des 2. deutschen evangelischen Kirchentages 1921, Berlin-Steglitz, Kirchenausschuss & Evangelischer Pressverband, 1921.

Verhandlungen des ersten deutschen evangelischen Kirchentages 1924, Berlin-Steglitz, Kirchenausschuss & Evangelischer Pressverband, 1924.

Verhandlungen des zweiten deutschen evangelischen Kirchentages 1927, Berlin-Steglitz, Kirchenausschuss & Evangelischer Pressverband, 1927.

PERIODIC LITERATURE (AND YEARS CONSULTED)

Research centered around periodicals from which a conceptual view of the church's role in society was likely to emerge. In selecting periodicals, the author relied on the judgments of August Hinderer, director of the Evangelischer Pressverband für Deutschland, whose analysis of the Evangelical church press is found in *RGG,* 4 (1930), 1448–56. The periodic literature examined for this book represented virtually every important church party or group and large free association that operated in the territory of the Old-Prussian church.

Allgemeine evangelisch-lutherische Kirchenzeitung (1916–27). Confessional Lutheran and nationalist conservative. Organ of the General Evangelical-Lutheran Conference. The most widely circulated Protestant church periodical in Germany.

Allgemeines Kirchenblatt für das evangelische Deutschland (1917–27). Official publication of the Church Federation.

Die christliche Welt (1916–27). Democratic liberal.

Deutsches Pfarrerblatt (1924–27). Professional journal of pastors' societies.

Die Deutschkirche (1922–27). Racist folkish. Organ of the League for a German Church.

Die Dorfkirche (1921–25). Cultural folkish. Organ of an association of country pastors.

Die Eiche (1914–28). Organ of the German Association of the World Alliance.

Eiserne Blätter (1919–27). Nationalist liberal.

Das evangelische Deutschland (1924–27). Semiofficial periodical of the Church Federation.

Evangelische Kirchen-Zeitung (1919–20). Confessional Lutheran and nationalist conservative. Organ of the confessional Lutheran church party.

Geisteskampf der Gegenwart (1918–27). Nationalist and apologetical monthly.

Gotthard-Briefe (1922–27). Pietist and nationalist conservative.

Die Innere Mission im evangelischen Deutschland (1920–27). Organ of Central Committee of the Inner Mission.

Licht und Leben (1917–27). Pietist and nationalist conservative.

Neue kirchliche Zeitschrift (1917–27). Scholarly Lutheran journal.

Preussische Kirchenzeitung (1920–27). Organ of the Middle church party.

Preussisches Pfarrarchiv (1918–27). Published church and state decrees and laws.

Positive Union (1917–19, 1925–27). Orthodox and nationalist conservative. Organ of the largest church party.

Protestantenblatt (1917–27). Church liberal.

Protestantische Monatshefte (1916–21). Church liberal.

Die Reformation (1917–22). Positive Unionist and nationalist conservative.

Reformirte Kirchenzeitung (1917–27). Organ of the Reformed (Calvinist) League of Germany.

Der Reichsbote (1919–20, 1924–27). Orthodox and nationalist conservative. Political daily that catered to rightist pastors (lacks pagination).

Die Wartburg (1917–27). Nationalist liberal. Oriented toward the antiultramontane Evangelical League.

Zeitwende (1925–27). Cultural monthly.

Der Zusammenschluss (1926–28). Promoted confessional peace and cooperation.

BOOKS AND ARTICLES

Included in this bibliography are only those entries in the notes that most directly aided the preparation of this book. Included as well are items, not cited in the notes, that cover important aspects of this study's general thesis.

Alexander, Thomas, *The Prussian Elementary Schools,* New York, Macmillan, 1918.

Althaus, Paul, *Staatsgedanken und Reich Gottes,* Langensalza, Gesellschaft "Deutscher Staat," 1923.

Andersen, Friedrich, *Der deutsche Heiland,* Munich, Deutscher Volksverlag, 1921.

Anschütz, Gerhard, *Die Verfassung des Deutschen Reichs vom 11. August 1919. Ein Kommentar für Wissenschaft und Praxis,* 4th ed. Berlin, G. Stilke, 1933.

Arndt, Ino, "Die Judenfrage im Licht der evangelischen Sonntagsblätter von 1918–1933," manuscript Ph.D. thesis, University of Tübingen, 1960.

Balzer, Friedrich-Martin, "Kirche und Klassenbindung in der Weimarer Republik," in *Kirche und Klassenbindung,* ed. Yorick Spiegel, Frankfurt/M., Suhrkamp, 1974.

Baumgarten, Otto et al., *Geistige und sittliche Wirkungen des Krieges in Deutschland,* Stuttgart, Deutsche Verlags-Anstalt, 1927.

Baumgarten, Otto, *Meine Lebensgeschichte,* Tübingen, J. C. B. Mohr (Paul Siebeck), 1929.

Bell, G.K.A., ed., *The Stockholm Conference 1925*, London, Humphrey Milford, 1926.

Bergsträsser, Ludwig, *Geschichte der politischen Parteien in Deutschland*, 11th ed. Munich, Günter Olzog, 1965.

Besier, Gerhard, *Krieg—Frieden—Abrüstung. Die Haltung der europäischen und amerikanischen Kirchen zur Frage der deutschen Kriegsschuld 1914–1933. Ein kirchenhistorischer Beitrag zur Friedensforschung und Friedenserziehung*, Göttingen, Vandenhoeck and Ruprecht, 1982.

Bien, Alexander, "Der moderne Antisemitismus und seine Bedeutung für die Judenfrage," *VfZ, 6* (1966), 340–60.

Bigler, Robert M., *The Politics of German Protestantism. The Rise of the Protestant Church Elite in Prussia, 1815–1848*, Berkeley, University of California Press, 1972.

Boelitz, Otto, *The Reorganization of Education in Prussia*, trans. I.L. Kandel and Thomas Alexander, New York, Teachers College, 1927.

Brakelmann, Günter, ed., *Der deutsche Protestantismus im Epochenjahr 1917*, Witten, Luther-Verlag, 1974.

Brakelmann, Günter, *Protestantische Kriegstheologie im Ersten Weltkrieg. Reinhold Seeberg als Theologe des deutschen Imperialismus*. Bielefeld, Luther-Verlag, 1974.

Bredt, Johannes Victor, *Neues evangelisches Kirchenrecht für Preussen*, 3 vols. Berlin, Georg Stilke, 1921–28.

Breipohl, Renate, *Religiöser Sozialismus und bürgerliches Geschichtsbewusstsein zur Zeit der Weimarer Republik*, Zürich, Theologischer Verlag, 1971.

Brunstäd, Friedrich, *Deutschland und der Sozialismus*, 2nd ed. Berlin, Otto Elener, 1927.

———, *Die Staatsideen der politischen Parteien*, Berlin, Vossische Buchhandlung, 1920.

———, *Völkisch-nationale Erneuerung*, Berlin, Deutschnationale Schriftenvertriebs-stelle, 1921.

Buchheim, Hans, *Glaubenskrise im dritten Reich*, Stuttgart, Deutsche Verlags-Anstalt, 1953.

Buchheim, Karl, *Geschichte der christlichen Parteien in Deutschland*, Munich, Kösel-Verlag, 1953.

Cazelles, Henri, *Église et état en Allemagne de Weimar aux premières années du IIIe Reich*, Paris, Rousseau et Cie., 1936.

Chanady, Attlia, "The Disintegration of the German National People's Party 1924–1930," *Journal of Modern History*, 39 (1967), 65–91.

Christ, Herbert, *Der politische Protestantismus in der Weimarer Republik. Eine Studie über die politische Meinungsbildung durch die evangelischen Kirchen im Spiegel der Literatur und der Presse*, Ph.D. thesis, University of Bonn, 1966.

Cohn, Norman, *Warrant for Genocide. The Myth of the Jewish World Conspiracy and the Protocols of the Elders of Zion*, London, Eyre & Spottiswoode, 1967.

Conway, John, trans., *The Path to Dictatorship 1918–1933. Ten Essays by German Scholars,* Garden City, N.Y., Doubleday, 1966.

Craig, Gorden A., *The Politics of the Prussian Army, 1640–1945,* Oxford, Clarendon Press, 1955.

Cranz, F. Edward, *An Essay on the Development of Luther's Thought on Justice, Law and Society,* Cambridge, Harvard University Press, 1959.

Dahm, Karl-Wilhelm, *Pfarrer und Politik. Soziale Position und politische Mentalität des deutschen evangelischen Pfarrerstandes zwischen 1918 und 1933,* Cologne, Westdeutscher Verlag, 1965.

Dehn, Günther, *Die alte Zeit, die vorigen Jahre. Lebenserinnerungen,* Munich, Christian Kaiser, 1962.

Diessmann, Adolf, *Die Stockholmer Bewegung. Die Weltkirchenkonferenzen zu Stockholm 1925 und Bern 1926 von Innen Betrachtet,* Berlin, Furche, 1927.

Deissmann, Adolf, ed., *Die Stockholmer Weltkirchenkonferenz,* Berlin, Furche, 1926.

Dibelius, Otto, *Friede auf Erden?* Berlin, Furche, 1930.

———, *Das Jahrhundert der Kirche,* Berlin, Furche, 1927.

———, *Nachspiel,* Berlin, Furche, 1928.

Dickmann, Fritz, "Die Kriegsschuldfrage auf der Friedenskonferenz von Paris 1919," *HZ, 197* (1963), 43–99.

Diehl, James M., *Paramilitary Politics in Weimar Germany,* Bloomington, Indiana University Press, 1977.

Dorpalen, Andreas, "The German Conservatives and the Parliamentarization of Imperial Germany," *JCEA, 11* (1951), 184–99.

———, "Wilhelmian Germany—A House Divided against Itself," *JCEA, 15* (1955), 240–47.

[Duske, Johannes], *Denkschrift über den Umfang der Staatsleistungen der deutschen Länder an die evangelischen Kirche bis zur Ablösung,* Berlin-Charlottenburg, Evangelische Kirche der Union, 1928.

Duske, Johannes, *Die Dotationspflicht des preussischen Staates für die allgemeine Verwaltung des evangelischen Kirche der altpreussischen Union,* Berlin, Martin Warneck, 1929.

Ebers, Godehard Josef, ed., *Evangelisches Kirchenrecht in Preussen,* 2 vols. Munich, Max Hueber, 1932.

Eger, Hans, *Der evangelisch-soziale Kongress,* Ph.D. thesis, University of Heidelberg, 1930.

Ehni, Hans-Peter, "Zum Parteienverhältnis in Preussen 1918–1932," *Archiv für Sozialgeschichte, 11* (1971), 241–88.

Elliger, Walter, et al., *Die evangelische Kirche der Union,* Witten, Luther-Verlag, 1967.

Epstein, Klaus, "Der Interfraktionelle Ausschuss und das Problem der Parlamentarisierung 1917–1918," *HZ, 191* (1960), 562–584.

Erbacher, Hermann, ed., *Zeitschriften-Verzeichnis evangelisch-kirchlicher Bibliotheken,* Hannover-Herrenhausen, Verlag des Amtsblattes der Evangelischen kirche in Deutschland, 1962.

Eyck, Erich, *A History of the Weimar Republic,* trans. Harlan P. Hanson and Robert G. L. Waite, 2 vols. Cambridge, Harvard University Press, 1962.

Fischer, Fritz, "Der deutsche Protestantismus und die Politik im 19. Jahrhundert," *HZ, 171* (1951), 473–518.

————, *Germany's Aims in the First World War,* New York, Norton, 1967.

Fischer, Hans Gerhard, *Evangelische Kirche und Demokratie nach 1945. Ein Beitrag zum Problem der politischen Theologie,* Lübeck, Matthiesen, 1970.

Foerster, Erich, *Kirche und Schule in der Weimarer Verfassung,* Gotha, Friedrich Andreas Perthes, 1925.

Frank, Walter, *Hofprediger Adolf Stoecker und die christlich-soziale Bewegung,* Berlin, Reimar Hobbing, 1928.

Führ, Christoph, *Zur Schulpolitik der Weimarer Republik: Darstellung und Quellen,* Weinheim, Julius Beltz, 1970.

Gaede, Reinhard, *Kirche—Christen—Krieg und Frieden. Die Diskussion im deutschen Protestantismus während der Weimarer Zeit,* Hamburg-Bergstedt, Herbert Reich evang. Verlag, 1975.

Gaede, Reinhard, "Die Stellung des deutschen Protestantismus zum Problem von Krieg und Frieden während der Zeit der Weimarer Republik," in *Kirche zwischen Krieg und Frieden. Studien zur Geschichte des deutschen Protestantismus,* ed. Wolfgang Huber and Johannes Schwerdtfeger, Stuttgart, Ernst Klett, 1976.

Gatzke, Hans W., *Germany's Drive to the West,* Baltimore, Johns Hopkins Press, 1950.

Giesecke, Hermann, "Zur Schulpolitik der Sozialdemokraten in Preussen und im Reich 1918/19," *VfZ, 13* (1965), 162–77.

Gordon, Frank Joseph, "The Evangelical Churches and the Weimar Republic, 1918–1933," manuscript Ph.D. thesis, University of Colorado, 1977.

Greschat, Martin, ed., *Der deutsche Protestantismus im Revolutionsjahr 1918/19,* Witten, Luther-Verlag, 1974.

Groh, John E. *Nineteenth Century German Protestantism. The Church as Social Model,* Washington, D.C., University Press of America, 1982.

Grünthal, Günther, *Reichsschulgesetz und Zentrumspartei in der Weimarer Republik,* Düsseldorf, Droste, 1968.

Gutteridge, Richard, *The German Evangelical Church and the Jews 1879–1950,* New York, Barnes & Noble, 1976.

Hartenstein, Wolfgang, *Die Anfänge der Deutschen Volkspartei 1918–1920,* Düsseldorf, Droste, 1962.

Hartung, Fritz, *Deutsche Verfassungsgeschichte,* 6th ed. Stuttgart, K.F. Koehler, 1950.

Hatfield, Douglas W., "Reform in the Prussian Evangelical Church and the Concept of the *Landesherr*," *Church History*, 24 (1982), 553–72.

Heckel, Martin, "Zur Entwicklung des deutschen Staatskirchenrechts von der Reformation bis zur Schwelle der Weimarer Verfassung," *Zeitschrift für evangelisches Kirchenrecht*, 12 (1966), 1–39.

Heienbrok, Wilhelm, ed., *Evangelische Kirchenkunde*, Bielefeld, Velhagen & Klasing, 1929.

Helmreich, Ernst Christian, *Religious Education in German Schools. An Historical Approach*, Cambridge, Harvard University Press, 1959.

Hermelink, Heinrich, *Katholizismus und Protestantismus in der Gegenwart*, Gotha, Friedrich Andreas Perthes, 1924.

Heuss, Theodor, *Friedrich Naumann. Der Mann, Das Werk, Die Zeit*, 2nd ed. Stuttgart, Rainer Wunderlich Verlag Hermann Leins, 1949.

Hintze, Otto, "Die Epochen des evangelischen Kirchenregiments in Preussen," *Regierung und Verwaltung*, 3, ed. Gerhard Oestreich, Göttingen, Vandenhoeck & Ruprecht, 1967.

Hirsch, Emanuel, *Deutschlands Schicksal*, Göttingen, Vandenhoeck & Ruprecht, 1920.

———, *Staat und Kirche im 19. und 20. Jahrhundert*, Göttingen, Vandenhoeck & Ruprecht, 1929.

Hoffmann, Georg, "Das Nachwirken deutscher staatskirchlicher Tradition im evangelischen Kirchenbewusstsein nach 1918," *Ecclesia und Res Publica*, ed. Georg Kretschmar and Bernhard Lohse, Göttingen, Vandenhoeck and Ruprecht, 1961.

Holl, Karl, "Luther und das landesherrliche Kirchenregiment," *Gesammelte Aufsätze zur Kirchengeschichte*, 1, Tübingen, J.C.B. Mohr (Paul Siebeck), 1932.

Holl, Karl, "Konfessionalität, Konfessionalismus, und demokratische Republik—Zu einigen Aspekten der Reichspräsidentenwahl von 1925," *VfZ*, 17 (1969), 254–75.

Holstein, Günther, *Luther und die deutsche Staatsidee*, Tübingen, J.C.B. Mohr (Paul Siebeck), 1926.

Horowitz, Arnold, "Prussian State and Protestant Church in the Reign of Wilhelm II," manuscript Ph.D. thesis, Yale University, 1976.

Israël, Carl, *Geschichte des Reichskirchenrechts dargestellt auf Grund der stenographischen Berichte über die Verhandlungen der Verfassunggebenden Deutschen Nationalversammlung in Weimar*, Berlin, Franz Vahlen, 1922.

Jacke, Jochen, *Kirche zwischen Monarchie und Republik. Der preussische Protestantismus nach dem Zusammenbruch von 1918*, Hamburg, Hans Christians Verlag, 1976.

Jacobi, Gerhard, *Tagebuch eines Grossstadtpfarrers. Briefe an einem Freund*, 9th ed. Berlin, Furche, 1930.

Jasper, Gotthard, *Der Schutz der Republik. Studien zur staatlichen Sicherung der*

Demokratie in der Weimarer Republik 1922–1930, Tübingen, J.C.B. Mohr (Paul Siebeck), 1963.

Jones, Larry Eugene, "Inflation, Revaluation, and the Crisis of Middle-Class Politics: A Study in the Dissolution of the German Party System, 1923–28" *CEH, 12* (1979), 143–68.

Kaufmann, Walter H., *Monarchism in the Weimar Republic,* New York, Bookman Associates, 1953.

Keller, Adolf, and George Stewart, *Protestant Europe. Its Crisis and Outlook,* New York, George H. Doran, 1927.

Kirchliches Jahrbuch für die evangelischen Landeskirchen Deutschlands, ed. Johannes Schneider, Gütersloh, Bertelsmann, 1914–29.

Köhler, Günter, *Die Auswirkungen der Novemberrevolution von 1918 auf die altpreussiche evangelische Landeskirche,* thesis, Kirchliche Hochschule in Berlin, 1967.

Krüger, Peter, "Die Reparationen und das Scheitern einer deutschen Verständigungspolitik auf der Pariser Friedenskonferenz im Jahre 1919," *HZ, 221* (Aug.–Dec. 1975), 326–72.

Kupisch, Karl, "Strömungen der Evangelischen Kirche in der Weimarer Republik," *Archiv für Sozialgeschichte, 11* (1971), 373–415.

———, *Zwischen Idealismus und Massendemokratie,* Berlin, Lettner-Verlad, 1955.

———, *Die deutschen Landeskirchen im 19. und 20. Jahrhundert,* Göttingen, Vandenhoeck & Ruprecht, 1966.

———, ed., *Quellen zur Geschichte des deutschen Protestantismus 1871–1945,* Munich, Siebenstern Taschenbuch Verlag, 1960.

Lidtke, Vernon L., "August Bebel and German Social Democracy's Relation to the Christian Churches," *JHI, 27* (1966), 245–64.

Liebe, Werner, *Die Deutschnationale Volkspartei 1918–1924,* Düsseldorf, Droste, 1956.

Luckau, Alma, ed., *The German Delegation at the Paris Peace Conference. A Documentary Study of Germany's Acceptance of the Treaty of Versailles,* New York, Columbia University Press, 1941.

Mehnert, Gottfried, *Evangelische Kirche und Politik, 1917–1919. Die politische Strömungen im deutschen Protestantismus von der Julikrise 1917 bis zum Herbst 1919,* Düsseldorf, Droste, 1959.

Meier, Kurt, *Der evangelische Kirchenkampf,* 2 vols. Halle/S and Göttingen, Vandenhoeck and Ruprecht, 1976.

Merz, Georg, *Religiöse Ansätze im modernen Sozialismus* in *Christentum und soziale Frage, 1,* Munich, Christian Kaiser, 1919.

Morsey, Rudolf, *Die Deutsche Zentrumspartei 1917–1923,* Düsseldorf, Droste, 1966.

Motschmann, Claus, *Evangelische Kirche und preussischer Staat in den Anfängen der Weimarer Republik. Möglichkeiten und Grenzen ihrer Zusammenarbeit*, Lübeck, Mattiesen, 1969.

Mumm, Reinhard, *Der christlich-soziale Gedanke. Bericht über eine Lebensarbeit in schwerer Zeit*, Berlin, E.S. Mittler & Sohn, 1933.

Naumann, Gottfried, *Sozialismus und Religion in Deutschland*, Leipzig, J.C. Hinrichs'sche Buchhandlung, 1921.

Niebuhr, H. Richard, *Christ and Culture*, New York, Harper & Brothers, 1956.

Niedner, Johannes, *Die Ausgaben des preussischen Staates für die evangelische Landeskirche der älteren Provinzen*, Stuttgart, Ferdinand Enke, 1904.

Nowak, Kurt, *Evangelische Kirche und Weimarer Republik. Zum politischen Weg des deutschen Protestantismus zwischen 1918 und 1932*, Göttingen, Vandenhoeck & Ruprecht, 1981.

Opitz, Günter, *Der Christlich-Soziale Volksdienst. Versuch einer protestantischen Partei in der Weimarer Republik*, Düsseldorf, Droste, 1969.

Oxenius, Hans Götz, *Die Entstehung der Verfassung der evangelischen Kirche der altpreussischen Union von 1922*, Ph.D. thesis, University of Cologne, 1959.

Patemann, Reinhard, *Der Kampf um die preussische Wahlreform im Ersten Weltkrieg*, Düsseldorf, Droste, 1964.

Pollmann, Klaus Erich, *Landesherrliches Kirchenregiment und soziale Frage. Der evangelische Oberkirchenrat der altpreussischen Landeskirche und die sozialpolitische Bewegung der Geistlichen nach 1890*, Berlin, Walter de Gruyter, 1973.

Pressel, Wilhelm, *Die Kriegspredigt 1914–1918 in der evangelischen Kirche Deutschlands*, Göttingen, Vandenhoeck & Ruprecht, 1967.

Rade, Martin, *Christentum und Frieden*, Tübingen, J. C. B. Mohr (Paul Siebeck), 1922.

Rathje, Johannes, *Die Welt des freien Protestantismus*, Stuttgart, Ehrenfried Klotz, 1952.

Real, Jean, "The Religious Conception of Race: Houston Stewart Chamberlain and Germanic Christianity," *The Third Reich*, ed. Maurice Baumont et al., New York, Frederick A. Praeger, 1955.

Die Religion in Geschichte und Gegenwart, 2nd ed. 5 vols. Tübingen, 1927–31.

Rosenberg, Arthur, *Imperial Germany. The Birth of the German Republic 1871–1918*, trans. Ian F. D. Morrow, Boston, Beacon Press, 1964.

Rouse, Ruth, and Stephen Charles Neill, eds., *A History of the Ecumenical Movement, 1517–1948*, London, S.P.C.K., 1954.

Schafft, Hermann, *Vom Kampf gegen die Kirche für die Kirche*, Habertshof bei Schlüchtern, Neuwerk-Verlag, 1925.

Schian, Martin, *Die deutsche evangelische Kirche im Weltkriege*, 2 vols. Berlin, E.S. Mittler & Sohn, 1921–25.

Schnabel, Franz, *Die religiösen Kräfte* in *Deutsche Geschichte im neunzehnten Jahrhundert*, 4, 3rd ed. Freiburg, Herder, 1955.

Schneider, J[ohannes], *Die Konfessionsschichtung der Bevölkerung Deutschlands nach den Ergebnissen der Volkszählung vom 16. Juni 1925,* Berlin, Verlag des Evangelischen Bundes, 1928.

Schoeps, Hans Joachim, ed., *Das Wilhelminische Zeitalter* in *Zeitgeist im Wandel, 1,* Stuttgart, Ernst Klett, 1967.

———, *Zeitgeist der Weimarer Republik* in *Zeitgeist im Wandel, 2,* Stuttgart, Ernst Klett, 1968.

Scholder, Klaus, *Vorgeschichte und Zeit der Illusionen 1918—1934* in *Die Kirchen und das Dritte Reich, 1,* Frankfurt/M., Ullstein, 1977.

Schulz, Heinrich, *Der Leidensweg des Reichsschulgesetzes,* Berlin, J. H. W. Dietz Nachf., 1925.

Seeberg, Reinhold, *System der Ethik,* 2nd ed. Leipzig, A. Deichertsche Verlagsbuchhandlung, Dr. Werner Scholl, 1920.

———, *Zum Verständnis der gegenwärtigen Krisis in der europäischen Geisteskultur,* Leipzig, A. Deichertsche Verlagsbuchhandlung, Dr. Werner Scholl, 1923.

Shanahan, William O., *German Protestants Face the Social Question, 1,* Notre Dame, University of Notre Dame Press, 1954.

Snell, John L., "Die Republik aus Versäumnissen," *Die Welt als Geschichte, 15,* (1955), 196—219.

Soecknick, Gerda, *Religiöser Sozialismus der neueren Zeit unter besonderer Berücksichtigung Deutschlands,* Jena, Gustav Fischer, 1926.

Söhngen, Oskar, ed., *Hundert Jahre Evangelischer Oberkirchenrat der altpreussischen Union 1850—1950,* Berlin-Spandau, Wichern-Verlag, 1950.

Sontheimer, Kurt, *Antidemokratisches Denken in der Weimarer Republik. Die politischen Ideen des deutschen Nationalismus zwischen 1918 und 1933,* Munich, Nymphenburger Verlagshandlung, 1962.

Spotts, Frederic, *The Churches and Politics in Germany,* Middletown, Conn., Wesleyan University Press, 1973.

Springer, Herbert, *Protestantische Kirche und Volksschule in Deutschland,* Leipzig, C. Schroeter, 1929.

Stoll, Gerhard E., *Die evangelische Zeitschriftenpresse im Jahre 1933,* Witten, Luther-Verlag, 1963.

Stürmer, Michael, *Koalition und Opposition in der Weimarer Republik 1924—1928,* Düsseldorf, Droste, 1967.

Tal, Uriel, *Christians and Jews in Germany. Religion, Politics, and Ideology in the Second Reich, 1870—1914,* trans. Noah Jonathan Jacobs, Ithaca, N.Y., Cornell University Press, 1975.

Thimme, Friedrich and Ernst Rolffs, eds., *Revolution und Kirche,* Berlin, Georg Reimar, 1919.

Tilgner, Wolfgang, "Volk, Nation und Vaterland im protestantischen Denken zwischen Kaiserreich und Nationalsozialismus (ca. 1870—1933)," *Volk—*

Nation—Vaterland. Der deutsche Protestantismus und der Nationalismus, Gütersloh, Güterloher Verlagshaus Gerd Mohn, 1970.

————, *Volksnomostheologie und Schöpfungsglaube. Ein Beitrag zur Geschichte des Kirchenkampfes*, Göttingen, Vandenhoeck & Ruprecht, 1966.

Treue, Wolfgang, ed., *Deutsche Parteiprogramme 1861–1956*, 2nd ed. Göttingen, Musterschmidt-Verlag, 1956.

Tribukait, Pfarrer, *Der Kirchen-Schulkampf in Westfalen. Seine Entstehung und sein Verlauf. Meine Stellungnahme und meine Erlebnisse in diesem Kampf*, 1928(?).

Troeltsch, Ernst, *The Social Teaching of the Christian Churches*, trans. Olive Wyon, 4th Eng. ed., 2 vols. London, George Allen & Unwin, 1956.

————, *Spektator-Briefe. Aufsätze über die deutsche Revolution und die Weltpolitik 1918/22*, ed. H. Baron, Tübingen, J.C.B. Mohr (Paul Siebeck), 1924.

Turner, Henry Ashby, Jr., *Stresemann and the Politics of the Weimar Republic*, Princeton, Princeton University Press, 1963.

von der Heydt, Fritz, *Gute Wehr. Werden, Wirken und Wollen des Evangelischen Bundes*, Berlin, Verlag des Evangelischen Bundes, 1936.

von Dryander, Ernst, *Erinnerungen aus meinem Leben*, Bielefeld, Velhagen & Klasing, 1922.

von Klemperer, Klemens, *Germany's New Conservatism: Its History and Dilemma in the Twentieth Century*, Princeton, Princeton University Press, 1957.

von Rittberg, Else Gräfin, "Der preussische Kirchenvertrag von 1931," Ph.D. thesis, University of Bonn, 1960.

von Zahn-Harnack, Agnes, *Adolf von Harnack*, 2nd ed. Berlin, Walter de Gruyter, 1951.

Ward, William Reginald, *Theology, Sociology and Politics. The German Protestant Social Conscience 1890–1933*, Berne, Peter Lang, 1979.

Wende, Erich, *C. H. Becker, Mensch und Politiker*, Stuttgart, Deutsche Verlags-Anstalt, 1959.

Wittram, Reinhard, *Das Nationale als europäisches Problem*, Göttingen, Vandenhoeck & Ruprecht, 1954.

Wright, J.R.C., *'Above Parties': The Political Attitudes of the German Protestant Church Leadership 1918–1922*, London, Oxford University Press, 1974.

Wünsch, Georg, *Der Zusammenbruch des Luthertums als Sozialgestaltung*, Tübingen, J. C. B. Mohr (Paul Siebeck), 1921.

Zeender, John K., "German Catholics and the Concept of an Interconfessional Party 1900–1922," *JCEA*, 23 (1964), 424–39.

Zimmermann, Ludwig, *Deutsche Aussenpolitik in der Ära de Weimarer Republik*, Göttingen, Musterschmidt-Verlag, 1958.

Zoellner, Wilhelm, *Die ökumenische Arbeit des Deutschen Evangelischen Kirchenausschuss und die Kriegsschuldfrage*, Berlin, 1931.

INDEX